Performing with

Microsoft® Office Excel 2003

Comprehensive Course

Iris Blanc
New York City Department of Education

Cathy Vento
Computer Education Consultant

THOMSON

COURSE TECHNOLOGY

COURSE TECHNOLOGY
25 THOMSON PLACE
BOSTON, MA 02210

Microsoft®
Office
Specialist
Approved Courseware

Australia • Canada • Mexico • Singapore • Spain • United Kingdom • United States

THOMSON
COURSE TECHNOLOGY

Kristen Honorst
Prof. Guttleiber

Performing with Microsoft Office Excel 2003: Comprehensive Course
by Iris Blanc and Cathy Vento

Executive Director:
Cheryl Costantini

Senior Editor:
Alexandra Arnold

Product Manager:
David Rivera

Development Editor:
Rose Marie Kuebbing
Custom Editorial Productions, Inc.

Senior Marketing Manager:
Kim Ryttel

Director of Production:
Patty Stephan

Production Editor:
Jean Findley
Custom Editorial Productions, Inc.

Senior Manufacturing Coordinator:
Trevor Kallop

Senior Designer:
Abby Scholz

Illustrations:
Ferruccio Sardella

Compositor:
GEX Publishing Services

Printer:
Banta Menasha

"Microsoft and the Microsoft Office Specialist Logo are registered trademarks of Microsoft Corporation in the United States and other countries. Course Technology is an independent entity from Microsoft Corporation, and not affiliated with Microsoft Corporation in any manner. This textbook may be used in assisting students to prepare for a Microsoft Office Specialist Exam. Neither Microsoft Corporation, its designated review company, or Course Technology warrants that use of this textbook will ensure passing the relevant Exam.

"Use of the Microsoft Office Specialist Approved Courseware Logo on this product signifies that it has been independently reviewed and approved in complying with the following standards: 'Acceptable coverage of all content related to the Microsoft Office Exam entitled "Microsoft Office Word 2003 Specialist Exam," and sufficient performance-based exercises that relate closely to all required content, based on sampling of text.'"

The *Performing with Microsoft® Office 2003* series teaches Office tools through a unique set of task-oriented exercises and project-based applications built around a business theme. Students focus on the skills they need to know to complete practical, realistic applications and create materials suitable for portfolio evaluation. In this Comprehensive Course text, the software skills developed meet Specialist and Expert level Microsoft Office Specialist certification requirements for Excel 2003. XP users may also use this text since XP procedures are noted where they differ from Office 2003.

Performing with Microsoft® Office 2003 is a new and different approach based on the premise that students successfully assimilate and retain computer skills when they understand why the skills are useful. *Performing with Microsoft® Office 2003* presents skill sets within the framework of engaging projects and tasks that teach the software and business competencies needed to succeed in the workplace, thus providing a real-life context for learning. Through this task- and project-based approach, students develop critical thinking, analysis, problem solving, and information and resource management skills. With the Internet activities that appear throughout the text, they learn research and communication skills—essential tools for today's workplace. College or college-bound students will find that these software, business, and thinking skills will serve them in their coursework, internships, and professional careers.

Rather than focus solely on software features, this series emphasizes the project or task and develops those software skill sets needed to accomplish it.

OBJECTIVES

Performing with Microsoft® Office Excel 2003: Comprehensive Course is intended for a half-year Computer Applications course. No experience with this software is assumed. The objectives of this book are:

- To use a three-phased approach to develop Office Specialist competencies:
  - ✶ **Tryouts:** Learners practice software skills using a step-by-step tutorial approach.
  - ✶ **Rehearsals:** Learners apply software skills to an illustrated business task.
  - ✶ **Performances:** Learners use technology to complete a business project.
- To use tasks and projects to develop SCANS competencies:
  - ✶ Acquire and evaluate data
  - ✶ Organize and maintain files

- ✶ Interpret and communicate information
- ✶ Apply technology to specific tasks
- ✶ Apply critical thinking and problem solving
- ✶ Work with members of a team
- To provide a text that may be used for independent study.

When students complete a Computer Applications course using this text, they will have Specialist and Expert level skills and workplace competencies.

ORGANIZATION OF THE TEXT

Performing with Microsoft® Office Excel 2003: Comprehensive Course begins with the Introductory Excel Lessons 1–7 and are followed by the Advanced Excel Lessons 8–13. If you class needs practice with basic Office skills, such as opening, saving, and printing files, as well as Internet basics, have students complete the three lessons in the Performing Basics unit found in *Performing with Microsoft Office 2003: Introductory Course.*

The lessons in Introductory and Advanced Excel are organized by a series of categories that cover the following types of outcome-based projects:
- Business Forms
- Accounting Records
- Data Analysis
- Financial Reports
- Charts
- Integration/Excel and the Web
- Budgets and Templates
- Data Tables
- Data Lists
- Marketing and Sales Reports

Lessons use a three-phased pedagogy. The first phase, **Tryout,** introduces the software features necessary to complete document production in the lesson category (e.g., correspondence). It also includes software concepts, illustrations, step-by-step directions, and short, easy exercises called **Try it Out**, which provide practice with software features. Students should read all software concepts on a topic before completing the related **Try it Out!** exercise.

In the second phase, **Rehearsal,** students apply the software skills practiced in the Tryout phase to a series of tasks in which they produce model professional documents. **What You Need to**

Know information and **Cues for Reference** guide learners in completing the activities on their own, thus helping them build skills and confidence in accomplishing the Rehearsal activity. The Rehearsal phase produces tangible results that represent actual professional documents within the lesson category.

In the third phase, **Performance,** students complete challenging work-related projects (either independently or as a team) for one of nine companies. In this phase, students must apply critical thinking and problem-solving skills and integrate the software skills and business concepts learned to produce the documents required by the company-related scenarios. This phase can be used as evidence of lesson mastery.

This text is an innovative approach to teaching software skills through a project-based, applied learning process. This approach is unique because it teaches skills by applying software features in various work-based contexts. The opportunity to use the skills independently and creatively will enable students to survive and thrive in a high-performance workplace.

SPECIAL FEATURES

- **Keyboarding Reinforcement Unit** (found on the Data CD) contains 18 exercises of drill and practice material covering the entire alphabet for those who wish to learn the keyboard or improve their keyboarding skills quickly.
- **End-of-Lesson Performance activities** use a project-based approach to reinforce the concepts and applications learned in the lesson and require critical thinking and Internet skills.
- **Final Capstone Project** applies the skills learned throughout the text.
- **Data files** (found on the Data CD) allow learners to complete many of the activities without keyboarding lengthy text.
- **Directories** list file names alphabetically with corresponding lesson numbers, as well as document sample pages.
- **Vocabulary words**—both software and project-related—for each lesson.
- **Portfolio-building projects** found in the Performance sections of each lesson.
- **Multiple-Choice, True/False, Matching and Completion Objective test questions** as part of the Encore review can be found on the Data CD.
- **Appendices** that include the following:
  - ✦ Microsoft® Office Correlation Chart
  - ✦ File Management
  - ✦ Using the Mouse
  - ✦ Toolbars, Menus, and Dialog Boxes
  - ✦ Selection Techniques
  - ✦ Portfolio Basics
  - ✦ Proofreader's Marks
  - ✦ Task Reference
  - ✦ Outlook Basics
- **Glossary**

A first course text is available: *Performing with Microsoft® Office 2003: Introductory Course.* This allows a full year's course on Introductory Microsoft Office instruction. Also, as part of this series, there is a stand-alone, comprehensive text on Microsoft Word.

To help with additional projects, there is *Projects for the Entrepreneur: Microsoft Office 2003.*

ACKNOWLEDGMENTS

For the many people who have played a role in the production of this quality book, we owe our gratitude and appreciation. First and foremost among them are Cheryl Costantini, Executive Director; Kim Ryttel, Senior Marketing Manager; Patty Stephan, Director of Production; Alexandra Arnold, Senior Editor; David Rivera, Product Manager; Trevor Kallop, Senior Manufacturing Coordinator; and Abby Scholz, Senior Designer for their professionalism, guidance, and support throughout this project.

Our heartfelt thanks go to those who have made significant contributions and assisted us with the production of this book:
- To the production team at Custom Editorial Productions: Rose Marie Kuebbing, Jean Findley, and Beckie Middendorf, who kept everyone on track and on time, and did so with support and guidance all along the way.
- To Marie Michele for her wonderful illustrations.
- To our families for their love, encouragement, inspiration, and above all, for their patience.

Iris Blanc
Cathy Vento

ABOUT THE AUTHORS

Iris Blanc is currently the Director of Virtual Enterprises, International, a New York City Department of Education program. Formerly, Ms. Blanc was assistant principal/department chair of Business Education at Tottenville High School, a New York City public high school.

Ms. Blanc has taught business education and computer applications at the high school and college levels for over 30 years. Ms. Blanc conducts seminars, workshops, and short courses in applied learning strategies and methods of teaching and integrating technology at conferences nationwide.

Catherine Vento is currently working as a consultant for the New York City Department of Education and as a staff developer for the district. She was formerly the assistant principal/department chair of Business Education at Susan Wagner High School, a New York City public high school.

Ms. Vento has taught business education, accounting, and computer applications at the high school level. She has presented seminars, workshops, and mini-courses at conferences, colleges, and business schools nationwide.

Ms. Blanc and Ms. Vento have co-authored numerous computer application texts and reference guides for over 20 years. The Performing series represents their combined pedagogical talents in an innovative, new approach to develop workplace skills and competencies. Over their many years as educators and authors, they have discovered that students learn best what they need to know!

LESSON 8

Budgets and Templates

In this lesson, you will learn to use Excel features to combine information across worksheets and workbooks, including consolidating, sharing, and merging workbooks. You will also learn to create and edit a workbook template to display a budget.

Upon completion of this lesson, you should have mastered the following skill sets:

* Create a workspace consisting of two or more workbooks
* Consolidate data from two or more worksheets
* Define and modify workbook properties
* Create a workbook template
* Create a new workbook based on a user-created template
* Change the default file location for templates
* Edit a workbook template
* Create a shared workbook
* Track, accept, and reject changes in workbooks
* Merge workbooks

Terms
Software-related
 Workspace
 Data consolidation
 Properties
 Template
 Shared workbook
 Track changes
 Merged workbook
Document-related
 Consolidated budget
 Quarterly budget
 Divisional sales report

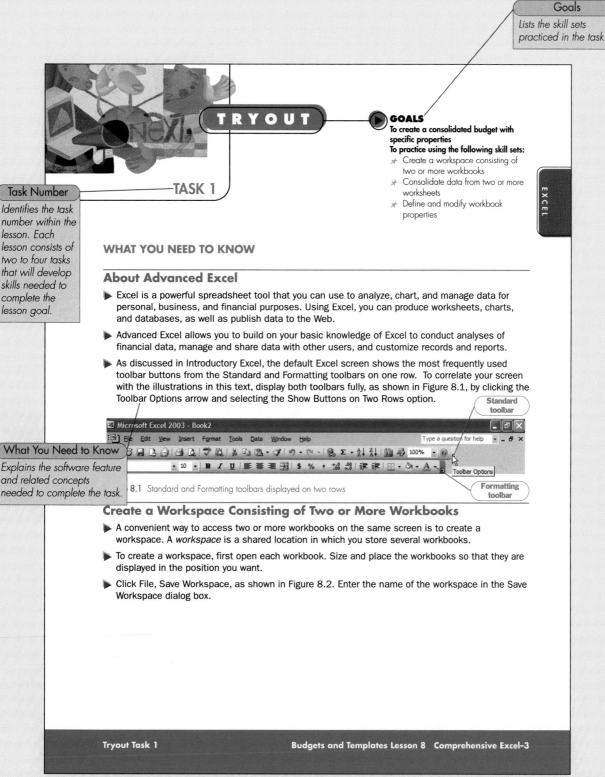

Goals

Lists the skill sets practiced in the task.

TRYOUT

▶ **GOALS**
To create a consolidated budget with specific properties
To practice using the following skill sets:
✳ Create a workspace consisting of two or more workbooks
✳ Consolidate data from two or more worksheets
✳ Define and modify workbook properties

EXCEL

TASK 1

Task Number

Identifies the task number within the lesson. Each lesson consists of two to four tasks that will develop skills needed to complete the lesson goal.

WHAT YOU NEED TO KNOW

About Advanced Excel

▶ Excel is a powerful spreadsheet tool that you can use to analyze, chart, and manage data for personal, business, and financial purposes. Using Excel, you can produce worksheets, charts, and databases, as well as publish data to the Web.

▶ Advanced Excel allows you to build on your basic knowledge of Excel to conduct analyses of financial data, manage and share data with other users, and customize records and reports.

▶ As discussed in Introductory Excel, the default Excel screen shows the most frequently used toolbar buttons from the Standard and Formatting toolbars on one row. To correlate your screen with the illustrations in this text, display both toolbars fully, as shown in Figure 8.1, by clicking the Toolbar Options arrow and selecting the Show Buttons on Two Rows option.

What You Need to Know

Explains the software feature and related concepts needed to complete the task.

Standard toolbar

Microsoft Excel 2003 - Book2

File Edit View Insert Format Tools Data Window Help   Type a question for help

100%

Toolbar Options

Formatting toolbar

8.1 Standard and Formatting toolbars displayed on two rows

Create a Workspace Consisting of Two or More Workbooks

▶ A convenient way to access two or more workbooks on the same screen is to create a workspace. A *workspace* is a shared location in which you store several workbooks.

▶ To create a workspace, first open each workbook. Size and place the workbooks so that they are displayed in the position you want.

▶ Click File, Save Workspace, as shown in Figure 8.2. Enter the name of the workspace in the Save Workspace dialog box.

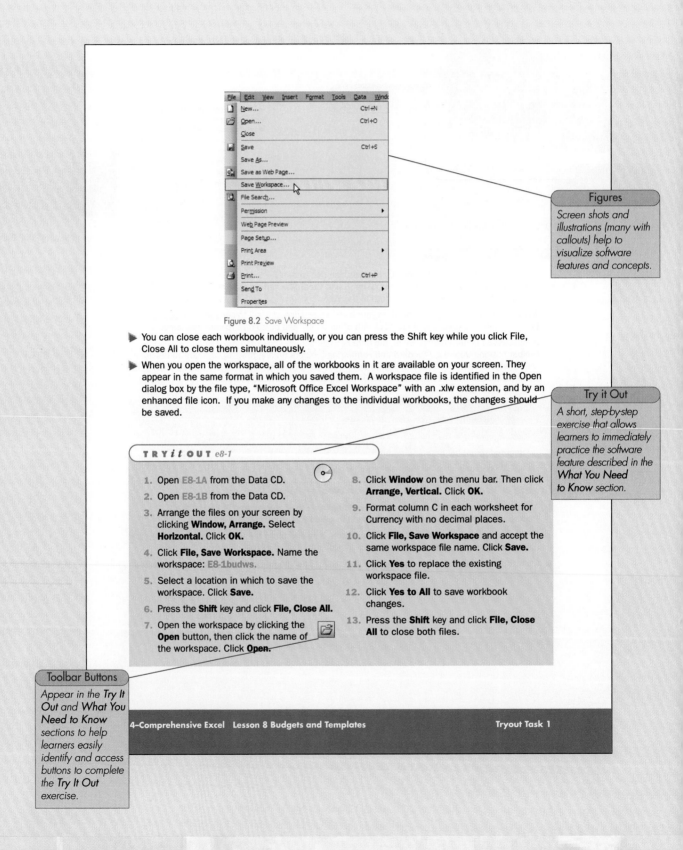

Figure 8.2 Save Workspace

▶ You can close each workbook individually, or you can press the Shift key while you click File, Close All to close them simultaneously.

▶ When you open the workspace, all of the workbooks in it are available on your screen. They appear in the same format in which you saved them. A workspace file is identified in the Open dialog box by the file type, "Microsoft Office Excel Workspace" with an .xlw extension, and by an enhanced file icon. If you make any changes to the individual workbooks, the changes should be saved.

Figures

Screen shots and illustrations (many with callouts) help to visualize software features and concepts.

Try it Out

A short, step-by-step exercise that allows learners to immediately practice the software feature described in the What You Need to Know section.

T R Y it O U T e8-1

1. Open **E8-1A** from the Data CD.
2. Open **E8-1B** from the Data CD.
3. Arrange the files on your screen by clicking **Window, Arrange.** Select **Horizontal.** Click **OK.**
4. Click **File, Save Workspace.** Name the workspace: **E8-1budws.**
5. Select a location in which to save the workspace. Click **Save.**
6. Press the **Shift** key and click **File, Close All.**
7. Open the workspace by clicking the **Open** button, then click the name of the workspace. Click **Open.**

8. Click **Window** on the menu bar. Then click **Arrange, Vertical.** Click **OK.**
9. Format column C in each worksheet for Currency with no decimal places.
10. Click **File, Save Workspace** and accept the same workspace file name. Click **Save.**
11. Click **Yes** to replace the existing workspace file.
12. Click **Yes to All** to save workbook changes.
13. Press the **Shift** key and click **File, Close All** to close both files.

Toolbar Buttons

Appear in the Try It Out and What You Need to Know sections to help learners easily identify and access buttons to complete the Try It Out exercise.

REHEARSAL

▶ GOAL
To create a consolidated budget with specific properties

SETTING THE STAGE/WRAPUP
File names: **8.1Sutton1**
8.1Sutton2
8.1CBws
8.1SuttonCB

TASK 1

WHAT YOU NEED TO KNOW

▶ Consolidated financial statements combine corresponding financial information from two or more sources, such as departments within a company or within affiliated companies owned by a larger corporation. A *consolidated budget* combines the planned or actual income and expenses from several departments or companies.

▶ A *quarterly budget* is prepared four times a year to reflect income and expense activity up to the end of each three-month period. These statements are usually dated the last day of March, June, September, and December. Quarterly budgets are often used to compare proposed income and expenditures with actual income and expenditures.

▶ In this Rehearsal activity, you will create a consolidated quarterly budget to show the accumulated activity for two departments that are part of the Sutton Investment Group. You will combine departmental data for the proposed and actual budgets for the second quarter and set worksheet properties.

▽ DIRECTIONS

1. Open **8.1Sutton1** and **8.1Sutton2** from the Data CD.

2. Enter formulas to calculate the Total Expenses and the Net Income for the Budget and Actual columns on both worksheets, as shown in Illustration A on the next page.

3. Size and position the two files according to your preference.

4. Save a workspace for these two files as **8.1CBws** and, when prompted, save **8.1Sutton1** and **8.1Sutton2**.

5. Copy the headings in Rows 1:4 from one of the files to a new workbook.

6. Copy the labels in Column A from one of the files to the new workbook.

7. Consolidate the data from each of the two departments for the columns labeled Budget and Actual.

8. Edit titles on the new sheet reflecting that it is a consolidated budget for the second quarter. Include the company name, report title, and quarter ending date.

9. Add border rulings, as necessary, as shown in Illustration B on the next page.

10. Set the following properties for the consolidated worksheet.
    a. Summary properties: Enter the title (business name), subject, and your name; use Budget as the category and Consolidated Budget as the keywords.
    b. Custom properties: Department: Mutual Funds and Securities; Forward to: Managers and Acctg. Depts.

11. Print a copy of the consolidated budget.

12. Save the file as **8.1SuttonCB** and close all files.

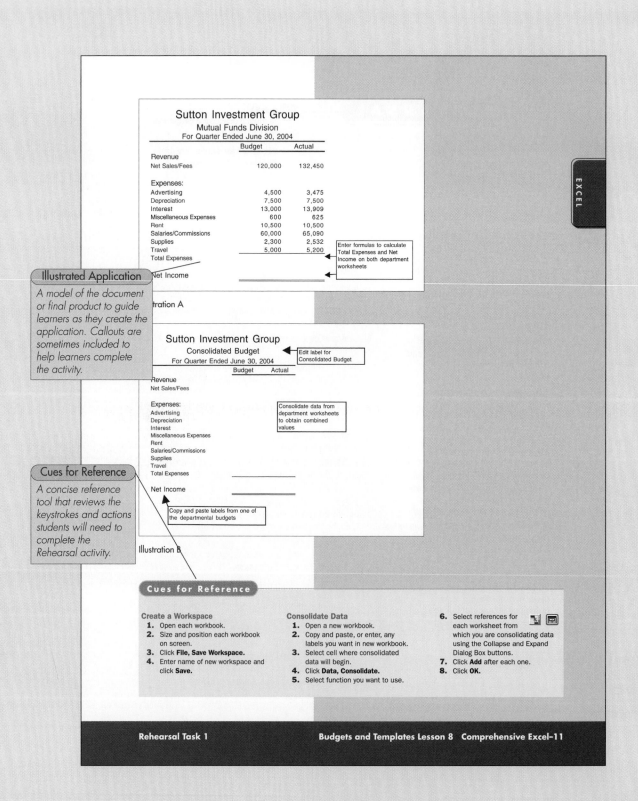

Illustrated Application

A model of the document or final product to guide learners as they create the application. Callouts are sometimes included to help learners complete the activity.

Cues for Reference

A concise reference tool that reviews the keystrokes and actions students will need to complete the Rehearsal activity.

Sutton Investment Group
Mutual Funds Division
For Quarter Ended June 30, 2004

	Budget	Actual
Revenue		
Net Sales/Fees	120,000	132,450
Expenses:		
Advertising	4,500	3,475
Depreciation	7,500	7,500
Interest	13,000	13,909
Miscellaneous Expenses	600	625
Rent	10,500	10,500
Salaries/Commissions	60,000	65,090
Supplies	2,300	2,532
Travel	5,000	5,200
Total Expenses		
Net Income		

Enter formulas to calculate Total Expenses and Net Income on both department worksheets

Illustration A

Sutton Investment Group
Consolidated Budget
For Quarter Ended June 30, 2004

Edit label for Consolidated Budget

	Budget	Actual
Revenue		
Net Sales/Fees		
Expenses:		
Advertising		
Depreciation		
Interest		
Miscellaneous Expenses		
Rent		
Salaries/Commissions		
Supplies		
Travel		
Total Expenses		
Net Income		

Consolidate data from department worksheets to obtain combined values

Copy and paste labels from one of the departmental budgets

Illustration B

Cues for Reference

Create a Workspace
1. Open each workbook.
2. Size and position each workbook on screen.
3. Click **File, Save Workspace.**
4. Enter name of new workspace and click **Save.**

Consolidate Data
1. Open a new workbook.
2. Copy and paste, or enter, any labels you want in new workbook.
3. Select cell where consolidated data will begin.
4. Click **Data, Consolidate.**
5. Select function you want to use.

6. Select references for each worksheet from which you are consolidating data using the Collapse and Expand Dialog Box buttons.
7. Click **Add** after each one.
8. Click **OK.**

EXCEL

PERFORMANCE

▶ **SETTING THE STAGE/WRAPUP**

⚡ Act I File names:
  8p1.budget
  8p1budtemp
  8p1budgroup
⚡ Act II File names:
  8p2.boston
  8p2.sandiego
  8p2.budtemp
  8p2consolbud
⚡ Act III File names:
  8p3.DivisionalSales
  8p3.DivSales
  8p3.DivSalesFairfax
  8p3.DivSalesAlexandria
  8p3.DivSalesFallsChurch
  8p3.DivSalesFinal

Setting the Stage

Identifies file names and/or settings needed to begin the activities, which are listed as Acts. There may be two to four Acts in this phase.

WHAT YOU NEED TO KNOW

Act I

The Air Land Sea Travel Group would like each department in the organization to use the same quarterly budget form to facilitate financial planning.

Prepare a template for the quarterly budget, using 8p1.budget on the Data CD as a starting point. You are also asked to prepare the budget for the Group Travel Department for the quarter ending September 30, 2004, and to revise the template.

air land sea
t r a v e l   g r o u p

Scenario

Introduces the business problem.

Company Logo

Identifies the company that the students are "working for" in the scenario. The company information is outlined on the To the Student pages and may be used for reference.

Follow these guidelines:

⚡ Format and enhance the title area in **Rows 1:4** by changing font size, and/or styles and adding color as desired. Make labels for Income, Expenses, and Net Income a bit larger than those in the rest of the budget.

⚡ Enter the formulas necessary to complete the budget template.

⚡ Apply the appropriate number formats to each column and adjust column width as necessary.

⚡ Apply borders to the appropriate cells to follow accounting styles and to enhance the column headings.

⚡ Save the form as a template in the Templates folder and name it: 8p1.budtemp.

⚡ Add a line for Supplies to the list of expenses by inserting a line on the template, in alphabetical order. Fill in formulas and check the formulas for totals. Resave the template using the same name. See the illustration of the completed template on the next page.

Guidelines

Lists the requirements, specifications, and/or tips needed to complete the project.

WHAT'S NEW AND IMPROVED IN MICROSOFT® OFFICE 2003

Microsoft Office 2003 has many powerful new features as well as significantly improved interfaces to the features with which you are already familiar. Complex operations such as mail merge are now much easier. Improved Web access from all applications means you can integrate Web resources with your Office files. Sharing the information or data in your Office applications via the Web is now practically seamless. Office 2003 includes improved tools to enhance collaboration when you work on projects with other people. Some of the new features are covered in the Introductory Course. Other features are taught in the *Performing with Microsoft® Office Word 2003* and *Performing with Microsoft® Office Excel 2003* comprehensive texts.

The many new and improved Office 2003 features include:

- New and improved task panes to improve access to special features.
- Research task pane offering a wide variety of reference information.
- Support for ink devices such as a Tablet PC.
- Better integration of Microsoft Office Online site features.
- Shared workspace task pane.

Microsoft® Office Word 2003 includes the following new features:

- Compare documents side by side.
- Improved readability using the new Reading Layout view.
- Improved document protection for formatting and content.
- Support for XML documents.

Microsoft® Office Excel 2003 includes the following new features:

- Compare workbooks side by side.
- Improved statistical functions.
- Improved list functions.
- Support for import and export of XML data.

Microsoft® Office PowerPoint® 2003 includes the following new features:

- Updated PowerPoint viewer for opening presentations without software installation.
- New Slide Show navigation tools.
- Ink feature to mark slides in a presentation.
- New SmartTag support.

Microsoft® Office Access 2003 includes the following new features:

- Can view information on object dependencies.
- Error checking for forms and reports.
- Back-up database feature.
- Improved sorting functions.
- Field properties can be propagated from tables to forms.

Start-up Checklist
HARDWARE
Minimum Configuration

- PC with Pentium 233 MHz or higher; Pentium III recommended.
- Microsoft Windows 2000, Service Pack 3 or later, or Windows XP or later (recommended)
- 64 MB RAM (minimum) 128 MB RAM (recommended)
- Hard disk with 350 MB free for typical installation
- CD-ROM drive
- Super VGA monitor (800 × 600) or higher resolution with 256 colors
- Microsoft Mouse, Microsoft IntelliMouse, or compatible pointing device
- 33,600 bps or higher modem
- Printer

Before you start to work, please read this introduction. Spending this time before you begin will enhance your learning experience.

Conventions: Different type styles have special meaning. You will save time by recognizing the nature of the text from the type style.

Type Style	Color	Use	Example
Bold Italics	**Black**	Key terms	*word processing*
Bold	**Black**	Action items	Press the **Enter** key
Bold	**Red**	File names	2.2to.xls
			3.3pf styles.doc

ANCILLARIES

Student Data Files: All data files mentioned in the text that are needed to complete the exercises for this book are located on on a separate CD called a Review Pack. They can also be downloaded for each title on www.course.com.

Instructor Resources (IR) CD-ROM: The Instructor Resources CD-ROM contains a wealth of instructional material you can use to prepare for and aid in your teaching of Office 2003. On the CD, you will find:

- Data files for the course.
- Solution files for the course.
- Answers to all exercises.
- Lesson plans for each lesson.
- Copies of the figures that appear in the student text, which can be used to prepare transparencies.
- A correlation grid that shows skills required for Microsoft Office Specialist certification.
- A correlation grid that shows the SCANS workplace competencies skills.
- PowerPoint presentations showing Office 2003 features for Word, Excel, Access, and PowerPoint®.
- Keyboarding Reinforcement unit.
- Multiple-Choice, True/False, Matching and Completion Objective test questions.

ExamView®

This textbook is accompanied by ExamView®, a powerful testing software package that allows instructors to create and administer printed, computer (LAN-based), and Internet exams. ExamView® includes hundreds of questions that correspond to the topics covered in this text, enabling students to generate detailed study guides that include page references for further review. The computer-based and Internet testing components allow students to take exams at their computers, and also save the instructor time by grading each exam automatically.

SAM 2003 Assessment & Training

SAM 2003 helps you energize your class exams and training assignments by allowing students to learn and test important computer skills in an active, hands-on environment.

With SAM 2003 Assessment, you create powerful interactive exam on critical applications such as Word, Outlook, PowerPoint, Windows, the Internet, and much more. The exams simulate the application environment, allowing your students to demonstrate their knowledge and think through the skill by performing real-world tasks.

- Build hands-on exams that allow the student to work in the simulated application environment
- Add more muscle to your lesson plan with SAM 2003 Training. Using highly interactive text, graphics, and sound, SAM 2003 Training gives your students the flexibility to learn computer applications by choosing the training method that fits them the best.
- Create customized training units that employ various approaches to teach computer skills
- Designed to be used with the Microsoft Office 2003 series, SAM 2003 Assessment & Training includes built-in page references so students can create study guides that match the Microsoft Office 2003 textbooks you use in class. Powerful administrative options allow you to schedule exams and assignments, secure your tests, and run reports with almost limitless flexibility.
- Deliver exams and training units that best fit the way you teach
- Choose from more than one dozen reports to track testing and learning progress

The Rehearsal and Performance phases of each lesson use various types of companies to demonstrate the kinds of documents that a real business might produce. A description of each company used in this text is outlined below. The Performance phase of each unit will identify the company you "work for" by the company logo illustrated. Use these pages as a reference if you need to find information about the company as you complete the project at hand.

Company Name and Contact Information	Description of Company	Logo
Air Land Sea Travel Group *New York* 505 Park Avenue New York, NY 10010 Phone 212-555-5555 Fax: 212-666-6767 E-mail: als@net.com *Boston* One Main Street Boston, MA 11111 Phone: 617-666-6666 Fax: 617-777-7777 E-mail: alsbos@net.com *California* Los Angeles 46 Beverly Drive Beverly Hills, CA 90210 Phone: 310-555-5555 Fax: 310-555-4444 E-mail: alsbh@net.com San Francisco 35 Market Street San Francisco, CA 99876 Phone: 415-888-8888 Fax: 415-222-2222 E-mail: alssf@net.com	The Air Land Sea Travel Group, also known as the ALS Travel Group, has offices in Boston, New York, and two in California. ALS specializes in both corporate and leisure travel packages. The Corporate Travel Department services business clients throughout the country. The company has been in business for over 40 years and is known for its reliable service, great prices, and exclusive offers. The president of the company is Ms. Janice Pierce. The director of the Corporate Travel Department in New York is Mr. Wilson Jones. The director of the Leisure Travel Department is Ms. Robin Byron.	air land sea travel group

Company Name and Contact Information	Description of Company	Logo
Green Brothers Gardening 32 Braddock Road Fairfax, VA 22030 Phone: 703-555-0005 Fax: 703-555-0015 E-mail: gbg@network.com Web: www.grenbros.com	Green Brothers Gardening, a full-service landscaping and nursery business, has three locations in and around Fairfax, Virginia. Calvin Green, the president and CEO, runs the business with his brother, Ralph Green, the chief financial officer. Maria Torres is their director of Marketing and Sales. They have an office and nursery staff in each store. They also employ workers on a daily basis. The firm handles lawn maintenance programs, tree and shrub planting, pruning, masonry, snow plowing, sanding, and landscape contracting. They carry unique specimen plants and cater to corporate as well as residential markets. They have a reputation for creating natural, lush landscaping.	GREEN BROTHERS GARDENING
Odyssey Travel Gear 445 Michigan Avenue Chicago, IL 60611 Phone: 630-222-8888 Fax: 630-666-8787 E-mail: otg@networld.com Web: www.otg.com	Odyssey Travel Gear offers products that make travel easier, such as luggage and luggage carts, garment bags, rain gear, money belts, sleep sacks, etc. The company has several retail stores, but most of their business comes from catalog and Internet sales. The retail stores are located in Chicago, Miami, Boston, Dallas, and San Diego. The company's headquarters are located in Chicago, Illinois. Ms. Jane McBride is the president and CEO. The Web site features new products, dozens of reduced-priced items from past catalogs, and lots of valuable information.	OTG odyssey travel group
Trilogy Productions California 101 Sunset Boulevard Beverly Hills, CA 90210 Phone (310) 505-0000 Fax (310) 606-0000 E-mail tpc@world.com New York 350 West 57 Street New York, NY 10106 Phone (212) 555-9999 Fax (212) 555-8900 E-mail: tpny@world.com	Trilogy Productions is a motion picture and television production company. John Alan, the current CEO (chief executive officer) and president, and Andrew Martin, the current CFO (chief financial officer) formed the company in 1990. Trilogy Productions deals with a number of Hollywood's top talent, including writers, directors, and filmmakers. They have released roughly 50 feature films and numerous Emmy-winning television programs. The Motion Picture and Television Divisions are located in the same building in Beverly Hills, California. Trilogy also maintains a small office in New York, which primarily handles all marketing and sales distribution. The director of Marketing and Sales is Christopher Manning. Ms. Cindy Napster is the manager of the Human Resources Department. She handles all employee-related matters for the New York and California offices.	TRILOGY PRODUCTIONS
In-Shape Fitness Centers 54 Cactus Drive Phoenix, AZ 85003 Phone: 602-555-1001 Fax: 602-555-1005 E-mail: inshape@net.com	In-Shape Fitness Centers began in Phoenix, Arizona with one location and quickly grew to four other locations within the Phoenix area. In-Shape Fitness is a high-quality health and fitness facility, which offers a wide range of exercise and fitness programs. The company's successful growth over a short time has been the result of its innovative fitness programs, well-trained staff, and dedication to quality and service. Mr. Robert Treadmill, president, retired this year and Ms. Alivea James has replaced him.	

Company Name and Contact Information	Description of Company	Logo
Occasions Event Planning *New York* 675 Third Avenue New York, NY 10017 Tel: 212-555-1234 Fax: 212-555-1230 *New Jersey* 1045 Palisades Avenue Fort Lee, NJ 07024 Phone: 201-555-4322 Fax: 201-555-4323 E-mail: oep@world.com	Occasions Event Planning offers full service gourmet catering, DJ's, live bands, recreational rentals, entertainment for children, vending machines, appliance rental, and more. Located in New York City, the Occasions Event Planning Company plans conferences, parties, seminars, and meetings. Recently, it opened a New Jersey office. Jane McBride is the president of the company.	
Four Corners Realty 450 Flora Boulevard Hollywood, FL 30025 Phone: 954-555-4433 Fax: 954-555-4412 E-mail: 4corners@world.net	Four Corners Realty is a real estate company located in Hollywood, Florida. It specializes in the sale and rental of residential and commercial properties. Dennis Halpern is the president and CEO (chief executive officer). The company has a large staff of associates servicing the Hollywood, Florida area and has been selling fine properties for more than 25 years.	
Time Out Sporting Goods *Barkely Store* 1412 Barkely Street Chicago, IL 60004 Phone: 874-555-1200 Fax: 874-555-1201 *Montrose Store* 235 Parsons Boulevard Chicago, IL 60075 Phone: 847-555-1950 Fax: 847-555-1951 E-mail: tosg@aom.com Web: www.timeout.com	Time Out Sporting Goods is a family-owned-and-operated retailer of sporting equipment, sporting apparel, and athletic footwear. Time Out has two stores in the Chicago area. The Barkely store is located in downtown Chicago, while the Montrose store is located in a suburb west of the city.	
Sutton Investment Group 34562 Corona Street Los Angeles, CA 90001 Phone: 213-555-6660 Fax: 213-555-6623 E-mail: Sutton@money.com Web: www.Sutton.com	Sutton Investment Group is a full-service investment company located in downtown Los Angeles. They service corporate and individual clients and provide investment, financial planning, and brokerage services. They offer their employees a full benefits package and have been in business for ten years.	

UNDERSTANDING MICROSOFT OFFICE SPECIALIST/SCANS

UNDERSTANDING MICROSOFT OFFICE SPECIALIST CERTIFICATION

What is certification?

The logo on the front cover indicates that the Microsoft Corporation has officially certified the book at the Specialist skill level for Office 2003 in Word, Excel, Access, and PowerPoint. This certification is part of the **Microsoft Office Specialist** program that validates your Office skills. For more information about the program, visit www.microsoft.com/learning/mcp/ OfficeSpecialist/. Appendix A provides a chart that lists skill sets and activities, and references the page numbers in this text where the skill sets are discussed.

Why would I want to become certified?

- The Microsoft Office Specialist Program provides an industry-recognized standard for measuring an individual's mastery of Office applications.
- By passing one or more Microsoft Office Specialist Program certification exams, you demonstrate your proficiency in a given Office application to employers.
- Individuals who pass one or more exams can gain a competitive edge in the job marketplace.

Where does testing take place?

To be certified, you will need to take an exam from a third-party testing company called an Authorization Certification Testing Center. Call **800-933-4493** at Nivo International to find the location of the testing center nearest you. Learn more about the criteria for testing and what is involved. Tests are conducted on different dates throughout the calendar year. Course Technology, a division of Thomson Learning, has developed an entire line of training materials.

Skills Assessment Software

Use SAM 2003, our skills assessment software, to gauge students' readiness for the Microsoft Office Specialist certification exams for Microsoft Office 2003. Through predefined prep exams that map back to skills taught in Course Technology textbooks, your students will have the tools they need to pass the certification exam with flying colors. For more information, visit www.course.com.

UNDERSTANDING SCANS: SECRETARY'S COMMISSION ON ACHIEVING NECESSARY SKILLS

The Secretary's Commission on Achieving Necessary Skills (SCANS) from the U.S. Department of Labor was asked to examine the demands of the workplace and whether new learners are capable of meeting those demands. Specifically, the Commission was directed to advise the Secretary on the level of skills required to enter employment. In carrying out this charge, the Commission was asked to do the following:

- Define the skills needed for employment.
- Propose acceptable levels of proficiency.
- Suggest effective ways to assess proficiency.
- Develop a dissemination strategy for the nation's schools, businesses, and homes.

SCANS research verified that what we call workplace know-how defines effective job performance today. This know-how has two elements: competencies and a foundation. The SCANS report defines five competencies and a three-part foundation of skills and personal qualities that lie at the heart of job performance. These eight requirements are essential preparation for all students, whether they are entering the workforce, continuing in a present work environment, or planning further education.

SCANS workplace competencies and foundation skills have been integrated into Microsoft Office 2003. The workplace competencies are identified as: 1) ability to use resources, 2) interpersonal skills, 3) ability to work with information, 4) understanding of systems, and 5) knowledge and understanding of technology. The foundation skills are identified as 1) basic communication skills, 2) thinking skills, and 3) personal qualities.

Please refer to the correlation document on the Instructor Resources CD-ROM for specifics on how the topics in this text meet these requirements.

DIRECTORIES

Continued on next page

Lesson	Section	Task No.	Data	Solution
	Rehearsal	3	11.3inventory	s.11.3inventory
	Performance	Act I	11p1.Pers	s.11p1.Pers
		Act II	11p2.Inven	s.11p2.Inven
12	Tryout	1	E12-1	
			E12-3	
	Rehearsal	1	12.1Personnel	
	Tryout	2	E12-4	
			E12-5	
			E12-6	s.E12-6
	Rehearsal	2	12.2Sales	
	Tryout	3	E12-7	s.E12-7
			E12-8	s.E12-8
			E12-9	
			E12-10	
			E12-11	s.E12-11
	Rehearsal	3	12.3Aging	s.12.3Aging
	Performance	Act I	12p1.TriPersonnel	s.12p1.TriPersonnel
		Act II	12p2.OdySales	s.12p2.OdySales
		Act III	12p3.ALSAging	s.12p3.ALSAging
13	Tryout	1	E13-1Homes.mdb	
			E13-2HomeText.doc	
			E13-4	E13-4text.doc
				E13-4text.txt
			E13-5	
			E13-6	s.13-6.mhtml
	Rehearsal	1	13.1Competition.html	
			13.1Seniors.mdb	s.13-1Seniors
	Tryout	2	13.7Transactions.mdb	s.E13-7
			E13-8	s.E13-8
			E13-9	s.E13-9
			NetSalesSchema.xsd	
			E13-Sales	E13-Sales
			E13-11	s.E13.11
			E13-PASales	
			E13-12	s.E13.12

Directory of Files

Lesson	Section	Task No.	Data	Solution
	Rehearsal	2	13.2Argentina	s.13.2ForeignOrders
			13.2Orderschema.xsd	
			13.2Argentina.xml	
			13.2Conversion	
			13.2ForeignOrders.mdb	
	Performance	Act I	13p1.national.doc	
			13p1.national	
			13p1.Travel.doc	s.13p1.travel
		Act II	13p2.Orders.mdb	s.13p2.orders
			13p2.Mexico.xml	
			13p2.orderschema.xsd	
Final Project				
	Job 1		Salesinv.xls	s.salesinv.tmp
			Musicmaxlogo.tif	
	Job 2			12345wil.xls
				12345ott.xls
	Job 3		emplist.xls	s.emplist3.xls
	Job 4		emplist4.xls	s.emplist4.xls
	Job 5		emplist5.xls	s.emplist5.xls
	Job 6		funding6.xls	s.funding6.xls
	Job 7			s.flyer7.xls
	Job 8		wilmington.xls	s.annualreport8.xls
			mktgsales.xls	
			fayetteville.doc	
			RevenueSchema.xsd	
			charlotte.xml	
	Job 9		annualreport9.xls	s.annualreport9.xls

TABLE OF CONTENTS

PREFACE

PERFORMING WITH EXCEL

PERFORMING WITH EXCEL

PERFORMING WITH EXCEL

FINAL PROJECT

PERFORMING WITH EXCEL
INTRODUCTORY UNIT

Excel Basics

In this lesson, you will learn about the Excel screen, including the toolbars, menus, and view preferences. You will use navigation techniques, express movements, and learn some basic worksheet concepts while exploring the Excel screen. You will also learn about creating and renaming folders for file management.

Upon completion of this lesson, you should have mastered the following skill sets:

- Start Excel
- Explore the Excel workbook
- Explore menus and toolbars
- Set view preferences
- Navigate the worksheet
- Use scroll bars
- Use the Go To command
- Create a folder for saving workbooks
- Rename a folder

Terms

Worksheet
Workbook
Status bar
Task pane
Title bar
Menu bar
Toolbar
Formula bar
Active cell
Name box
Column
Row
Cell
Cell address
Active cell reference
Scroll bars
Working folder
Folder

TRYOUT

GOALS
To explore the Excel workbook
To practice using the following skill sets:
- Start Excel
- Explore the Excel workbook
- Explore menus and toolbars
- Set view preferences

TASK 1

WHAT YOU NEED TO KNOW

About Excel

▶ Excel is a powerful spreadsheet tool you can use to analyze, chart, and manage data for personal, business, and financial use. You can also use Excel to produce worksheets, charts, and databases, and to publish data to the Web.

Start Excel

▶ To start Excel, on the Windows taskbar, click Start, select All Programs, select Microsoft Office, and Microsoft Office Excel 2003. If you have customized your desktop or Start menu, just double-click the Excel icon.

T R Y *it* O U T *E1-1*

1. Click **Start** on the Windows taskbar.

2. Select **All Programs.**

3. Select **Microsoft Office.**

4. Click **Microsoft Office Excel 2003.**

Explore the Excel Workbook

▶ When you start Excel, a new *workbook*, called Book1, appears containing three *worksheets* identified by the sheet tabs at the bottom of the workbook. The active sheet in Figure 1.1 is Sheet1, but you can click another sheet tab to make it the active sheet. You can increase the number of sheets in a workbook, as discussed in Lesson 4, to two hundred fifty-five.

▶ The bottom of the screen also contains the *status bar,* which displays the condition of worksheet calculations and settings. This bar shows items such as the setting for caps or number lock.

▶ The *task pane* appears on startup on the right side of the screen and shows options for the task at hand. In the Getting Started task pane, the Microsoft Office Online section provides current links to online content and the Open section shows the last four files opened. You can close the task pane using the Close button on the top right corner of the pane. If the task pane does not display, use the View menu, as discussed on the next page.

1. Click **Sheet2**.
2. Click **Sheet3**.

3. Click **Sheet1**.
4. Click the **Close** button on the task pane to close the pane.

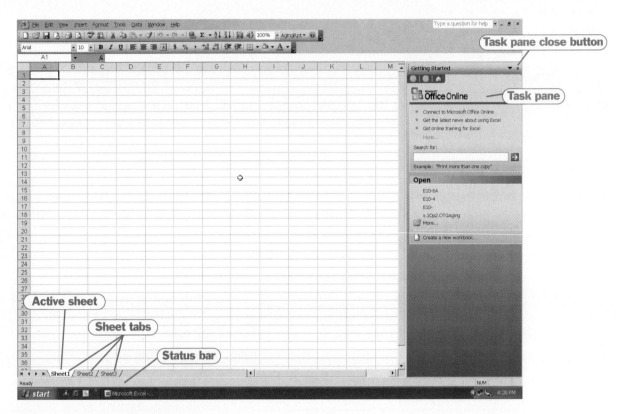

Figure 1.1 Excel workbook screen

Explore Menus and Toolbars

▶ The top portion of the screen contains the *title bar,* the *menu bar,* and two *toolbars.* The toolbars are the Standard and Formatting toolbars, as shown in Figure 1.2.

▶ Excel also has a *formula bar,* which contains the *Name box* on the left, the Insert Function button, and an area that displays the contents of the active cell. The *active cell* is the location of the worksheet insertion point, which shows where you are currently working. The name of the active cell appears in the *Name box.*

▶ Click the Toolbar Options arrow at the end of the toolbar to show the most frequently used buttons on one row or to add buttons that are not displayed.

Figure 1.2 Excel title bar, menu bar, toolbar, and formula bar

T R Y *i t* **O U T** *E1-3*

1. In Cell A1, type **test**. Press Enter.

2. Click in Cell A1. Notice the text and the reference to A1, the active cell, in the Name box.

3. Click **File**.

4. Position the mouse pointer over all other menu headings to display the menu items.

5. Click the **Toolbar Options** arrow button on the Standard toolbar.

6. Click the **Show Buttons on One Row** option. Note that the Standard and Formatting toolbars are consolidated into one row.

7. Click the **Toolbar options** arrow button and click the **Show Buttons on Two Rows** option.

8. Position the mouse pointer over each button to view its function.

Set View Preferences

▶ Use the View menu to set display options for your Excel workbook. As shown in Figure 1.3, Task Pane, Formula Bar, and Status Bar are checked on the menu, which means they are displayed. Click the check marks to remove the features from the display.

▶ If you are working on a large worksheet or have difficulty seeing all the data, two View options will help:

- The Full Screen option on the View menu expands the worksheet to fill the screen while closing the toolbars and the formula bar.

- The Zoom option on the View menu lets you set the magnification of cells in a worksheet, as shown in Figure 1.4.

▶ To further customize view preferences, click Tools, Options, and then the View tab in the Options dialog box, as shown in Figure 1.5. Here, you can set display options for the Excel window, including showing formulas, gridlines, and setting gridline colors.

Figure 1.3 View menu

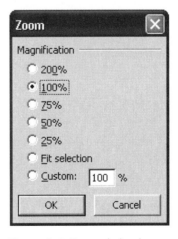

Figure 1.4 Zoom dialog box

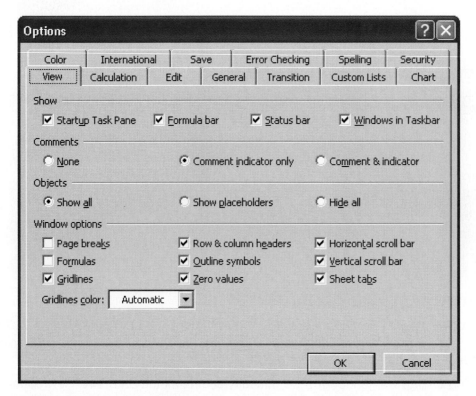

Figure 1.5 Options dialog box

TRY it OUT E1-4

1. Click the **View** menu and deselect the **Status bar**.

2. Click **View** and select the **Task Pane.**

3. Click **View, Toolbars**. Notice the checked and available toolbars.

4. Select the **Drawing Toolbar**.

5. Click **View, Full Screen.**

6. Click **Close Full Screen** (on the Full Screen toolbar on the worksheet) to return to the normal view.

7. Click **View, Zoom** to see the dialog box.

8. Select **200%** magnification and click **OK.**

9. Restore the magnification to **100%.**

10. Click **Tools, Options,** and then the **View** tab, if not already selected.

11. Click the **Status bar** check box to restore it. Click **OK.**

12. Click **View, Toolbars** and deselect the **Drawing Toolbar.**

13. Click the **Close** button to close Excel. Do not save the file.

REHEARSAL

TASK 1

WHAT YOU NEED TO KNOW

▶ If you have a shortcut to Excel on your desktop, double-click it to start the application, or click Start, All Programs, Microsoft Office, and Microsoft Office Excel 2003.

▶ In this Rehearsal activity, you will explore the Excel workbook, toolbars, and menus. You will use the View menu to set and reset preferences.

 DIRECTIONS

1. Click **File**. Notice the menu selections.
2. Click away from the File menu once to close it.
3. Select and view the commands on each menu.
4. Click **Sheet3**.
5. Click **Sheet1.**
6. Rest the mouse pointer on a toolbar button to display its name.
7. Find the toolbar buttons for **Bold, Print,** and **Save.**
8. Click **View, Toolbars.**
9. Deselect the **Formatting** and **Standard** toolbars.
10. Restore the toolbars.
11. Click **View, Zoom.**
12. Select other magnifications to view the effect.
13. Return to **100%** magnification.
14. Use the View menu to deselect the **Task Pane, Formula Bar,** and **Status Bar.**
15. Use the View menu to reselect the **Formula Bar,** the **Task Pane,** and the **Status Bar.**
16. Click **Tools, Options** to open the dialog box and make the following changes. In the View tab:
    a. Deselect the vertical and horizontal scroll bars.
    b. Set the gridline color to **Red.**
17. Restore the vertical and horizontal scroll bars and set the color back to **Automatic.**

Cues for Reference

Start Excel
- Double-click the **Microsoft Excel** icon on the desktop or Shortcut Bar.
  or
- Click **Start, All Programs, Microsoft Office, Microsoft Office Excel 2003.**

Office XP Click **Start, Programs, Microsoft Excel.**

Set Zoom
1. Click **View, Zoom.**
2. Select percentage of magnification.
3. Click **OK.**

Select Toolbars
1. Click **View, Toolbars.**
2. Select or deselect toolbars.

Set Options
1. Click **Tools, Options.**
2. Select appropriate tab.
3. Select or deselect options.
4. Click **OK.**

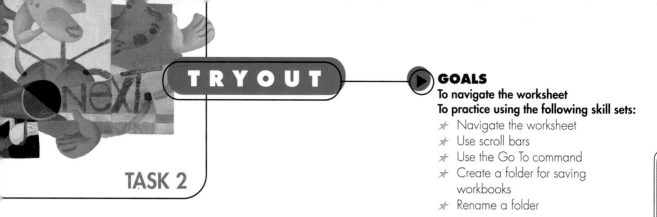

TRYOUT

TASK 2

▶ **GOALS**
To navigate the worksheet
To practice using the following skill sets:
* ✴ Navigate the worksheet
* ✴ Use scroll bars
* ✴ Use the Go To command
* ✴ Create a folder for saving workbooks
* ✴ Rename a folder

EXCEL

WHAT YOU NEED TO KNOW

Navigate the Worksheet

▶ A worksheet has alphabetical *column* headings and numbered *rows*. The intersection of a column and row is called a *cell*. A worksheet contains 256 columns and 65,536 rows, which means that over 16 million cells are available for data. As you will see after the tryout, only a small part of the worksheet is visible on the screen at one time.

▶ A cell is referenced (referred to) by its unique *cell address*, which is made up of the column and row number. Cell B2, as shown in Figure 1.6, has a heavy border indicating that it is the active cell. The *active cell* is also identified in the *Name box* on the formula bar, which always displays the *active cell reference*, and by the highlighted column and row of the active cell. The mouse pointer is a plus sign when on the worksheet, as shown below.

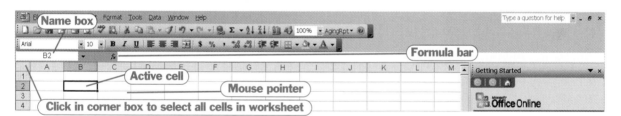

Figure 1.6 Worksheet with active Cell B2 in Name box

T R Y *it* O U T *E1-5*

1. Click **Cell D5** to make it active.

2. Press the left arrow key until **Cell B5** is selected.

3. Press the arrow keys to select **Cell H20**.

▶ To move around the worksheet, press the arrow keys or press both an arrow key and the Ctrl key for express (fast) movements. As you move through the worksheet, the active cell changes, as does the active cell reference in the Name box. A table of keystrokes to select cells and to navigate the worksheet is shown below.

SELECT WORKSHEET CELLS	
Select a cell	Click the cell
Select the worksheet	Ctrl+A, or click corner box
Select a row	Shift+Space
Select a column	Ctrl+Space
NAVIGATE THE WORKSHEET	
Move one cell	Use the left, right, up, or down arrow
Move one screen up or down	Page Up or Page Down
First cell in worksheet	Ctrl+Home
First cell in current row	Home
First cell in current column	Ctrl+↑
Last cell in current row	Ctrl+→
Last cell in current column	Ctrl+↓

T R Y *it* O U T *E1-6*

Note: *H20 should be the active cell.*

1. Press the **Shift** key + **spacebar** to select **Row 20.**

2. Press the **Ctrl+Home** keys.

3. Use navigation express shortcuts to go to:
   Last cell in current row: **Ctrl+→**
   First cell in current row: **Home**
   Last cell in current column: **Ctrl+↓**

4. Return to the first cell in the worksheet.

5. Click the corner box to the left of the Column A heading, as shown in Figure 1.6, to select the entire worksheet.

6. Click any cell to deselect it.

Use Scroll Bars

▶ To scroll to different areas in a worksheet, use the mouse pointer and the *scroll bars* at the right and bottom of the worksheet window, as shown in Figure 1.7, and summarized in the table below. Scrolling does not change the active cell.

USE SCROLL BARS	
One column left or right	Click left or right scroll arrows
One row up or down	Click up or down scroll arrows
Scroll quickly	Click and drag scroll bar, press and hold Shift

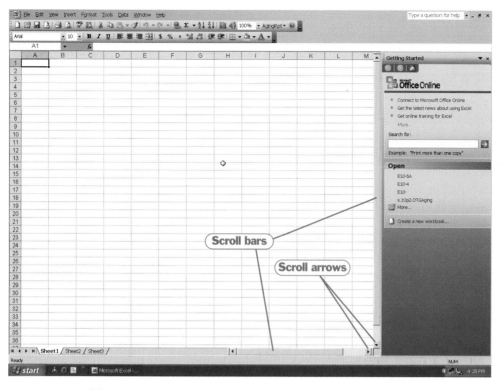

Figure 1.7 Scroll bars

TRY it OUT E1-7

1. Click the **down** scroll arrow on the vertical scroll bar.

2. Click the **right** scroll arrow on the horizontal scroll bar.

3. Click the **horizontal** scroll bar, press the **Shift** key, and drag to the right.

4. Click and drag the **horizontal** scroll bar to the left, back to Column A.

5. Click the **up** scroll arrow on the vertical scroll bar.

Use the Go To Command

▶ You can move directly to a specific cell by entering the cell address in the Name box or by using the Go To command.

▶ Click Edit, Go To or press the F5 key to display the Go To dialog box, as shown in Figure 1.8. You can enter the desired cell address, or select a location from your list of previously selected locations. The dollar signs displayed with the cell addresses indicate that the address is an absolute reference (see Lesson 4) to that specific location.

Figure 1.8 Go To dialog box

1. Click **Edit**, **Go To**.

2. In the Reference text box, enter **J122** and press the **Enter** key.

3. Press the **F5** key and go to **Cell AB321**. Click **OK**.

4. Click the **Name box** on the left side of the formula bar.

5. Enter **E15** and press the **Enter** key.

6. Press the **F5** key and double-click to select **Cell J122** from the Go To list.

7. To return to Cell A1 press the **Ctrl+Home** keys.

Create a Folder for Saving Workbooks

▶ The *working folder,* or default location for saving your files, is usually the My Documents folder. A *folder* is a location on a drive that you create to hold files that are related to each other. See Appendix B for more file management procedures.

▶ Use the Open dialog box to create folders or subfolders to organize your workbook files. Click the Open button on the Standard toolbar and click the down arrow to select the location for your new folder. Click the Create New Folder button on the Open dialog box toolbar, as shown in Figure 1.9, and name the folder. You will then be able to select this folder so that it is in the Look in box. Use the same procedure to create subfolders within the new folder.

▶ Once you have selected a folder for opening and saving, it remains in the Look in box until you turn off the computer.

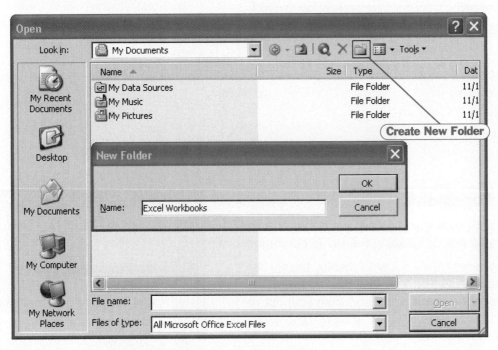

Figure 1.9 Open dialog box, opening a new folder

Renaming Folders

▶ To rename any folder, right-click the folder and select Rename from the shortcut menu as shown in Figure 1.10. Type the new folder name and press Enter.

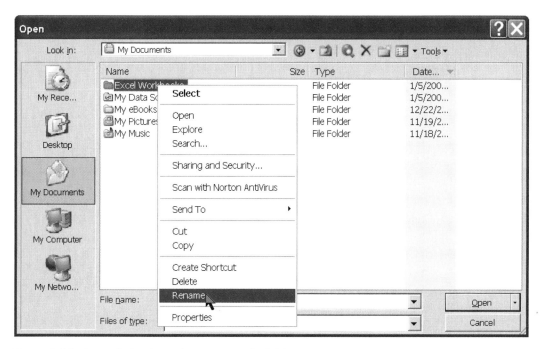

Figure 1.10 Open dialog box, shortcut menu for folders

T R Y *it* O U T *E1-9*

1. Click the **Open** button on the Standard toolbar.

2. Click the **Create New Folder** button on the Open dialog box toolbar.

3. Type the name of the folder: **Excel Workbooks.** Click **OK.** (Notice that the folder is empty and the folder name is in the Look in box.)

4. Click the **Up One Level** button to return to the main folder.

5. Right-click the **Excel Workbooks** folder.

6. Select **Rename** from the shortcut menu.

7. Type **Excel Solutions,** and press **Enter.**

8. Click the **Cancel** button on the Open dialog box.

9. Click the **Save** button on the Standard toolbar. Notice your new working folder.

10. Click **Cancel**.

REHEARSAL

GOAL
To navigate the worksheet

SETTING THE STAGE/WRAPUP
Start Excel

TASK 2

WHAT YOU NEED TO KNOW

▶ Notice the active cell reference in the Name box as you move through the worksheet.

▶ In this Rehearsal activity, you will navigate the worksheet using shortcut keys and express movements. You will also create and rename a subfolder in your Excel Workbooks folder.

▼ DIRECTIONS

1. Click **Cell E5** to make it active.

2. Press the arrow keys to select **Cell AA45.**

3. Use express keystrokes to go to the following locations:
   a. Last cell in current row
   b. Last cell in current column
   c. First cell in current row
   d. First cell in worksheet

4. Click the **horizontal** scroll bar, press the **Shift** key, and drag to the right.

5. Click the **horizontal** scroll bar and press the **Shift** key until you can see **Column BZ.**

6. Drag the **horizontal** scroll bar to the left, back to **Column A.**

7. Press the **F5** key to go to **Cell J33.**

8. Repeat Step 7 to go to **Cell BB159** and **Cell J33** again.

9. In the Name box, enter **G5**. Press **Enter.**

10. Press the **Ctrl** key + spacebar to select **Column J.**

11. Select the entire worksheet.

12. Select any cell.

13. Move one screen down.

14. Press the **Ctrl+Home** keys to return to **Cell A1.**

15. Click the **Open** button on the Standard toolbar; then, if Excel Solutions is not in the Look in box, select it from the list of folders and double-click the folder.

16. Create a new folder and name it **Lesson 1**.

17. Move up one level in the Open dialog box and rename the new folder **Lesson 2.**

18. Click **Cancel**.

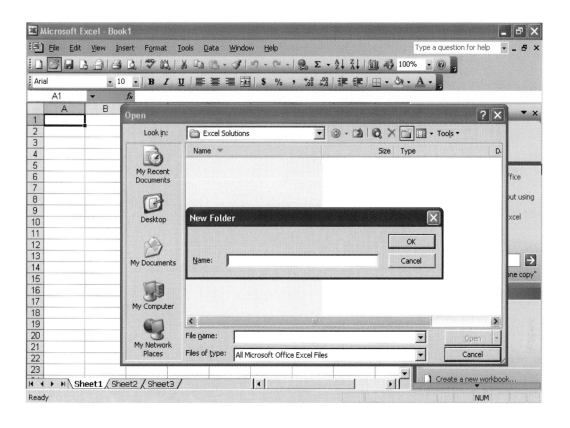

Cues for Reference

Scroll Through a Worksheet
- Click **scroll bar arrow** to move worksheet view.
  or
- Click **Shift**+**scroll bar arrow** to quickly scroll through worksheet.

Use Go To (Express Navigation)
1. Click F5.
2. Enter cell address.
3. Click **OK**.

Use Navigation Express Shortcuts

Select a row	**Shift+spacebar**
Select a column	**Ctrl+spacebar**
Move one cell	Use the **left, right, up,** or **down arrow**

Move one screen up or down	**Page Up** or **Page Down**
First cell in worksheet	**Ctrl+Home**
First cell in current row	**Home**
First cell in current column	**Ctrl+↑**
Last cell in current row	**Ctrl+→**
Last cell in current column	**Ctrl+↓**

Create New Folder
1. Click the **Open** button.
2. If necessary, click the list arrow in Look in box, or double-click a listed folder to select location.
3. Click the **Create New Folder** button.
4. Enter the folder name.
5. Click **OK**.

Rename a Folder
1. Right-click the folder.
2. Enter the new folder name.
3. Press **Enter**.

Business Forms

In this lesson, you will learn to use Excel to design business forms and to customize both software and online templates. You will use the Internet to e-mail a form and to access Microsoft Office Online.

Upon completion of this lesson, you should have mastered the following skill sets:

- Enter text, dates, and numbers
- Use Smart Tags
- Format cell data
  - Format dates
  - Format for currency
  - Format text
- Use Save and Save As
- Edit cell data
  - Edit cell contents
  - Align cell data
  - Clear cell contents
  - Check spelling
  - Use the Thesaurus
- Use AutoComplete
- Use Print Preview
- Select a range of cells
- Print
  - Set Print Area
  - Change print settings
- Work with templates
- Save a file as a template
- View Web templates

Terms
Software-related
Label
Left-aligned
Value
Right-aligned
Edit mode
Thesaurus
AutoComplete
Range
Template

Document-related
Business form
Transaction
Professional invoice
Purchase order
Vendor
Sales invoice

TRYOUT

TASK 1

 GOALS

To create an invoice for services
To practice using the following skill sets:

* ✶ Enter text, dates, and numbers
* ✶ Use Smart Tags
* ✶ Format cell data
  * ✶ Format dates
  * ✶ Format for currency
  * ✶ Format text
* ✶ Use Save and Save As

WHAT YOU NEED TO KNOW

Enter Text, Dates, and Numbers

▶ When you enter an alphabetic character or symbol (text) as the first character in a cell, the cell contains a *label*. Labels are *left-aligned* in the cell by default.

▶ When you enter a number or date as the first character in a cell, the cell contains a *value*. Values are *right-aligned* in the cell by default.

▶ After you enter a label or value in a cell, press the Enter key or the arrow key that points to the location of the next data entry to enter the data. Notice the following in Figure 2.1:

* Labels are left-aligned.
* Dates and values are right-aligned.

▶ The default cell width displays approximately nine characters, depending on the font, but you can enter over 32,000 characters in each cell. If you enter text beyond the default cell width, it appears in the next cell's space as long as no other data is there. Notice in Figure 2.1 that the label AV Equipment in Cell A4 would be truncated if there were data in the next cell. However, the formula bar would show that the full label is stored in the cell.

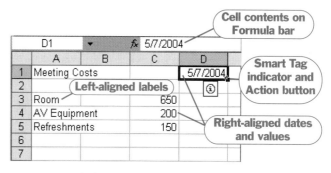

Figure 2.1 Label and value entries

TRYi**t OUT** E2-1

1. Start Excel.

2. Enter the label in **Cell A1,** as shown in Figure 2.1.

3. Press the **right arrow** key to enter the data and move to cell D1.

4. Enter the date in **Cell D1,** as shown on the formula bar.

5. Enter the data in **Row 3** of the illustration. Notice the alignment of data.

6. Enter the data in **Row 4** of the illustration.

7. Click **Cell A4** and **Cell B4**. Notice that the label is stored only in Cell A4.

8. Enter data for **Row 5.**

9. Do not close or save the file.

Use Smart Tags

▶ As shown in Figure 2.1, Excel labels certain types of data with Smart Tags. The Smart Tag indicator, a purple triangle, displays in the cell and the Actions button displays nearby on the worksheet. Click the list arrow on the button to display custom actions associated with that data element, as shown in Figure 2.2. If Smart Tags do not display on your screen, click Tools, AutoCorrect options, and then click the Smart Tags tab, select Label data with smart tags, and click OK.

▶ In Excel, you can activate a Smart Tag when you enter dates, stock symbols, Outlook e-mail recipients, and numeric labels.

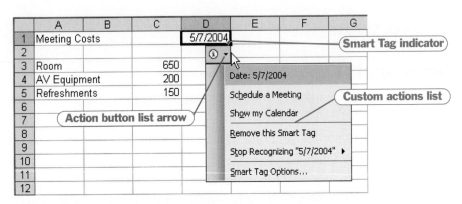

Figure 2.2 Smart Tag actions for dates

TRY it OUT E2-2

1. Continue to work in the open file or open **E2-2** from the Data CD.

2. Select **Cell D1.** Click the list arrow on the Smart Tag options button that displays below the date.

3. Click **Show my Calendar.** Your calendar in Outlook will display.

4. Close the calendar.

5. Enter **MSFT** in **Cell E1.** Press **Enter** and then move the mouse over the cell.

6. View the Smart Tag options for the stock symbol.

7. Do not close or save the file.

Format Cell Data

Format Dates

▶ You can enter a date in any format and reformat it in one of 17 date formats. For example, if you enter the date in the mm/dd/yyyy format, you can change it to mm/dd/yy.

▶ To format dates, select the date and click Format, Cells. In the Format Cells dialog box, click the Number tab, click Date from the Category list, and click a date format from the Type list, as shown in Figure 2.3.

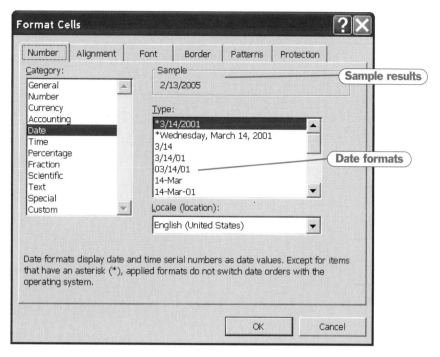

Figure 2.3 Format Cells dialog box

T R Y *i t* **O U T** *E2-3*

1. Continue to work in the open file or open **E2-3** from the Data CD.

2. Click **Cell D1.**

3. Click **Format, Cells.**

4. On the Number tab, click **Date,** if necessary.

5. Scroll down and select the **March 14, 2001,** or full date format.

6. Click **OK.**

7. Do not close or save the file.

Format for Currency

▶ When you enter numbers or values, they are in the General format, which means that decimal places are only shown if there are decimal values. To add a dollar sign and two decimal places (Currency format) for the selected cell, click the Currency Style button on the Formatting toolbar, as shown in Figure 2.4.

Format Text

▶ The default font is Arial, 10 point. To change font and font size, select the cell(s) and click the Font and Font Size list arrows on the Formatting toolbar and choose the desired settings. Bold, Italic, and Underline styles may also be set.

Figure 2.4 Formatting toolbar – font list

TRY it OUT *E2-4*

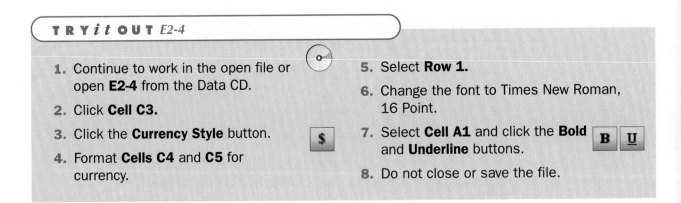

1. Continue to work in the open file or open **E2-4** from the Data CD.

2. Click **Cell C3**.

3. Click the **Currency Style** button.

4. Format **Cells C4** and **C5** for currency.

5. Select **Row 1**.

6. Change the font to Times New Roman, 16 Point.

7. Select **Cell A1** and click the **Bold** and **Underline** buttons.

8. Do not close or save the file.

Use Save and Save As

▶ Excel workbooks are named Book1, Book2, and so forth, until you save them with your own file names. Click the Save button on the Standard toolbar to save a new file or to overwrite an existing file.

▶ When you click the Save button to save a new file, the Save As dialog box opens. Naming a file in the Save As dialog box creates an Excel Worksheet file with an .xls extension.

▶ You can save Excel files with different names, in different locations, and in different file formats using the settings in the Save As dialog box. To save a file with any of these changes, click File, Save As, and select the appropriate settings. Notice the Save as type list, as shown in Figure 2.5.

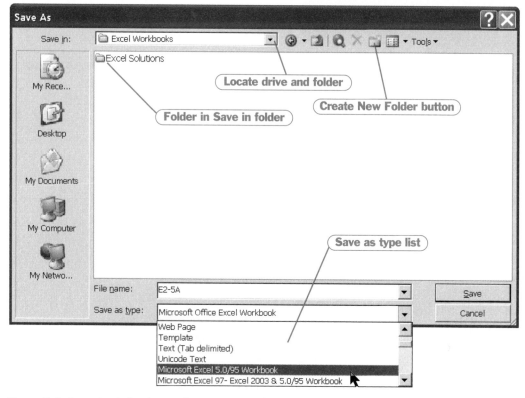

Figure 2.5 Save As dialog box with Save as type list

TRY*it*OUT E2-5

1. Continue to work in the open file or open **E2-5** from the Data CD.

2. Click the **Save** button.

3. Double-click the name of your working folder, **Lesson 2,** if it is listed, or locate your folder using the list arrow in the Save in box.

4. Enter **E2-5** as the file name.

5. Click **Save.** Notice the file name on the title bar.

6. Enter Total in **Cell A6.**

7. Click the **Save** button. The new data is saved in that file.

8. Click **File, Save As.**

9. Enter **E2-5A** as the file name, to save the file under a new name.

10. In the Save as type box, click **Microsoft Excel 97-Excel 2003 & 5.0/95 Workbook,** for use with the earlier version of the software.

11. Click **Save.** Click **File, Close.**

REHEARSAL

TASK 1

 GOAL
To create an invoice for services

SETTING THE STAGE/WRAPUP
File names: 2.1proinv
2.1solution

WHAT YOU NEED TO KNOW

▶ A *business form* is a document format that you develop for a business activity that occurs often. Once you create the form, you always use it to record that particular *transaction*, or business event, in a uniform manner. Many business forms are numbered consecutively for reference in records or communications.

▶ Consultants and professionals in fee-based businesses use a *professional invoice* to bill their clients for the services provided.

▶ You can use preprinted forms or predesigned Excel worksheets for business forms or you can create your own forms with Excel.

▶ In this Rehearsal activity, you will use the model illustration to create an invoice for planning services for Occasions Event Planning.

▼ DIRECTIONS

1. Open a new blank worksheet. In **Cell C1,** enter the label as illustrated on the facing page. (Press the arrow keys to move to **Cell A3.**)

2. Enter the long label in **Cell A3.**

3. Enter the label in **Cell E3** and the date with the current year in **Cell F3.**

4. Click **Cell F3** to make it the active cell.

5. Click the Smart Tag button to view the list of actions. Click **Remove this Smart Tag.**

6. Click **Format, Cells,** to set the date format, as illustrated.

7. Enter the remaining data in the exact locations illustrated.

8. Format the date in **Cell B14** using the same date format.

9. In **Cell F16,** enter the value and format for currency.

10. Save the file in your **Lesson 2** folder; name it **2.1proinv.**

11. Resave the file as **2.1solution,** as an Excel 97 file type.

12. Close the file.

	A	B	C	D	E	F
1			INVOICE			
2						
3	Occasions Event Planning				Date:	5-Mar-04
4	675 Third Avenue					
5	New York, NY 10017				212-555-1234	
6						
7						
8	Bill to:		Mr. Martin Meyers			
9			1050 Greenway Street			
10			Brooklyn, NY 12015			
11						
12	Description					Amount
13	Event:	Training Seminar				
14	Date:	5-Mar-04				
15						
16			Professional event planning services			$ 525.00

Cues for Reference

Enter a Label or Value
1. Click cell to receive data.
2. Enter the label or value.
3. Press **Enter** or press an **arrow** key to move to next cell.

Format Dates
1. Select the date.
2. Click **Format, Cells.**
3. In the Number tab, click **Date.**
4. Select a date format.
5. Click **OK.**

Format Currency
1. Select the value to format.
2. Click the **Currency Style** button.

Use Smart Tag
1. Click the **Smart Tag** button list arrow.
2. Select the action.

Save
- For a new file, click the **Save** button; see Save As, Steps 2 through 5, at right.

or
- To resave an existing file, click the **Save** button.

Save As
1. Click **File, Save As.**
2. In Save in box, select location.
   or
   Double-click folder in current folder.
3. Enter file name in File name box.
4. Click **Save as type** down arrow, and click file type, if necessary.
5. Click **Save.**

TRYOUT

TASK 2

GOALS
To create a purchase order
To practice using the following skill sets:
- ✶ Edit cell data
  - ✶ Edit cell contents
  - ✶ Align cell data
  - ✶ Clear cell contents
  - ✶ Check spelling
  - ✶ Use the Thesaurus
- ✶ Use AutoComplete
- ✶ Use Print Preview
- ✶ Select a range of cells
- ✶ Print
  - ✶ Set Print Area
  - ✶ Change print settings

WHAT YOU NEED TO KNOW

Edit Cell Data

Edit Cell Contents

▶ If you notice an error *before* you complete an entry, press the Backspace key to edit data before you press the Enter key. Once you press the Enter key, the data is entered in the cell.

▶ If you notice an error *after* you enter the data, you can redo the entry so that the new data overwrites the original data. To correct an entry in *Edit mode*, press the F2 key, which places the insertion point at the end of the incorrect label. Or, double-click in the cell at the edit location. Note the items to be edited in Figure 2.6.

	B	C	D	E	F	G
1		10/12/2004				
2	Number	Units	Item			
3	125	Boxes	Envelopes	Change to: #10 Envelopes		
4	85	Reams	Legal Pads			
5						
6			Change to: Legal Size Paper			
7						

Dates and values right-aligned — *Labels left-aligned*

Figure 2.6 Default alignments with items for edit

TRY *it* OUT E2-6

1. Open **E2-6** from the Data CD.

2. Change "Legal Pads" to "Legal Size Paper":
   a. Click **Cell C4**.

b. Press the **F2** key. The insertion point is at the end of the label.

c. Press the **Backspace** key to delete "Pads" and enter `Size Paper`.

Continued on next page

3. Change "Envelopes" to "#10 Envelopes":
   a. Place the mouse pointer at the beginning of **Cell C3** and double-click the cell. You should be in Edit mode with the insertion point at the beginning of the cell.
   b. Enter #10 and a space.
4. In **Cell A6,** enter 130. Before it is entered, press the **Backspace** key once

and enter 5 to make it 135. Then press the **Enter** key.

5. In **Cell A7,** enter 182 and then press the **Enter** key.
6. In **Cell A7,** enter 185 to overwrite. Then, press the **Enter** key.
7. Do not close or save the file.

EXCEL

Align Data

▶ As discussed in Task 1, by default, label text is left-aligned, whereas values and dates are right-aligned in the cell, as shown in Figure 2.6.

▶ However, you can change the alignment of data to improve the appearance of the worksheet by using the alignment buttons on the Formatting toolbar, shown in Figure 2.7. Select the cell and click the appropriate alignment button to left-align, center, or right-align data.

Figure 2.7 Alignment buttons on Formatting toolbar

1. Continue working in the open file or open **E2-7** from the Data CD.
2. Click **Cell A2** and click the **Center** alignment button.
3. Center the label in **Cell B2.**
4. Center the label in **Cell C2.**
5. Left-align the data in **Cell A6.**
6. Right-align the data in **Cell A6.**
7. Do not close the file.

Clear Cell Contents

▶ If you want to remove data you enter in a cell, select the cell and press the Delete key.
▶ You can also remove data by clicking Edit, Clear, and Contents.

TRY *it* OUT E2-8

1. Continue working in the open file or open **E2-8** from the Data CD.
2. Click **Cell A6**.
3. Press the **Delete** key.

4. Click **Cell A7**.
5. Click **Edit, Clear,** and **Contents**.
6. Do not close the file.

Check Spelling

▶ The Spelling feature compares the words in your file to the words in the application's dictionary. In Excel, there is no indication of a spelling error until you use the Spelling feature. Click the Spelling button on the Standard toolbar to check the spelling of worksheet labels.

TRY *it* OUT E2-9

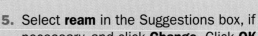

1. Continue working in the open file or open **E2-9** from the Data CD.
2. In **Cell B6,** type the word **reem** and then press the Enter key.
3. Click the **Spelling** button.
4. Click **Yes** to start at the beginning of the worksheet.

5. Select **ream** in the Suggestions box, if necessary, and click **Change**. Click **OK**.
6. Delete the text in **Cell B6**.
7. Do not save or close the file.

Use the Thesaurus

▶ Excel has a new Research tool that includes thesaurus references in English, French, and Spanish. A *thesaurus* provides synonyms for the selected word that may better express the intended meaning. Type the word to be researched, click the Research button on the Standard toolbar, and select the appropriate reference book from the Research task pane, as shown in Figure 2.8. Click the green arrow to start the search and view the results of your research. Replace the word, if you wish, by overwriting it with the appropriate synonym.

▶ You can change or update the list of reference books that display using the Research options hyperlink.

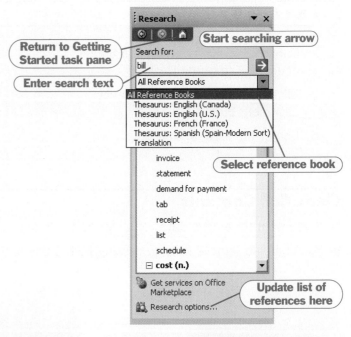

Figure 2.8 Research task pane.

TRY *it* OUT *E2-10*

1. Continue working in the open file or open **E2-10** from the Data CD.

2. In **Cell A1,** enter the word `bill` and then select **Cell A1.**

3. Click the **Research** button. The Research task pane appears.

4. Click the list arrow and select **Thesaurus: English (U.S.).** Click the green Go arrow and notice the synonyms.

5. Click the list arrow and check the results in the **French Thesaurus** and in the **Translation** reference. *Note: If you do not have these references, check others available to you.*

6. Close the Research task pane.

7. In **Cell A1,** enter the word `Invoice.`

8. Do not save or close the file.

Use AutoComplete

▶ The *AutoComplete* feature lets you enter labels automatically if you have previously entered them in the same column.

▶ When you enter the first letter or letters of repeated data, Excel AutoCompletes the label from your previously entered data. If the label is correct, press the Enter key to confirm the entry. If it is not correct, continue entering the new label.

TRY *it* OUT *E2-11*

1. Continue working in the open file or open **E2-11** from the Data CD.

2. Follow the steps below to add 10 Boxes Pencils in **Row 5.**
   a. In **Cell A5,** enter `10.`
   b. In **Cell B5,** start to enter `Boxes.` TheAutoComplete feature will complete the label.
   c. Press the **Enter** key to accept the completed label.

3. In **Cell C5,** enter `Pencils.`

4. Do not save or close the file.

Use Print Preview

▶ Before printing, it is advisable to preview the worksheet because worksheets can become too large for one page. Click the Print Preview button on the Standard toolbar to open Print Preview.

▶ If the preview is satisfactory, you can print the worksheet using the Print button on the Preview screen as shown in Figure 2.9.

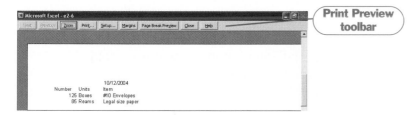

Figure 2.9 Print Preview screen

1. Continue working in the open file or open **E2-12** from the Data CD.

2. Click the **Print Preview** button.

3. Click the data to get a better view.

4. Click the **Print** button on the Preview toolbar.

5. Click **OK** in the Print dialog box. The worksheet prints as previewed.

Select a Range of Cells

▶ A _range_ is a group of cells in a row, column, or block. The beginning and ending cell addresses identify a range. For example, A2:C5 is selected in Figure 2.10. To select a range, click the first cell in the range, hold down the mouse, and drag the selection until all the cells in the range are selected. Notice that a dark border outlines the range and, except for the first cell, all cells are shaded.

1	Invoice		10/12/2004
2	Number	Units	Item
3	125	Boxes	#10 Envelopes
4	85	Reams	Legal Size Pap
5	10	Boxes	Pencils
6		Selected range A2:C5	

Figure 2.10 Selected cells in a range

1. Continue working in the open file or open **E2-13** from the Data CD.

2. Select the cells in the range **A2:C5.**

3. Click on any cell to deselect the range.

Print

▶ Use the Print button on the Standard toolbar to print a worksheet. Printing with the toolbar button prints the worksheet with default settings. The entire worksheet prints in portrait orientation without gridlines or row and column headings. If this is satisfactory, the Print button is the most efficient way to print.

Set Print Area

▶ To print only part of a worksheet, you must define the print area. With the mouse, select the block of cells you want to print, and click File, Print Area, and Set Print Area. You must clear this setting if you wish to print any other selection. You can clear the print area by clicking File, Print Area, and Clear Print Area.

Change Print Settings

▶ Click File, Page Setup to customize print settings. The Page Setup dialog box contains tabs for setting Page, Margins, Header/Footer, and Sheet options. For example, to set up gridline printing click File, Page Setup, click the Sheet tab, and select Gridlines in the Print section, as shown in Figure 2.11.

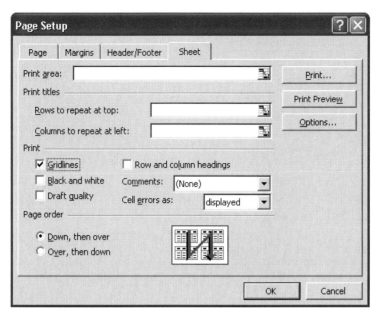

Figure 2.11 Page Setup dialog box with Sheet tab and Gridlines selected

TRY*it***OUT** *E2-14*

1. Continue working in the open file or open **E2-14** from the Data CD.

2. Click the **Print** button on the toolbar. The worksheet prints with default settings.

3. Click in **Cell A2,** select the block of cells from **A2** to **D5.**

4. Click **File, Print Area,** and **Set Print Area.** The area is outlined.

5. Click **File, Page Setup,** and click the **Sheet** tab.

6. Click the **Gridlines** check box in the Print section, and click **OK.**

7. Click the **Print Preview** button.

8. Click the **Print** button on the Preview toolbar.

9. Click **OK.** The worksheet prints as previewed with area and gridline settings.

10. Save the file as **E2-14** in the **Lesson 2** folder you created in Lesson 1; close the file.

REHEARSAL

TASK 2

GOAL
To create a purchase order

SETTING THE STAGE/WRAPUP
File name: **2.2purord**

WHAT YOU NEED TO KNOW

▶ A *purchase order* is a business form that a firm completes and sends to a *vendor*, or supplier, when merchandise or supplies are needed.

▶ The Received column is left blank, because it is used to check the order when it is received. The terms of the purchase define the agreement for payment. You can obtain the stock or item numbers and descriptions for the purchase order from the vendor's catalog, quotations, or Web site.

▶ When you enter data in a cell containing both values and text, such as an address, Excel formats the entry as a label.

▶ In this Rehearsal activity, you will create a purchase order for supplies for Time Out Sporting Goods. You must enter formulas to calculate the purchase order amounts and total. Therefore, you will not complete the purchase order until the next lesson.

▼ DIRECTIONS

1. Open a new blank worksheet. Create the purchase order illustrated on the facing page by entering the values, date with the current year, and labels in the appropriate cell locations. Press the arrow keys to enter the data and move to the cell you need for the next data item.

2. In **Cell B15,** notice the AutoComplete effect as you begin to enter the label.

3. Go to **Cell A13.**

4. Double-click the cell to switch to Edit mode and change the value to **3.**

5. Center and bold the labels in the range **A12:C12.**

6. Right-align the labels in the range **G12:H12.**

7. Select **Cell D15.** Press the **F2** key to go into Edit mode. Change the cell data to **#2345 Folders - Green.**

8. Overwrite data in **Cell H5;** Change "30 days" to **Check.**

9. Remove the Smart Tag that appears in **Cell H4** for UPS.

10. Place your cursor in **Cell A1** and use Spell Check. Ignore any errors that arise for proper names.

11. Bold column headings and text in **Cells F2** to **F6, A8,** and **D1.**

12. Change the font size in **Cell D1** to **12.**

13. Set the print area for the range **A1:H6** to print the heading.

14. Check the Print Preview screen.

15. Clear the print area.

16. Use Page Setup to set and print the entire purchase order with gridlines.

17. Save the file and name it **2.2purord.** Close the file.

	A	B	C	D	E	F	G	H	I	J
1				PURCHASE ORDER						
2	Time Out Sporting Goods					Date:		10/15/04	Remove	
3	1412 Barkely Street					Order #:		1000	SmartTag	
4	Chicago, IL 60064					Ship Via:		UPS		
5						Terms:		30 days	Change to:	
6	Phone:	847-555-1200				Ordered by:		Bill	Check	
7										
8	TO:	Supplies Unlimited								
9		545 Industrial Way								
10		Chicago, IL 60064								
11										
12	Quantity	Unit	Received	Description			Price	Amount		
13	5	Boxes		#2343 Folders			10.55			
14	4	Cartons		#654 Copy Paper			23.85			
15	2	Boxes		#2345 Folders			11.95			
16										
17	Change to: 3			Change to:						
18				#2345 Folders - Green						
19										
20										

T R Y O U T

GOALS
To create a sales invoice from a customized template
To practice using the following skill sets:
* ✴ Work with templates
* ✴ Save a file as a template
* ✴ View Web templates

WHAT YOU NEED TO KNOW

Work with Templates

▶ Excel provides model worksheet designs, or *templates,* for common business forms. A template contains worksheet settings, such as fonts, formatting, styles, and formulas, that are not changed or overwritten.

▶ You can open Excel templates using the New Workbook task pane in the Templates section, as shown in Figure 2.12. Click File, New, if the task pane is not displayed. Click On my computer to open the Templates dialog box and click the Spreadsheet Solutions tab, as shown in Figure 2.13.

Figure 2.12 New Workbook task pane

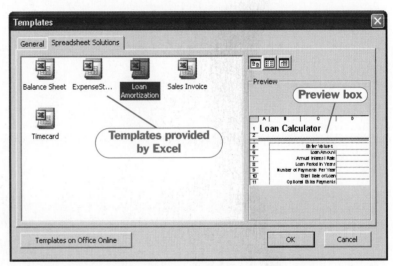

Figure 2.13 Templates dialog box, Spreadsheet Solutions tab

T R Y *i t* O U T E2-15

1. If the New task pane is not displayed, click **File, New.**

2. Click **On my computer** on the New Workbook task pane to open the Templates dialog box.

3. Click the **Spreadsheet Solutions** tab.

4. Click each icon and view a sample in the Preview box.

5. Double-click the **ExpenseStatement** template.

6. Double-click the **Name** box, then enter your name on the expense statement. Press the **Enter** key.

7. Do not save or close the file.

Save a File as a Template

▶ If you customize a template, save it as a template file so that it will remain intact after each use.

▶ Save a file as a template in the Save As dialog box by clicking Template in the Save as type drop-down list, as shown in Figure 2.14. The new template file, with an .xlt extension, is automatically saved in the Templates folder. Your template can be found in the General tab in the Templates dialog box.

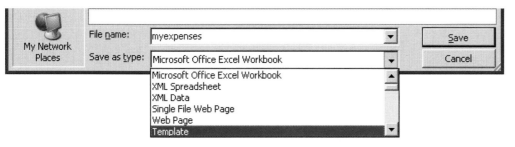

Figure 2.14 Saving a file as a template

T R Y it O U T E2-16

1. Continue to work in the open file or open **E2-16** from the Data CD.

2. Click **File, Save As.**

3. Name the file **myexpenses.**

4. Click the **Save as type** list arrow and click **Template.**

5. Click **Save.** Close the file.

6. Click **On my computer** in the New Workbook task pane.

7. Click the **General** tab in the Templates dialog box. Notice the location of your template.

8. Right-click your template's icon and click **Delete.** Click **Yes** to send the template to the Recycle Bin.

9. Close the Templates dialog box.

View Web Templates

▶ Additional templates are available at Microsoft Office Online or at Web sites you have personally located. You can view, customize, and save them to your computer. If you are online, you can select Templates on Office Online from the New Workbook task pane, which will directly link you through Internet Explorer to the appropriate Web site, as shown in Figure 2.15.

▶ To save time searching for the appropriate Web template on the site, you should use the **Search online for:** box in the Task pane, as shown in Figure 2.12. Enter the name of the template you wish to find and click Go. This will connect you to the site and display the results of the search.

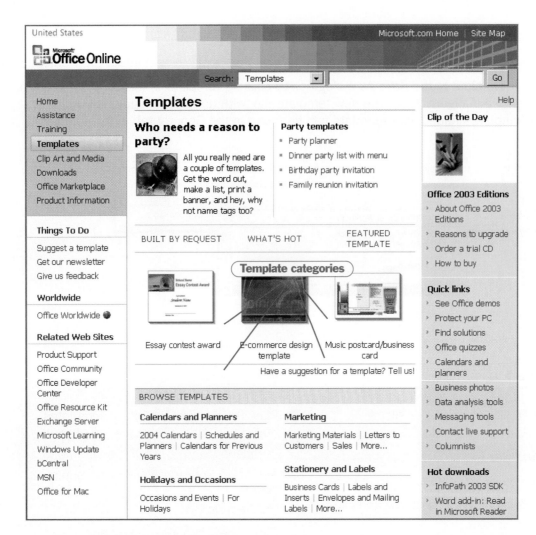

Figure 2.15 Office Online Templates page

TRY*it*OUT *E2-17*

Note: You need Internet capabilities for this Try it Out.

1. Click **File, New** to display the task pane.

2. Click **Templates on Office Online.**

3. Click **Orders and Inventory,** and under Order Management, click **Invoices and Purchase Orders.**

4. Select and view the template **Invoice that Calculates Total.**

5. Exit the browser.

6. Place cursor in the **Search online for** box.

7. Enter **Invoice.** Click **Go.** Notice the results.

8. Exit the browser and close Excel.

REHEARSAL

TASK 3

SETTING THE STAGE/WRAPUP
File names: **2.3invoice**
                 2.3timeout

WHAT YOU NEED TO KNOW

▶ A *sales invoice* is a bill that a seller prepares and sends to a customer for goods supplied by the seller. It usually contains an itemized list of items sold, as well as shipping and payment information, and may contain the customer's purchase order number.

▶ After you customize a sales invoice Excel template for your company and save it as a template, you can use it to prepare all company invoices in the future. Because the template contains formulas, it automatically calculates the total bill.

▶ In this Rehearsal activity, you will customize the invoice template, as shown in Figure 2.16, for Supplies Unlimited. The company will ship office supplies ordered by Time Out Sporting Goods and needs to prepare the invoice for the sale.

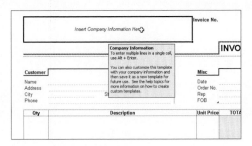

Figure 2.16 Sales Invoice template, company information

DIRECTIONS

1. Open the **Sales Invoice** template in the Spreadsheet Solutions tab of the Templates dialog box.

2. Click in the **Company Information** box at the top of the invoice and enter the company information as illustrated on the facing page. As indicated in the comment box, use **Alt+Enter** to move to a new line in the company letterhead.

3. Scroll to the bottom of the invoice to the **Insert Fine Print Here** section.

4. Select the box and use the **Edit** menu to clear the contents of this box.

5. Click in the **Insert Farewell Statement Here** box and enter the slogan, as illustrated.

6. Save the file as a template; name it **2.3invoice.**

7. Close the file.

8. Open the new **2.3invoice** template file in the General tab of the Templates dialog box.

9. Complete the invoice, as illustrated. Notice that the totals are automatically calculated.

10. Enter shipping charges of **$10.** Click the **Undo** button and change the amount by entering **$15.**

11. Enter the tax rate of **6.25%** in Cell L38, the white box closest to the **Tax Rate** label.

12. Print the invoice.

13. Save the file as an Excel workbook file in your solutions folder and name it **2.3timeout.**

Supplies Unlimited
545 Industrial Way
Chicago, IL 60064
847-555-6545

Invoice No.

INVOICE

Customer		Misc	
Name	Time Out Sporting Goods	Date	10/20/XX
Address	1412 Barkely Street	Order No.	1000
City	Chicago State IL ZIP 60064	Rep	Joe
Phone	847-555-1200	FOB	

Qty	Description	Unit Price		TOTAL
3	Boxes #2543 Folders	$ 10.55	$	31.65
4	Cartons #654 Copy Paper	$ 23.85	$	95.40
2	Boxes #2545 Folders	$ 11.95	$	23.90

> Enter shipping charges as directed

		SubTotal	$	150.95
		Shipping		
	Tax Rate(s)	6.25%	$	9.43
		TOTAL	$	160.38

Payment	Select One...

Comments
Name
CC #
Expires

Office Use Only

> This value will change when shipping charges are added

Your unlimited resource for supplies!

> Enter farewell statement here

Open Templates Dialog Box
1. Click **File, New** to display the New Workbook task pane.
2. Click **On my computer** in the New Workbook task pane template section.
- **Office XP:** Click **General Templates** in the New Workbook task pane.

Customize Template
1. Select area to customize.
2. Double-click on placeholder text, and drag mouse to select it.
3. Enter the custom information.
   or
1. Click placeholder.
2. Enter the custom information.

Save File as Template
1. Click **Save.**
2. Enter the file name.
3. Click **Template** in the Save as type box.
4. Click **Save.**

PERFORMANCE

SETTING THE STAGE/WRAPUP

✶ Act I File names: **2p1proinv**
2p1.bill

✶ Act II File names: **2p2.otginv**
2p2.bertle

✶ Act III File name: **2p3.quote**

WHAT YOU NEED TO KNOW

Act I

Wilson Jones, the director of the Corporate Travel Group at Air Land Sea Travel Group, has just completed arrangements and travel bookings for a corporate conference in Scottsdale, Arizona. The conference is planned for February 10–13 for Garrison Games, Inc, 342 Third Avenue, New York, NY 10017. You are to prepare a bill for $2200 using a Professional Invoice form to bill for conference-planning services.

✶ In the New Workbook task pane, click **From existing workbook,** and open the file **2p1proinv** from the Data CD. This opens the Professional Invoice file from Task 1 as a new file.

✶ Edit the file using the current information. Use today's date on the invoice.

✶ Save the file; name it **2p1.bill.**

Act II

You work for Marilyn Healy in the Marketing Department at Odyssey Travel Gear. Odyssey has started to use a catalog to market its merchandise wholesale to hotel gift shops. You are asked to prepare a customized invoice template for wholesale catalog sales and an invoice for a sale made today.

✶ Use the Sales Invoice template to create a new invoice template for Odyssey Travel Gear. Enter the company name and address, and the "Fine Print" and "Farewell Statement" as listed below:

Fine Print: For questions, call Customer Service at 630-555-8888, Extension 15.

Farewell Statement: Thank you for choosing Odyssey Travel Gear.

Save the file as a new template; name it **2p2.otginv.**

✶ Use the new template to create an invoice for the sale made today:

Use today's date.

The sale was made to the Bertleson Hotel, 2356 Lakeshore Drive, Chicago, IL 60611, 800-555-8787.

Invoice No. 2000, Order No. BH543, Rep. Marilyn

Qty	Description	Unit Price
12	Leather waist packs #432	12.35
6	Collapsible luggage carts #1654	18.50
12	Travel Alarm Clock #211	14.50

Shipping is $18.50.

There is no sales tax, because this is a wholesale transaction.

Payment method is Credit. Select it from drop-down list.

Save the document; name it **2p2.bertle.**

✴ Attach the invoice to an e-mail to Mr. Mark at the Bertleson Hotel (but send it to your teacher). Tell Mr. Mark that his order is being shipped, that the invoice is attached, and that the invoice will also be included with the shipment.

Act III

You work for the sales manager, Kiley Thompson, in the New York office of Trilogy Productions. A small independent film company has requested a quotation of rates for use of the studios and editing facilities. Locate a template for a price quotation using the Template Home Page on Microsoft Office Online or the Search online feature. *If you are using Office XP, click Templates on Microsoft.com in the New Workbook task pane.*

✴ When you locate the Price Quotation form, click the hyperlink to open the form and select **Download** to bring the template into Excel. Click Yes if a dialog box appears. Note the Template help task pane.

Enter the name and address for Trilogy Productions. Delete the company slogan line. Save the file as a template; name it **2p3.quote** and disconnect from the Internet.

✴ Use the template to create a quotation for Mr. Thompson using the following information:

Date: 8/10/2004, Quotation valid until: 9/10/2004, Quotation: 100, Customer ID: 346

Prepared by: Your name

Bill to: Jamal Carson, Carson Films, Inc 432 Christopher Street NY, NY 10012, 212-555-4388

2 days	Use of studio for filming short subject	$4200.00
1 day	Use of editing facilities	$1000.00

Customer will provide personnel.

✴ Use Edit mode to edit the line below the total to read: `If you have any questions concerning this quotation, contact Kiley Thompson, Extension 420.`

✴ Save the worksheet as **2p3.quotecarson.**

LESSON 3

▶ # Accounting Records

In this lesson, you will learn to use Excel to create accounting records and statements. You will use formulas, functions, and formatting to complete the tasks. You will use the Internet to locate tax forms and rates.

Upon completion of this lesson, you should have mastered the following skill sets:

- ✵ Change row or column size
- ✵ Cut, copy, and paste
- ✵ Apply and clear number formats
- ✵ Use the Office Clipboard to cut, copy, and paste
- ✵ Use formula basics
- ✵ Enter functions
  - ✱ AutoSum
  - ✱ Enter the range in a formula
  - ✱ AutoSum List
  - ✱ Formula bar
- ✵ Use the Fill Handle tool
- ✵ Modify page setup options
  - ✱ Orientation
  - ✱ Set page margins and centering

- ✵ Edit formulas using the Formula bar
- ✵ Move selected cells
- ✵ Insert, view, and edit cell comments
- ✵ Apply and modify cell formats with the Format Cells dialog box
- ✵ Use the Format Painter

Terms

Software-related
- AutoFit
- Office Clipboard
- Formulas
- Order of mathematical operations
- Function
- AutoSum
- Insert Function button
- Function arguments
- AutoFill
- Fill handle
- Series
- Drag-and-drop
- Cell comment
- Format Painter
- Research tools

Document-related
- Account
- General ledger
- Accounts receivable
- Accounts payable
- Account statement
- Journal
- Sales journal
- Tax status
- Payroll register
- Reimburse
- Expense report

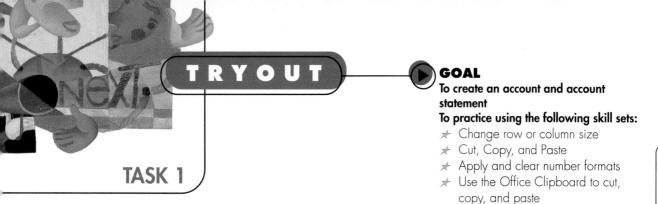

TRYOUT

GOAL

To create an account and account statement

To practice using the following skill sets:

* ✴ Change row or column size
* ✴ Cut, Copy, and Paste
* ✴ Apply and clear number formats
* ✴ Use the Office Clipboard to cut, copy, and paste
* ✴ Use formula basics

EXCEL

TASK 1

WHAT YOU NEED TO KNOW

Change Row or Column Size and Alignment

▶ Columns are set for a standard column width of 8.43, the number of characters displayed using the standard font. When you enter long labels, they appear in the next cell, if it is empty. When you enter long values, Excel fills the cell with number signs (#), or displays the number in scientific notation to indicate the need to widen the column.

▶ To change the width of a column, place the mouse pointer on the line between the column letter headings and, when the mouse pointer changes to a double-headed arrow, drag the column to size. The width is displayed as you make this adjustment, as shown in Figure 3.1. However, the most efficient way is to double-click the column header line, and the column will *AutoFit,* or widen to fit the data in that column.

Figure 3.1 Column width indicator display

▶ By default, row height is automatically determined by the font point size and cell data is vertically aligned at the bottom of the row. However, you may change row height by dragging the row to the desired size.

▶ Use the alignment buttons to align data horizontally. Data in a row can be aligned vertically to the top, middle, or bottom of a row by clicking Format, Cells, and setting the vertical alignment on the Alignment tab.

1. Open **E3-1** from the Data CD. Notice the cells with errors due to column width.

2. Double-click the line between **Columns A** and **B** to AutoFit the text in **Column A.**

3. Place the insertion point between **Columns C** and **D**.

4. When you see the double-headed arrow, drag to increase the column width to **18.43**.

5. Select **Cell C1** and change the font size to **14**. Notice the change in the row height.

6. Select **Cells A1 to C1**.

7. Click **Format, Cells, Alignment** tab and set the Vertical alignment to **Center.** Click **OK.**

8. Select **Cell C1** and change the font size back to **10**.

9. Select **Rows 1** and **2,** place the insertion point between **Rows 2** and **3,** and drag to set both row heights to **18.00.**

10. Do not close the file.

Cut, Copy, and Paste Data

▶ Cut and Paste are tools to move text or data from one location and place it in another. To remove data, select it and click the Cut button on the Standard toolbar. The data is placed temporarily on the Office Clipboard, a temporary storage area.

▶ Copy and Paste are tools to copy data from one location and place it in another. To copy data, select it and click the Copy button on the Standard toolbar.

▶ In both cases, to place the data in a new location, select the first cell of the range and click the Paste button on the Standard toolbar.

▶ Because Cut, Copy, and Paste commands are used frequently, you can use shortcut methods for performing these tasks: Ctrl+X = cut; Ctrl+C = copy; Ctrl+V = paste.

1. Use the open file or open **E3-2** from the Data CD.

2. Select **Cells A3 to A7** and click the **Cut** button on the toolbar.

3. Select **Cell A10** and click the **Paste** button on the toolbar to move the data.

4. Click the **Undo** button to restore the data.

5. Select **Cells B3 to B7** and click the **Copy** button on the toolbar.

6. Select **Cell C3** and click the **Paste** button on the toolbar to copy the data.

7. Do not close the file.

Apply and Clear Number Formats

▶ You can format numbers with the Formatting toolbar buttons. Select the data to format and then click the appropriate button, as shown in Figure 3.2 and demonstrated in Figure 3.3.

Figure 3.2 Formatting toolbar, number format buttons

► The number format buttons on the Formatting toolbar are listed and illustrated below:

- Currency Style adds two decimal places and a dollar sign. $

- Percent Style changes the value to a percentage. %

- Comma Style adds commas and two decimal places. ,

- Increase Decimal adds one decimal place.

- Decrease Decimal decreases one decimal place.

Note: Decreasing decimals causes the values to be rounded.

► To clear number formats without deleting the values, click Edit, Clear, and Formats.

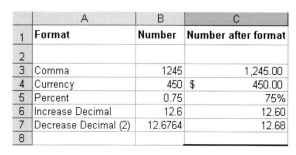

	A	B	C
1	Format	Number	Number after format
2			
3	Comma	1245	1,245.00
4	Currency	450 $	450.00
5	Percent	0.75	75%
6	Increase Decimal	12.6	12.60
7	Decrease Decimal (2)	12.6764	12.68
8			

Figure 3.3 Sample number formats

T R Y i t O U T *E3-3*

1. Use the open file or open **E3-3** from the Data CD.

2. Format the cells in **Column C** to match the illustration in Figure 3.3.

3. Select **Cells C3** to **C7** and clear all formats by clicking **Edit, Clear,** and **Formats.**

4. Click the **Undo** button to reverse the Clear Formats command.

5. Deselect the range by clicking another cell.

6. Do not close the file.

Use the Office Clipboard to Cut, Copy, and Paste

► When you copy data in Excel, it is stored in a memory location called the *Office Clipboard.* If you plan to copy more than one group of data, you can display the Office Clipboard task pane by clicking Edit, Office Clipboard. This is useful if you are reordering or reassigning locations for several items of data, or if you want to paste items several times. As shown in Figure 3.4, after each row is copied the sample appears on the Clipboard, with the last selection shown on top.

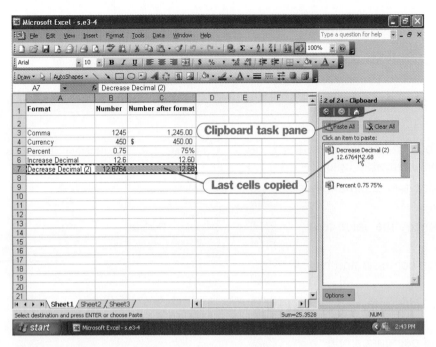

Figure 3.4 Office Clipboard task pane

TRY *it* **OUT** *E3-4*

1. Use the open file or open **E3-4** from the Data CD.

2. Click **Edit, Office Clipboard** and click **Clear All,** if necessary.

3. Cut the data in the range **A5:C5.**

4. Cut the data in the range **A7:C7.**

5. Copy the data in the range **A1:C1.**

6. Select **Cell A5** and click the **Decrease Decimal** data on the Clipboard. The data is pasted.

7. Select **Cell A7** and click the **Percent** data on the Clipboard.

8. Save the file; name it **E3-4.** Close the file.

Use Formula Basics

▶ *Formulas* are equations or instructions to calculate values on the worksheet. All formulas start with an equal sign (=), contain no spaces, and include the cell addresses and mathematical operators necessary to complete the formula. For example, =B5+B6 adds the values in B5 and B6.

▶ The standard mathematical operators used in formulas are:

+ Addition   − Subtraction   * Multiplication

/ Division   ^ Exponentiation

▶ To enter formulas correctly, you should understand the way the computer processes an equation. The computer executes all operations from left to right, in order of appearance and mathematical priority. The *order of mathematical operations*, or *priority*, is listed below:

1. Parentheses   ( )
2. Exponents   ^
3. Multiplication *   Division   /
4. Addition   +   Subtraction −

▶ For example, in the formula =A1*(B1+C1), B1+C1, the values in parentheses are calculated first, before the multiplication is performed. If the parentheses were omitted, A1*B1 would be calculated first and C1 would be added to that answer. This would result in a different outcome.

▶ You can enter a formula directly by keying the symbols and cell addresses. You can also enter the symbols and select the cell addresses as they appear in the formula. Selecting the cell addresses minimizes the possibility of entry errors. As you enter the formula, it appears in the Formula bar. After the formula is entered into the cell, the answer appears in the cell and you can see the formula in the Formula bar, as shown in Figure 3.5.

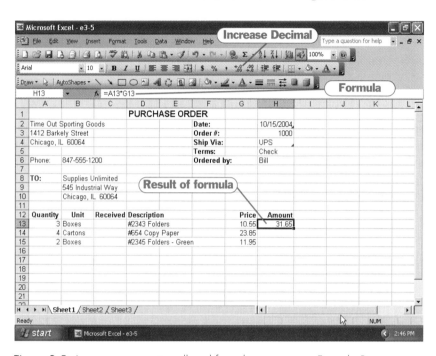

Figure 3.5 Answer appears in cell and formula appears on Formula Bar

TRY it OUT E3-5

1. Open **2.2purord** from your files or **E3-5** from the Data CD.

2. In **Cell H13,** enter a formula to multiply the quantity by the price:
   a. Enter = (equal sign).
   b. Click **Cell A13.**
   c. Enter * (asterisk).
   d. Click **Cell G13.**
   e. Press the **Enter** key.

3. Click **Cell H13** and notice the formula in the Formula bar.

4. Enter the appropriate formula in **Cell H14.** *(Hint: =A14*G14)*

5. Click **Cell H14,** copy the formula, and paste it to **Cell H15.** Notice that the formula in **Cell H15** copies relative to the new location.

6. Select the range **H14:H15** and click the **Increase Decimal** button to add one decimal place.

7. Enter a formula in **Cell H17** to add the three values in Column H. *(Hint: =H13+H14+H15)*

8. Format the total for currency.

9. Save the file; name it **E3-5.** Close the file.

REHEARSAL

Again

TASK 1

 GOAL
To create an acount and account statement

SETTING THE STAGE/WRAPUP
File names: 3.1account
3.1statement

WHAT YOU NEED TO KNOW

▶ An *account* is an accounting record that keeps track of the increases and decreases in the value of an item in a business. It is set up in a bankbook-style arrangement that contains columns for increases, decreases, and balances. Accounts are used to record transactions from journals, as you will learn in Task 2.

▶ The *general ledger* contains all the accounts of a business. In addition, there are supplemental ledgers; the *accounts receivable (AR)* ledger containing records of customers, the people who owe the business money, and the *accounts payable (AP)* ledger containing records of creditors, the people to whom the business owes money.

▶ Customers' accounts are used to create the *account statements* or bills that are sent out each month.

▶ In this Rehearsal activity, you will create an account and an account statement for a Time Out Sporting Goods customer. On accounts receivable accounts, invoices (which increase the account) and credits and returns (which decrease the account) are used to tabulate the account balance. The account statement or bill is sent out at the end of the month to every customer, based on the activity in the account.

▼ DIRECTIONS

1. Open **3.1account** from the Data CD.

2. Adjust column width as necessary.

3. As shown in Illustration A below, in **Cell F8,** calculate the balance on 5/3. Because the first invoice is also the balance on 5/3, enter =D8 in **Cell F8.**

	A	B	C	D	E	F	G
1	Accounts Receivable Ledger						
2							
3	Customer:		Central High School - Health Ed. Dept.				
4			2382 Margate Avenue				
5	No: C15		Chicago, IL 60064				
6							
7	Date	Explanation	Reference	Charges	Credits	Balance	
8	5/3/2004	Invoice #2325	S5	434.56			
9	5/15/2004	Return - #CM450	J9		65.35		
10	5/22/2004	Invoice #2336	S5	1045.32			
11	5/25/2004	Damaged #CM501	J9		150		
12							
13		Adjust column width				Enter formulas here to calculate daily balance	
14							
15							

Illustration A

4. Calculate the balance on 5/15 in **Cell F9.** The formula should subtract the return in **Cell E9** from the previous balance in **Cell F8.** *(Hint: =F8-E9)*

5. Enter a formula in **Cell F10** that can be used for any balance calculation in this account. *(Hint: Previous balance+charges–credits =F9+D10-E10)*

6. Format the credit in **Cell E11** by adding two decimal places.

7. Clear all formats in **Cell E11.** Click **Undo** to keep the format.

8. Copy the formula from **Cell F10,** and paste it to **Cell F11.**

9. Select and format the values in **Column F** for commas.

10. Save the file as **3.1 account.**

Continued on next page

11. As shown in Illustration B below, copy the following ranges to the clipboard to create the account statement:

   a. **C3:C5** Name and address of customer

   b. **A7:F7** Column headings

   c. **A8:F11** Account data

12. Open **3.1statement** from the Data CD.

13. Paste the following data to the locations listed below:

   a. Name and address to **Cell A9**

   b. Column headings to **Cell A13**

   c. Account data to **Cell A15**

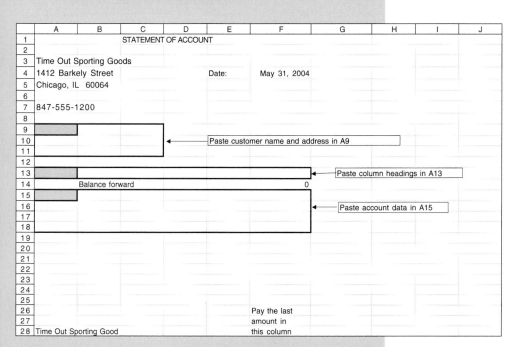

Illustration B

14. Adjust column width as necessary.

15. Format the final balance in **Cell F18** for currency.

16. Print the account statement without gridlines.

17. Save the file as **3.1 statement.** Close both files.

Cues for Reference

Apply Number Formats
1. Select cell or range of cells.
2. Click format button:

   Percentage Style

   Currency Style

   Comma Style

   Increase Decimal

   Decrease Decimal

Clear Number Formats
1. Select cell or range of cells.
2. Click **Edit, Clear, Formats.**

Use Office Clipboard Task Pane
1. Click **Edit, Office Clipboard.**
2. Cut or copy data.
3. Select location for pasted data.
4. Click data sample on Office Clipboard.

Enter Formulas
1. Enter = (equal sign)
2. Select formula data.
3. Enter a mathematical operator.
4. Select formula data.
5. Repeat Steps 3 and 4 until formula is complete.
6. Press **Enter.**

TRYOUT

GOAL
To create a Sales Journal
To practice using the following skill sets:
* Enter functions
    * AutoSum
    * Enter the range in a formula
    * AutoSum List
    * Formula bar

TASK 2

WHAT YOU NEED TO KNOW

Enter Functions

▶ A *function* is a built-in formula that performs a special calculation automatically. Function formulas, for example, =SUM(B4:B7), add all the values, or arguments, in the range specified. A function contains an equal sign, function name, open parenthesis, range or arguments, and then close parenthesis.

AutoSum

▶ The *AutoSum* feature automatically enters a function to find the total of a group of cells. To add a column of data, make the location of the total the active cell and click the AutoSum button on the Standard toolbar. Excel selects the cells it thinks you want to add and surrounds them with a moving dotted line, as shown in Figure 3.6.

▶ In the cell where the total is to appear, you see the automatic sum formula to add the cells, =SUM(B4:B47). If the cells selected are the ones you want to add, just press the Enter key; if not, revise the selected range of data.

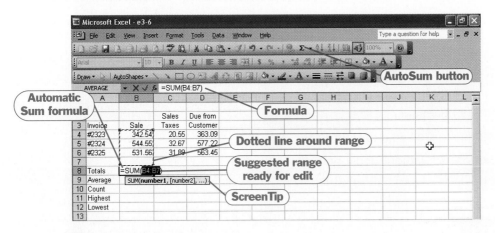

Figure 3.6 AutoSum feature

Enter the Range in a Formula

▶ If the range suggested by AutoSum is not correct, you must enter the correct range. An accurate way to enter a range address in any formula is to drag through the range with the mouse pointer.

1. Open **E3-6** from the Data CD.

2. Go to **Cell B8.**

3. Click the **AutoSum** button. Notice the formula in the cell and on the Formula bar.

4. Press the **Enter** key.

5. Repeat steps 3 and 4 for Cells C8 and D8. If the range is incorrect, then correct it by dragging the dotted line to the appropriate location.

6. Select Cells **B8** to **D8** and format for commas.

7. Add the Sales Taxes and Sales totals horizontally to see if they equal the "Due from Customer" total. Go to **Cell E8.**
   a. Click the **AutoSum** button. Notice that the range is incorrect.
   b. Drag to select the range **B8:C8,** the correct range.
   c. Press the **Enter** key.

8. Do not close the file.

AutoSum List

▶ At the right of the AutoSum button is a list arrow, as shown in Figure 3.7, that provides other commonly used functions you can select for the range of data. The functions available are listed below:

Sum   Calculates the total of numbers in a range

Average   Calculates the average, or mean, of numbers in a range

Count   Counts the number of values in a range

Max   Calculates the highest value in a range

Min   Calculates the lowest value in a range

Figure 3.7 AutoSum options list

1. Use the open file or open **E3-7** from the Data CD.

2. Go to **Cell B9.**

3. Click the **AutoSum** list arrow.

4. Click **Average.**

5. Drag through to correct the range to **B4:B6** and press the **Enter** key.

6. For the following, be sure to correct the range to **B4:B6** before pressing the **Enter** key:
   a. In **Cell B10,** find the COUNT, or number of values.
   b. In **Cell B11,** find the MAX, or highest value.
   c. In **Cell B12,** find the MIN, or lowest value.

7. Do not close the file.

Formula Bar

▶ Formulas may be entered using the Formula bar. When you press the equal sign, the Formula bar provides a drop-down list of commonly used functions, Cancel and Enter buttons, and the *Insert Function button*, as shown in Figure 3.8. The **fx** button will be discussed in Lesson 4.

▶ When you select a function from the list, Excel enters the function name automatically in the formula and prompts you for the *function arguments*, the cell ranges that supply the data for the formula. The Function Arguments dialog box, shown in Figure 3.9, displays the arguments or range, explains the function, the result of the formula, and provides Help features.

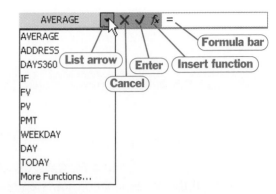

Figure 3.8 Formula bar function list

▶ The Collapse Dialog Box button, at the right of the range, collapses the dialog box to help you select the correct range. When the dialog box is collapsed, it still may obstruct the range, but you can move it away by dragging its title bar with the mouse pointer. After you make your selection, you can click the Expand Dialog Box button to redisplay the dialog box.

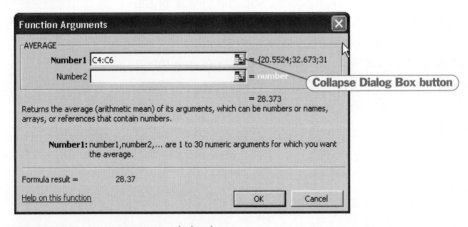

Figure 3.9 Function Arguments dialog box

T R Y *it* O U T *E3-8*

1. Use the open file or open **E3-8** from the Data CD.

2. Enter the equal sign (=) in **Cell C9.**

3. Click **Average** from the drop-down list of functions.

4. Click the **Collapse Dialog Box** button.

5. Drag the dialog box title bar out of the way, if necessary.

6. Select the range **C4:C6.**

7. Click the **Expand Dialog Box** button.

8. Click **OK.**

9. Use the same method to complete the formulas for **Cells C10, C11,** and **C12.** *Note:* If the Count, Max, and Min functions are not visible, click more functions to locate them.

10. Format the values in **Cells B11** to **C12** for two decimal places.

11. Copy the formulas from Cells **C9:C12** to **D9.**

12. Save the file **E3-8.** Close the file.

R E H E A R S A L

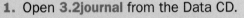

TASK 2

GOAL
To create a Sales Journal

SETTING THE STAGE/WRAPUP
File name: **3.2journal**

WHAT YOU NEED TO KNOW

▶ Accounting records, such as *journals*, keep track of financial events or transactions for money management and decision-making purposes. One type of journal, a *sales journal*, is a record of the sales made to customers on credit.

▶ The sales invoice, created when a sale is made on credit, is the basis for the entry in the journal. Entries from the journal are then transferred to each customer's account, as discussed in Task 1. In some businesses, the journal and ledger accounts are generated from the preparation of the invoice, using accounting system software.

▶ The final (retail) consumer of merchandise pays sales tax while wholesale customers who are resellers and nonprofit organizations are tax exempt.

▶ In this Rehearsal activity, you will prepare a sales journal for Time Out Sporting Goods to record sales for its credit business, which is a small part of its sales.

▼ DIRECTIONS

1. Open **3.2journal** from the Data CD.

2. Adjust column width for **Column C**.

3. Select the range **A3:F4**. Center and italicize the column headings.

4. Format **Cell C2** to Arial, 14 point, bold, and format the date column to mm/dd/yy.

5. Enter the additional invoices as follows:
   a. Enter data in columns A, B, C, and F as shown in the illustration on the facing page. Note that AutoComplete will help you enter the customers' names.
   b. Copy the formulas from **Columns E and D** down for the new invoices. Notice that the Sales Tax formula is applied only to the Kelly Klinger invoice.

6. Select the range **D5:F18** and format for two decimal places using the Comma format.

7. Use the AutoSum feature to find the total in **Cell D20**.

8. Use the AutoSum feature to find the average of the range **D5:D18** in **Cell D22.** Use the mouse to correct the range in the function.

9. Enter the **equal sign** in **Cell D23** and use the function list on the Formula bar to find the highest value (Max). Click the **Collapse Dialog Box** button to select the range **D5:D18.**

10. Use the method you prefer to find the remaining data.

11. Select the range **D20:D25** and format for two decimal places using the Comma format.

12. Copy the range of summary data in **D20:D25.**

13. As illustrated on the facing page, paste the range twice to **Cells E20** and **F20.**

14. Print the journal with gridlines.

15. Save the file **3.2journal.** Close the file.

	A	B	C	D	E	F
1	**Arial, 14 point, bold**				**Centered and italicized**	
2			**SALES JOURNAL**			Page 5
3				*Accounts*	*Sales*	*Sales*
4	*Date*	*Invoice #*	*Customer*	*Receivable*	*Taxes*	*Income*
5	5/3/04	2325	Central H.S. Health Ed Dept	434.56		434.56
6	5/4/04	2326	Jason Gym	550.00		550.00
7	5/7/04	2327	Eastern H.S. - Gym	515.00		515.00
8	5/9/04	2328	Fitness King	1,255.00		1,255.00
9	5/11/04	2329	Harry Putter	185.94	10.94	175.00
10	5/14/04	2330	Eastern H.S. - Gym	325.00		325.00
11	5/14/04	2331	Jason Gym	385.00		385.00
12	5/16/04	2332	Fitness King	155.00		155.00
13	5/17/04	2333	Harry Putter	313.44	18.44	295.00
14	5/18/04	2334	Eastern H.S. - Gym	660.00		660.00
15	5/21/04	2335	Kelly Klinger	143.44	8.44	135.00
16	5/22/04	2336	Central H.S. Health Ed Dept	1,045.32		1,045.32
17	5/24/04	2337	Jason Gym	451.56		451.56
18	5/31/04	2338	Kelly Klinger	90.31	5.31	85.00
19						
20	**Enter new sales**		Totals			
21						
22			Averages			
23			Highest			
24			Lowest			
25			Count			
26					Copy D20:D25 to E20 and F20	
27						
28						

Cues for Reference

Use Auto Sum
1. Select cell to display answer.
2. Click the **AutoSum** button. Σ
3. If range is correct, press **Enter.**
4. If not, use mouse pointer to reselect the correct range and press **Enter.**

Enter Range in a Formula
1. Place mouse pointer on first cell in range.
2. Click, hold, and drag to last cell in range.

Use Functions on AutoSum List
1. Select cell to display answer.
2. Click **AutoSum** list arrow.
3. Select function.
4. Correct the range.
5. Press **Enter.**

Use Functions from the Formula bar
1. Select cell to display answer.
2. Enter **Equals (=).**
3. Select function from drop-down list.

4. Click the **Collapse Dialog Box** button.
5. Drag the dialog box title bar out of the way, if necessary.
6. Select the range.
7. Click the **Expand Dialog Box** button.
8. Press **OK.**

TRYOUT

GOAL
To create a payroll
To practice using the following skill sets:
* Use the Fill Handle tool
* Modify page setup options
  * Orientation
  * Set page margins and centering
* Edit formulas using the Formula bar

TASK 3

WHAT YOU NEED TO KNOW

Use the Fill Handle Tool

▶ You can use the *AutoFill* tool to copy labels, values, or formulas or to create sequential lists of values or labels.

▶ To use AutoFill as a copy tool, select the cell to be copied and place your insertion point on the *fill handle*, the small square at the bottom right of the cell to copy, as shown in Figure 3.10. When the mouse pointer changes to a thin black plus sign, click and drag the cell border to fill the appropriate range. You will find this to be an easy way to copy formulas. You can also click Edit, Fill to access this feature.

	A	B	C	D	E
1					
2		Gross	Taxes	Union	Net
3	Employee	Pay		Dues	Pay
4					
5	1000	280	67	10	203
6	1001	300	79	10	211
7	1002	295	72		
8	1003	655	146		
9	1004	432	96		
10	1005	425	89		
11					

Fill handle

Figure 3.10 AutoFill activated

Create a Series

▶ To create a *series* of values or labels, such as check numbers, days of the week, months, years, etc., enter the first two items in the series and then use the fill handle to complete the column.

TRY it OUT *E3-9*

1. Open **E3-9** from the Data CD.
2. AutoFill a value:
   a. Click **Cell D6** and place your mouse pointer on the fill handle.
   b. When the insertion point changes to a black plus sign, click and drag the border down to **Cell D10.**

3. AutoFill a formula: In **Cell E6,** use the fill handle to fill the formula down to **Cell E10.**
4. Fill a formula from **Cells B12 to E12:**
   a. Select the range **B12:E12.**
   b. Click **Edit, Fill,** and **Right.**

Continued on next page

5. Enter 1000 in **Cell A5** and 1001 **in Cell A6.**

6. Select both values and use the fill handle to create a sequential list to **Cell A10.**

7. Enter January in **Cell F1** and February in **Cell G1.**

8. Select **both values** and use the fill handle to fill to **Cell K1.**

9. Do not close the file.

Modify Page Setup Options

Orientation

▶ If you Print Preview your worksheet and note that it is wider than the page width, use landscape orientation to print the worksheet horizontally on the page. Or, you can scale the data to fit on one page, which reduces the font size.

▶ In the Page Setup dialog box with the Page tab selected, shown in Figure 3.11, you can set page orientation and scaling.

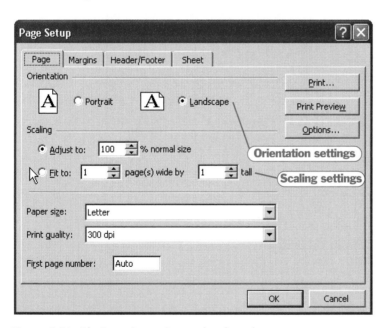

Figure 3.11 File Page Setup, Page tab selected

---

1. Continue working in the open file or open **E3-10** from the Data CD.

2. Click **File, Page Setup,** and click the **Page** tab, if not already displayed.

3. Click the **Print Preview** button. Notice that the worksheet is not completely

visible. Click **Setup** on the Print Preview toolbar.

4. Click **Fit to 1 page wide by 1 tall** in the Page tab of the Page Setup dialog box.

Continued on next page

5. Click **OK.** Notice that the full worksheet displays with a smaller font.

6. Click **Setup** on the Print Preview toolbar.

7. Select **Adjust to 100% normal size** and click **Landscape** orientation in the Page tab of the Page Setup dialog box.

8. Click **OK.**

9. Click **Close** on the Print Preview toolbar.

10. Do not close the file.

Set Page Margins and Centering

▶ On the Margins tab, as shown in Figure 3.12, you can center the worksheet on the page and set margins. You can also set Margins manually, in Print Preview mode, by clicking the Margins button on the Print Preview toolbar.

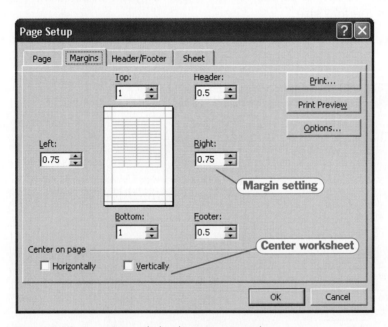

Figure 3.12 Page Setup dialog box, Margins tab

1. Continue working in the open file or open **E3-11** from the Data CD.

2. Click **File, Page Setup,** and click the **Margins** tab.

3. Under **Center on page,** click **Horizontally** and **Vertically.**

4. Click the **Print Preview** button.

5. Click the **Margins** button on the Print Preview toolbar.

6. Drag the margin grids to move the margins closer to the data.

7. Click **Close** on the Print Preview toolbar.

8. Do not close the file.

Edit Formulas Using the Formula Bar

▶ To edit or revise a formula in Edit mode, press the F2 key or double-click the formula. Excel then color codes the arguments in the cell formula and on the Formula bar to match a box around the actual arguments. This clearly identifies each part of the formula and may clarify the errors that need correction.

▶ Once you are in Edit mode, you can drag the border of the range or cell, or backspace to correct errors. Figures 3.13 and 3.14 show how formula arguments and a range appear in Edit mode.

	A	B	C	D	E	
1						Jan
2		Gross	Taxes	Union	Net	
3	Employee	Pay		Dues	Pay	
4			Cursor in edit location			
5	1000	280	67	10	=B5+C5-D5	
6	1001	300	79	10		
7	1002	295	72	10	Color-coded formula	
8	1003	655	146	10	arguments	
9	1004	432	96	10		
10	1005	425	89	10		

Figure 3.13 Edit mode for formula arguments

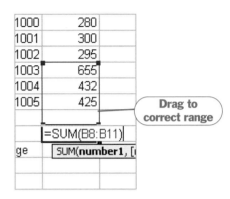

1000	280
1001	300
1002	295
1003	655
1004	432
1005	425

Drag to correct range

=SUM(B8:B11)

ge | SUM(**number1**, [

Figure 3.14 Edit mode for arguments in a range

T R Y *i t* **O U T** *E3-12*

1. Continue working in the open file or open **E3-12** from the Data CD.

2. Double-click **Cell E5** to edit the formula.

3. Revise the formula to read =B5-C5-D5 because both the taxes and dues should be subtracted. Use the **left arrow** and the **backspace** keys to make the change from plus to minus.

4. Press the **Enter** key.

5. In **Cell E5,** click the **fill handle** to AutoFill the revised formula from **Cell E5** down to **E10.**

6. Double-click **Cell B12** and notice the range.

7. Drag the range border to correct it so that it adds the range **B5:B10.**

8. In **Cell B12,** click the **fill handle** to AutoFill the revised formula across from **Cells B12** to **E12.**

9. Find the Averages in **Row 13** and format the data for no decimal places.

10. Save the file as **E3-12.** Close the file.

REHEARSAL

GOAL
To create a payroll

SETTING THE STAGE/WRAPUP
File name: **3.3payroll**

TASK 3

WHAT YOU NEED TO KNOW

▶ To complete payroll calculations, you need to know the employee's *tax status* data, i.e., marital status and the number of dependents claimed. Use the tax status and the salary to look up the federal withholding tax on tax tables. State tax rates vary with each state having different tables and rules. Social Security and Medicare taxes are deducted from all payrolls at the rates of 6.2% and 1.45%, respectively. You can use a percent in an Excel formula.

▶ Payrolls may be completed by outside services or by the Accounting Department in a large firm. A *payroll register* is a form used to calculate the salaries, taxes, and net pay due each employee for the pay period. You will calculate gross pay (the salary before taxes), the taxes on gross pay, and the net pay (the salary less all the deductions). Once you complete a payroll register, you can save the worksheet as a template to use for each week's payroll. Internet sites also provide paycheck calculators for small businesses.

▶ In this Rehearsal activity, you will prepare a weekly payroll for WorkOut Centers, located in Austin, Texas. There is no state or local withholding tax in this state.

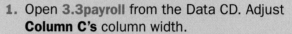

DIRECTIONS

1. Open **3.3payroll** from the Data CD. Adjust **Column C's** column width.

2. *Employee Number:* Select the range **A7:A8** and use the fill handle to drag the series of numbers to every employee.

3. *Gross Pay:* In **Cell F7,** enter a formula to find gross pay.

   (Hint: =Regular Earnings+Overtime – use cell addresses in the formula)

4. Use the fill handle in **Cell F7** to copy the formula down to each employee's payroll.

5. *Social Security:* In **Cell H7,** enter a formula to find the Social Security tax, which is 6.2% of the gross pay. *(Hint: =Gross Pay*6.2%)*

6. *Medicare:* In **Cell I7,** enter a formula to find the Medicare tax, which is 1.45% of the gross pay.

7. *Total Deductions:* In **Cell J7,** use AutoSum to enter a formula to find the total of all the payroll deductions from the range **G7:I7.**

8. *Net Pay:* In **Cell K7,** enter a formula to find net pay, which is the gross pay less the total deductions.

9. As shown in the illustration on the facing page, select the range **H7:K7,** and use the fill handle to fill all the formulas for the payroll.

10. In **Cell D15,** use AutoSum to find the total of the column.

11. In **Cell D17,** press **equal (=)** and use the Formula bar drop-down function list to enter the formula for the column average. Be sure to select the correct range.

12. In **Cell D18,** use the AutoSum drop-down list to find the count. Be sure to correct the range.

Continued on next page

13. Double-click each formula just completed in Steps 10, 11, and 12 to check the ranges in Edit mode.

14. Select the range **D15:D18** and use the fill handle to copy the formulas across to all columns.

15. Format payroll data in the range **D7:K17** in comma format.

16. Center column headings for the range **D5:K6.**

17. Format the worksheet: Italicize and bold all column headings. Bold text in Cells A3, F3, and C15 to C18. Change the font for the title in Cell E1 as illustrated or to a similar font, and increase the font size to 14.

18. Use Page Setup to print the payroll in landscape orientation, centered horizontally. Print one copy.

19. Save the file **3.3payroll.** Close the file.

	A	B	C	D	E	F	G	H	I	J	K
1			Lucida Sans, 14 point →		PAYROLL REGISTER						
2										Bold and Italics	
3	For Pay Period Ended:			15-Jun-04		Date of Payment:		20-Jun-04			
4											
5	Employee			Regular		Gross	Federal	Social		Total	Net
6	Number	Status	Name	Earnings	Overtime	Pay	W.T.	Security	Medicare	Deductions	Pay
7	225	S1	Bosco, Vince	280.00	85.00		32.63				
8	226	M2	Ingram, Sally	800.00	200.00		102.26				
9		S2	Josephs, Ted	250.00			8.17				
10		M2	Lee, Gina	435.00			19.37				
11		M4	Montez, Maria	475.00			11.63				
12		S0	Pasternak, Joan	250.00			24.18				
13		S1	Thompson, John	450.00	100.00		60.38				
14											
15			Totals								
16											
17			Average								
18			Count								

Edit Formulas
1. Select formula.
2. Press **F2.**
3. Edit range by dragging border, or Edit operators in formula.

Use AutoFill
1. For series, select first two cells in series. For formulas, values, and text, select a cell.
2. Point cursor to fill handle in bottom right corner.
3. Drag to fill series.

Modify Page Orientation
1. Click **File, Page Setup,** and click **Page** tab.
2. Click **Landscape.**
3. Click **OK.**

Set Page Margins and Centering
1. Click **Print Preview** button.
2. Click **Margins** button on the Print Preview toolbar.

3. Drag margins to appropriate location.
4. Click **Close** on the Print Preview toolbar.
   or
1. Click **File, Page Setup,** and click **Margins** tab.
2. Set margins or centering.
3. Click **OK.**

TRYOUT

GOAL

To create an expense report
To practice using the following skill sets:
- ✳ Moving selected cells
- ✳ Insert, view, and edit cell comments
- ✳ Apply and modify cell formats with the Format Cells dialog box
- ✳ Use the Format Painter

TASK 4

WHAT YOU NEED TO KNOW

Moving Selected Cells

▶ You can move data by using the Cut and Paste buttons on the Standard toolbar, or by selecting the range and dragging it to the paste location (known as *drag-and-drop*). Moving data removes it from the first location and pastes it to the new location. This will overwrite any data in the new location.

▶ To drag-and-drop data, select the data to move and place the mouse pointer on the edge of the range until it changes to a four-headed arrow. Drag the outline of the range to the first cell in the new location's range. As shown in Figure 3.15, as you drag the data, the new range or location appears. Data formats move with the data, but you must check that formulas are correct after a move operation.

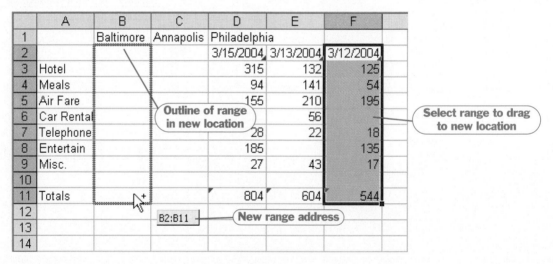

Figure 3.15 Selected range moved to new location

T R Y *it* O U T *E3-13*

1. Open **E3-13** from the Data CD.

2. Select the range **E2:E11.**

3. Click the **Cut** button.

4. Select **Cell C2,** and then click the **Paste** button.

5. Select the range **F2:F11.**

6. Place the mouse pointer at the edge of the range until the pointer becomes a four-headed arrow.

7. Click, hold, and drag-and-drop the range to **B2:B11.**

8. Do not close the file.

Insert, View, and Edit Cell Comments

▶ You can attach a text comment in a cell to document formulas or assumptions built into the worksheet, or to comment on data sent to you by someone else. Because this feature is used when sharing workbooks, the user's name will also be on the comment.

▶ Insert a comment in the cell by clicking Insert, Comment and entering the comment in the comment box. A red triangle appears in the top corner of the cell to indicate the presence of a *cell comment,* as shown in Figure 3.16.

▶ When the mouse moves over a cell with a comment indicator, you can view the comment. If this does not occur, click Comment indicator only on the Tools, Options, View tab.

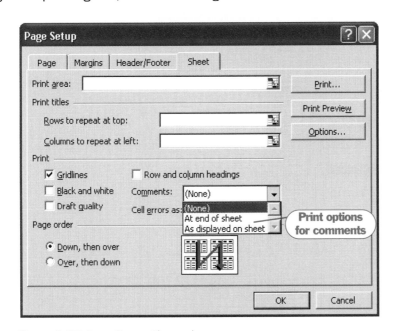

Cell comment

	A	B	C	D
1	Comment indicator	Baltimore A	Your Name: Meeting with J & R Equipment Supply	
2		3/12/2004	3	
3	Hotel	125.00		
4	Meals	54.00	141.00	94.00
5	Air Fare	195.00	210.00	155.00
6	Car Rental		56.00	
7	Telephone	18.00	22.00	28.00
8	Entertain	135.00		185.00
9	Misc.	17.00	43.00	27.00
10				
11	Totals	544.00	604.00	804.00

Figure 3.16 Cell comment

▶ To edit or delete a comment, right-click the comment cell and select the desired action.

▶ To print comments, select one of the Comments drop-down list print options on the Sheet tab of the Page Setup dialog box, as shown in Figure 3.17.

Figure 3.17 Page Setup, Sheet tab

Continued on next page

T R Y *i t* **O U T** *E3-14*

1. Continue working in the open file or open **E3-14** from the Data CD.

2. In **Cell B1**, click **Insert, Comment.**

3. Enter this text:

   J&R Equipment Supply

4. Click on any cell to come out of Comment mode.

5. Right-click **Cell C1,** select **Insert Comment,** and enter:

   `Sailboat Show and Conference`

6. Right-click **Cell B1,** select **Edit Comment.**

7. Edit the comment to read: `Meeting with J&R Equipment Supply.`

8. Click on any cell to come out of Comment mode.

9. Enter a comment in **Cell D1:** `Meeting with Michael Collins.`

10. Right-click **Cell D1** and select **Delete Comment**.

11. Use the Page Setup dialog box to print the worksheet. Select **Comments: At end of sheet.**

12. Do not close the file.

Apply and Modify Cell Formats with the Format Cells Dialog Box

▶ You have been using the Formatting toolbar buttons to format cells. You can set all formats at once and have additional formatting options if you use the Format Cells dialog box as shown in Figure 3.18. Click Format, Cells, or the Ctrl+1 keys and notice the six cell formatting tabs that appear. Format a cell by selecting the appropriate options from any or all tabs and click OK.

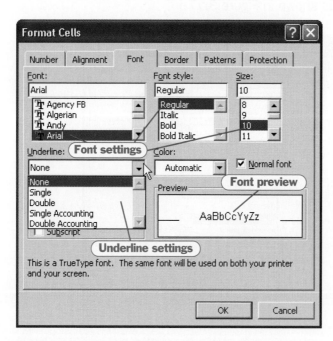

Figure 3.18 Format Cells dialog box, Font tab

1. Continue working in the open file or open **E3-15** from the Data CD.

2. Select the range **B1:D1.**

3. Click **Format, Cells,** and click the **Font** tab in the Format Cells dialog box.

4. Format for the Book Antiqua font, bold, Single Accounting Underline. Note the Preview box.

5. Click **OK.**

Continued on next page

6. Select the range **B3:D9** and press the **Ctrl+1** keys.

7. In the **Number** tab, select a number format with two decimals.

8. Click **OK.**

9. Do not close the file.

Use the Format Painter

▶ Once you have set formats for text or values, you can copy formats from one cell to another by using the *Format Painter* button on the Formatting toolbar. When you are in Format Painter mode, the mouse pointer includes a paintbrush icon, as shown in Figure 3.19.

▶ To format more than one area of the worksheet with the Format Painter option, double-click the button. After formatting is complete, click the Format Painter button again to exit Format Painter mode.

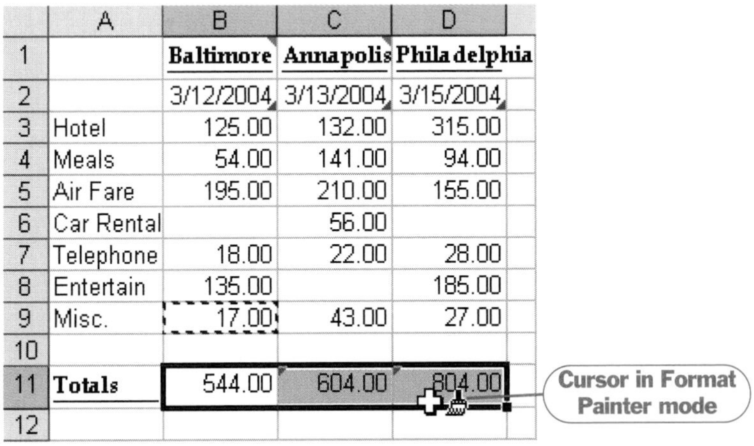

	A	B	C	D
1		**Baltimore**	**Annapolis**	**Philadelphia**
2		3/12/2004	3/13/2004	3/15/2004
3	Hotel	125.00	132.00	315.00
4	Meals	54.00	141.00	94.00
5	Air Fare	195.00	210.00	155.00
6	Car Rental		56.00	
7	Telephone	18.00	22.00	28.00
8	Entertain	135.00		185.00
9	Misc.	17.00	43.00	27.00
10				
11	**Totals**	544.00	604.00	804.00
12				

Cursor in Format Painter mode

Figure 3.19 Format Painter

1. Continue working in the open file or open **E3-16** from the Data CD.

2. Select **Cell B9.**

3. Click the **Format Painter** button.

4. Select and apply the format to the range **B11:D11.**

5. Select **B1** and click **Format Painter.**

6. Select and apply the format to **Cell A11.**

7. Save the file **E3-16.** Close the file.

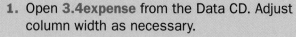

REHEARSAL

TASK 4

GOAL
To create an expense report

SETTING THE STAGE/WRAPUP
File name: **3.4expense**

WHAT YOU NEED TO KNOW

▶ When employees travel on company business, the company usually *reimburses,* or refunds, their expenses. They may get a cash advance before the trip, which reduces the reimbursement amount.

▶ After the trip, they must submit all expenses and receipts for reimbursement with an *expense report.* The tax laws require detailed records for business entertainment because business travel expenses are part of the costs of doing business.

▶ In this Rehearsal activity, you will prepare an expense report for Sara Vikers, an employee of Occasions Event Planning. She is applying for reimbursement of expenses for her business trip to Rochester, N.Y., to meet with the hotels, vendors, and co-sponsor of the photography conference she is planning.

▼ DIRECTIONS

1. Open **3.4expense** from the Data CD. Adjust column width as necessary.

2. Select the range **A1:A3** and use the Format Cells dialog box to format for Tahoma, bold, 12 point.

3. Move the letterhead, using drag-and-drop, to **Cell C1.**

4. Use **Format Painter** to apply the font format from **Cell C1** to the EXPENSE REPORT title.

5. Select the labels in the range **A6:A8** and format them for bold.

6. Double-click the **Format Painter** button and apply bold format to the column headings in **Rows 10, 24,** and **25,** as shown on the facing page.

7. Click **Format Painter** to turn off multiple cell format.

8. Center the column headings in the range **C10:H10.**

9. Format the dates as shown in the illustration on the facing page.

10. Select the range **A23:H31** and move the range to **Cell A18.**

11. As illustrated on the facing page, in **Cell C18,** use AutoSum to find the total of the column.

12. Use the fill handle to extend the formula to **Cell H18.**

13. In **Cell H21,** enter a formula to find the amount due Sara Vikers. *(Hint: =Total-Advance)*

14. Select the range **C11:H21** and format for two decimals.

15. Use **Format Painter** to apply the same format to **Cell G26.**

16. Click **Cell H20,** click **Insert, Comment,** and enter the comment `Receipt #86 9/10`.

17. Click **Cell H21,** click **Format, Cells,** and click the **Font** tab to add a Double Accounting underline.

Continued on next page

18. Edit the comment to add the current year.

19. Print the expense report with the comment displayed at the end of the sheet.

20. Save the file **3.4expense**. Close the file.

	A	B	C	D	E	F	G	H
1			**Occasions Event Planning**					
2			**675 Third Avenue**					
3			**New York, NY 10017**					
4	**EXPENSE REPORT**							
5								
6	**Employee:**		Sara Vikers					
7	**Purpose:**		Trip to Rochester, NY to plan Photography Conference					
8	**Date (s):**		September 12 and 13, 2004					
9								
10	**Date**	**Description**	**Meals**	**Travel**	**Lodging**	**Telephone**	**Other**	**Total**
11	9/12	Employee	35		96	23	15	169
12	9/12	Entertainment*	137					137
13	9/13	Car Rental Charges		75				75
14	9/13	Fuel		35				35
15	9/13	Tolls		8.5				8.5
16	9/13	Employee	52			21	22	95
17								
18		Totals						→
19								
20						Less: Advance		250
21						Net due		
22								
23								
24	**Entertainment Expenses Detail***							
25	**Date**	**Client/Company Entertained**	**Purpose**		**Restaurant**		**Amount**	
26	9/12/04	R. Frank, Vision Camera Co.	Conference planning		Blue Hill Restaurant		137	

PERFORMANCE

Act I

Ralph Green, the CFO of Green Brothers Gardening, has asked you to work on the sales journal to record credit sales. This sales journal for Green Brothers' smallest nursery divides sales into the services provided at that location, i.e., nursery, maintenance contracts, and landscaping. Use 4.5% for the sales tax rate for Virginia and apply it only to nursery sales. Although the sales journal normally provides totals at the end of the month, Mr. Green wants data on June 15 to help with business decisions.

* Open **3p1.salejour** from the Data CD and adjust column width as necessary.

* Sales Income column: Enter formula to add all services.

* Sales Tax column: Enter formula to calculate taxes on nursery sales only. Zero should appear if there is no tax.

* Accounts Receivable column: Enter formula to add tax to sales.

* Fill the formulas down the columns.

* Invoice number column: Use AutoFill.

* Find totals and statistics for all columns.

* Format numbers for commas, except for the Count row, and set alignments, column widths, and text formats to improve the appearance of the worksheet.

* Print the journal using landscape orientation.

* Save and close the file **3p1.salejour**.

Act II

Odyssey Travel Gear has asked you to complete the weekly payroll for the Chicago store for the week ending July 20. Store employees are paid based on an hourly rate.

The deductions for federal and state income taxes are based on the salary and tax status of the employee and are obtained from tax tables or from online services. The tax status M2, for example, is made up of the marital staus (M = married, S = single) and the number of federal exemptions. Social Security (6.2%) and Medicare (1.45%) taxes are calculated using the current tax rate.

Name	Status	Hours	Rate	Gross Pay	Federal W.T.	State W.T.	Social Security Tax	Medicare Tax	Total Deductions	Net Pay
Odyssey Travel Gear									Chicago Store #01	
Payroll Register									For the week ended: 20-Jul-04	
Miller, Carson	M 2	40	14.50		39.26	17.40				
Vaughn, Tamika	M 1	40	10.95		26.76	13.14				
Sanchez, Linda	S 0	35	9.00		33.93	9.45				
Frommel, Sam	S 2	38	9.00							
Witnaur, Mary	M 0	40	8.25							
	Total									
	Average									
	Highest									
	Lowest									

✳ Open **3p2.payroll** from the Data CD and adjust column widths as necessary.

✳ The employees' hours for the week are shown below:

Name	Status	Hours	Rate
Miller, Carson	M 2	40	14.50
Vaughn, Tamika	M 1	40	10.95
Sanchez, Linda	S 0	35	9.00
Frommel, Sam	S 2	38	9.00
Witnaur, Mary	M 0	40	8.25

✳ The federal and state taxes are included for the first three employees. Use the Paycheck Calculator on the Personal Calculator link on www.paycheckcity.com to look up the federal and state taxes for the last two employees. On the Web site, you will have to enter the State (Illinois), Gross Pay, Pay Frequency (weekly), Married or Single for federal filing status and enter the number of federal exemptions. When you click Calculate, the detailed paycheck will appear. Copy the state and federal taxes and enter them on your worksheet.

✳ Enter formulas for Gross Pay *(Hint: Hours*Rate)*, Social Security Tax, Medicare Tax, Total Deductions, and Net Pay. Fill the formulas for all employees and format values.

✳ Find summary values for the payroll, including Totals, Averages, Highest, and Lowest. Format all values for commas.

✳ Print Preview, change the orientation to print the worksheet on one page, print, save, and close the file **3p2.payroll.**

Act III

Carl Westfield, from the Television Division in the California office of Trilogy Productions, has just returned from a business trip to San Diego, California where he met with local stations and writers. He needs an expense report for the trip made October 12 to October 15, 2004. The company reimburses him for mileage driven at $.36 per mile.

		Trilogy Productions						
		101 Sunset Boulevard						
		Beverly Hills, CA 90211						
EXPENSE REPORT								
Employee:								
Purpose:								
Date (s):								
Date	Description	Transport	Fuel	Meals	Lodging	Phone	Other	Total
						Total		
						Less: Advance		
						Net due		
(Mileage reimbursed at $.36 per mile.)								
Entertainment Expenses Detail"								
Date	Client/Company Entertained		Purpose		Restaurant/Event			Amount

* Open **3p3.expense** from the Data CD, and format font, font size and style, as you want, for the Trilogy Productions heading and report title. Center the column headings and save the file as a template.

* Mr. Westfield provides you with the following receipts and list of expenses. Enter and place the expense amounts in the appropriate columns.

  10/12 Fuel $20.76

  10/13 Entertainment: $325.64 - Dinner meeting - Ocean View Restaurant, SDTV Marketing Team

10/14 Entertainment: $114.95 - Luncheon, XY Project - Carson Willers, screenwriter, at LaTavola

10/15 Other expenses: $72.89, Hotel $389.85, Meals $412.65, Telephone $45.89, Fuel $23.54

10/15 Mileage: 300 miles @ $.36 per mile (Enter a formula to multiply the mileage by $.36 in the Transport column to find the expense.)

✴ Mr. Westfield drove from Sunset Boulevard in Beverly Hills, CA 90210 to Federal Boulevard in San Diego, CA 92102. Mr. Westfield just estimated the mileage. You have been asked to check the distance of this trip on the Internet by going to www.mappoint.msn.com. Use the Directions tab to determine the one-way mileage for this trip. Then, on an unused area of the worksheet, calculate the mileage by doubling the one-way mileage and adding 50 miles for in-town driving. (Edit the formula and the label to show the new mileage figure.)

✴ Enter a comment in the Transport calculation cell to note the number of trip miles and the number of in-town miles.

✴ Mr. Westfield received an advance of $300 before the trip and would like to be reimbursed for the balance.

✴ Complete formulas to add values across and down and format as necessary.

✴ Print the expense report, changing the print settings if necessary. Save the file as an Excel workbook file; name it **3p3.exp1012.**

Data Analysis

In this lesson, you will learn to use Excel features, functions, and multiple worksheet workbooks to create and complete analyses of business data. Completed worksheets and workbooks will be saved as a Web page.

Upon completion of this lesson, you should have mastered the following skill sets:

✻ Apply and modify cell formats
  ✱ Cell borders
  ✱ Decimal place and negative number format
✻ Insert a page break
✻ Lists
  ✱ Sort lists
  ✱ Filter lists using AutoFilter
✻ Use numeric labels
✻ Indent text
✻ Insert and delete rows and columns
✻ Use formulas with absolute and relative reference
✻ Convert workbooks into Web pages
  ✱ Add a Background Pattern
  ✱ Use Web Page Preview
  ✱ Save a workbook as a Web page

✻ Apply and modify worksheet formats
  ✱ AutoFormat
  ✱ Fill color and font color
✻ Modify workbooks
  ✱ Insert and delete worksheets
  ✱ Move and copy worksheets
  ✱ Rename and format worksheet tabs
  ✱ Group worksheets
✻ Use date formats and functions
✻ Use financial functions
  ✱ The PMT function
  ✱ The FV function
  ✱ The PV function
✻ Use Paste Special, Values

Terms
Software-related
Border
Negative numbers
Page break
Sort
AutoFilter
Numeric label
Label prefix
Relative reference
Absolute reference
Web page
Interactivity
AutoFormat
Tab Scrolling buttons
Group sheets
Serial value
Date function
Financial functions
PMT
Principal
Rate
Annual interest rate
Nper
FV
PV
Paste values

Document-related
Budget
Quarterly
Income statement
Revenue
Credit terms
Reciprocal

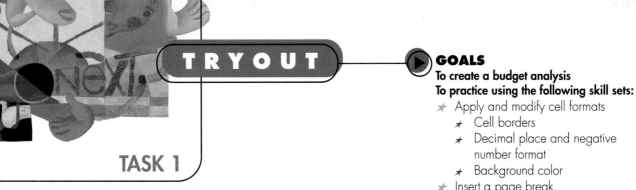

TRYOUT

TASK 1

▶ **GOALS**
To create a budget analysis
To practice using the following skill sets:
* Apply and modify cell formats
  * Cell borders
  * Decimal place and negative number format
  * Background color
* Insert a page break
* Lists
  * Filter lists using AutoFilter
  * Sort lists

EXCEL

WHAT YOU NEED TO KNOW

Apply and Modify Cell Formats

▶ Excel provides several ways for you to format the cells in a worksheet to create professional-looking documents. You can add a variety of borders and format numeric values appropriately.

Cell Borders

▶ To outline or separate data, you can include a variety of line styles that *border* the edge of a cell or range of cells. You add borders by selecting the range, clicking the Borders button on the Formatting toolbar, as shown in Figure 4.1, and selecting the border style.

▶ Click the last Border button option to open the Draw Borders toolbar, as shown in Figure 4.2. To draw your borders, select the line style, use the pencil cursor to draw the border, and use the eraser button to make corrections.

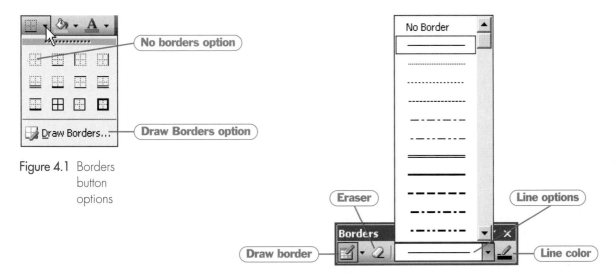

Figure 4.1 Borders button options

Figure 4.2 Draw Borders toolbar and line options

▶ Borders can also be set and previewed using the Border tab in the Format Cells dialog box, as shown in Figure 4.3. The dialog box contains three preset border formats and other border styles illustrated around the preview box. Line Style and Color boxes allow you to set these features for the selected border style.

► Border formats remain when you clear cell contents. Therefore, you must clear border settings separately. To clear borders, select the No Border option from the Borders button drop-down list, or the None style in the Border tab of the Format Cells dialog box.

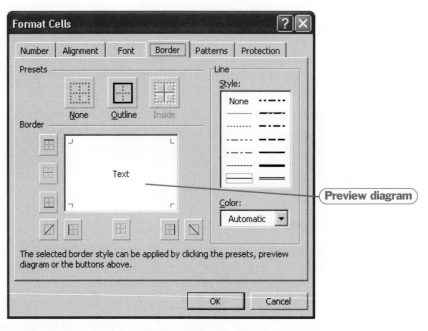

Figure 4.3 Format Cells dialog box, Border tab

TRY *it* OUT *E4-1*

1. Open **E4-1** from the Data CD.

2. Select columns **B:F** and double-click between columns **F** and **G** to AutoFit the data.

3. Select the range **A4:F4** and click the **Borders** button list arrow.

4. Select the **Thick Bottom Border** style.

5. Select the range **C36:F36.**

6. Click **Format, Cells,** and click the **Border** tab.

7. Select the **Double Line** style and click the preset **Outline** style. Notice the preview box. Click **OK.**

8. With the range **C36:F36** still selected, click the **No Border** style on the Borders button menu to clear the borders.

9. Click **Undo** to reverse the **No Border** style.

10. Click the **Borders** button and the **Draw Borders** option.

11. Select the thick line style and use the pencil cursor to outline the range **A5:F7.**

12. Click the **Erase** button on the Borders toolbar and erase the border in the ranges **A5:A7** and **F5:F7.**

13. Close the Borders toolbar but do not close the file.

Decimal Place and Negative Number Format

► Make settings for decimal places and commas with the toolbar buttons discussed earlier. However, formats for decimal places, commas, and for negative numbers, may be set by clicking the Number tab in the Format Cells dialog box, as shown in Figure 4.4.

▶ When *negative numbers* are the result of a calculation, the default format displays the value with parentheses. However, you can set negative values to display with a minus sign, in red with parentheses, or both. You need a color printer to print red numbers.

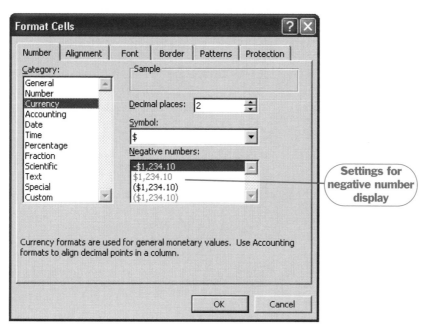

Figure 4.4 Format Cells dialog box, Number tab

Insert a Page Break

▶ A *page break* is the location on the page where one page ends and another begins. Excel automatically inserts a page break when data goes beyond the bottom and right margins of a page.

▶ Use the View, Page Break Preview commands to go into Page Break Preview, as shown in Figure 4.5, to view the existing page breaks to see if your worksheet will fit on one page. You can adjust the page breaks by dragging the dotted lines that represent the breaks. If you move the page breaks to include more rows, the cell size decreases to fit all rows on the page. Use the View menu to return to normal view.

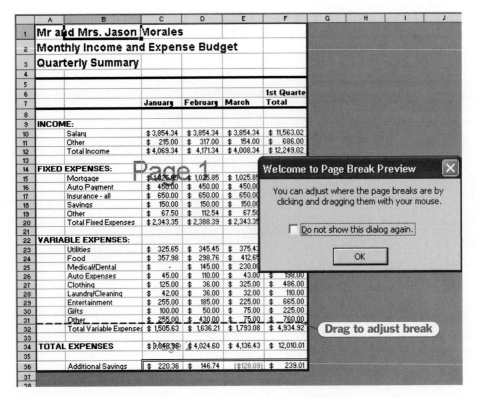

Figure 4.5 Page Break Preview

TRY it OUT E4-3

1. Continue to work in the open file, or open **E4-3** from the Data CD.

2. Click **File, Page Setup,** and click **Landscape** on the Page tab. Click **OK.**

3. Click **View, Page Break Preview** and close the Welcome to Page Break Preview dialog box.

4. Scroll down, if necessary, and notice the blue dotted line that breaks page 1 from page 2.

5. Drag the line down so that all the data appears on page 1.

6. Click **File, Page Setup,** and notice that the worksheet has been scaled to 84%. Note: The scaling percentage may vary depending on your system.

7. Print Preview the file and return to **Normal** on the View menu. Note that Portrait orientation would be a better choice for this worksheet.

8. Save the file **E4-3.** Close the file.

Lists

▶ Data arranged in columns with headers or in a table is called a list. You can sort or filter lists to arrange or find data.

Sort Lists

▶ You can use the Sort Ascending or Sort Descending buttons on the toolbar for quick sorts or use the Sort dialog box for additional features.

► To sort tables, select the entire table without the column headings and click Data, Sort. The Sort dialog box displays, as shown in Figure 4.6. Select the first-, second-, and third-level sort data and select ascending or descending sorts. The header row becomes the column names as long as the Header row option is selected and the headers are in the row above the table. You can re-sort or use the Undo and/or Redo buttons to return to the original settings.

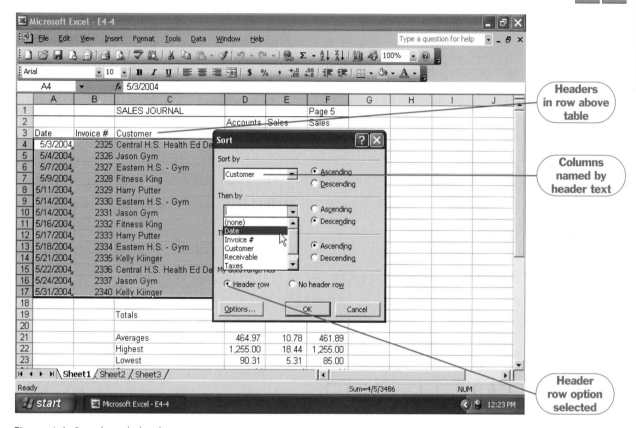

Figure 4.6 Sort data dialog box

T R Y *it* **O U T** *E4-4*

1. Open **E4-4** from the Data CD.

2. Select the range **B26:B29.**

3. Click the **Sort Descending** button. Click the **Sort Ascending** button.

4. Select the range **A4:F17.**

5. Click **Data, Sort** to display the Sort dialog box.

6. Use the list arrows to Sort by **Customer** (ascending), and then by **Date** (descending).

7. Click **OK.** Note that the customers are in alphabetical order and the dates are in reverse chronological order by customer.

8. Click **Data, Sort** and Sort by **Invoice #** (ascending), and then by **(none).**

9. Click **Undo** and then click **Redo.**

10. Do not close the file.

Filter Lists Using AutoFilter

▶ *AutoFilter* is an Excel data list feature that applies a filter that hides all items that do not meet the criteria you set. To apply AutoFilter, select any cell in a list or the entire list and click Data, Filter, AutoFilter. A series of arrows appears at the top of each column. When you select a column and an item from the drop-down list, you are setting a criterion, which will filter the list and show only the items you select.

▶ For example, in the sales journal shown in Figure 4.7, after you select a customer's name from the drop-down list in the Customers column, you see all the sales made to that customer. All others are filtered out. To remove the filter, click All on the drop-down list, and deselect AutoFilter on the Data, Filter menu.

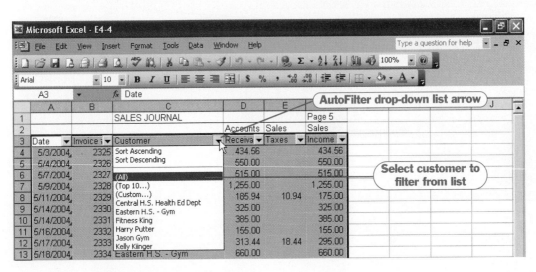

Figure 4.7 AutoFilter and drop-down filter list

TRY*it* OUT E4-5

1. Continue to work in the open file, or open **E4-5** from the Data CD.

2. Select the range **A3:F17** and click **Data, Filter,** and **AutoFilter.**

3. Click the list arrow in the **Customer** column, and select **Fitness King.** Sales to Fitness King appear.

4. Click the same **list arrow,** and select **Eastern H.S. - Gym.**

5. Click the **list arrow** again and select **All** to remove the filter.

6. Click **Data, Filter** and **AutoFilter** to remove the filter arrows.

7. Open your solution to E4-3 or open **E4-5a** from the Data CD.

8. Apply **AutoFilter** in the **VARIABLE EXPENSES** section.

9. Filter to find the amount of Medical/Dental expenses.

10. Remove the filter and deselect **AutoFilter.**

11. Close both files. Do not save.

REHEARSAL

GOAL
To create a budget analysis

SETTING THE STAGE/WRAPUP
File name: **4.1budget**

TASK 1

WHAT YOU NEED TO KNOW

▶ A *budget* is an analysis of the projected income and expenses for a future period. Companies create budgets based on past history and projections of future trends. Budgets are the basis for management decisions and plans for expenditures.

▶ Businesses analyze data *quarterly,* which is every three months, or four times a year, using percentages for ease of comparison.

▶ In this Rehearsal activity, you will create a budget analysis for the quarter ending September 30, 2004, for Time Out Sporting Goods. This company is comparing its budget for the third quarter, prepared earlier, with the actual expenditures to note the items that created the change in expected profits.

▼ DIRECTIONS

1. Open **4.1budget** from the Data CD.

2. Drag column borders to make width changes as follows: **Column A** to **23.00**, **Columns B:E** to **12.00.**

3. Set the following formats as illustrated on the facing page:
   a. Select **Cell B1** and format for 18 point, Arial.
   b. Select the range **A3:F3** and apply a Thick Bottom Border for the row.
   c. Use the Draw Borders tool to add a Thick Bottom Border to the range **A7:F7.**
   d. Format **Columns B** and **C** for commas with no decimal places.

4. Enter a formula in **Cell D9** to find the Increase/Decrease from Budget. *(Hint: Actual-Budget)*

5. Click **Format, Cells,** and click the **Number** tab in the Format Cells dialog box. Click Number and format **Cell D9** for red negative numbers with parentheses and for commas with no decimal places. (Set the decimal places, and check the comma separator.)

6. Copy the formula down to **Cell D33.** Delete dashes or zeros where there are no entries in **Columns B** and **C.**

7. Enter a formula in **Cell E9** to find the % Increase/Decrease from Budget. *(Hint: D9/Budget)*

8. Format **Cell E9** for percent with two decimal places. (Click the **Percent** and **Increase or Decrease Decimal** buttons.)

9. Copy the formula down to **Cell E33.** Delete error messages as necessary.

10. Use the Draw border tool or the **Border** button to:
    • Add a Bottom Border under the values for **Rows 12** and **28.**
    • Add a single Top and Double Bottom border under the values for **Row 33.**

Continued on next page

11. Select the expenses in the range **A17:E28** and sort in ascending order by **Column A.**

12. Use AutoFilter on the Expenses list to find the Supplies data.

13. Display all the data and remove the AutoFilter.

14. In Page Setup, set to print in landscape mode and set Margins to horizontally and vertically center the worksheet. Click **OK.**

15. In Page Break Preview, extend the margins to fit the worksheet on one page.

16. Return to Normal view, Print Preview, and print the worksheet.

17. Save the file **4.1budget.** Close the file.

	A	B	C	D	E	F	G	H
1		Time Out Sporting Goods				18 point Arial		
2	Comparison of Budgeted Income Statement with Actual Income Statement							
3		For Quarter Ended September 30, 2004						
4					% of			
5				Increase/	Increase/	Thick bottom borders		
6		Budget	Actual	Decrease	Decrease			
7		3rd Qtr	3rd Qtr	from Budget	from Budget			
8	Revenue:							
9	Net Sales	442,500	443,780					
10								
11	Cost of Goods Sold:							
12	Cost of Goods Sold	287,625	291,456			Bottom border		
13								
14	Gross Profit	154,875	152,324					
15								
16	Expenses:							
17	Advertising/promotions	3,750	3,795					
18	Depreciation	5,625	5,625					
19	Insurance	4,500	4,500					
20	Legal/accounting	4,125	4,075					
21	Loan interest payments	6,375	6,375					
22	Miscellaneous expenses	2,850	2,815					
23	Payroll expenses	3,150	3,165					
24	Rent	56,250	56,250					
25	Repairs/maintenance	1,350	1,858					
26	Salaries/wages	20,738	20,805					
27	Supplies	1,988	1,850					
28	Utilities	1,935	1,925					
29	Total Expenses	112,635	113,038					
30								
31	Net Income before Taxes	42,240	39,286			Top and bottom double border		
32	Taxes	12,672	11,786					
33	Net Income after Taxes	29,568	27,500					
34								

Cues for Reference

Apply Borders
1. Select area to receive border.
2. Click **Border** button list arrow.
3. Click border style.
   or
1. Click **Format, Cells,** and click the **Border** tab.
2. Select line, color, and style.
3. Click **OK.**
   or
1. Click **Border** button list arrow.
2. Click **Draw Borders.**
3. Click the list arrow to set the line style.
4. Draw the border.

Format Decimals and Negative Numbers
1. Select data to format.
2. Click **Format, Cells,** and click the **Number** tab.
3. Click the **Number** category.

4. Use list arrows to select decimal settings.
5. Use list arrows to select negative number setting.
6. Select comma indicator, if appropriate.

Correct Page Break
1. Click **View, Page Break Preview.**
2. Drag margin line(s) to correct page break.
3. Click **View, Normal** to leave Page Break Preview.

Sort
1. Select the table data without the column headings.
2. Click **Data, Sort.**
3. Select the first, second, and third sort columns and sort order.
4. Click **OK.**

   or
1. Select column to sort.
2. Click the **Sort Ascending** or **Sort Descending** button.

Apply AutoFilter
1. Select any cell in the list to filter or select the data.
2. Click **Data, Filter, AutoFilter.**
3. Click the list arrow in column to filter.

Show All Data in Filtered List
1. Click the list arrow in filtered column.
2. Select **All.**

End AutoFilter
• Click **Data, Filter,** and **AutoFilter** to deselect the feature.

TRYOUT

TASK 2

GOALS
To create an income statement analysis and publish it to the Web
To practice using the following skill sets:
- ✴ Use numeric labels
- ✴ Indent text
- ✴ Insert and delete rows and columns
- ✴ Use formulas with absolute and relative reference
- ✴ Convert workbooks into Web pages
    - ✴ Add a background pattern
    - ✴ Use Web Page Preview
    - ✴ Save a workbook as a Web page
    - ✴ Publish to the Web

WHAT YOU NEED TO KNOW

Use Numeric Labels

▶ A *numeric label* is a value or number that is not used for calculations and is treated as a label or text. It is wise to enter numeric column headings as numeric labels so the values are not included in the total by mistake.

▶ To enter a number as a numeric label, begin the entry with an apostrophe ('), which serves as the *label prefix*. For example, to enter the year 2005, you would enter '2005. The label prefix appears only on the formula bar, and the number is formatted as left-aligned text, as shown in Figure 4.8. Note the Smart Tag indicator and message.

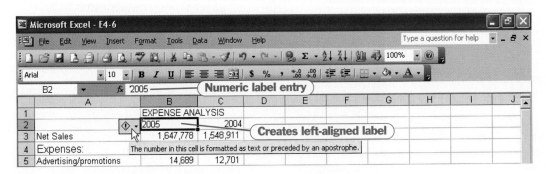

Figure 4.8 Numeric label and related smart tag

TRY*it*OUT *E4-6*

1. Open **E4-6** from the Data CD.

2. In **Cell B2,** overtype the value with a numeric label: **'2005.**

3. Enter a numeric label in **Cell C2** for 2004: **'2004.**

4. Center the labels.

5. Do not close the file.

Indent Text

▶ The indent text feature allows you to align text away from the left edge of the cell. Indent text quickly by clicking the Increase Indent button on the Formatting toolbar, and adjust or undo indentation by clicking the Decrease Indent button. Use indentations to set off lists of text from heading labels.

TRY *it* OUT *E4-7*

1. Continue to work in the open file, or open **E4-7** from the Data CD.

2. Select the range **A5:A16.**

3. Click the **Increase Indent button.**

4. Do not close the file.

Insert and Delete Rows and Columns

▶ You can insert or delete columns or rows to change the structure of a worksheet. Always save a workbook before doing this to avoid deleting data in error.

▶ When you insert a column or row, existing data shifts to allow for the new space. Select the column or row where you want the new space to be and click Insert, Columns or Rows, or you can right-click to use the shortcut menu. If you want to insert more than one column or row, select that number of rows or columns, starting with the location where the new column or row begins. An Insert Options Smart Tag will appear with format options when columns or rows are inserted.

▶ When you delete a column or row, all data in that space is eliminated and existing data shifts to fill in the space. If you attempt to delete data by selecting cells, and not the entire row or column, the Delete dialog box opens, as shown in Figure 4.9, to provide options to clarify the request.

Figure 4.9 Delete dialog box

TRY *it* OUT *E4-8*

1. Continue to work in the open file, or open **E4-8** from the Data CD.

2. Select **Column C.**

3. Click **Insert, Columns** and note the Insert Options Smart Tag.

4. Select **Clear Formatting** on the Insert Options Smart Tag.

5. Select **Row 3,** right-click, and select **Delete** on the shortcut menu. The row and the data are deleted.

6. Select **Row 2** and insert a row.

7. Select the range **B5:C5** and click **Edit, Delete.** (Notice the Delete dialog box.)

8. Click **Cancel.**

9. Do not close the file.

Use Formulas with Absolute and Relative Reference

▶ When you copy formulas from one cell to another, the cell references change, relative to their new location. This is called *relative reference,* the most commonly used technique of entering and copying formulas.

▶ However, in some cases a value in a formula must remain constant when copied to other locations. This is called an *absolute reference.* To identify a value as an absolute reference, or constant, a dollar sign ($) must precede the column and row references for that cell.

▶ For example, you need an absolute reference to find the percentage each value in a list represents of the total, because the total must be the constant in each formula. Therefore, in the formula =B5/$B$17, B17 represents the total and is an absolute reference. When this formula is copied, B17 remains constant in the formula but B5, with no absolute reference code, changes relative to the formula location. You can enter the dollar signs ($) in the formula by keying them in or by pressing the F4 key.

T R Y *it* O U T *E4-9*

1. Continue to work in the open file, or open **E4-9** from the Data CD.

2. In **Cell B17,** check the formula on the formula bar.

3. Copy the formula to **Cell D17** and check the formula (copied with relative reference).

4. Enter a label in **Cells C3** and **E3:** % of Total.

5. Enter a formula in **Cell C5** to find the percentage each expense is of the total. (Hint: **=B5/$B$17:** press the equal sign, click **B5,** press **/,** click **B17,** press the **F4** key to enter the dollar signs.)

6. Format the value for percent with no decimal places.

7. Use the fill handle to copy the formula down to **Cell C16** for all expenses.

8. Check the formulas for each expense (copied with absolute reference).

9. Find the total in **Cell C17** and format for percent (100%).

10. Complete the formulas for Column E.

11. Save the file as **E4-9.** Do not close the file.

Convert a Workbook into a Web Page

▶ You can make workbooks available to employees or stockholders who may be in various locations by saving all or part of a workbook as a Web page. A *Web page* is a location on an Internet server, part of the World Wide Web, which can be reached and identified by a Web address. Web pages have an .mht or .html file extension.

Add a Background Pattern

▶ A background may be added to a worksheet to enhance its display. The background pattern does not print, but will be retained if the worksheet is published as a Web page. Click Format, Sheet, Background and select a graphic to use for the pattern. The graphic will fill the sheet. Remove the background by clicking Format, Sheet, Delete Background.

Use Web Page Preview

▶ Before you save an Excel workbook as a Web page, carefully edit and check the content, then save the file. You can preview your worksheet without publishing it, as shown in Figure 4.10, by clicking File, Web Page Preview. Close the Web Page Preview window to edit the worksheet as necessary.

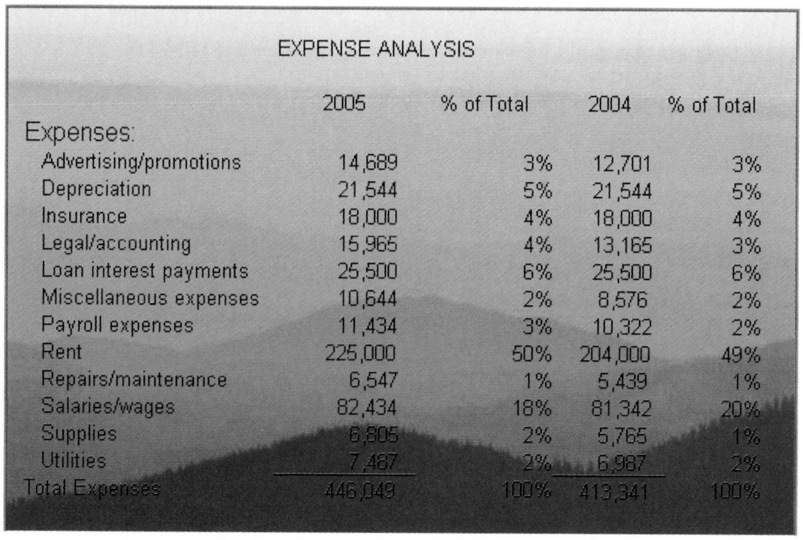

EXPENSE ANALYSIS

	2005	% of Total	2004	% of Total
Expenses:				
Advertising/promotions	14,689	3%	12,701	3%
Depreciation	21,544	5%	21,544	5%
Insurance	18,000	4%	18,000	4%
Legal/accounting	15,965	4%	13,165	3%
Loan interest payments	25,500	6%	25,500	6%
Miscellaneous expenses	10,644	2%	8,576	2%
Payroll expenses	11,434	3%	10,322	2%
Rent	225,000	50%	204,000	49%
Repairs/maintenance	6,547	1%	5,439	1%
Salaries/wages	82,434	18%	81,342	20%
Supplies	6,805	2%	5,765	1%
Utilities	7,487	2%	6,987	2%
Total Expenses	446,049	100%	413,341	100%

Figure 4.10 Worksheet with background in Web page preview

TRY it OUT E4-10

1. Continue to work in the open file, or open **E4-10** from the Data CD.

2. Click **Format, Sheet, Background** and open the Sample Pictures folder.

3. Select the **Blue hills** picture file and click **Insert.**

4. Click the **Print Preview** button and note that the background does not print. Close the Print Preview window.

5. Click **File, Web Page Preview.** (The worksheet with its background is displayed as a Web page.) Close the Web Page Preview window.

6. Save the file as **E4-10**.

Save a Workbook as a Web Page

▶ To save your workbook as a Web page, click File, Save As Web Page to open the Save As dialog box with Web page settings. You can save the entire workbook or the selected sheet, and add interactivity. The *Interactivity* setting allows users to make changes to the workbook on the Web site.

▶ To create a title for your Web page, click the Change Title button. The Set Page Title dialog box opens, as shown in Figure 4.11, and the title you enter appears centered over your worksheet on the Web page.

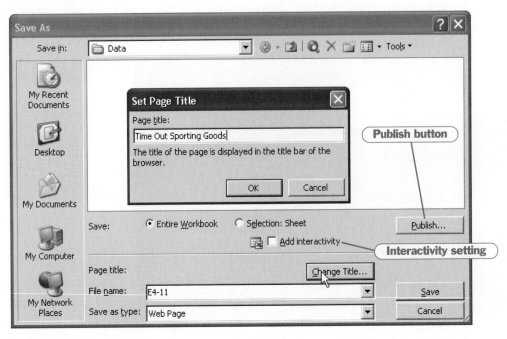

Figure 4.11 Save As Web Page and Set Title dialog box

TRY*it*OUT *E4-11*

1. Continue to work in the open file, or open **E4-11** from the Data CD.

2. Click **File, Save as Web Page.**

3. Click **Selection: Sheet.**

4. Click **Change Title.**

5. Enter **Time Out Sporting Goods** and click **OK.**

6. In the File name box, enter the file name: **test.**

7. Do not close the file or the Save As dialog box.

Publish to the Web

▶ After you name the file and choose the save settings, click Publish, and click Browse to select a local disk folder as the publish location. On the Publish as Web Page dialog box, as shown in Figure 4.12, check Open published web page in browser, and click Publish. The published page is saved to your local drive and the Web page opens in Internet Explorer or your Web browser for you to preview.

▶ If you added interactivity, you can now make changes to the workbook in the browser; otherwise, you need to go back to the Excel file to make any changes. When your edits are complete, you can republish the Web page to your public location.

▶ Some Web site hosting companies let you publish Web pages directly to the Internet, but you or your facility must sign up for an account. Some accounts are free if you accept advertisements that automatically appear on your site.

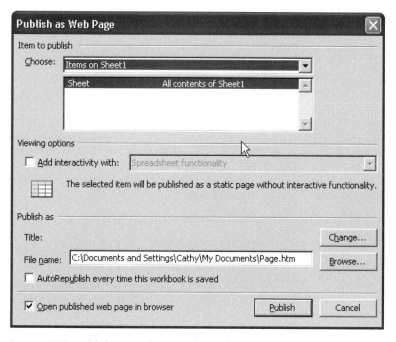

Figure 4.12 Publish as Web Page dialog box

T R Y _it_ O U T _E4-12_

1. Continue to work in the open file.
2. Click **Publish.**
3. Click **Browse** and select location for the file. Click **OK.**
4. Check **Open published web page in browser.** Click **Publish.** (The file will open in Internet Explorer or your default browser.)
5. Review the data, and then click the **Close** button.
6. In the worksheet, bold the title in **Cell B1.**

7. Format the totals in **Cells B17** and **D17** for currency with no decimal places, adjusting column width as necessary.
8. Republish the worksheet:
   a. Click **File, Save as Web Page.**
   b. Click **test.**
   c. Check **Republish:Sheet.**
   d. Click **Publish** on the Save As dialog box.
   e. Click **Publish** on the Publish as Web Page dialog box.
9. Note the edits and close the browser.
10. Save the file as E4-12. Close the file.

REHEARSAL

 GOAL
To create an income statement analysis with absolute reference formulas and to save the file as a Web page

SETTING THE STAGE/WRAPUP
File name: 4.2is

TASK 2

WHAT YOU NEED TO KNOW

▶ At the end of the year companies prepare an *income statement* to show the income, expenses, and profits for the year. The current income statement data is compared to the statement for the previous year to determine trends.

▶ To analyze the data, we compare the percentage each item is of net sales for each period. Because net sales are used as a constant in every formula for this analysis, it is necessary to use an absolute reference.

▶ In this Rehearsal activity, you will prepare a comparison of summary income statements for Time Out Sporting Goods for two years, and save it as a Web page.

▽ DIRECTIONS

1. Open **4.2is** from the Data CD and adjust column width as necessary.

2. Insert two rows at **Row 5.**

3. Indent text in the range **A8:A9.**

4. Select **Column C** and insert two columns. Create column headings as illustrated on the facing page, using numeric labels where necessary.

5. Enter a formula in **Cell C8,** using an absolute reference, to find the percentage each line is of net sales.

6. Format the result for Percent style. (The answer in **Cell C8** should be 100%, because this is the net sales value.)

7. Copy the formula down for each item.

8. Delete unnecessary formula results.

9. Delete **Row 12.**

10. Enter a formula in **Cell F8** to find the percentage of net sales.

11. Format the result for percent, copy the formula, and clear unwanted results.

12. Add borders as shown in the illustration on the facing page.

13. Check your formats and results.

14. Save the file as **4.2is.**

15. Add a background pattern. Preview the worksheet as a Web page. Close the preview.

16. Save the file as a Web page with the same file name. Change the title to: `Financial Data.`

17. Publish the file to your directory and open the published Web site in your browser.

18. Close the browser and the file.

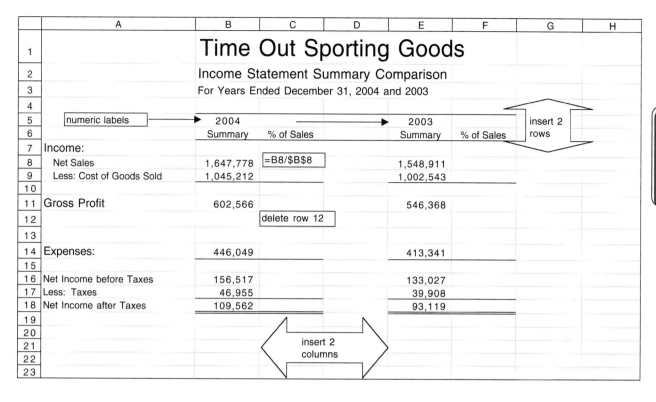

Time Out Sporting Goods

Income Statement Summary Comparison

For Years Ended December 31, 2004 and 2003

	A	B	C	D	E	F	G	H
5	numeric labels →	2004 →			2003		insert 2	
6		Summary	% of Sales		Summary	% of Sales	rows	
7	Income:							
8	Net Sales	1,647,778	=B8/$B$8		1,548,911			
9	Less: Cost of Goods Sold	1,045,212			1,002,543			
10								
11	Gross Profit	602,566			546,368			
12			delete row 12					
13								
14	Expenses:	446,049			413,341			
15								
16	Net Income before Taxes	156,517			133,027			
17	Less: Taxes	46,955			39,908			
18	Net Income after Taxes	109,562			93,119			
19								
20								
21			insert 2					
22			columns					
23								

Cues for Reference

Indent Text
1. Select cells with data to indent.
2. Click **Increase Indent** button.

Insert Rows or Columns
1. Select row(s) or column(s) at the insertion point.
2. Click **Insert, Column** or **Insert, Row.**

Enter Numeric Label
1. Enter apostrophe (').
2. Enter a value.
3. Press **Enter.**

Delete Rows or Columns
1. Select row(s) or column(s) to delete.
2. Click **Edit, Delete.**

Use Absolute Reference Formulas
1. Enter formula, including absolute reference cell.
2. Press **F4** to insert dollar signs.

Add Background Pattern
1. Click **Format, Sheet, Background.**
2. Select the graphic.
3. Click **Insert.**

Save as Web Page and View in Browser
1. Click **File, Save as Web Page.**
2. Click **Change Title.**
3. Enter Web page title.
4. Click **OK.**
5. Name file.
6. Click selection: **Worksheet.**
7. Click **Publish.**
8. Click **Open published web page in browser.**
9. Click **Publish.**

▶ **GOALS**
To create a revenue analysis on multiple worksheets
To practice using the following skill sets:
✳ Apply and modify worksheet formats
  ✳ AutoFormat
  ✳ Fill Color and Font Color
✳ Modify workbooks
  ✳ Insert and delete worksheets
  ✳ Move and copy worksheets
  ✳ Rename and format worksheet tabs
  ✳ Group worksheets

WHAT YOU NEED TO KNOW

Apply and Modify Worksheet Formats

▶ Excel provides built-in formats that you can apply to a range of data.

AutoFormat

▶ The *AutoFormat* feature includes automatic formats for numbers, fonts, borders, patterns, colors, alignments, row heights, and column widths.

▶ When you select a range and click Format, AutoFormat, you find a selection of 16 table formats on the AutoFormat dialog box. As shown in Figure 4.13, all formats include only column headings and data. When you use AutoFormat, you must format title rows separately.

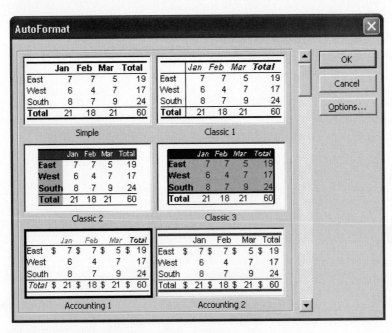

Figure 4.13 AutoFormat dialog box

1. Open **E4-13** from the Data CD.
2. Select the range **A4:F17.**
3. Click **Format, AutoFormat.**
4. View the AutoFormat selections.

5. Select the **Classic 3** AutoFormat.
6. Click **OK.**
7. Do not close the file.

EXCEL

Fill Color and Font Color

▶ The Fill Color and Font Color buttons on the Formatting toolbar provide a palette of colors to format a selected cell or range of cells. You can use them to format sections of an entire worksheet or titles on an AutoFormat worksheet.

▶ You can also apply shading or patterns to a selected range by clicking Format, Cells, and the Patterns tab. Select a color from the Cell shading color palette or a pattern from the Pattern palette, as shown in Figure 4.14. If you place your mouse pointer over a pattern or color in the Patterns tab, or over a color on the toolbar palettes, the name of the pattern or color will appear.

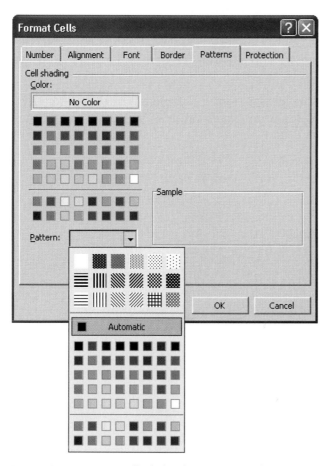

Figure 4.14 Format, Cells dialog box, Patterns tab

1. Continue to work in the open file, or open **E4-14** from the Data CD.

2. Select the range **A1:F3.**

3. Click the **Format, Cells, Patterns** tab, and click the **Pattern** list arrow to select the **12.5% Gray** pattern. Click **OK.**

4. Click elsewhere to view the setting. Click **Undo.**

5. Re-select the range **A1:F3.**

6. Click the **Fill Color** button list arrow and select **Gray 25%.**

7. Click the **Font Color** button list arrow and select **Dark Blue.**

8. Save the file **E4-14**. Close the file.

Modify Workbooks

▶ You can create the same worksheet for several months or for several divisions of the same company by using multiple worksheets in the same workbook. Excel lets you work with sheets in many ways. For example, you can delete, insert, rename, move, copy, and hide sheets.

Insert and Delete Worksheets

▶ There are three sheets, labeled Sheet1 through Sheet3, on the sheet tabs. The active sheet tab is white, and the inactive sheets are shaded. The *Tab Scrolling buttons* allow you to scroll hidden sheets into view.

▶ Select Insert, Worksheet to insert a worksheet. Or, you can insert and delete sheets by right-clicking a sheet tab and clicking Insert or Delete on the shortcut menu, as shown in Figure 4.15.

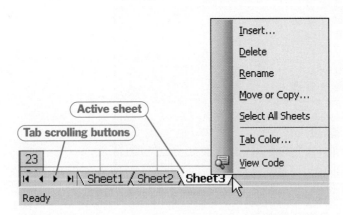

Figure 4.15 Sheet tabs and worksheet shortcut menu

TRY*it* OUT *E4-15*

1. Open **E4-15** from the Data CD.

2. Click **Insert, Worksheet.** A new sheet appears.

3. Right-click any sheet tab.

4. Click **Insert** and click **OK** in the Insert dialog box. A new sheet appears.

5. Right-click **Sheet4.** Click **Delete.**

6. Delete **Sheet1.**

7. Do not close the file.

Move and Copy Worksheets

▶ You can move sheets by using the drag-and-drop method. When you drag the sheet tab, the mouse pointer displays a sheet that you can drop in any location.

▶ To move or copy a sheet, right-click the sheet tab and select Move or Copy. When the Move or Copy dialog box opens, as shown in Figure 4.16, notice that you have the option of moving or copying the sheet to another workbook, or to a location in the current workbook. When you copy a sheet, it will copy with the same sheet name, identified with a (2) to show it is a second copy.

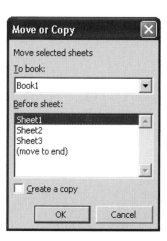

Figure 4.16 Move or Copy dialog box

TRY*it* OUT *E4-16*

1. Continue to work in the open file, or open **E4-16** from the Data CD.

2. Make a copy of the January sheet, and move it to the end:
   a. Right-click the **JANUARY** tab.
   b. Select **Move or Copy.**
   c. Click **Create a copy.**
   d. Select **(move to end).**
   e. Click **OK.**

3. On Sheet2, which shows February data, copy the sales in range **D7:D12,** then

   paste them into the **JANUARY (2)** sheet in **Cell D7.**

4. Click the **Match Destination Formatting** option on the Paste Options Smart Tag button.

5. Select and drag the **JANUARY (2)** sheet to the second worksheet position.

6. Do not close the file.

Rename and Format Worksheet Tabs

▶ To rename a sheet, you can select Rename on the shortcut menu, as shown in Figure 4.15, or double-click the sheet tab and enter the new name.

▶ You can format the color of the sheet tab by clicking Format, Sheet, Tab Color, or clicking Tab Color on the shortcut menu. Then, select the color from the Format Tab Color dialog box, as shown in Figure 4.17. The color will display at the bottom of the tab if it is active; otherwise, the color will fill the tab.

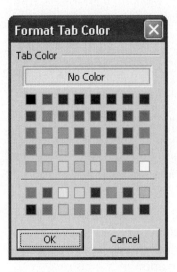

Figure 4.17 Format Tab Color dialog box

T R Y *it* **O U T** *E4-17*

1. Continue to work in the open file, or open **E4-17** from the Data CD.

2. Double-click the **JANUARY(2)** sheet and rename it: FEBRUARY.

3. In **Cell F4,** enter FEBRUARY and widen the column.

4. Click **Sheet2,** right-click, and delete the sheet. Click **Delete** again to confirm deletion.

5. Click the **JANUARY** sheet, then click **Format, Sheet, Tab Color, Blue.** Click **OK.**

6. Right-click the **FEBRUARY** sheet, and click **Tab Color, Red.** Click **OK.**

7. Do not close the file.

Group and Print Worksheets

▶ If you are creating a worksheet that you want to copy to one or more worksheets, you can group the sheets and make the entries on all sheets simultaneously. To *group sheets,* click the first sheet, press and hold the Ctrl key, and select all other sheets. Or, if the sheets you want to select are next to one another, you can click the first sheet, press and hold the Shift key, and click the last sheet.

▶ To print a multiple worksheet file or to make print settings for the entire workbook, first group all sheets. Make print settings with sheets grouped, and click Entire workbook in the Print what section in the Print dialog box, as shown in Figure 4.18.

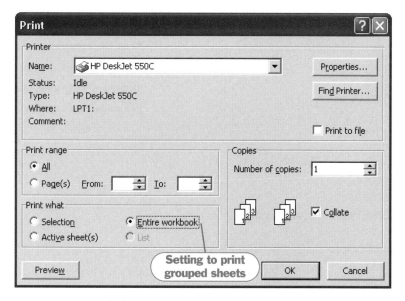

Figure 4.18 Print dialog box

T R Y *i t* **O U T** *E4-18*

1. Continue to work in the open file, or open **E4-18** from the Data CD.

2. Select the **JANUARY** tab, press and hold the **Shift** key, and click **FEBRUARY.** Notice that both sheets are active.

3. In **B3,** enter: **Boston Store.** Check both sheets.

4. With sheets still grouped, click **File, Page Setup.**

5. Deselect the **Gridlines** and the **Row and column** settings on the Sheet tab.

6. Click **OK.**

7. Click **File, Print.**

8. Click **Entire workbook, OK.**

9. Click **Sheet3** to clear grouping and check the **January** and **February** sheets.

10. Save the file **E4-18.** Close the file.

REHEARSAL

TASK 3

 GOAL
To create a revenue analysis on multiple worksheets

SETTING THE STAGE
File name: **4.3revenue**

WHAT YOU NEED TO KNOW

▶ Income or revenue for a business will vary depending on seasonal or economic factors. Business owners analyze revenue figures to note trends, warning signs, and to make management decisions.

▶ Occasions Event Planning plans conferences, parties, seminars, meetings, etc. The company makes arrangements with vendors such as hotels, food caterers, printers, etc., to plan clients' events. Its revenues come from charges for consultation hours and a charge of 18% of all contract vendor bills.

▶ In this Rehearsal activity, you will create a revenue analysis workbook using a quarterly analysis on multiple worksheets.

DIRECTIONS

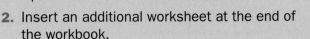

1. Open **4.3revenue** from the Data CD.
2. Insert an additional worksheet at the end of the workbook.
3. Copy Column A from Sheet1 to remaining sheets:
   a. Copy **Column A** on Sheet 1.
   b. Group Sheets 2–4 by clicking **Sheet2,** pressing and holding the **Shift** key, and clicking **Sheet4.**
   c. Paste data to **Cell A1** on Sheet2. (Column A data will be on all sheets.)
   d. Widen **Column A** by double-clicking the column edge, if necessary.
4. Rename Sheets 1–4: 1st Qtr., 2nd Qtr., 3rd Qtr., and 4th Qtr.
5. Cut and paste **April, May,** and **June** data as illustrated on the facing page, from 1st Qtr. sheet to 2nd Qtr. sheet in **Cell B3.**
6. Group all sheets. (Select **1st Qtr.,** press and hold the **Shift** key, and click **4th Qtr.)**
7. Enter the following labels, formats, and formulas on all grouped sheets:
   a. In **Cell E3,** enter a column heading: `Total.`
   b. In **Cell E5,** enter a formula to add the values for the three months.
   c. AutoFill the formula down to Cell **E18.**
   d. In **Cell B13,** enter a formula to add the values for the month.
   e. AutoFill the formula for all months and the Total column.
   f. In **Cell B16,** enter a formula to find Fees on Contracts. (Hint: 18% of total billings for the month: =Total*18%.) AutoFill across for all months.
   g. In **Cell B18,** enter a formula to find Total Revenue by adding Fees and Consultation Revenues. AutoFill across for all months.
   h. Format all values for commas with no decimal places.

Continued on next page

i. Select the range **A3:E18** and AutoFormat the sheets using the List 1 format.

j. Select the range and **A1:E2,** and Fill Color the range using a light turquoise.

8. Ungroup sheets by clicking the **3rd Qtr.** sheet tab.

9. Group 3rd and 4th Qtr. sheets and widen **Columns B:E** to **8.00.** (These sheets have no data yet.)

10. Color sheet tabs as you prefer.

11. Group all sheets and print workbook by clicking **Entire workbook** in the Print dialog box in the Print what section.

12. Save the file **4.3revenue.** Close the workbook.

	A	B	C	D	E	F	G
1	OCCASIONS EVENT PLANNING						
2	**Revenue and Billings Analysis**						
3		January	February	March	April	May	June
4	Billings for Contract Vendors:						
5	Food/Catering	53445	43766	33232	56433	49876	65876
6	Hotels/Venues	87543	65888	73455	98665	82565	98665
7	Printing/Advertising	13232	10533	8564	11654	10112	14323
8	Music/Entertainment	45865	45865	45865	45865	45865	45865
9	Personnel/Speakers/Security	56454	43566	44345	53888	48975	57645
10	Audio/Visual	17654	15433	13245	16543	14987	17909
11	Computers/Special Equipment	54333	54678	32122	50323	42945	44567
12	Miscellaneous	11342	9453	6590	7645	6588	9856
13	Total						
14							
15	Revenue:						
16	Fees on Contracts						
17	Consultation Revenues	10540	11450	11340	12500	12600	11800
18	Total						
19							
20							
21							

\1st Qtr. / 2nd Qtr. / 3rd Qtr. / 4th Qtr. /

Cues for Reference

AutoFormat Data
1. Select worksheet data beginning with column headers.
2. Click **Format, AutoFormat.**
3. Click **AutoFormat style.**
4. Click **OK.**

Group Consecutive Sheets
1. Click the first sheet to group.
2. Press and hold **Shift.**
3. Click last sheet to group.

Group Nonconsecutive Sheets
1. Click the first sheet to group.
2. Press and hold **Ctrl.**

3. Click the second sheet to group.
4. Repeat as necessary.

Delete Sheet
1. Right-click sheet tab of sheet to delete.
2. Click **Delete.**
3. Click **OK.**

Insert Sheet
1. Right-click any sheet tab.
2. Click **Insert.**
3. Click **OK.**

Rename Sheet
• Double-click sheet and type new name
or
1. Right-click sheet tab of sheet to rename.
2. Click **Rename.**
3. Enter new name.

Format Tab Color
1. Right-click sheet tab to format.
2. Click **Tab Color.**
3. Click color.
4. Click **OK.**

TRYOUT

GOALS
To analyze purchase options using financial and date functions
To practice using the following skill sets:
* Use date formats and functions
    * Use the Insert Function button
    * Use financial functions
        * The PMT function
        * The FV function
        * The PV function
    * Use Paste Special, Values

TASK 4

WHAT YOU NEED TO KNOW

Use Date Format and Functions

▶ When you enter a date, Excel automatically creates a *serial value,* or you can use the date function, =DATE(year, month, day), to do so. The serial, or numeric, value allows you to use dates in formulas and represents the number of days from January 1, 1900, to the date entered. To view a date's serial value, format the date as a number using the General format, as shown in Figure 4.19.

	A	B	C	D	E
1	Date Functions:	Test dates:	1/1/1900	1/30/1900	1/30/2005
2	Serial or numeric values when dates formatted as General numbers			1	30	38382
3					

Figure 4.19 Dates formatted to show serial values

▶ Once you enter a date, you can change the format, as discussed in Lesson 1, by clicking Format, Cells, the Number tab, and then clicking Date from the Category list. The format of the date does not affect or change its serial value.

▶ You can enter the current date, based on the computer's clock, by pressing the Ctrl + ; (semicolon) keys. This method will retain the date entered today in the file. Or you can enter the current date and time by using =NOW(). This will change to the current date whenever the file is reopened.

TRY*it*OUT *E4-19*

1. Open **E4-19** from the Data CD.

2. Notice the test dates and select the range **C1:E1**.

3. Click **Format, Cells,** and the **Number** tab. Select **General** to format the dates as numbers. (These are the serial values.)

4. Reformat the range **C1:E1** as dates in a format that shows a four-digit year.

5. In **Cell C2**, press the **Ctrl + ;** keys, to get today's date.

6. In **Cell D2**, enter **=Now( )**, to get today's date and time.

7. In **Cell B7**, enter a formula to calculate 15 days after the date in **Cell B5**. *(Hint: =B5+15.)*

Continued on next page

---

8. In **Cells B8, B9,** and **B10,** enter formulas to calculate the dates for 30, 45, and 90 days after the purchase date in B5.

9. If dates did not appear as the answers in the range B7:B10, format the serial values in a date format.

10. Do not close the file.

Use the Insert Function button

▶ If you want to view all the functions available in Excel, you can click the AutoSum list arrow and click More Functions or use the Insert Function button on the formula bar.

▶ When you click the Insert Function button, an equal sign appears and the Insert Function dialog box opens, as shown in Figure 4.20. You can state what you want to accomplish in the Search for a function box, or find the function you need in the Or select a category box. The Function Arguments dialog box, shown in Figure 4.21 on the next page, appears after you select the function.

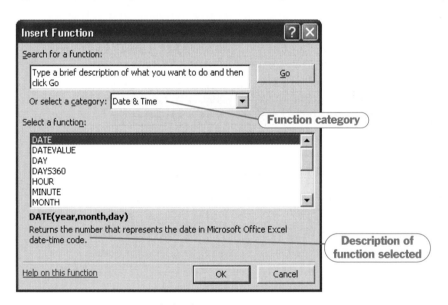

Figure 4.20 Insert Function dialog box

1. Continue working in the open file or open **E4-20** from the Data CD.

2. In **Cell E2,** click the **Insert Function** button on the formula bar to open the Insert Function dialog box.

3. In the Or select a category box, click the list arrow and select **All.** Scroll to view the functions.

4. Select the **Date & Time** category.

5. Scroll and double-click the **TODAY** function from the Select a function box and click **OK.**

6. Save the file as **E4-20.** Close the file.

Financial Functions

▶ *Financial functions* are used to analyze loans, calculate payments, and compute depreciation on assets. The financial functions most frequently used for analyzing loans are the PMT, FV, and PV functions.

The PMT Function

▶ The *PMT* (payment) function is used to calculate a loan payment when you know the principal (present value of loan), interest rate, and number of payments. The function and required arguments are =PMT(Rate, Nper, Pv).

• *Rate* =interest rate per period. Because rates are generally stated as *annual interest* rates, you must divide the annual interest rate by 12 when calculating a monthly payment. For example, you would enter 7% annual interest rate as 7%/12.

• *Nper* =number of payments.

• *Pv* =present value or principal of loan.

▶ To enter financial functions, click the Insert Function button on the Standard toolbar, select the Financial category and the function. Once you select the function, the Function Argument box appears where you use the Collapse Dialog Box buttons to select function arguments. You may have to enter absolute reference codes or divide the annual interest rate after you select the appropriate argument, as shown in Figure 4.21. (Note: The last two arguments are optional here and in the other financial functions in this lesson.)

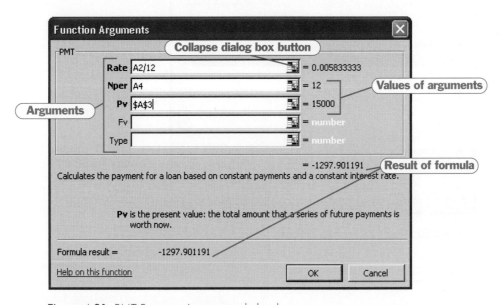

Figure 4.21 PMT Function Arguments dialog box

TRY *it* OUT *E4-21*

Note: You will find the monthly payment to repay $15000 over 12 months at 7% interest.

1. Open **E4-21** from the Data CD.

2. In **Cell E2,** click the **Insert Function** button on the formula bar, and select the

Financial category in the Insert Function dialog box.

3. Click **PMT,** under Select a function, and click **OK.**

Continued on next page

4. In the Rate box, click the **Collapse dialog box** button and 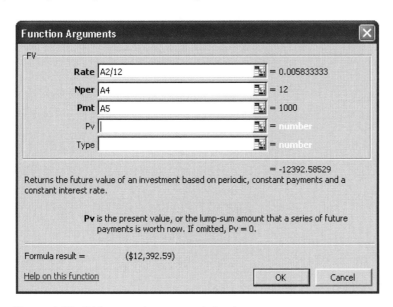 select **Cell A2.** Click the **Restore dialog box** button.

5. Next to **A2** in the Rate box, enter **/12** to divide the annual rate into a monthly rate.

6. In the Nper box, for number of payments, select **A4.**

7. In the Pv box, the principal, select **Cell A3,** and click **F4** to make it absolute. (For practice, not necessary here. Note the result.)

8. Click **OK.** (The payment is stated as a negative number that reduces the loan.)

9. Do not close the file.

The FV Function

▶ The *FV* (future value) function is used to calculate the future value of a series of equal payments, at a fixed interest rate, for a specific number of payments. You can use this function to calculate the value of equal savings deposits at the end of a period. The function and required arguments are =FV(Rate,Nper,Pmt), as shown in Figure 4.22.

Function Arguments ☒

FV

Rate	A2/12	= 0.005833333
Nper	A4	= 12
Pmt	A5	= 1000
Pv		= number
Type		= number

= -12392.58529

Returns the future value of an investment based on periodic, constant payments and a constant interest rate.

Pv is the present value, or the lump-sum amount that a series of future payments is worth now. If omitted, Pv = 0.

Formula result =   ($12,392.59)

Help on this function   OK   Cancel

Figure 4.22 FV Function Arguments dialog box

Note: You will find the future value of 12 payments of $1000 earning 7% interest.

1. Continue to work in the open file or open **E4-22** from the Data CD.

2. In **Cell E3,** enter the FV function as follows:
   a. Click the **Insert Function** button and in the **Financial** category select **FV** function.

b. For Rate, select **Cell A2,** an annual rate, which should be divided by 12.

c. For Nper, select **Cell A4,** for 12 payments.

d. For Pmt, select **Cell A5,** for $1000.

3. Click **OK.**

4. Do not close the file.

The PV Function

▶ The *PV* (present value) function is used to calculate the present value of a series of equal payments, at a fixed interest rate, for a specific number of payments. Therefore, you can calculate the principal, or money needed now, to generate equal payments in the future. The function and arguments are =PV(Rate,Nper,Pmt), as shown in Figure 4.23.

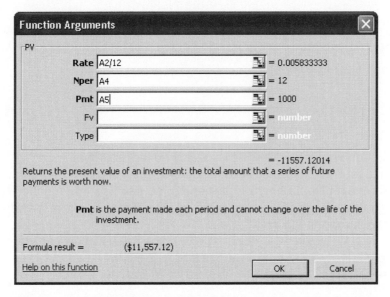

Figure 4.23 PV Function Arguments dialog box

T R Y *it* **O U T** *E4-23*

Note: You will find the present value or money needed now at a 7% rate, to generate equal payments of $1000 in the future.

1. Continue to work in the open file or open **E4-23** from the Data CD.

2. In **Cell E4,** enter the PV function to find the present value of 12, $1000 payments, at 7%. (Divide the annual rate by 12.)

3. Check your formulas and answers against the Check column. (Absolute references, as shown in Figure 4.21, would be necessary if the formulas were to be copied.)

4. Do not close the file.

Use Paste Special, Values

▶ When you used the Copy and Paste functions in previous tasks, you copied the entire contents of a cell. If you want to copy and paste specific cell contents, use the Paste Options button, the Smart Tag that appears on the worksheet, or use the Paste button options list on the Formatting toolbar, as shown in Figure 4.24.

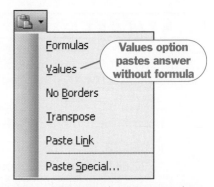

Figure 4.24 Paste button options list on the Formatting toolbar

► The Values option will paste the numeric value or answer without including the formula in cases where the formula will not work in the new location. You can also paste values and formats by selecting Paste Special on the Paste button options list shown in Figure 4.24, and then select Values and number formats. Or, it is faster to use the Paste Options button list on the worksheet, as shown in Figure 4.25, and select Values and Number Formatting.

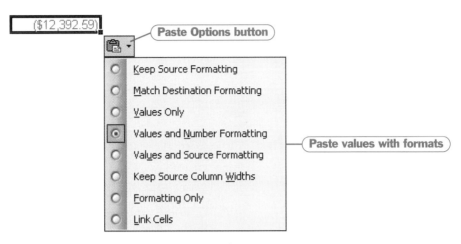

Figure 4.25 Paste Options button, options list

T R Y *it* **O U T** *E4-24*

1. Continue to work in the open file or open **E4-24** on the Data CD.

2. Click **Cell E2,** which includes a formula and answer, and click **Copy.**

3. Click **Cell B8** and click **Paste.** (Zeros or a #REF error appears.)

4. Click the list arrow on the **Paste** button, and click **Values Only.** (The answer appears.)

5. Check the formula bar for **Cells B8** and **E2.** Notice the difference.

6. Click **Cell E3,** which includes a formula and an answer, and click **Copy.**

7. Click **Cell B9,** click the **Paste** list arrow on the Standard toolbar, and click **Paste Special, Values and Number Formatting** and click **OK.**

8. Use the Paste Options button on the worksheet to copy and paste (**Values and Number Formatting**) the answer from **Cell E4** into **Cell B10.**

9. Save the file **E4-24.** Close the file.

REHEARSAL

TASK 4

GOAL
To use financial and date functions to analyze the options for the purchase of equipment

SETTING THE STAGE/WRAPUP
File name: **4.4loan**

WHAT YOU NEED TO KNOW

▶ When making a large purchase, individuals and businesses should analyze all the options for payment. Use financial functions to calculate the costs of the money over the time of the loan at the prevailing interest rates.

▶ Sellers often give buyers credit *terms* that involve discounts for early payment. Thus, the notation 2/30, 1/60, n/90 means that the buyer will get 2% off the bill if paid in 30 days, 1% if paid in 60 days, or the full amount is due in 90 days.

▶ When calculating the amount due after a 2% discount is taken, you can multiply by the *reciprocal,* the difference from 100%, or 98%, to calculate the discounted payment.

▶ In this Rehearsal activity, you will prepare a multiple sheet analysis to help In-Shape Fitness Centers consider payment options for additional equipment for the gym. The options include paying cash, taking a loan, or saving for the purchase.

▼ DIRECTIONS

1. Open **4.4options** from the Data CD.
2. First view each sheet, select the **Purchase** sheet, and then group all sheets.
3. On the **Purchase** sheet, adjust column width and format the titles as illustrated on the facing page using **Blue** fill color and **White** font color. Note: Use another font if Eurostyle is not available.
4. In **Cell B9,** find the total amount of the purchase and format the row as illustrated in **Pale blue.**
5. Click any sheet to ungroup the sheets.
6. On the **Cash Options** sheet:
   a. In **Cell B15, B16,** and **B17,** enter formulas to calculate the dates for each discount and for full payment, using the Purchase Date plus the appropriate number of days.
   b. In **Cell C15,** enter a formula to find the purchase price after a 2% discount. *(Hint: Total Loan Principal*98%.)*
   c. In **Cell C16,** enter a formula to find the purchase price after a 1% discount.
   d. In **Cell C17,** enter the full payment amount.
   e. Copy **Cells B15:C17** and switch to the Loan Options sheet.
7. On the **Loan Options** sheet:
   a. In **Cell A13,** click the **Paste Options** button, **Values and Number Formatting** and click **OK.**
   b. All loan calculations are for 12 months. In **Cell C13,** enter a financial function to find the monthly payment (PMT), using the annual interest rate in **Cell C12** divided by 12, 12 payments, and the principal in **Cell B13** with an absolute reference.

Continued on next page

c. Copy the formula across for all interest rate choices to **Cell G13.**

d. Enter formulas in Cells **C14** and **C15** and fill each formula across. *Note: Use absolute reference for the principal amounts in B14 and B15, and divide the annual rate by 12.*

8. On the **Fund Options** sheet: (saving for the purchase):

a. In **Cell B14,** enter a formula to calculate the Total Payments if you make 12 payments of $1125.

b. In **Cell B16,** enter a financial function to calculate the future value (FV) of the annual interest in **Cell A16** divided by 12, for 12 payments (absolute reference), for the payment in **Cell B12** (absolute reference).

c. Copy the formula down for all interest rates.

9. Color the worksheet tabs in shades of blue.

10. Group all sheets and print the workbook.

11. Save the file **4.4options.** Close the file.

In-Shape Fitness Centers
Analysis of Equipment Purchase Options

Date of Purchase	4/24/04	
Equipment		
QXR All Weight Trainer	10,765.00	
HiClimb Stair Climber	1,525.00	
Pacer Treadmill W14	1,450.00	
Total		

Eurostyle 18 Bold

Format font and fill colors

Find total

Purchase Sheet

11	**Cash Options**		
12	**Purchase Date:**	4/24/2004	
13	**Terms: 2/30, 1/60, n/90**		
14		**Date Due**	**Amount Due**
15	2% discount date - 30 days		
16	1% discount date - 60 days		
17	90 days full payment date		
18		Calculate due dates	Calculate amounts due after discount
19			
20			
21			
22			

Cash Options Sheet

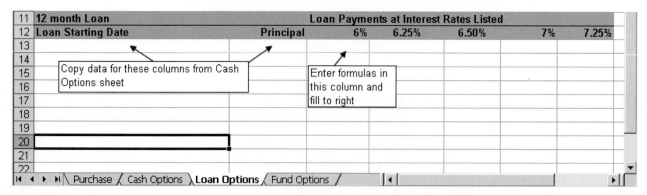

Loan Options Sheet

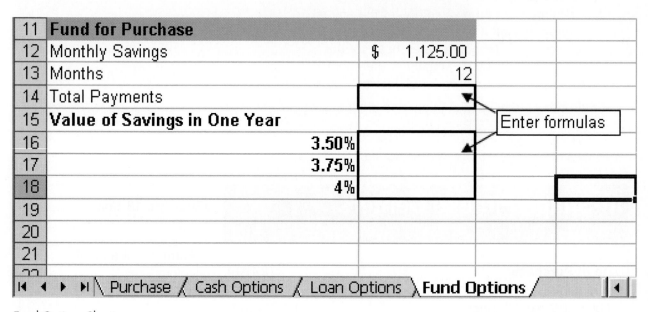

Fund Options Sheet

Paste Special, Values and Formatting
1. Select item to copy.
2. Click **Copy** button.
3. Select paste location.
4. Click **Paste** button.

For Paste button on Toolbar
5. Click list arrow on **Paste** button.
6. Select **Values and Number Formatting** option and click **OK**.

For Paste Options button on worksheet
5. Click the **Paste Options** button.
6. Select the **Values and Number Formatting** option.

Insert a Financial Function
1. Click **Insert Function** button on formula bar.
2. Click list arrow to select **Financial** category.

3. Select **Function**.
4. Click **OK**.
5. Click the **Collapse Dialog Box** button to select each argument from the worksheet.
6. Add any additional formula items, as necessary (absolute reference or division of annual interest rates by 12).
7. Click **OK**.

PERFORMANCE

SETTING THE STAGE/WRAPUP

Act I File name: **4p1.budget**
Act II File name: **4p2.incomebk**
Act III File name: **4p3.loanoptions**

EXCEL

Act I

You prepare accounting data for the Boston office of the Air Land Sea Travel Group. The office manager has asked you to develop an analysis of expenses for the last two years and has provided his estimate of expenses for the year 2005. This report will be e-mailed to the other offices in California and New York, so that they can complete similar analyses for consolidation into one report.

	A	B	C	D	E	F
1		Air Land Sea Travel Group				
2	Boston Office	Expense Budget Analysis				
3						
4		2003	2004	2005	Projected	
5	**Expense**	**Actual**	**Actual**	**Budget**	**Change**	**% Change**
6	Advertising	36,736	39,055	42,450		
7	Depreciation	10,200	10,790	10,790		
8	Insurance	5,640	5,855	6,140		
9	Miscellaneous	5,500	6,050	6,660		
10	Payroll	175,450	193,100	223,997		
11	Rent	39,500	41,500	41,500		
12	Supplies	8,800	9,350	9,900		
13	Utilities	6,820	7,015	7,535		
14	Total	288,646	312,715	348,972		

Follow these guidelines:

✴ Open **4p1.budget** from the Data CD.

✴ Create title lines for the report that include the company name, report name "Expense Budget Analysis," and "Boston Office." Insert rows if necessary, and format text using any desired font and font size.

✴ Reenter year column headings as numeric labels.

✴ Adjust column widths as necessary.

✴ Enter and fill formulas to complete Projected Change and % Change columns, and Totals row.

• The Projected Change column shows the change the 2005 budget is from the 2004 actual numbers.

• The % Change is the percentage the Projected Change is of the 2004 Actual data. Include the Totals line when you copy down the formula in Cell F5, to get the % Change for the Totals line.

✴ Total Cells B14:E14.

✴ Format numbers and percentages as appropriate.

✴ AutoFormat the column headings and data in one of the styles provided.

✴ Use color buttons to format the area above the column headings to match the AutoFormat selected.

✴ Check your work and save the file.

✳ Attach the worksheet to an e-mail to the other offices (using an address provided by your instructor). Write a note to accounting personnel requesting that they complete a similar analysis for their office so that all the reports can be consolidated.

✳ Save the file **4p1.budget**. Close the file.

Act II

You work in the company headquarters of Odyssey Travel Gear. All the retail stores have sent in income statement data over the last year. You have been asked to format the existing raw data and to create an analysis for each store on a separate worksheet. The resulting workbook will be saved as a Web page to provide corporate information.

Follow these guidelines:

✳ Use the file **4p2.incomebk** from the Data CD.

	A	B	C	D	E	F	G
1			Odyssey Travel Gear				
2			Income Statement				
3			For the six months ended December 31, 2004				
4							
5			Boston	Chicago	Dallas	Miami	San Diego	Totals
6	Income						
7	Net Sales Income		625,206	743,036	350,510	362,232	499,854	2,580,838
8	Less: Cost of Goods Sold		393,822	467,307	228,765	231,575	315,752	1,637,221
9	Gross Profit on Sales		231,383	275,729	121,745	130,657	184,102	943,617
10							
11	Expenses						
12	Selling		79,978	92,019	45,323	45,403	62,852	325,575
13	Administrative		44,343	53,456	24,324	27,564	34,567	184,254
14	Miscellaneous		9,980	10,936	7,104	5,425	5,942	39,387
15	Total		134,301	156,411	76,751	78,392	103,361	549,216
16							
17	Net Income Before Taxes		97,083	119,318	44,993	52,265	80,741	394,401

✳ Group the June 30 and December 31 worksheets, add a "Totals" heading in Column G, and calculate the totals.

✳ Add additional worksheets to create one for each store; rename and color the tabs accordingly.

✳ Group the store worksheets and paste Rows 1:3 and Column A data to all the store worksheets. On the store worksheets create columns named "June 30," "December 31," "Totals," and "% of Sales."

✳ Copy the data from the June and December sheets to the appropriate columns on each sheet.

✳ Group store worksheets and complete the Totals and % of Sales columns. You will need to use an absolute reference formula to find % of Sales.

✳ Format all store worksheets as a group. Use the AutoFormat and color and fill buttons to format the worksheet. Print a copy of the entire workbook.

✳ Save the file **4p2.incomebk** and save the workbook as a Web page with an appropriate title. Preview the workbook on your browser.

Act III

Trilogy Productions is contemplating the purchase or lease of warehouse space in Brooklyn, New York, to service its New York distribution center. The price of the building has been negotiated at $550,000. The company has researched loan costs and has determined that for 10-year loans, the interest rate decreases as the amount of the down payment increases. As an alternative, Trilogy could also sign a 10-year

	A	B	C	D	E	F
1		Trilogy Productions				
2		Property Purchase or Lease Options				
3						
4	Property Purchase					
5		Down	Down	Net		FV of Down
6	Price	Payment %	Payment	Principal		Payment @ 8%
7	550,000	20%				
8	550,000	25%				
9	550,000	30%				
10						
11				Monthly		
12	Net Principal	Interest	Payments	Payment		
13		8%	120			
14		7.75%	120			
15		7.5%	120			

lease for the property. The company has asked you to develop an analysis of the options to help it make this decision.

Follow these guidelines:

✦ Use the file **4p3.warehouse** from the Data CD.

✦ Group both sheets and format the headings in Rows 1 and 2 using any color and/or font settings of your choice.

✦ On the Purchase sheet:

- Calculate the Down Payment and Net Principal columns. (Hint: Down Payment %*Principal=Downpayment.)

- Use Paste Options to copy the range D7:D9 to Cell A13.

- Calculate the monthly payments beginning in Cell D13 for each set of loan terms using the PMT function.

- Optional: Find the future value (FV) of each down payment in Column C, beginning in Cell F7, to show what the funds could do if they were invested in the business and not spent on the building. Use 8% as the growth Rate, 10 (years) for Nper, omit the Pmt argument, and use the down payment as the Pv.

✦ On the Lease sheet:

- In Cell A7 find the total cost of the lease. (Hint: Payments*Monthly payment.)

- To analyze the real cost of the lease payments, calculate the present and future value of the lease payments at a rate of 8%. The interest rate must be divided by 12 since these are monthly payments.

✦ Format both worksheet column headings using color, border, and/or font settings.

✦ Preview and print a copy of the workbook.

✦ Save the file **4p3.warehouse.**

Financial Reports

In this lesson, you will learn to use logical functions, 3-D formulas, print settings, and the linking and formatting features in Excel to prepare financial reports.

Upon completion of this lesson, you should have mastered the following skill sets:

- ✴ Merge, center, and split cells
- ✴ Workbook layout and links
  - ✴ Split and arrange multiple workbooks
  - ✴ Paste link between workbooks
  - ✴ Hide workbooks
- ✴ Work with hyperlinks
  - ✴ Insert a hyperlink
  - ✴ Use a hyperlink
  - ✴ Edit a hyperlink
- ✴ Modify row and column layout
  - ✴ Hide and unhide rows and columns
  - ✴ Freeze and unfreeze rows and columns
- ✴ Modify page set up options
  - ✴ Print nonadjacent sections of a worksheet

- ✴ Print titles
- ✴ Use logical functions in formulas
- ✴ Add headers and footers to worksheets
  - ✴ Add customized headers and footers
- ✴ Enter 3-D references
- ✴ Use styles
  - ✴ Apply a style
  - ✴ Define a new style
  - ✴ Modify a style
  - ✴ Remove a style
- ✴ Find and replace cell data and formats
  - ✴ Find cell data
  - ✴ Find and replace data and formats

Terms
Software-related
Merge and Center button
Splitting cells
Paste Link option
Hyperlink
Freeze Panes
Print Titles
IF statement
Headers and footers
3-D references
Styles
Find and Replace
Document-related
Schedule of accounts receivable
Schedule of accounts payable
Trial balance
Worksheet
Consolidated income statement
Balance sheet

GOALS

To create a trial balance with linked accounts receivable and payable schedules

To practice using the following skill sets:

✴ Merge, center, and split cells
✴ Workbook layout and links
  ✴ Split and arrange multiple workbooks
  ✴ Paste link between workbooks
  ✴ Hide workbooks
✴ Work with hyperlinks
  ✴ Insert a hyperlink
  ✴ Use a hyperlink
  ✴ Edit a hyperlink

EXCEL

WHAT YOU NEED TO KNOW

Merge, Center, and Split Cells

▶ The *Merge and Center* button on the Formatting toolbar centers text over a selected range by merging the cells. To center a title across the top of a worksheet, enter the title in Column A, select the title and the range over which to center it, and click the Merge and Center button. The title is still in Column A, but it is centered in one large cell you created by merging the cells across the range. You can merge only one line at a time.

▶ Returning the cells to their normal width is called *splitting* the cells. You can set or remove these features in the Alignment tab of the Format Cells dialog box, as shown in Figure 5.1. Or, reselect the range and click the Merge and Center button to split the cells.

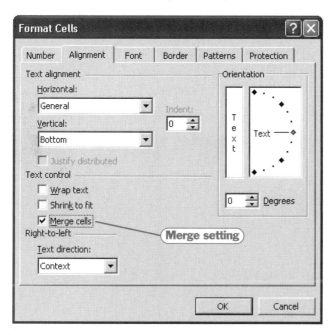

Figure 5.1 Format Cells dialog box, Alignment tab, Merge setting

1. Open **E5-1** from the Data CD.

2. Group the AR and AP worksheets.

3. Select the range **A1:B1** and change the font size to 14 point.

4. Click the **Merge and Center** button to merge the cells and center the text.

5. Click the **Merge and Center** button again to split the cells.

6. Click the **Undo** button to keep the merge and center setting.

7. Select the range **A2:B2.** Change the font size to 12 point and merge and center the text.

8. Select Cell **A2** and click **Format, Cells** and the **Alignment** tab.

9. Deselect Merge cells and click **OK.**

10. Click the **Undo** button to keep the center setting.

11. Do not close the file.

Workbook Layout and Links

Split and Arrange Multiple Workbooks

▶ When working with more than one workbook, you can switch between workbooks using the file buttons on the taskbar or by selecting the file name from the list of open files on the Window menu, as shown in Figure 5.2.

▶ To view multiple workbooks, you can click Window, Compare Side by Side. Or click Window, Arrange to display the Arrange Windows dialog box, shown in Figure 5.3, which provides other options for arranging multiple files as well as for viewing windows of the active workbook.

▶ When you click Compare Side by Side, the files are arranged on the screen, as shown in Figure 5.4. The active file is indicated by the blue title bar. Click any cell in a worksheet to make that the active file. Click Close Side by Side on the Window menu to return to your previous view.

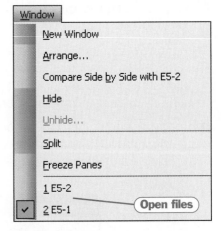

Figure 5.2 Window menu with list of open files

Figure 5.3 Arrange Windows dialog box

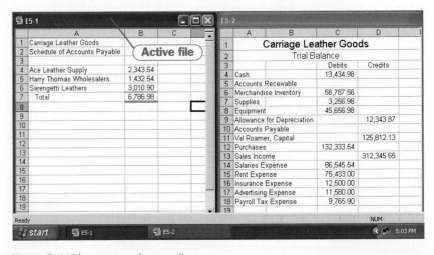

Figure 5.4 Files arranged vertically

1. Continue to work in the open file or open **E5-2A** from the Data CD.

2. Open **E5-2** from the Data CD and notice the totals. They should be in balance, but are not at this time.

3. Switch to the original file using the Window menu.

4. To arrange both files on the screen, click **Window, Compare Side by Side with E5-2.xls.**

5. To change the arrangement option, click **Window, Arrange,** and **Horizontal**. Click **OK**.

6. On any worksheet, click the scroll bar and notice the synchronous scroll.

7. Close the files without saving them.

Paste Link Between Workbooks

▶ In the last lesson, you used the Paste Special, Values feature to copy and paste the values or answer in a formula cell. Another Paste Special feature is the *Paste Link* option. This option links cells to another worksheet or workbook so that if you change the original data, it changes in the linked location as well.

▶ This feature is invaluable when combining schedules or data from various workbooks into a summary workbook, because any corrections you make to the source data will be reflected in the summary worksheet.

▶ To link a cell or cells, copy the cell(s), go to the location to link (which may be in another workbook), and click the Paste button list arrow on the Standard toolbar and click Paste Link from the drop-down list.

▶ On the formula bar of a linked cell you will see a reference to the original file. For example, =[E5-3A.xls]AR!$B$10, means that the cell is linked to Cell B10 on the AR sheet of the E5-3A file.

▶ Links between files are saved when you save and close the files. When you open a linked file, a prompt appears, as shown in Figure 5.5, requesting permission to update the file by activating the link. The file updates automatically, without a prompt, if you select that option in the Tools, Options menu.

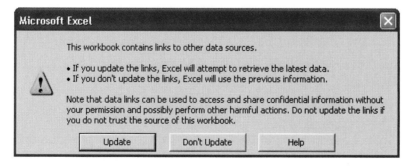

Figure 5.5 Prompt to update linked files

1. Open **E5-3** and **E5-3A** from the Data CD. Make sure they are both arranged vertically on the screen.

2. In **E5-3A** on the **AR** sheet, copy the total in **Cell B10.**

3. In **E5-3** in **Cell C5,** click the list arrow on the **Paste** button and click **Paste Link** to link the data.

4. Click **Cell C5** and notice the paste link reference on the formula bar.

5. In **E5-3A**, select the **AP** sheet and copy **Cell B7.**

6. In **E5-3** in **Cell D10,** click the list arrow on the **Paste** button and click **Paste Link** to link the data. Notice the totals now.

7. In **E5-3A**, select the **AR** sheet and correct Mary Cainter's balance (**Cell B5**) to: $1311.55.

8. Notice the updated Accounts Receivable total on both worksheets and the grand totals in **E5-3.**

9. Save both files **E5-3** and **E5-3A.** Do not close the files.

Hide Workbooks or Worksheets

▶ You may wish to hide a workbook or worksheet for presentation purposes. To hide a worksheet, select the sheet and click Format, Sheet, Hide. To redisplay a sheet, click Format, Sheet, Unhide and select the sheet to unhide. To hide a workbook, click Window, Hide and click Window, Unhide to redisplay the workbook.

1. Use the open files or open **E5-4** and **E5-4A** from the Data CD. If you open the files, select the Update option and make sure they are both arranged vertically on the screen.

2. Click anywhere in the AR worksheet and click **Format, Sheet, Hide.** The AR sheet is hidden.

3. In the same file, click **Window, Hide.** The workbook is hidden.

4. Click **Window, Unhide** and click **OK** to accept the file name.

5. Click **Format, Sheet, Unhide** and click **OK** to accept the sheet name.

6. Close both files without saving them.

Work with Hyperlinks

Insert a Hyperlink

▶ A *hyperlink* is a shortcut that allows you to jump to another location that provides additional or related information. When you click a hyperlink, it can open another workbook, a file on your hard drive or network, or an Internet address.

▶ To insert a hyperlink, first enter the text that will lead to the link. Then, click the Insert Hyperlink button on the Standard toolbar to open the Insert Hyperlink dialog box. As you can see in Figure 5.6, in the Link to pane on the left side of the dialog box you can select the location to hyperlink to, then select the file or location in the Look in box.

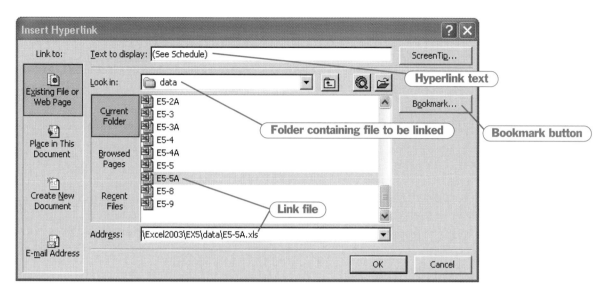

Figure 5.6 Insert Hyperlink dialog box

► To link to a specific location in a workbook, click the Bookmark button on the Insert Hyperlink dialog box to open the Select Place in Document dialog box. Figure 5.7 shows the dialog box and the sheet names in the file, as well as any other defined names.

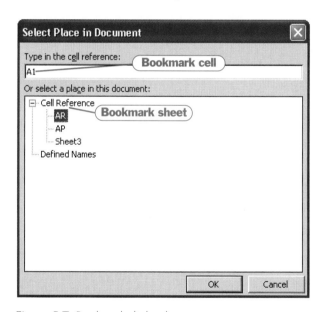

Figure 5.7 Bookmark dialog box

TRY it OUT *E5-5*

1. Open **E5-5** and **E5-5A** from the Data CD, select **Update** and arrange them on the screen vertically.

2. In **Cells B5** and **B10** of **E5-5,** enter: **(See Schedule).**

3. Widen **Columns A** and **B** to fit the widest entry.

4. In **Cell B5,** click the **Insert Hyperlink** button.

5. In the Insert Hyperlink box, click **E5-5A** in the current folder.

Continued on next page

TRY *it* OUT *E5-5 Continued*

6. Click **Bookmark** and click the **AR** sheet. *(A specific cell is not necessary in this case.)*
7. Click **OK** twice.
8. Repeat Steps 4–7 for **Cell B10,** except change Step 6 to select the **AP** sheet.
9. Do not close the files.

Use a Hyperlink

▶ When you point to text or a graphic that contains a hyperlink, the mouse pointer becomes a hand to indicate the link. A ScreenTip also appears, stating the link reference and instructions for using a hyperlink, as shown in Figure 5.8. You can click once to follow the link or click and hold to select and edit the cell.

▶ After you view and close the file referenced by the hyperlink, you return to the original location.

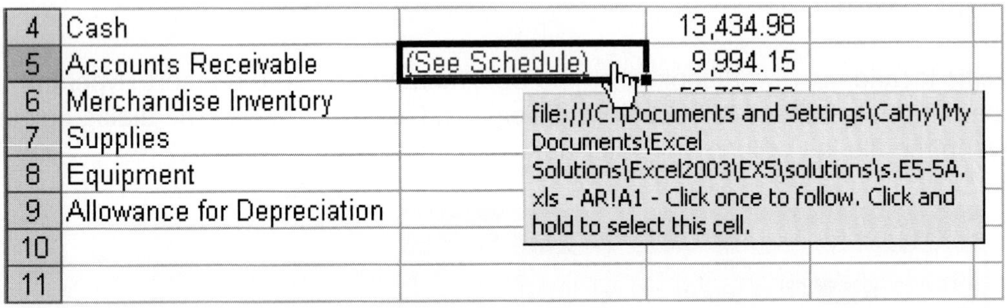

4 Cash 13,434.98
5 Accounts Receivable (See Schedule) 9,994.15
6 Merchandise Inventory
7 Supplies
8 Equipment
9 Allowance for Depreciation
10
11
file:///C:\Documents and Settings\Cathy\My Documents\Excel Solutions\Excel2003\EX5\solutions\s.E5-5A.xls - AR!A1 - Click once to follow. Click and hold to select this cell.

Figure 5.8 ScreenTip display for a hyperlink

TRY *it* OUT *E5-6*

1. Continue to work in the open files.
2. In **E5-5,** move your mouse pointer near **Cell B5** to view the ScreenTip.
3. Click **Cell B5** to jump to the AR sheet in **E5-5A.**
4. Close the file **E5-5A.**
5. In **E5-5,** click **Cell B10** to jump to the AP sheet in **E5-5A.**
6. Close the file **E5-5A.**
7. Do not close **E5-5.**

Edit a Hyperlink

▶ To edit only the hyperlink text, click the hyperlink, hold the mouse button down until the hand pointer changes to a plus sign, as shown in Figure 5.9, then edit the text on the formula bar.

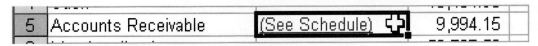

5 Accounts Receivable (See Schedule) 9,994.15

Figure 5.9 Hold mouse pointer down for edit mode

▶ To edit any part of the hyperlink, right-click the hyperlink and click Edit Hyperlink from the shortcut menu. Use the Edit Hyperlink dialog box, shown in Figure 5.10, to edit any part of the hyperlink. It looks like the Insert Hyperlink dialog box, except that it has a Remove Link button.

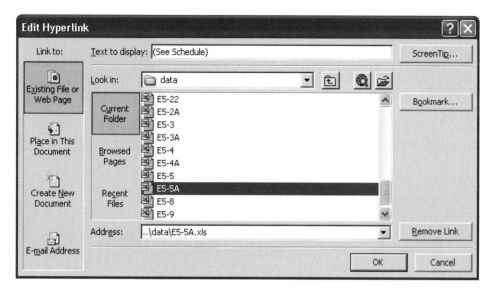

Figure 5.10 Edit Hyperlink dialog box

TRY it OUT *E5-7*

1. Continue to work in the open file.

2. Click and hold the mouse pointer on the hyperlink text in **Cell B5** until it changes to a plus sign.

3. In the formula bar, edit the hyperlink text to read: **(See AR Schedule).**

4. Right-click the hyperlink text in **Cell B10** and click **Edit Hyperlink.**

5. In the Text to display box, edit the text to read: **(See AP Schedule).** Adjust column width.

6. Click **OK.**

7. Save the **E5-5** file. Close the file.

REHEARSAL

Again

TASK 1

GOAL
To create a trial balance with linked accounts receivable and payable schedules

SETTING THE STAGE/WRAPUP
File names: 5.1sched
5.1tb

WHAT YOU NEED TO KNOW

▶ Schedules and trial balances are lists of account balances that a business prepares at the end of each month to check the accuracy of its accounts.

▶ The *schedule of accounts receivable* (AR) is a list of all the customers that owe the business money. The *schedule of accounts payable* (AP) is a list of all the business's creditors, or vendors, that it must pay.

▶ The *trial balance* is a list of all the accounts in a business ledger and their balances for the end of the month. Accounts either have debit (left side) or credit (right side) balances, depending on the type of account. For example, Accounts Receivable and Cash have debit balances and Accounts Payable and Sales have credit balances. In a trial balance, the debit and credit balances must be equal to prove the accuracy of the ledger, or book of accounts.

▶ In this rehearsal activity, Green Brothers Gardening wants to check its schedules and trial balance for the year ended December 31, 2004. You will merge and center the headings, paste link the schedule totals, correct the schedules, and create and edit hyperlinks on the trial balance.

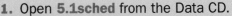

DIRECTIONS

1. Open **5.1sched** from the Data CD.

2. Group both the Schedule of AR and the Schedule of AP sheets (Illustrations A and B).

3. Merge and center each of the three title rows over **Columns A** to **E.**

4. Bold titles in **Rows 1** and **2.**

5. Click **Sheet3** to ungroup the sheets and check the titles on both sheets.

6. Use AutoSum to find the totals on each schedule and format for currency.

7. Open **5.1tb** from the Data CD (Illustration C).

8. Merge and center each of the three title rows over **Columns A** to **E.**

9. Practice splitting the cells for **Row1** to return to the original settings.

10. Merge and center **Row1** again.

11. Use AutoSum to find the total of all the debits in **Column D** and all the credits in **Column E.**

12. Arrange both worksheets on the screen side by side.

13. Copy the total of the Schedule of AR (**5.1sched, Cell D22**) and paste link it to **Cell D7** on the trial balance, as illustrated on the facing page.

14. Copy the total of the Schedule of AP (**5.1sched, Cell D14**) and paste link it to **Cell E15** on the trial balance, as illustrated on the facing page.

15. Check to see if the trial balance actually balances; debits should equal credits.

Continued on next page

16. To find the error, the bookkeeper first checked the schedule accounts and found an error in the Miller Plant Supply AP account. The business owes $950, not $1950. Make the correction on the Schedule of AP sheet as illustrated and notice the automatic update to the trial balance.

17. Save the **5.1sched** and **5.1tb** files. Hide the **5.1sched** file.

18. Enter hyperlink text in **Column C** of the Trial Balance to refer users to the schedules, as illustrated.
   a. In **Cell C7**, enter: **(see Schedule of AR).**
   b. In **Cell C15**, enter: **(see Schedule of AP).**

19. Create hyperlinks for each text string, using bookmarks to send the user to the correct sheet.

20. Check the hyperlinks.

21. Edit the hyperlink text to delete the word "see" on both hyperlinks.

22. Print a copy of the Trial Balance.

23. Save the **5.1tb** file. Unhide the **5.1sched** file and save the file. Close both files.

	A	B	C	D	E	F	G
1		**Green Brothers Gardening**					
2		**Schedule of Accounts Receivable**					
3		For the Year Ended December 31, 2004					
4							
5		Abermarle, Kelly		2144.65			
6		Capital Bank		5434.54			
7		Drury, David		1232.87			
8		Engle, Dr. Carrie		346.87			
9		Fairfax Water Co		1124.75			
10		Grinder, Sam		769.76			
11		Harrison Tools Co		2212.77			
12		Johnson, Linda		435.87			
13		Logan, Harry		909.56			
14		Loomis, Bart		212.87			
15		Samson, Peter		543.98			
16		Samuels, Larry		634.87			
17		Souten, Willem G.		540.00			
18		Toomey, Martin		563.55			
19		United Cars		2389.00			
20		Whiticomb, Roger		1876.98			
21							
22				21372.89	← Copy total and paste link to Trial Balance		
23							

⊩ ◀ ▶ ▶⊩ \ Schedule of AR ╱ Schedule of AP ╱ Sheet3 ╱

Illustration A

	A	B	C	D	E	F	G
1		**Green Brothers Gardening**					
2		**Schedule of Accounts Payable**					
3		For the Year Ended December 31, 2004					
4							
5		Bulbs Unlimited		1439.55			
6		Nursery Supply Inc		976.65			
7		Varsity Nurseries		3426.98			
8		Grollier Farms		1549.75			
9		KCG Supply Co		549.45			
10		Pride Farms		1290.67			
11		Miller Plant Supply		950.00	← correct value		
12		Jay's Perrenials		1540.00			
13							
14				11723.05	← Copy total and paste link to Trial Balance		
15							

Illustration B

	A	B	C	D	E	F	G
1		Green Brothers Gardening					
2		Trial Balance					
3		For the Year Ended December 31, 2004					
4							
5	**Account N**	**Acount**		**Debit**	**Credit**		
6	110	Cash		12,807.67			
7	120	Accounts Receivable	(Schedule of AR)	21,372.89			
8	150	Nursery Inventory		22,876.90			
9	155	Merchandise Inventory		18,765.89			
10	160	Supplies		3,915.89			
11	180	Equipment		28,650.00			
12	181	Accumulated Depreciation			1,640.30		
13	190	Buildings		535,000.00			
14	191	Accumulated Depreciation			56,565.00		
15	200	Accounts Payable	(Schedule of AP)		11,723.05		
16	210	Payroll Taxes Payable			82,765.96		
17	230	Mortgage Payable			422,000.00		
18	300	Calvin Green, Capital			80,610.40		
19	350	Raph Green, Capital			80,610.40		
20	400	Sales Income			586,000.00		
21	510	Purchases - Nursery		196,879.93			
22	520	Purchases - Mdse		97,876.76			
23	610	Advertising Expense		36,788.00			
24	620	Lease Expenses		16,755.00			
25	630	Insurance Expense		8,986.00			
26	640	Salary Expense		290,876.78			
27	650	Supplies Expense		3,657.87			
28	660	Miscellaneous Expense		1,876.98			
29	670	Payroll Taxes Expense		24,828.55			
30							
31				1,321,915.11	1,321,915.11		
32							

Hyperlinks to 5.1sched

AR and AP values linked to schedule totals

Illustration C

TRYOUT

TASK 2

GOALS

To create a sales and commissions analysis and link the data to a worksheet

To complete a quarterly worksheet

To practice using the following skill sets:

* Modify row and column layout
  * Hide and unhide rows and columns
  * Freeze and unfreeze rows and columns
* Modify page setup options
  * Print nonadjacent sections of a worksheet
  * Print titles
* Use logical functions in formulas

EXCEL

WHAT YOU NEED TO KNOW

Modify Row and Column Layout

Hide and Unhide Rows and Columns

▶ You can hide detail columns and rows on the screen display to simplify a complicated worksheet, or for security purposes. Hidden columns and rows do not print.

▶ To hide columns or rows, select the rows or columns to hide, click Format, Column or Row, and click Hide. You can also drag the border of the row or column to hide it. When you hide a column or row, the worksheet border does not display the column letter or row number.

▶ You can display hidden columns by selecting the columns or rows before and after the hidden area and dragging right for columns or down for rows, as shown in Figure 5.11. You can also click Format, Columns or Rows, and select Unhide.

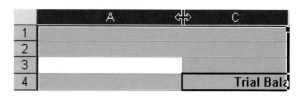

Figure 5.11 Display hidden column – drag to right

T R Y *it* O U T E5-8

1. Open **E5-8** from the Data CD.

2. Click **Don't Update** at the update prompt.

3. Select **Column B.**

4. Click **Format, Column,** and **Hide.**

5. Click **Format, Column,** and **Unhide.**

6. Select **Rows 23:28.**

7. Click **Format, Row,** and **Hide.**

8. Select **Rows 22** and **29,** and drag down to unhide the rows.

Note: Be sure to return rows to normal height.

9. Click at the right edge of **Column B** and drag to the left to hide the column.

10. Do not close the file.

Freeze and Unfreeze Rows and Columns

▶ When you work with a large worksheet, you may find that the column headings or row labels that identify the data scroll out of view. You can keep them in view by freezing them. Select the row below or the column to the right of the data to freeze, and click Window, Freeze Panes.

▶ The *Freeze Panes* command locks the pane, a group of rows or columns above or to the left of the cell you select, so that area does not move during scrolling. To remove the freeze, click Windows, Unfreeze.

T R Y *i t* O U T *E5-9*

1. Continue to work in the open file or open **E5-9** from the Data CD. *Click Don't Update if you open E5-9.*

2. Click in **Cell A6** and click **Window, Freeze Panes.**

3. Use the vertical scroll bar to scroll down the page and notice the frozen rows at the top of the screen.

4. Click **Window, Unfreeze Panes.**

5. Click in **Cell E6** and freeze the panes.

6. Use the horizontal scroll bar to scroll to the right to view the entire worksheet in comparison to the Trial Balance columns.

7. Clear the freeze.

8. Do not close the file.

Modify Page Setup Options

Print Nonadjacent Sections of a Worksheet

▶ To print sections of a worksheet that are not adjacent, you can hide the columns or rows that are not needed and print the data as displayed.

▶ If a worksheet is wider or longer than the width of the page, you can adjust the page break lines, or you can use the Page Setup dialog box and click the Page tab, to select the Fit to 1 page wide by 1 page tall scaling option, as shown in Figure 5.12.

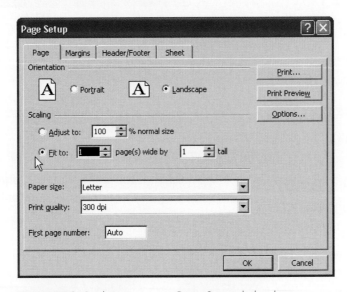

Figure 5.12 Scaling options in Page Setup dialog box

1. Continue to work in the open file or open **E5-10** from the Data CD. Click **Don't Update** if you open **E5-10**.

2. Hide Columns **C:F.**

3. Click **View, Page Break Preview.** (Notice that the worksheet is wider than the page.)

4. Click **OK** to the Welcome to Page Break Preview dialog box.

5. Click **View, Normal.**

6. Click **File, Page Setup.**

7. On the **Page** tab, with the Scaling option displayed, click **Fit to 1 page wide.** Click **OK**.

8. Print the worksheet as displayed. Only Columns A, G, H, I, J, K, and L will print.

9. Select Columns **A** and **G** and unhide the columns. (Keep Column B hidden.)

10. Click **File, Page Setup.** Click **Adjust to,** and change the size back to 100% normal size. Click **OK.**

11. Do not close the file.

Print Titles

▶ The *Print Titles* feature allows you to print column or row titles on subsequent pages of a multiple page worksheet. For example, if the worksheet in E5-9 were fully displayed, it would require two pages to print. You can set column titles to repeat at the left of the second page so that you can identify the values on each page.

▶ To print titles, click File, Page Setup, select the Sheet tab, and use the Collapse Dialog Box button to select the rows or columns to repeat in the Print titles section, as shown in Figure 5.13. If you have merged cells for the title rows, you must undo the merge first.

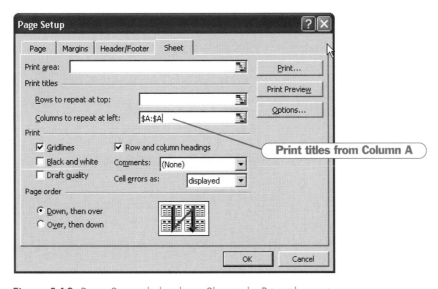

Figure 5.13 Page Setup dialog box, Sheet tab, Print titles setting

1. Continue to work in the open file or open **E5-11** from the Data CD. *Click Don't Update if you open E5-11.*

2. Click each merged title row and click the **Merge and Center** button to undo the merge.

Continued on next page

3. Click **File**, **Page Setup**, and click the **Sheet** tab.

4. Click the **Collapse Dialog Box** button for columns to repeat at left.

5. Click **Column A** and click the **Restore Dialog Box** button.

6. Click **OK.**

7. Click the **Print Preview** button.

8. Click **Next** on the preview screen to see Page 2.

9. Click **Close** to close the preview.

10. Save the file **E5.11**. Close the file.

Use Logical Functions in Formulas

▶ You can use an *IF statement* in a formula to test a situation and determine a value based on the outcome of the test. An IF statement is a function in the Logical Functions category. The format for an IF statement is:

=IF(CONDITION,X,Y) If a condition you are testing for is true, then the result is X. If the condition is false, then the result is Y. Notice that the parts of the function are separated by commas.

▶ For example, we will calculate the bonus for salespeople who get a 1% bonus on sales when they make sales over $30,000. In other words, if sales are greater than $30,000, then their bonus equals their sales multiplied by 1%, otherwise their bonus equals zero. The IF statement would read as follows if the sales amount resides in Cell B2:

=IF(B2>30000,B2*1%,0)

▶ The following table shows how to translate this statement:

FORMULA	FUNCTION	CONDITION	X	Y
English	If	Sales are greater than $30,000	Then multiply sales by 1% to calculate the bonus	Else the bonus equals 0
Excel	=IF	(B2>30000,	B2*1%,	0)

▶ IF statements use the following conditional operators to state the conditional question:

= Equal

> Greater than

< Less than

<> Not equal to

<= Less than or equal to

>= Greater than or equal to

▶ To enter an IF statement, click the Insert Function button on the formula bar and select IF from the Logical category.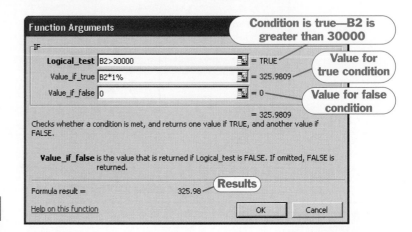

Figure 5.14 IF statement function arguments

There are Collapse Dialog Box buttons to select cells from the worksheet, or you can enter the function directly into the cell. Notice the entries in the dialog box in Figure 5.14.

1. Open **E5-12** from the Data CD. Notice the sales in Column B.

2. In **Cell D2,** enter an IF statement to calculate the bonus.
   a. Click the **fx (Insert Function) button.**
   b. Select the **Logical** category and the **IF** function. Click **OK.**
   c. In Logical test, enter: **B2>30000.**
   d. In the Value_if_ true, enter: **B2*1%.**

   e. In the Value_if_false, enter: **0.**
   f. Click **OK.**

3. In **Cell D2,** view the resulting formula on the formula bar.

4. Use the fill handle to copy the formula for all salespeople. Notice how the bonuses were applied.

5. Do not close the file.

EXCEL

▶ You can use an IF statement to insert text depending on a condition. For example, if the sales are greater than a certain amount, you can insert "Great work"; if not, you can insert "Sales seminar on Thursday." When you use an IF statement to enter text, the text must be placed within quotation marks. Excel automatically inserts quotation marks if you use the Insert Function dialog box; however, you must enter them if you enter the formula directly into the cell. Notice the formula bar and the Sales and Note columns in Figure 5.15.

	G2	▼	*fx*	=IF(B2>30000,"Great work!","Sales seminar on Thursday")				
	A	B	C	D	E	F	G	H	I
1	SALES STAFF	SALES	COMMISSION	BONUS	SALARY	EARNINGS	NOTE		
2	Acosta, Sam	32,598.09	651.96	325.98	1,500.00	2,477.94	Great work!		
3	Billings, Mary	28,321.32	566.43	-	1,500.00	2,066.43	Sales seminar on Thursday		
4	Camino, Juan	18,545.77	370.92	-	1,500.00	1,870.92	Sales seminar on Thursday		
5	Kelly, Joe	51,567.54	1,031.35	515.68	1,500.00	3,047.03	Great work!		
6	Lincoln, Terry	29,921.22	598.42	-	1,500.00	2,098.42	Sales seminar on Thursday		
7	Parson, Alice	35,325.78	706.52	353.26	1,500.00	2,559.77	Great work!		
8	Sulfa, Sally	55,896.95	1,117.94	558.97	1,500.00	3,176.91	Great work!		
9									

Figure 5.15 IF statement to enter text

1. Continue to work in the open file or open **E5-13.**

2. In **Cell G2,** enter an **IF** statement to generate the notes.
   a. Click the **fx (Insert Function)** button.
   b. Select the **Logical** category and **IF** function. Click **OK.**
   c. In the Logical_test box, enter: **B2>30000.**
   d. In the Value_if_true box, enter: **Great work!**

   e. In the Value_if_false box, enter: **Sales seminar on Thursday.**
   f. Click **OK.**

3. In **Cell G2,** view the resulting formula on the formula bar.

4. Use the fill handle to copy the formula for all salespeople.

5. Save the **E5-13** file. Close the file.

GOALS
To create a sales and commissions schedule
and to link the data into a worksheet
To complete a quarterly worksheet

SETTING THE STAGE/WRAPUP

File names: **5.2bonus**
 5.2worksheet

Format: All values should be
 formatted for commas with
 no decimal places

WHAT YOU NEED TO KNOW

▶ In Excel, spreadsheets are called
worksheets. In accounting
terminology, however, a *worksheet* is
a form used to gather trial balance
and adjustments information at the
end of an accounting period to plan
the preparation of the income
statement and balance sheet. It is
for the accountant's use.

▶ The worksheet adjustments, usually
prepared by the accountant, are
corrections that are made at the
end of the period so that the
accounts will reflect their true
balances. The net income is
calculated and the income
statement and balance sheet are
planned on the worksheet using the
adjusted trial balance data. Many
corporations round numbers on
financial reports, as noted in the
Setting the Stage directions above.

▶ The sales and commission
schedule calculates the sales,
commissions, and bonuses for the
period. IF statements are used to
calculate the commissions and
bonus for each salesperson. The
commission expense for the
period is linked to the appropriate
location on the worksheet.

▶ In this Rehearsal activity, Sutton
Investment Group wants you to
prepare and format the quarterly
Sales and Commissions Schedule
(Illustration A) and link the data to
the worksheet (Illustration B). On
the worksheet, you will format and
complete totals, modify the
columns and rows, and print part of
the worksheet.

▼ DIRECTIONS

1. Open **5.2bonus** from the Data CD.

2. Set font sizes for titles, as indicated in
Illustration A on the next page, and merge and center
the title rows.

3. Bold all column headings, center headings in
Columns B:F, and adjust column width, as
illustrated.

4. Enter a formula in **Cell C6** to calculate a 1.5%
commission on sales. (Hint: Sales*1.5%.)

5. Enter an IF statement in **Cell D6** to calculate a .5%
bonus on sales greater than $2,000,000.

 (Hint: Condition: Sales>2000000 If True: Sales*.5%
If False: 0.)

6. Enter a formula in **Cell E6** to calculate the total paid
to the employee. (Hint: Commission + Bonus.)

7. Enter an IF statement in **Cell F6** to enter an asterisk
(*) if the sales were over $2,500,000 and nothing if
they were not. (Hint: Use quotation marks around
the asterisk and around the blank, i.e., "*" or " ")

8. Copy formulas down for all salespersons and total
the columns.

9. Save the file **5.2bonus.**

10. Copy the total in **Cell E19.**

11. Open **5.2worksheet** from the Data CD.

12. Paste link the total of Column E to the Commissions
Expense location in **Cell B22.**

13. Format titles and column headings, as shown in
Illustration B on page 128.

14. Insert a column after Column A.

15. In **Cell B22,** enter a hyperlink to **5.2bonus** using
"(See Schedule)" as the hyperlink text.

Continued on next page

16. Freeze panes in **Cell B7** and find totals for **Columns C:L.**

    Note: Columns C and D, E and F, and G and H should match or balance with each other.

17. In a blank area below the worksheet, subtract the Income Statement totals, Column I from Column J (J-I). This value, the net income, should be placed in **Cells I31** and **L31.**

18. In **Cell I32,** add **Cells I30** and **I31.** Copy this formula to **Columns J:L.**

    Note: Columns I and J and K and L should balance with each other.

19. Include borders and lines, as shown in Illustration B.

20. Unfreeze panes, hide **Columns B:F,** and print the worksheet to fit on one page.

21. Unhide the columns and print the worksheet on two pages with column titles.

22. Save the file **5.2worksheet.** Close both files.

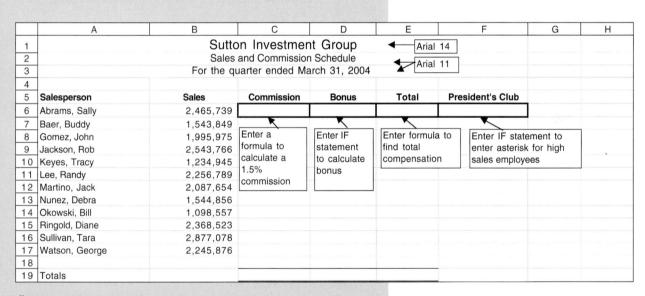

Illustration A

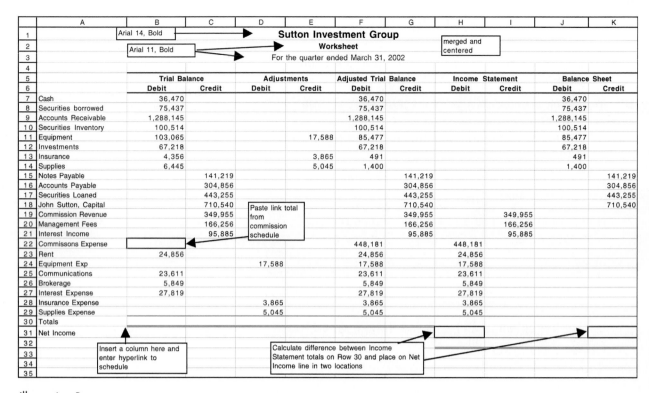

	A	B	C	D	E	F	G	H	I	J	K
1		Arial 14, Bold				Sutton Investment Group		merged and centered			
2		Arial 11, Bold				Worksheet					
3						For the quarter ended March 31, 2002					
4											
5			Trial Balance		Adjustments		Adjusted Trial Balance		Income Statement		Balance Sheet	
6		Debit	Credit	Debit	Credit	Debit	Credit	Debit	Credit	Debit	Credit
7	Cash	36,470				36,470				36,470	
8	Securities borrowed	75,437				75,437				75,437	
9	Accounts Receivable	1,288,145				1,288,145				1,288,145	
10	Securities Inventory	100,514				100,514				100,514	
11	Equipment	103,065			17,588	85,477				85,477	
12	Investments	67,218				67,218				67,218	
13	Insurance	4,356			3,865	491				491	
14	Supplies	6,445			5,045	1,400				1,400	
15	Notes Payable		141,219				141,219				141,219
16	Accounts Payable		304,856				304,856				304,856
17	Securities Loaned		443,255				443,255				443,255
18	John Sutton, Capital		710,540	Paste link total from commission schedule			710,540				710,540
19	Commission Revenue		349,955				349,955		349,955		
20	Management Fees		166,256				166,256		166,256		
21	Interest Income		95,885				95,885		95,885		
22	Commissons Expense					448,181		448,181			
23	Rent	24,856				24,856		24,856			
24	Equipment Exp			17,588		17,588		17,588			
25	Communications	23,611				23,611		23,611			
26	Brokerage	5,849				5,849		5,849			
27	Interest Expense	27,819				27,819		27,819			
28	Insurance Expense			3,865		3,865		3,865			
29	Supplies Expense			5,045		5,045		5,045			
30	Totals										
31	Net Income										
32											
33		Insert a column here and enter hyperlink to schedule				Calculate difference between Income Statement totals on Row 30 and place on Net Income line in two locations					
34											
35											

Illustration B

TRYOUT

GOALS
To create a consolidated income statement using 3-D references and a custom footer
To practice using the following skill sets:
* Add headers and footers to worksheets
    * Add customized headers and footers
* Enter 3-D references

EXCEL

TASK 3

WHAT YOU NEED TO KNOW

Add Headers and Footers to Worksheets

▶ *Headers and footers* allow you to repeat the same information at the top (header) or bottom (footer) of every page. You use this feature to enter a company name, date, file name, sheet name, etc. You can select from built-in headers or footers, or you can customize your own.

▶ To add a header or footer, click View, Header and Footer to display the Header/Footer tab of the Page Setup dialog box. You can select built-in header and footer text from the drop-down lists in each section. In Figure 5.16, notice the built-in footers that are displayed.

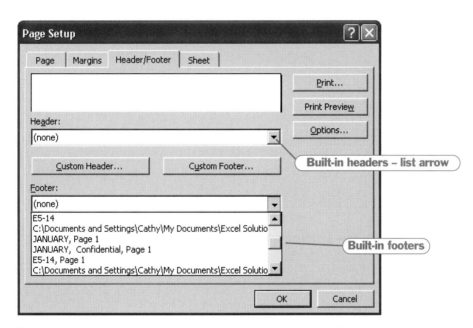

Figure 5.16 Header and Footer dialog box displaying built-in footers

---

T R Y *i t* O U T *E5-14*

1. Open **E5-14** from the Data CD and verify that the January tab is selected.

2. Click **View, Header and Footer.**

3. Click the list arrow in the Header section, and select the **JANUARY, Page 1** header.

4. Click the list arrow in the Footer section and select the file name or the **E5-14** footer.

5. Click **OK.**

Continued on next page

---

6. Click the **Print Preview** button. Notice the headers and footers.

7. Click **Close** to close the preview screen.

8. Close the file. Do not save.

Add Customized Headers and Footers

▶ To enter a customized header or footer, click the Custom Header or Custom Footer button on the Header/Footer page, (see Figure 5.16), and the Header or Footer custom dialog box opens.

▶ As shown in Figure 5.17, text entered into the left, center, and right sections is aligned in that section. You may click the appropriate button to include the date, time, page number, tab name, file name, or picture. You can use the picture option to insert a logo or graphic and the Format Picture button to customize settings once the picture is in place.

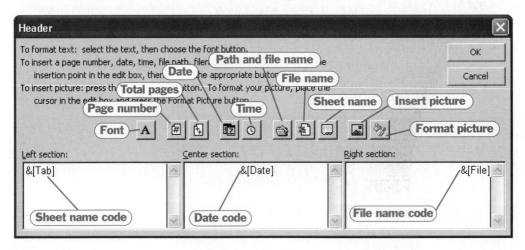

Figure 5.17 Custom Header dialog box

1. Open **E5-15** from the Data CD.

2. Click **View, Header and Footer.** Click **Custom Header.**

3. In the left section, click the **Sheet Name** button; in the center section, click the **Date** button; in the right section, click the **File Name** button. Click **OK.**

4. Click **Custom Footer**, and in the left section, click the **Insert Picture** button.

5. From your data folder, select the **E5-13logo** and click **Insert.**

6. Click the **Format Picture** button.

7. Set picture height to .79″ and click **OK.**

8. Enter `Trainor's Department Store` in the left section after the picture code. Click **OK.**

9. Click the **Print Preview** button.

10. Click **Close** to close the preview screen.

11. Do not close the file.

Enter 3-D References

▶ If you want to summarize data from several sheets onto a totals sheet within a workbook, you can use a formula in the *3-D reference* style. The style is called three dimensional because it calculates values through the sheets of a workbook to a summary worksheet at the end of the workbook.

▶ A 3-D reference includes the range of sheet names, an exclamation point, and the cell or range reference.

EXAMPLE OF 3-D REFERENCES	EXPLANATIONS
=SUM(Sheet1:Sheet3!D7)	Adds the values in D7 from sheets 1 to 3.
=AVERAGE(Sheet3:Sheet5!D7:D12)	Averages values in D7:D12 from sheets 3 to 5.
=January!D8+February!D8	Adds the values in D8 from the January and February sheets.

▶ To enter a 3-D reference, either enter the reference in the formula, or select the sheets and cells involved, and enter the mathematical operators, as necessary. Notice the formula in Figure 5.18, which was entered by selection. When 3-D references are copied, the cell references change, relative to the new location, but the sheet names remain constant.

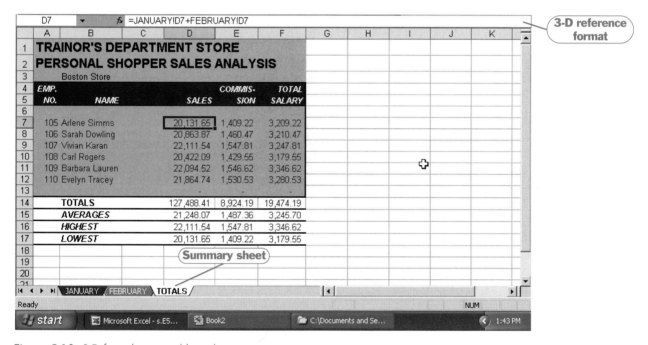

Figure 5.18 3-D formula entered by selection

1. Continue to work in the open file or open **E5-16** from the Data CD.

2. Rename Sheet3: **TOTALS.**

3. Use the selection method to enter a 3-D reference in **Cell D7** to add the values from the JANUARY and FEBRUARY sheets:
   a. In **Cell D7** on the Totals sheet, enter: = .
   b. Click **Cell D7** on the JANUARY sheet.
   c. Enter: + .
   d. Click **Cell D7** on the FEBRUARY sheet.
   e. Press the **Enter** key and go to **Cell D7** to view the formula.

4. In **Cell E7,** enter in a 3-D reference to add the values in **Cell E7** from the JANUARY and FEBRUARY sheets. (Hint: =Sum(January:February!E7.)

5. Use AutoFill to copy **Cell E7** to **Cell F7,** and copy all three formulas down to, and including the Totals, **Row 14.**

6. Adjust color and line formats.

7. Save the **E5-16** file. Close the file.

REHEARSAL

TASK 3

GOAL
To create a consolidated income statement using 3-D references and a custom footer

SETTING THE STAGE/WRAPUP
File name: **5.3income**
Format: All values should be formatted
           for commas with no
           decimal places

WHAT YOU NEED TO KNOW

▶ Corporations must report their financial data to their stockholders quarterly and annually. If a company has branches or divisions in various parts of the country, they need to combine income statement data into one financial report called a *consolidated income statement.*

▶ An income statement is prepared at the end of a financial period using income, cost, and expense accounts from the trial balance. It calculates gross profit, the markup on your product or service, and net profit, which is the final profit for the period after deducting expenses. It is a valuable source of information for stockholders or owners and for potential investors or lenders.

▶ In this Rehearsal activity, you will create a consolidated income statement for Time Out Sporting Goods. You will combine the numbers from the Barkely and Montrose stores into one income statement using 3-D references, and add a custom footer to the report.

DIRECTIONS

1. Open **5.3income** from the Data CD.

2. Group the Barkely and Montrose sheets and format as shown in the illustration on the facing page. (Font and bold settings, borders and lines, fill color, and values in comma format with no decimals.)

3. With the sheets still grouped, enter formulas in the cells listed below to calculate the following income statement items. (Hints are listed for some formulas.)
   C9:   Net Sales (Hint: Sales - Sales Returns)
   C13:   Gross Profit (Hint: Net Sales - Cost of Goods Sold)
   C25:   Total Expenses
   C27:   Net Income before Taxes (Hint: Gross Profit - Total Expenses)
   C29:   Net Income after Taxes

4. Ungroup the sheets using the worksheet tab shortcut menu.

5. Copy the entire Barkely worksheet.

6. Use the worksheet tab shortcut menu to insert a new sheet.

7. Paste the Barkely worksheet to **Cell A1** on the new sheet.

8. Move the new sheet to the last position; rename it: `Consolidated Income Statement.`

9. Adjust column widths as necessary and change the second title to read: `Consolidated Income Statement.`

10. Delete the values in **Column B** on the Consolidated Income Statement sheet.

Continued on next page

11. Group the sheets and freeze panes in **Cell A4** so that you can view the length of the report without losing the title. Ungroup the sheets using the shortcut menu.

12. In **Cell B7,** on the Consolidated Income Statement sheet, enter a 3-D formula to add the values from the Barkely sheet and the Montrose sheet in **Cell B7.** (Hint: =Barkely!B7+Montrose!B7.)

13. Use AutoFill to copy the formula down to **Cell B28.** Delete all zeros or dashes where the formula did not find values.

14. Check your work by looking at a value on the consolidated sheet to see if it totals the two sheets correctly.

15. Format the worksheet tabs with colors, as appropriate.

16. Group the sheets and set a custom footer to print the sheet name, date, and file name.

17. Save the file **5.3income** and print a copy of all worksheets.

18. Close the file.

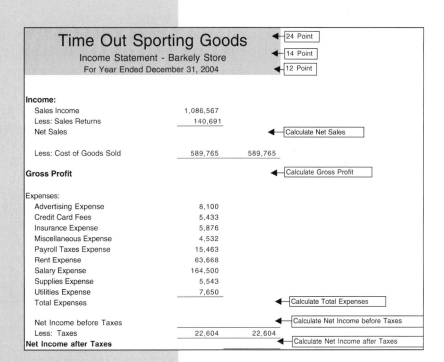

Cues for Reference

Add Headers and Footers
1. Click **View, Header and Footer.**
2. To select a built-in header or footer:
   - Click **Header** or **Footer** drop-down list.
   - Select header/footer.

Add Customized Headers and Footers
1. Click **View, Header and Footer.**

2. Click **Custom Header** or **Custom Footer.**
3. Click in section.
4. Enter text or insert header or footer code.
5. Repeat as necessary.
6. Click **OK.**
7. Click **OK.**

Enter 3-D References
- Enter the reference.

or
Use the mouse:
1. Enter equal sign, function, and parentheses, if necessary.
2. Select sheet and cell to reference.
3. Enter mathematical operator.
4. Repeat Steps 2 and 3 and close parentheses, if necessary.
5. Press **Enter.**

TRYOUT

TASK 4

▶ **GOALS**
To create a balance sheet using styles and the Find and Replace features
To practice using the following skill sets:
* Use styles
  * Apply a style
  * Define a new style
  * Modify a style
  * Remove a style
* Find and replace cell data and formats
  * Find cell data
  * Find and replace data and formats

WHAT YOU NEED TO KNOW

Use Styles

Apply a Style

▶ A *style* is a defined collection of data formats, such as font, font size, indentation, number formats, alignments, etc., that you name and store so that you can apply all those formats at once.

▶ Excel provides basic styles for numbers, as listed in the Style dialog box. To apply a basic style, select the cells to format, click Format, Style, and click the style from the Style name list. When you apply a style, you apply all the defined formats. Notice the Normal, or default, style formats for data, as shown in Figure 5.19.

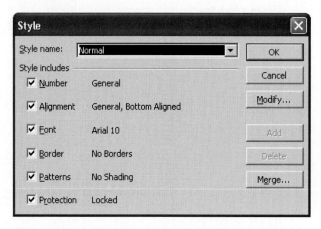

Figure 5.19 Style dialog box, Normal style

TRY *it* OUT E5-17

1. Open **E5-17** from the Data CD.

2. Select the range **C6:C10** and click **Format**, **Style.** Notice the settings for Comma style.

3. Click the **Style name** list arrow and select the **Normal** style. Notice the settings for Normal style.

4. Click **OK.** Notice the changes in the numbers.

Continued on next page

5. Click **Format**, **Style**, and apply the **Comma [0]** style (commas with no decimal places).

6. Click **OK**.

7. Use the Format Painter feature to copy the style to **Cell D11.**

8. Do not close the file.

Define a New Style

▶ If you find that you need a combination of formats in your work, you can define a new style. You can specify the formats in the Style dialog box or select a cell with the formats you want and name it in the Style dialog box. Once you name the style, the cell formats appear in the dialog box. Notice the "title" style in the Style dialog box in Figure 5.20.

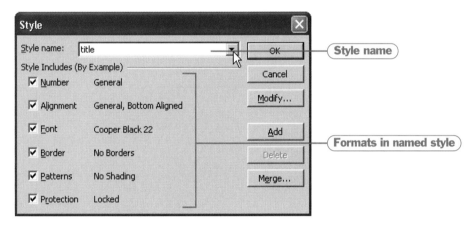

Figure 5.20 Style dialog box, Title style

1. Continue to work in the open file or open **E5-18** from the Data CD.

2. In **Cell A1,** change the font to **Cooper Black, 22 point.** (If this font is not installed, use another heavy, dark font.)

3. Click **Format**, **Style.**

4. Select **Title** in the Style name box, and notice the settings.

5. Click **OK**.

6. Click **Cell A2** and apply the **Title** style setting.

7. Do not close the file.

Modify a Style

▶ Use the Style dialog box to modify existing formats by clicking the format to change and then clicking Modify. In the Format cells dialog box that opens, click a tab to select the format you want and click OK. Repeat this procedure as necessary, and click OK to return to the Style dialog box. Click OK to apply the style or, if you just want to add the style to your styles list without applying it, click Add.

▶ If you modify a style, all the data using that style automatically changes. The Style feature provides consistency and saves reformatting the entire worksheet for a format modification.

TRY *it* OUT *E5-19*

1. Continue to work in the open file or open **E5-19** from the Data CD.

2. In **Cell A2,** click **Format**, **Style.**

3. Change "Title" to read `Title2` in the Style name box.

4. Click **Modify.**

5. In the Format Cells dialog box, with the **Font** tab selected, click **16 point.**

6. Click **OK** to set the format.

7. Click **OK** to apply.

8. Do not close the file.

Remove a Style

▶ You can remove a style from selected cells by clicking Format, Style, and click Normal style.

▶ You can remove a style from the Style name list by clicking the style and clicking the Delete button. Any cells set with that style revert to the Normal style setting.

TRY *it* OUT *E5-20*

1. Continue to work in the open file or open **E5-20** from the Data CD.

2. In **Cell D11,** click **Format**, **Style**, and **Normal.**

3. Click **OK.**

4. Click the **Undo** button.

5. Click **Format**, **Style**, and **Title2.**

6. Click **Delete.**

7. Click **OK.**

8. Apply the **Title** style to **Cell A2.**

9. Save the **E5-20** file. Close the file.

Find and Replace Cell Data and Formats

▶ If you want to review or edit specific text or numbers, you can search for the data and replace it, if necessary. This is called the *Find and Replace* feature. You can also find cells that match a format of a cell you specify. This feature is helpful if you want to change a format, because you can replace all occurrences as you find them.

Find Cell Data

▶ To find data, click Edit, Find and the Find and Replace dialog box opens in the Find tab. If you click the Options button, you notice, as shown in Figure 5.21, that you can define your search by looking in the sheet, in the workbook, searching by columns or rows, and looking for formulas, values, or comments. In addition, you can select options to match the case or the contents of the entire cell, and you can search for specific formats.

▶ Once you set your options, you can click Find All or Find Next. When you click Find All, you get a list of all the cell addresses that contain a match. When you click Find Next, you go to each location as it appears in the worksheet.

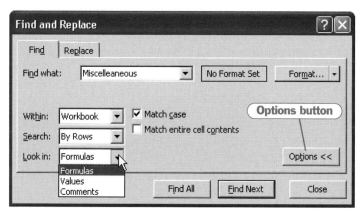

Figure 5.21 Find and Replace dialog box, Find tab, Look in list

TRY *it* OUT *E5-21*

1. Open **E5-21** from the Data CD.

2. Click **Edit**, **Find**, and the **Options** button.

3. Enter **Miscellaneous** in the Find what box.

4. Set the search **Within** the Workbook and click the **Match case** check box.

5. Click **Find Next** and keep clicking it until you find all occurrences.

6. Click **Find All** to see a list of all the locations.

7. Click the **Close** button in the dialog box.

8. Do not close the file.

Find and Replace Data and Formats

▶ To find specific data and replace it, click Edit, Replace, and the Find and Replace dialog box opens in the Replace tab as shown in Figure 5.22.

▶ After entering the Find and Replace information, you can click Replace All or just Replace. Clicking Replace All replaces all occurrences without giving you a chance to view each change. Clicking Replace lets you view each replacement before it is made, so you can be sure you want to replace it. You can undo a Find and Replace operation.

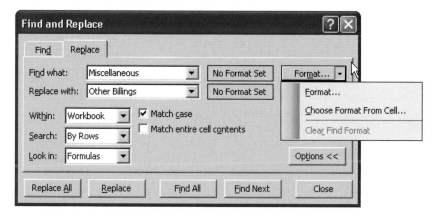

Figure 5.22 Find and Replace dialog box, Replace tab

▶ To search for a certain format, you can select a cell with the format you want, click the Format list arrow, click Choose Format From Cell, and that format becomes the search criteria. You can then change the format on the Replace with line by clicking Format to set the new format.

T R Y *it* **O U T** *E5-22*

1. Continue to work in the open file or open **E5-22** from the Data CD.

2. Click **Edit**, **Replace**, and **More** to display the Options buttons if they are not displayed.

3. Enter the information as shown in Figure 5.22, but do not press the Format button.

4. Click **Replace All** and notice the changes. Click **OK.**

5. Click the **Undo** button and click the **Redo** button.

6. Select and delete the text in the Find what and Replace with boxes.

7. Click the **Format** button list arrow on the Find what line and click **Choose Format From Cell.**

8. With the Choose cell pointer, click **Cell B3.**

9. Click the **Format** button list arrow on the Replace with line and click **Format**.

10. In the **Font** tab, set the format for **Arial, 10 point, bold, Dark Blue** color, and click **OK.** Notice the preview.

11. Click **Replace** each time to view the corrections.

12. Click the **Format** button list arrow on the Find what line and click **Clear Find Format.**

13. Click the **Format** button list arrow on the Replace with line and click **Clear Replace Format.**

14. Click the **Close button.**

15. Save the **E5-22** file. Close the file.

REHEARSAL

TASK 4

WHAT YOU NEED TO KNOW

▶ A business prepares a *balance sheet*, which is a financial report that shows the value of the firm's assets and liabilities, owner's worth, or stockholder's equity on a certain date. The balance sheet is based on the basic accounting equation: assets = liabilities + capital (owner's worth).

▶ The figures for the balance sheet come from the accounts and the worksheet. The owner's worth includes the profit for the period and shows the owner's share of the business. According to the formula, the creditors, or liabilities listed, and the owner share in the ownership of the assets. The proportion of ownership and the types of assets and liabilities listed are valuable information for a stockholder or owner, and for potential investors or lenders.

▶ In this Rehearsal activity, you will complete a balance sheet for Sutton Investment Group, set styles for enhancing the report, and find and replace data and formats.

DIRECTIONS

1. Open **5.4balsheet** from the Data CD.

2. Using the illustration on the facing page as a guide, enter the formulas to complete the balance sheet. The values in Total Assets, **Cell E21,** and in Total Liabilities and Owner's Equity, **Cell E38,** should balance or be equal.

3. Include lines under the numbers to indicate the additions, as illustrated.

4. In **Cell A1,** merge and center the title, and set the font for **Photina Casual Black, 16 point, bold.** (If this font is not installed, select a font similar to that shown in the illustration.)

5. Use Format Painter to format **Cell A2** with the same formats.

6. In **Cell A2,** change the font size to **14 point.**

7. Click **Cell A2** and define a style using that format; name it: `header2`.

8. Apply the **header2** format to **Cells A3, A6, A23,** and **A33.** (Hint: You can select each of these cells while pressing and holding the **Ctrl** key so that you can apply the style all at once.)

9. Format **Cell B7** for **Arial, 12 point, bold,** and define it as a style named: `header3`.

10. Apply the **header3** format to **Cells B16, B21, B24, B29,** and **B38.**

11. As shown in the illustration, indent labels that have not been formatted.

12. Select all the values in **Columns C, D,** and **E,** and format for commas with no decimal places.

13. Modify the **header2** style so that it includes a double-accounting underline. (All cells formatted with the header2 style will change.)

Continued on next page

14. Use the Find and Replace feature to find the word "Capital" and replace it with the word **Equity** in all occurrences.

15. Select **Cell E21** and format the cell for Currency with no decimals and a bold font. Define the style as **Totals.**

16. Apply the Totals style to **Cell E38.**

17. Select the entire report, the range **A1:E38,** and use Fill Color to shade it a light green.

18. Enter a footer that contains the file name and date.

19. Center the report vertically and horizontally using the Page Setup dialog box.

20. Print one copy.

21. Save the **5.4balsheet** file. Close the file.

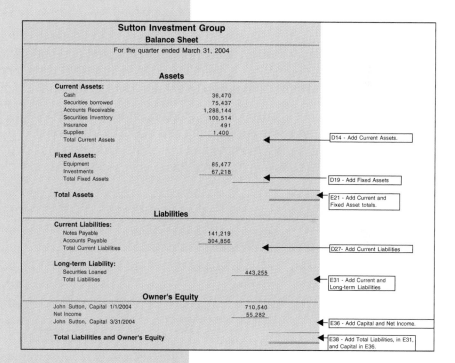

Define a New Style
1. Click a cell that contains the style you want.
2. Click **Format, Style.**
3. Enter a name for the style in the Style name box.
4. Click **Add.**
5. Click **OK.**

Apply a Style
1. Select cell(s) to receive style.
2. Click **Format, Style.**
3. Click the **Style** list arrow and click style to apply.
4. Click **OK.**

Modify a Style
1. Click **Format, Style.**
2. Click the **Style** list arrow and click style to modify.
3. Click **Modify.**
4. In the Format Cells dialog box, set the format.
5. Click **OK** twice.

Find and Replace Data
1. Click **Edit, Replace.**
2. Enter data in Find what box.
3. Enter data in Replace with box.
4. Click Options and set, if appropriate.
5. Click **Replace** to do one at a time.

or
• Click **Replace All** to replace all occurrences.

Find and Replace Formats
1. Click **Edit, Replace.**
2. Clear text in Find and Replace boxes.
3. On the Find what line, click **Format, Choose Format From Cell.**
4. Select cell with format to find.
5. On Replace with line, click **Format** and select **Format.**
6. Set the new format.
7. Click **Replace** or **Replace All.**

SETTING THE
STAGE/WRAPUP

Act I File names: **5p1.sched**
                   5p1.trialbal

Act II File name: **5p2.cis3d**

Act III File names: **5p3.worksheet**
                    5p3.balsheet

WHAT YOU NEED TO KNOW

Act I

You work in the Accounting Department of Odyssey Travel Gear in Chicago, and at the end of the year your department combines accounts from all stores and outlets into one Trial Balance. You have been asked to prepare the Schedules of Accounts Receivable and Accounts Payable and use the Paste Link and Hyperlink features to link the data to the Trial Balance.

Odyssey Travel Gear has thousands of customers, or accounts receivable, that are billed on a 20-day cycle. The business organizes the accounts alphabetically into billing groups; for example, customers with names from Aa to Be are billed on the first day of the cycle. The total due from each billing group is summarized on the Schedule of Accounts Receivable, which represents the total due from all customers.

	A	B	C	D	E
1		Odyssey Travel Gear			
2		**Schedule of Accounts Receivable**			
3		**December 31, 2004**			
4					
5	**Cycle**	**Customer Billing Group**	**Amount**		
6	1	Aa-Be	45,346		
7	2	Bf-Cr	46,543		
8	3	Cr-D	50,764		
9	4	E-F	29,765		
10	5	G	32,456		
11	6	H	43,566		
12	7	I-J	43,235		
13	8	K	38,796		
14	9	L	42,687		
15	10	M	48,769		
16			40,443		
17			34,561		
18			29,432		
19			50,840		
20			26,544		
21			49,076		
22			23,343		
23	18	T	31,854		
24	19	U-V	24,345		
25	20	W-Z	36,543		
26		Total	768,908		
27					
28					
29					
30					
31					
32					

Represents total amounts due from customers in each alphabetical group listed.

Each group of customers is billed on different day of the month to create the billing cycle. There are too many customers to bill them all on the same day.

Accounts Receivable / Accounts Payable / Sheet

Ready

start   5 Microsoft Office E...   C:\Documents

Follow these guidelines:

✴ Open the files **5p1.sched** and **5p1.trialbal** from the Data CD. In
both files, group sheets where possible, and format the titles and
column headings using Merge and Center, bold and font formats, lines,
colors, or borders. Format workbook values for commas with no
decimal places.

✴ In the schedules file, rename and color the tabs. Find the total for each
schedule, and add single and double lines.

✴ Copy the Accounts Receivable and Accounts Payable totals from the
schedules and paste link them to the proper location on the Trial
Balance. Link the totals next to the account title, in the Debit column
for Accounts Receivable and in the Credit column for Accounts Payable.

✴ Total the Trial Balance and include a single line for adding and double
lines under totals. The Debits and Credits should balance. Add a
column to the right of the account titles. Insert hyperlinks to the correct
schedule sheet in the file **5p1.sched,** using appropriate hyperlink text.

✴ Enter appropriate footers, save both files, print a copy of the Trial
Balance and both schedules, and close the files.

✴ Attach both files to an e-mail to the managers of the five retail stores.
(You can use the Internet addresses of other students in your class or
addresses provided by your instructor.) Inform them that you are
sending the trial balance and schedule data for the year ending
December 31, 2004, for their records.

Act II

The Air Land Sea Travel Group has agencies in Boston, New York, Los Angeles, and San Francisco.
Each agency has sent its quarterly income statement data, which has been copied into one
worksheet. Ms. Janice Pierce, the president of the company, would like a consolidated report along
with the supporting agency reports.

Follow these guidelines:

✴ Open the file **5p2.cis** from the Data CD.

✴ Copy any sheet and place it at the end of the worksheets. Rename and
color-format each tab using the city name, and name the last tab:
Consolidated Income Statement.

- Group sheets to enter formulas for calculating Total Income (D11), Total Expenses (D25), and Net Income (D27). Include lines for adding and double lines for totals, where necesasary.

- Ungroup the sheets, and on the last sheet, clear the data from Column C, which belonged to one of the agencies, leaving the formulas in Column D. Correct the title to read: `Consolidated Income Statement.` Use 3-D references in Column C to combine all the data from the four agencies onto the Consolidated Income Statement sheet. Clear any unnecessary formulas, and check to make sure the existing formulas in Column D are working correctly.

- Group the sheets to format values for commas with no decimals, use color buttons to format the Income Statements as desired, format the Net Income value for currency with no decimals, include headers and/or footers, and include the sheet name, date, file name, and company logo.

- Save the workbook, print copies of all sheets, and close the file.

- *Optional:* Insert another sheet and create an Income Analysis comparing the total and net income from the agency in each city. Calculate what percentage the net income is of total income so you can compare the results.

Act III

Green Brothers Gardening's chief financial officer, Ralph Green, has started to prepare the worksheet and Balance Sheet for the year. He has asked you to complete and format the reports. Ralph Green needs the Balance Sheet for meetings with bankers and the president, Calvin Green, because Green Brothers is contemplating an expansion and requires additional funding.

Follow these guidelines:

- Open the files **5p3.worksheet** and **5.p3balsheet** from the Data CD.

- Format worksheet titles and column headings using fonts, merge and center, and bold settings. Format worksheet values for commas with no decimal places.

- In Cell B5 of the worksheet, freeze panes to be able to work in the worksheet. The yellow areas show where you should place formulas. Find totals in cells B30:C30 and in cells D32:K32. In Cell H33, find Net Income by subtracting the total in Cell H32 from Cell I32. Enter the Net Income value in Cell K33 and find the totals in the range H34:K34. The values in each set of debit and credit columns, beginning with Columns B and C, should be equal. After formulas are completed, remove the color.

	A	B	C	D	E	F	G	H	I	J	K
1	Green Brothers Gardening										
2	Worksheet										
3	For the year ended December 31, 2004										
4											
5		Trial Balance		Adjustments		Adjusted Trial Balance		Income Statement		Balance Sheet	
6		Debit	Credit	Debit	Credit	Debit	Credit	Debit	Credit	Debit	Credit
7	Cash	34565				34565				34565	
8	Accounts Receivable	145765				145765				145765	
9	Nursery Inventory	257654		205444	257654	205444				205444	
10	Supplies	5456			3234	2222				2222	
11	Equipment	568433				568433				568433	
12	Allowance for Depreciation		181900		54678		236578				236578
13	Accounts Payable		142789				142789				142789
14	Loan Payable		25000				25000				25000
15	Ralph Green, Capital		386944				386944				386944
16	Calvin Green, Capital										
17	Purchases	865789				865789		865789			
18	Contracts Income		345765				345765		345765		
19	Nursery Sales Income		739872				739872		739872		
20	Landscaping Fees Income		673657				673657		673657		
21	Advertising Expense	36543				36543		36543			
22	Depreciation Expense			54678		54678		54678			
23	Equipment Maintenance	8745				8745		8745			
24	Interest Expense	2309				2309		2309			
25	Insurance Expense	11574				11574		11574			
26	Payroll Tax Expense	36546				36546		36546			
27	Rent Expense	89759				89759		89759			
28	Salary Expense	432789				432789		432789			
29	Supplies Expense			3234		3234		3234			
30	Totals										
31	Income Summary			257654	205444	257654	205444	257654	205444		
32	Totals										
33	Net Income										
34	Totals										
35											
36				Enter formulas in							
37				yellow areas							
38											
39											

* On the Balance Sheet, format the titles and values and establish styles for the headings in Cells A6, A21, and A29, and for the section headings in Cells B7, B14, B19, B22, B25, B27, B37, and B39.

* Subtract the Allowance for Depreciation from the Equipment account balance. Divide the Net Income (H33) from the worksheet in half, and place it under each partner's equity to calculate their new equity. Enter all formulas necessary to complete the Balance Sheet.

* Find and replace all occurrences of the word "Equity" with "Capital."

* Ralph Green needs the following printouts:

Balance sheet.

Partial worksheet with the Trial Balance and Adjustments columns hidden.

Full worksheet on two pages using the Print Titles feature.

* Save and close all files.

* Search the www.entrepreneurmag.com site to develop a list of the "best banks for small businesses" for the state of Virginia.

* Group Project: Use the same Web site to research the characteristics, problems, and advantages of organizing a business as a partnership (as in this family business) or as a corporation. The Green brothers are discussing incorporation and would like more information about this type of business organization. Write an essay that summarizes the aspects of organizing a business as a partnership, as compared to a corporate form of organization. (Hint: You can use "advantages of incorporation" as keywords.)

LESSON 6

Charts and Diagrams

In this lesson, you will learn to use features in Excel to create, modify, print, and position charts, diagrams, and graphics.

Upon completion of this lesson, you should have mastered the following skill sets:

* Create, modify, and position charts
* About charts
* Create charts
* Apply chart options
* Create pie chart
* Position a chart
* Chart types and subtypes
* Modify charts
* Copy and paste charts
* Format charts
* Print charts
* Create, position, and modify graphics
* Insert and download graphics and clip art
* Create, modify, and position diagrams
* Create stock charts

Terms

Software-related

Charts
Nonadjacent selection
Series labels
Legend
Y-axis or value axis
X-axis or category axis
Category labels
Data series
Chart Wizard
Embedded chart
Chart sheet
Pie chart
Column chart
Line chart
Graphics
AutoShapes
Diagrams

Document-related

Portfolio
S&P 500

GOALS

To use charts to analyze sales and income data

To create charts to compare expense data for several years

To practice using the following skill sets:

- ✴ Create, modify, and position charts
- ✴ About charts
- ✴ Create charts
- ✴ Apply chart options
- ✴ Create pie chart
- ✴ Position a chart
- ✴ Chart types and subtypes
- ✴ Modify charts
- ✴ Copy and paste charts
- ✴ Format charts
- ✴ Print charts

TASK 1

WHAT YOU NEED TO KNOW

Create, Modify, and Position Charts

About Charts

▶ *Charts* present and compare data in a graphic format so that you can compare information visually.

▶ To create a chart, you must first select the data to plot. Figure 6.1 shows two selections of data; each selection produces the chart shown in Figure 6.2. The list of guidelines below refer to the selection of chart data:

- The selection should be rectangular.

- The selection should not contain blank or unrelated columns or rows. (See Selection A in Figure 6.1.)

- Use a *nonadjacent selection* when data is not contiguous (see Selection B in Figure 6.1). Select data while pressing and holding the Ctrl key to eliminate blanks or unrelated data. You can also hide columns you do not want to select.

- The blank cell in the upper left corner of a selection indicates that the data to the right are *series labels* and the data below are category labels for the values.

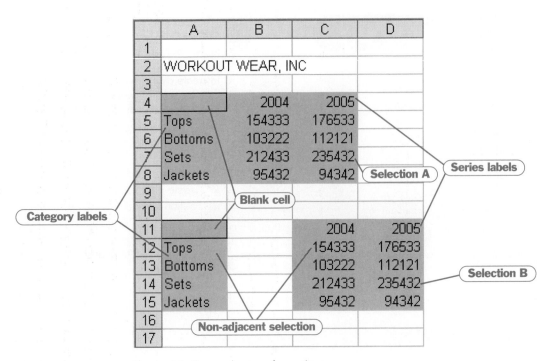

Figure 6.1 Data selections for a chart

▶ The chart in Figure 6.2 is a column chart produced from either selection in Figure 6.1 (because the same data is selected). Move the mouse pointer over the parts of a chart to view the ScreenTip that displays the name of the chart object. The objects in the column chart are labeled on Figure 6.2 and defined below:

- The chart title—identifies the data in the chart and is entered using the Chart Wizard.
- The *y-axis* or *value axis*—typically represents the vertical scale. The scale values are entered automatically by Excel.
- The y-axis or value axis title—identifies the values and is entered using the Chart Wizard.
- The *x-axis* or *category axis*—typically represents the horizontal scale and the data series categories.
- The *category labels*—identify each category and are obtained from the selected data (see Figure 6.1).
- The x-axis or category axis title—identifies the category and is entered using the Chart Wizard.
- The series labels-legend—identifies each data series and is obtained from the selected data (see Figure 6.1).
- The *data series*—groups of values identified by a label, such as 2004 data in the illustration.
- The plot area—the space where the values are charted.

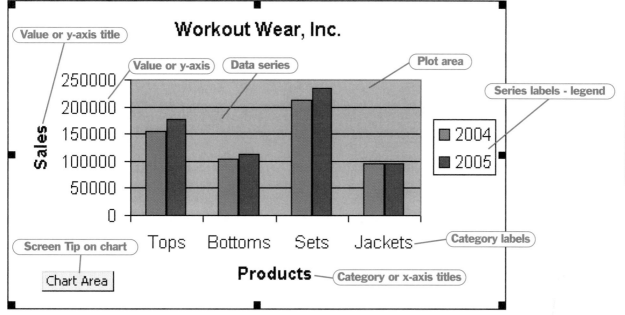

Figure 6.2 Column chart objects

T R Y *it* O U T *E6-1*

1. Open **E6-1** from the Data CD.

2. Select the range **A4:C8.** This is the charted data.

3. Select the range **A11:A15,** press and hold the **Ctrl** key, and select the range **C11:D15.** This is also the charted data, using a nonadjacent selection.

4. Move the mouse pointer over all the chart objects to locate each ScreenTip, one of which is shown in Figure 6.2.

5. Close the file. Do not save.

Create Charts

▶ The *Chart Wizard* makes creating charts easy by providing step-by-step instructions.

▶ The basic steps to create a chart are:
  • Select the worksheet data to chart.
  • Click the Chart Wizard button.
  • Follow the Chart Wizard prompts on four screens:
    Screen 1. Select chart type.
    Screen 2. Check chart source data range.
    Screen 3. Select chart options.
    Screen 4. Select chart location.

▶ The Chart Wizard takes you through the four screens to create a chart. Each screen consists of tabbed dialog boxes that allow you to select and format all the objects in your chart. As you make selections, the Chart Wizard shows you exactly how the chart looks so you can select the format that is best for presenting your data.

▶ On Screen 4, when you select the chart location, you create either an *embedded chart,* which exists as an object on your worksheet, or a *chart sheet,* which exists on a separate sheet within the workbook. Figure 6.3 shows Screen 4 displaying the chart placement options. Excel names chart sheets as Chart1, Chart2, etc, however, when you select As new sheet you can name the chart sheet to describe the chart better.

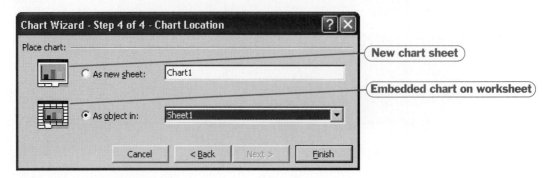

Figure 6.3 Chart Wizard, Screen 4

T R Y *it* **O U T** *E6-2*

1. Open **E6-2** from the Data CD.

2. Select the range **A4:C7.** This is the data range to chart.

3. Click the **Chart Wizard** button.

4. Click **Next** to accept the Column chart type.

5. Click **Next** to accept the data range.

6. In the Step 3 dialog box on the Titles tab, enter **Art 'n Stuff - Sales by Store** as the chart title.

7. Click **Next** to accept the title.

8. Select **As new sheet** for the chart location.

9. Enter **Column Chart** as the sheet name.

10. Click **Finish** to complete the chart. The chart appears on Column Chart, a new sheet.

11. Do not close the file.

Apply Chart Options

▶ Screen 3 of the Chart Wizard allows you to set chart options on six options tabs. You can change or enter chart titles, axes, gridlines, legends, data labels, and a data table for most charts. The number of tabs and options vary with the type of chart selected. For example, pie charts have only three option tabs.

▶ In Figure 6.4, you can see Screen 3 on the Titles tab for the column chart in E6-2. You can set and view each option on your chart in the preview window as you add the option.

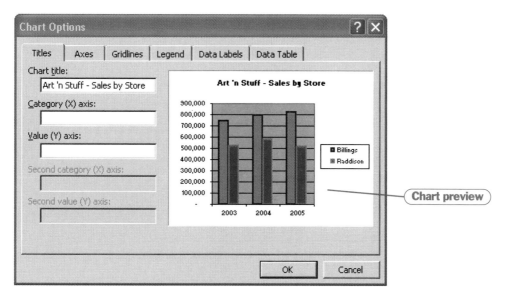

Figure 6.4 Chart Wizard, Screen 3, Chart Options, Titles tab

Create Pie Chart

▶ The *pie chart,* shown in Figure 6.5, is a circular graph you can use to show the relationship of each value in a data range to the entire range. The size of each slice of the pie represents the percentage each value contributes to the total. Select only one numeric data range for a pie chart.

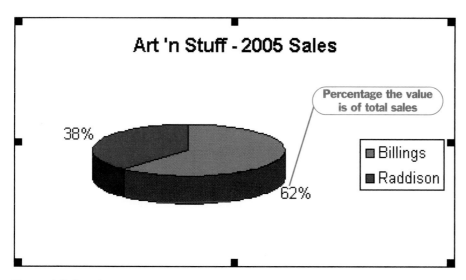

Figure 6.5 Pie chart

Position a Chart

▶ You have placed a chart on a new sheet. However, on the last screen of the Chart Wizard, you can also elect to embed the chart on the worksheet, which requires you to size and position the chart.

▶ To position, size, edit, move, and copy a chart on a worksheet, click the chart once to select it. As shown in Figure 6.6, handles appear around the chart border to indicate that the chart is selected and in Edit mode. Notice that Excel highlights the charted data as well.

▶ To move a chart, you must select the chart, click it, and drag it to its new location. The mouse pointer changes to a four-headed arrow during the move. You can size the chart by dragging the handles to the desired size.

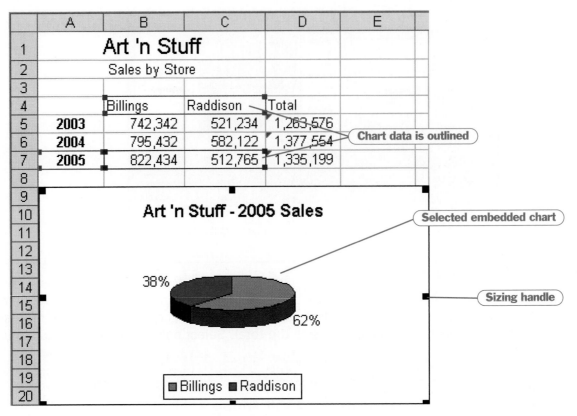

Figure 6.6 Selected embedded chart

T R Y *it* **O U T** *E6-3*

1. Continue to work in the open file on Sheet1 or open **E6-3** from the Data CD.

2. Select the range **A4:C4**, press and hold the **Ctrl** key, and select the range **A7:C7.**

3. Click the **Chart Wizard** button.

4. Select **Pie** chart, **second** sub-type, **3-D visual effect,** and click **Next.**

5. Click **Next** to accept the data range.

6. On the Titles tab, enter: `Art 'n Stuff — 2005 Sales`

7. On the Legend tab, select **Bottom placement** for the legend.

8. On the Data Labels tab, select **Percentage.**

9. Click **Finish.** The pie chart appears on the worksheet, as shown in Figure 6.6

10. Click and drag the chart to **A9,** a blank location on the worksheet.

11. Do not close the file.

Chart Types and Subtypes

▶ The *column chart* (see Figure 6.2) compares individual or sets of values. The height of each bar is proportional to its corresponding value in the worksheet.

▶ Fourteen standard chart types are available in the Chart Wizard. Each of these types offers at least two subtypes. The subtypes for the Column chart are shown in Figure 6.7.

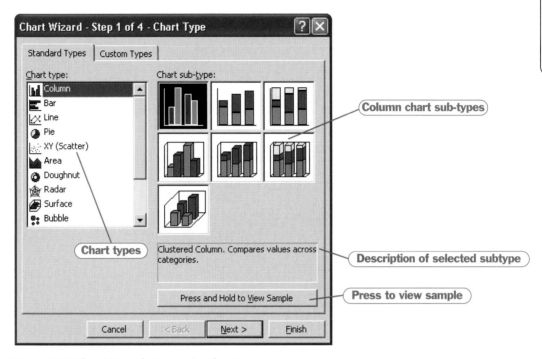

Figure 6.7 Chart Wizard, Screen 1, Chart Type

▶ A *line chart,* shown in Figure 6.8, is like a column chart because it compares individual sets of values, but lines connect the points of data. This is useful if you want to show a progression over time.

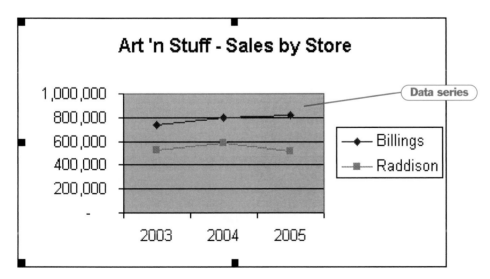

Figure 6.8 Line chart

1. Continue to work in the open file on Sheet1 or open **E6-4** from the Data CD.

2. Select the range **A4:C7** and click the **Chart Wizard** button.

3. Select each of the Column chart sub-types, and click and hold the **Press and Hold to View Sample** button.

4. Switch to Bar charts and test the subtypes as described in Step 3 above.

5. Switch to Line charts and select the **Line with Markers** subtype. Click Next.

6. Click **Next** to accept the data range.

7. Enter the title: `Art 'n Stuff — Sales by Store`. Click **Next.**

8. Place the chart as an embedded object on the sheet and position it in Cell F9 or next to the pie chart.

9. Do not close the file.

Modify Charts

▶ Use the Chart menu, which appears when you select a chart, to modify or edit your chart settings. The Chart menu, as shown in Figure 6.9, lists commands to revisit each of the steps in the Chart Wizard, where you can change your settings as necessary. You can also display the Chart menu by right-clicking the chart.

▶ You can modify the Source Data on Screen 2 and change the orientation of the data. By selecting rows or columns on the Source Data screen, you will change the emphasis of the charted data.

Copy and Paste Charts

▶ Once you select a chart, you can copy and paste it. Use the Copy and Paste buttons as you do with any other data.

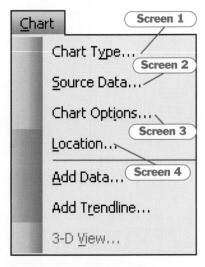

Figure 6.9 Chart menu

1. Continue to work in the open file or open **E6-5** from the Data CD.

2. Select and copy the line chart and paste it in **Cell A22** or to a location under the chart in Column A. A second chart, selected, appears.

3. Click **Chart, Chart Type,** and change the type to **Bar.** Click **OK.**

4. Right-click the chart and select **Source Data.**

5. In the **Series in** option area, change the orientation from columns to rows. Click **OK.**

6. Do not close the file.

Format Charts

▶ You can format every object on a chart using the Format Chart dialog box. You can open the dialog box, as shown in Figure 6.10, by double-clicking a chart or any object in a chart. When you double-click a chart object, Excel marks it with a border and handles and displays the name of the object in the name box.

▶ The Format Chart dialog box varies, depending on which chart object you want to format. Figure 6.10 shows the Format Chart Area dialog box.

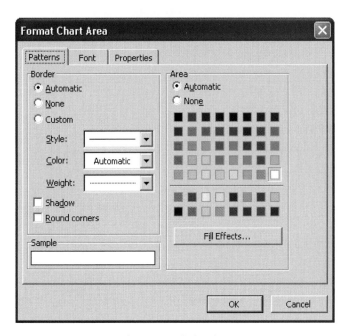

Figure 6.10 Format Chart Area dialog box

▶ In addition, every object in a chart has a shortcut menu that lets you change the chart type and the source data, format the object, or use other commands relevant to the object. Figure 6.11 shows the shortcut menu for the data series in a pie chart.

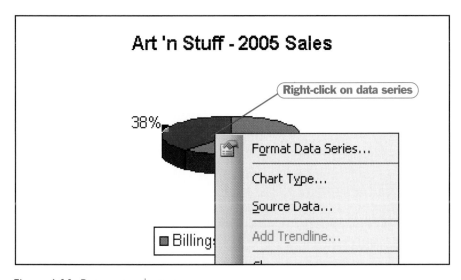

Figure 6.11 Data series shortcut menu

1. Continue to work in the open file or open **E6-6** from the Data CD.

2. Double-click the chart title of the pie chart. The title is bordered and the Format Chart Title dialog box appears.

3. In the Font tab, change the font to **Century, 16 point, bold, blue.** *Note:* Use another font if Century is not available.

4. Click **OK.**

5. Select the **embedded line chart** and right-click the **value axis** labels on the left.

6. On the shortcut menu, click **Format Axis** and click the **Alignment** tab.

7. Set the text alignment to **16 degrees** rotation. Click **OK.**

8. Return the Value Axis alignment to **0 degrees** rotation.

9. Double-click the Plot area and change the area color to **White** in the Format Plot Area dialog box. Click **OK.**

10. Select the Bar chart and double-click on the legend. Change the background color of the area to **Grey.** Click **OK.**

11. Do not close the file.

Print Charts

▶ You can print charts with the worksheet, or on a separate sheet. If you select an embedded chart on a worksheet or a chart sheet, it will print on a separate sheet to fit one page. If you print charts with the worksheet, use Print Preview to be sure everything fits on the page.

▶ Excel selects the page orientation (portrait or landscape) that matches the shape of the chart. On the Page Setup dialog box, the Chart tab replaces the Sheet tab, as shown in Figure 6.12. Chart setup options include chart size and printing quality.

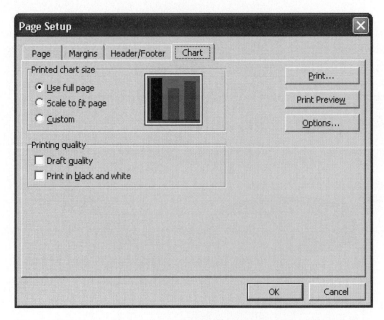

Figure 6.12 Page Setup dialog box, Chart tab

1. Continue to work in the open file or open **E6-7** from the Data CD.

2. Select the **Column Chart** sheet.

3. Click the **Print Preview** button.

4. Click **Print** and **OK.**

5. On Sheet1, select the pie chart.

6. Click the **Print Preview** button.

7. Click **Setup** and click the **Chart** tab.

8. Click **Print in black and white** and click **OK.**

9. Click **Print, OK.**

10. Select the range **A1:L34,** and click the **Print Preview** button.

11. Click **Setup** and change the orientation to **Landscape.** Close the preview screen.

12. Save the file as **E6-7.** Close the file.

EXCEL

REHEARSAL

TASK 1A

GOAL
To use charts to analyze sales and income data

SETTING THE STAGE/WRAPUP
File name: **6.1salechart**

WHAT YOU NEED TO KNOW

▶ Although detailed data is found on financial reports and analysis worksheets, businesses frequently use charts to summarize data for meetings, presentations, and annual reports. The chart type you select often determines the impression the data makes.

▶ Column and bar charts are similar, except that the data markers are vertical in column charts and horizontal in bar charts. You can copy and paste a chart and change the chart type to provide a different display.

▶ In this Rehearsal activity, you will create and modify charts using various chart types on chart sheets, and in the workbook for Time Out Sporting Goods. They are testing chart types to determine which chart makes the best impression.

▼ DIRECTIONS

1. Open **6.1salechart** from the Data CD.

2. On the Chart data sheet, use a nonadjacent selection to select the ranges **A3:A6** and **C3:D6**.

3. Create a column chart with the following options on the Chart Wizard screens:
   Screen 1: In the **Column** chart type, select the Clustered column with a 3-D visual effect subtype (Row 2, Column 1); click **Next**.
   Screen 2: Setting should be for **Series in: Columns**, check the data range and, if correct, click **Next**.
   Screen 3: In the Titles tab, enter **Time Out Sporting Goods** for the Chart title. Enter **Stores** for the x-axis title. On the Legend tab, place the legend at the bottom of the chart. Click **Next**.
   Screen 4: Place the chart as a new sheet and enter **Column Chart** as the chart name. Click **Finish**.

4. Select the chart title and format it for Arial Black, Regular style, 24 point.

5. Format the text in the legend and both axes for bold. Expand the legend box as necessary.

6. Select the **Chart data** sheet. Using the same data, create a bar chart with the following options on the Chart Wizard screens:
   Screen 1: Click **Bar** chart. Use the Clustered bar with a 3-D visual effect subtype (Row 2, Column 1); click **Next**.
   Screen 2: Check the data range and, if correct, click **Next**.
   Screen 3: In the Titles tab, enter **Time Out Sporting Goods** for the chart title. On the Legend tab, place the legend at the bottom of the chart. Click **Next**.

Continued on next page

Screen 4. Place the chart as a new sheet and enter **Bar Chart** as the chart name. Click **Finish.**

7. Format title, legend, and axes as you did in steps 4 and 5.

8. Insert a new worksheet and copy the bar chart to the new sheet.

9. Select the new chart and use the Chart menu to modify the type of chart to a line chart. Name the sheet **Line Chart.**

10. Select the **Chart Data** sheet. Use a nonadjacent selection to select ranges **A3:D3** and **A6:D6.**

11. Create a pie chart with the following options on the Chart Wizard screens:

    Screen 1: Click **Pie** chart. Use the Pie with a 3-D visual effect subtype (Row 1, Column 2); click **Next.**

    Screen 2: Check the data range and, if correct, click **Next.**

    Screen 3: In the Titles tab enter **Time Out Sporting Goods — Net Income** for the chart title. On the Legend tab, place the legend at the bottom of the chart. Set data labels to show percentage and category name; click **Next.**

    Screen 4: Place the chart as an object in Chart Data. Click **Finish.**

12. Drag the pie chart to **Cell A11.**

13. Select and print Column Chart, Bar Chart, and Chart Data sheets.

14. Delete the line chart sheet, because it was not the best way to present the data.

15. Save the file **6.1salechart.** Close the file.

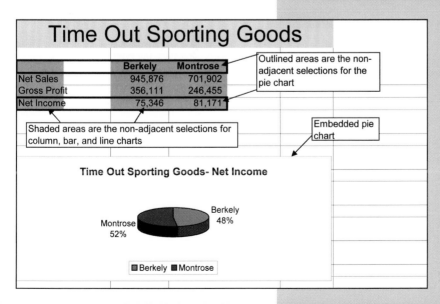

	Berkely	Montrose
Net Sales	945,876	701,902
Gross Profit	356,111	246,455
Net Income	75,346	81,171

Time Out Sporting Goods

Outlined areas are the non-adjacent selections for the pie chart

Shaded areas are the non-adjacent selections for column, bar, and line charts

Embedded pie chart

Time Out Sporting Goods- Net Income

Berkely 48%

Montrose 52%

☐ Berkely ☐ Montrose

Select Chart Data
1. Always keep a blank cell in top-left corner.
2. Select rectangular data to chart.
   or
   Press and hold **Ctrl** while selecting nonadjacent data.

Create a Chart
1. Select chart data.
2. Click **Chart Wizard** button.
3. Select chart type and subtype.
4. Click **Next.**
5. Check data range and reenter if incorrect.
6. Click **Next.**
7. Click appropriate tab and set chart options.
8. Click **Next.**
9. Select placement: Click **As new sheet** and enter sheet name in text box.
   or
   Click **As object in**, accept option offered, or enter sheet name.
10. Click **Finish.**

Select Chart
Embedded Chart
- Click chart. (A border with handles surrounds the chart.)

Chart Sheet
- Select sheet

Position Chart
1. Select the embedded chart.
2. Drag to new location. (Mouse pointer changes to four-headed arrow.)

Size Embedded Charts
1. Select chart.
2. Place mouse pointer on the handle on side of border to size. Use corner to size proportionally. The mouse pointer becomes a double-headed arrow when positioned correctly.
3. Drag border outline until you reach the required size.

Format Charts
1. Double-click the chart object to format.
2. Click the appropriate Format dialog box tab.
3. Set the format.
4. Click **OK.**

Modify Charts
1. Select chart.
2. Click **Chart** and chart option to modify.
   or
   Right-click chart and select chart option to modify.
3. Make modification.
4. Click **OK.**

Print Charts
Chart Sheet
1. Select sheet.
2. Click the **Print** button.

Embedded Chart on a Full Sheet
1. Select chart.
2. Click the **Print** button.

Embedded Chart on the Worksheet
1. Select worksheet range including chart.
2. Click **Print** button.

REHEARSAL

Again

TASK 1B

GOAL
To create charts to compare expense data for several years

SETTING THE STAGE/WRAPUP
File name: **6.1expchart**

WHAT YOU NEED TO KNOW

▶ In this Rehearsal activity, you will create, format, and modify charts using various chart types on chart sheets and embedded in the worksheet for the Sutton Investment Group. This company is comparing expenses for the past three years to see the developing trends and to determine where it can make changes.

DIRECTIONS

1. Open **6.1expchart** from the Data CD.

2. Use nonadjacent selection to select the labels and data in the ranges **C4:C11** and **E4:G11,** as shown in Illustration C on page 164.

3. Create a column chart, as shown in Illustration A. Include the following:
   a. 3-D visual effect (clustered column) subtype
   b. Enter the chart title: **Sutton Investment Group**
   c. X-axis title: **Expenses**
   d. Legend: Place at the top of the chart
   e. Place the chart on a chart sheet named: **Expense Column Chart**

4. Modify the x-axis data series labels to an **8 point** font.

5. Modify the chart title to a **16 point** font. Select the title area and add – **Expense Analysis** so that the title reads: **Sutton Investment Group – Expense Analysis**

6. Use the shortcut menu on the Expense Column Chart Sheet tab to create a copy of the chart sheet and move it to the end.

7. Select the chart copy and change the chart type to an Area chart with 3-D visual effect, as shown in Illustration B.

8. Select **Chart, Chart Options** and on the Gridlines tab, add major and minor gridlines to the x-axis.

9. Rename the Expense Column Chart(2) sheet to **Expense Area Chart.**

10. Delete Sheet2 and Sheet3.

11. On Sheet1, select the data labels in the range **C4:C11** and the data in **Column G** to create a pie chart for 2005 data. Use the following options:
    a. Apply the 3-D Visual Effect subtype.
    b. Enter the chart title: **Sutton Investment Group 2005 Expense Dollar.**

Continued on next page

c. Place the legend at the bottom of the chart.

d. Set data labels to show percentages.

e. Place the chart as an object on Sheet1.

12. Drag and size the chart so it fits in the range **A13:I41.**

13. Select the chart title, click after "Group," and press the **Enter** key so that the title is arranged on two lines, as shown in Illustration C.

14. Modify the legend so that it has a light yellow background.

15. Use the Patterns tab of the Format Chart Area dialog box to modify the color of the chart background and the border color to a light green.

16. Select the range **A1:I41** and change the background to a light green.

17. Rename Sheet1 as **Expense Data and Pie Chart.**

18. Group all the sheets and print the entire workbook.

19. Ungroup the sheets.

20. Save the file **6.1expchart** and close the file.

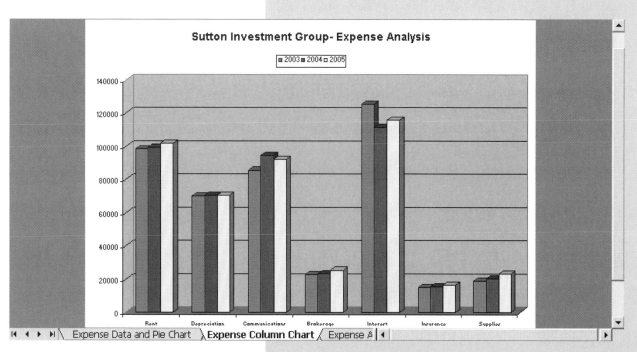

Illustration A

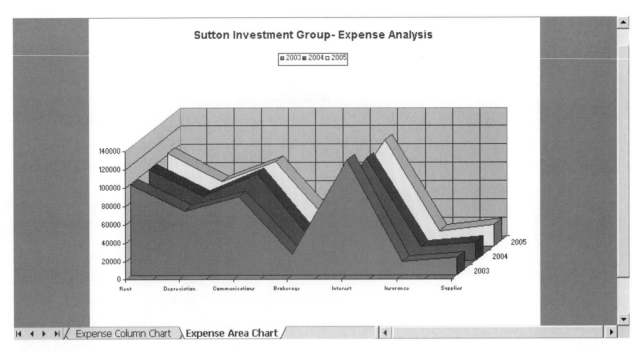

Illustration B

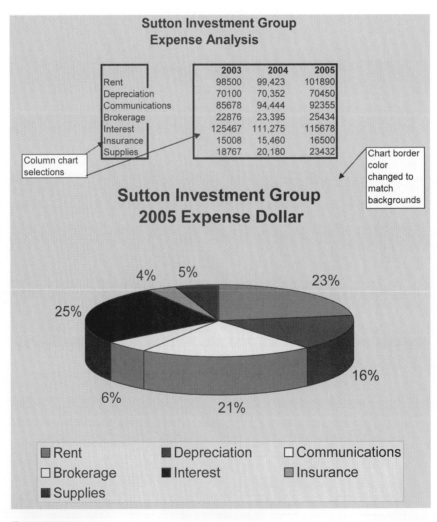

Illustration C

GOALS
To create graphics, diagrams, and stock charts for a presentation
To practice using the following skill sets:
 ✴ Create, position, and modify graphics
   ✴ Position graphics
   ✴ Modify graphics
 ✴ Insert and download graphics and clip art
 ✴ Create, modify, and position diagrams
 ✴ Create stock charts

EXCEL

WHAT YOU NEED TO KNOW

Create, Position, and Modify Graphics

▶ Drawing objects or pictures are *graphics*, or graphical images, that you can create or insert into your worksheets. If you want to add drawing objects to a worksheet or to a chart, you can create a customized object by using the tools available on the Drawing toolbar.

▶ Click View, Toolbars, and Drawing to display the Drawing toolbar, as shown in Figure 6.13. You can draw lines, arcs, arrows, rectangles, polygons, and a selection of shapes or freehand graphics on any area of a worksheet or chart. You can also add text boxes and shadows or three-dimensional enhancements to shapes.

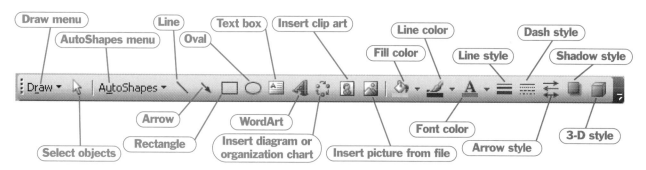

Figure 6.13 Drawing toolbar

▶ *AutoShapes* are predefined graphical images that you can place and size. When you place your mouse pointer over an AutoShape, the name of the shape appears as a ScreenTip, as shown in Figure 6.14.

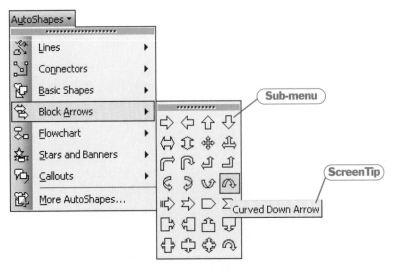

Figure 6.14 AutoShapes menu

▶ Select a Drawing Toolbar button to draw or format an object. The Line, Arrow, Rectangle, Text Box, and Oval buttons enable the mouse pointer to draw those objects as you drag them to the appropriate size. Figure 6.15 shows some of the graphic objects you can create with the Drawing toolbar.

▶ You can place graphics or drawing objects anywhere on a worksheet, as well as on charts. However, you must display, create, and modify graphics with charts deselected because they disappear when the chart is selected.

Position Graphics

▶ A selected graphic has small, white circles at the ends or on the border of the graphic, as seen in the text box graphic selected in Figure 6.15. Click a graphic to select it. However, notice that to select a graphic you do not select the chart.

▶ To move a selected graphic, place the mouse pointer over the graphic until you see a four-headed arrow, then click and drag to the new position. As with handles on charts, you can use the white circles to size the object.

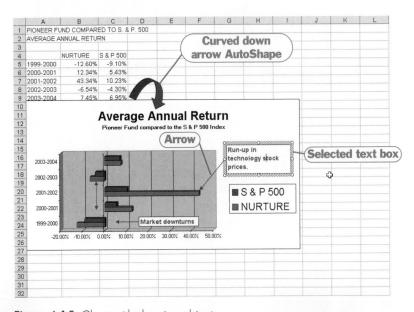

Figure 6.15 Chart with drawing objects

1. Open **E6-8** from the Data CD.

2. If necessary, click **View, Toolbars**, and **Drawing.**

3. On the Drawing toolbar, click the **Text Box** button.

4. Draw a text box on the chart above the legend box, as shown in Figure 6.15, and enter the text shown. (Do not select the chart.)

5. On the Drawing toolbar, click the **Arrow** button.

6. Draw a single arrow as shown, starting at the text box and dragging to the area where the arrow should point.

7. Repeat steps 3-6 and create the "Market downturns" text box and arrow.

8. On the Drawing toolbar, click the **AutoShapes** button, select **Lines,** and click the **Double Arrow.** Place as shown.

9. On the Drawing toolbar, click the **AutoShapes** button, select **Block Arrows,** and click the **Curved Down Arrow.** Place it starting in **Cell D7,** as shown in Figure 6.15.

10. Do not close the file.

Modify Graphics

▶ To modify or change a graphic, select it and press the Ctrl + 1 keys, or right-click and select the Format option. The Format dialog box, appropriate to the type of graphic selected, appears. For example, Figure 6.16 shows the Format AutoShape dialog box. You can modify all the items indicated in the tabs, including properties, where you can set the object to move and size proportionally with the chart.

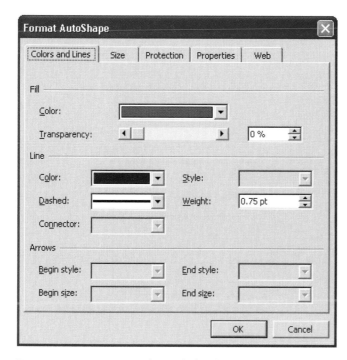

Figure 6.16 Format AutoShape dialog box

1. Continue to work in the open file or open **E6-9** from the Data CD.

2. Click the **Curved Down Arrow** to select it.

3. Press the **Ctrl + 1** keys and make the following changes:
   a. Change Fill Color to **Plum.**
   b. Change Line Color to **Navy.**
   c. In the Size tab, change Rotation to **30 degrees.**
   d. Click **OK.**

4. Position the graphic by dragging it so that the graphic starts in **Cell D9** and the arrow is on the chart.

5. Right-click each graphic arrow on the chart, select **Format Autoshape**, and change the Line Color to **Plum.**

6. Right-click each text box and change the font to bold and the color to **Plum.**

7. Resize the text boxes, if necessary.

8. Save the file as **E6-9.** Close the file.

Insert and Download Graphics and Clip Art

▶ You can use the Insert menu to insert pictures from various sources. Notice the Picture options on the Insert menu, as shown in Figure 6.17, and refer to Figure 6.13 to see the corresponding buttons on the Drawing toolbar. You can use the Insert Picture From File button to insert a company logo, or any picture file.

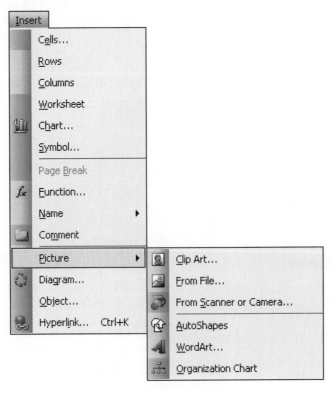

Figure 6.17 Insert menu

▶ When you click the Insert Clip Art button or the Clip Art option on the Insert, Picture menu, the Insert Clip Art task pane appears with search options for clip art, as shown in Figure 6.18.

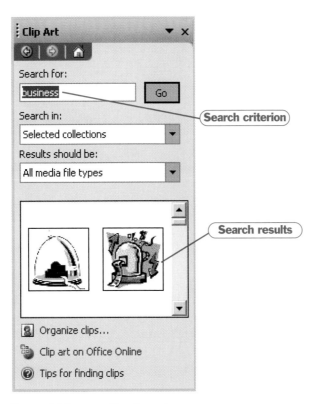

Figure 6.18 Insert Clip Art task pane

▶ Each clip art graphic that appears in the task pane contains an arrow that displays a menu of options. Insert is the first option, and you must click it to place the clip art on your worksheet. Notice the Clip Art list arrow menu in Figure 6.19.

▶ You can view clip art collections directly by clicking Organize clips or, if you have an Internet connection, click Clip art on Office Online. You can select graphics to download from the Web, in Microsoft Clip Art and Media.

▶ Once you select a picture from the collections and insert it, use the set of handles that appear to position and size the object. The Picture toolbar, as shown in Figure 6.20, appears when you select a picture with buttons to modify all aspects of the picture.

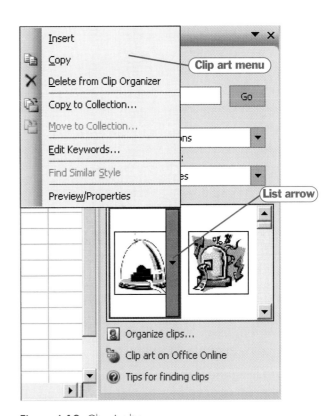

Figure 6.19 Clip Art list arrow menu

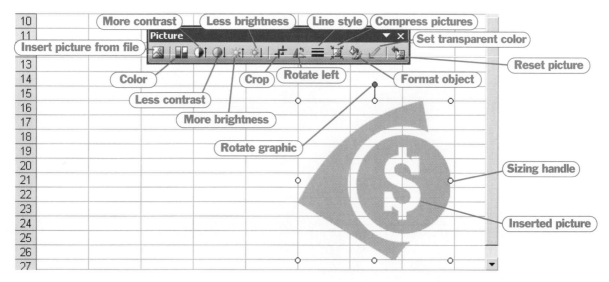

Figure 6.20 Picture toolbar

TRY *it* OUT *E6-10*

1. Open **E6-10** from the Data CD.

2. Click **Insert, Picture,** and **Clip Art.**

3. In the Insert Clip Art task pane, enter **Business** as the search text. Be sure that **All collections** is the Search in value.

4. Click **Go** and locate the clip art, as shown in Figure 6.20. *Note:* If you do not have this graphic, use another appropriate clip art.

5. Click **the list arrow** on the Clip Art menu and click **Insert.**

6. Place the clip art to the right of the data in the range G1:I12.

7. On the Picture toolbar, click the **Less Brightness** button several times to darken the graphic.

8. If you have an Internet connection, view graphics on Office Online:
   a. Click **Insert, Picture,** and **Clip Art.** In the task pane; click **Clip art on Office Online.**
   b. Enter a search criterion for Business and view available clip art.
   c. Close Office Online.

9. Save the file **E6-10.** Close the file.

Create, Modify, and Position Diagrams

▶ *Diagrams* can be added to spreadsheet reports to illustrate materials. They are not based on number values, but can clarify concepts or organization. To add a diagram to a worksheet, click Insert, Diagram, or click the Insert Diagram or Organization Chart button on the Drawing toolbar.

▶ In the Diagram Gallery dialog box that appears, the name and description of each diagram appears as it is selected, as shown in Figure 6.21. The diagram types are organization chart, cycle, radial, pyramid, Venn (showing areas of overlap), and target.

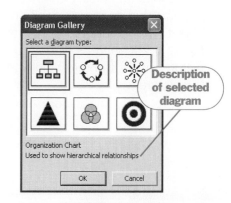

Figure 6.21 Diagram Gallery dialog box

► When you select a diagram and click OK, the Diagram toolbar appears and the diagram is displayed in a frame. You can add text to complete the diagram. Diagrams can be moved, sized, and positioned using the handles and mouse as discussed for charts and graphics.

► To format elements of a diagram, select the element(s) and right-click to open the format dialog box. Or, on the Diagram or Organization Chart toolbar that displays, as shown in Figure 6.22, you can select the AutoFormat button to view and select a series of preset formats.

Figure 6.22 Organization chart and Diagram toolbar

T R Y _it_ O U T *E6-11*

1. Open **E6-11** from the Data CD.

2. If necessary, display the Drawing toolbar by clicking **View, Toolbars, Drawing.**

3. Switch to the Company sheet and click the **Insert Diagram or Organization Chart** button.

4. With the Organization Chart selected, click **OK.**

5. Size and move the chart so that it is placed within the range **A3:G17.**

6. Click the **Autoformat** button on the Organization Chart toolbar.

7. Select the **Beveled Gradient** style. Click **OK.**

8. Enter the text as shown in Figure 6.22.

9. Create the Target diagram using the Text tool, as illustrated in Figure 6.22, and place it within the range **A19:G32.**

10. AutoFormat the diagram using the **Square Shadows** style.

11. Save the **E6-11** file. Do not close the file.

Create Stock Charts

▶ Excel provides four chart subtypes for stock market and price analysis, as shown in Figure 6.23. The High-Low-Close, Open-High-Low-Close, Volume-High-Low-Close, and Volume-Open-High-Low-Close charts can track the changes in stock data during a specific period. The terms used in stock charts are:

Volume: sales volume for the stock for the day

Open: opening price of the stock

High: the highest price for the day

Low: the lowest price for the day

Close: closing price of the stock

▶ In the Open-High-Low-Close chart shown in Figure 6.24, white bars indicate a close that is up in price and black bars indicate a close that is down in price. The data table is a chart option that you can add to show the charted data. To display the table, click the Data Table tab on the Step 3 Chart Options screen and select the Show data table option.

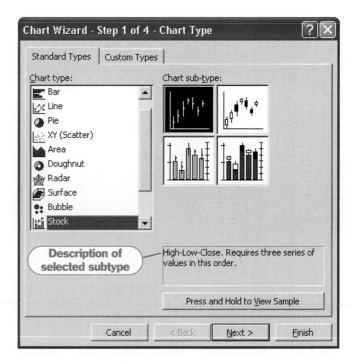

Figure 6.23 Stock chart subtypes

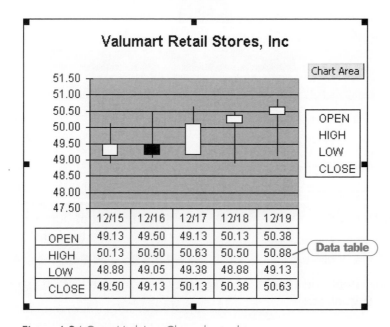

Figure 6.24 Open-High-Low-Close chart subtype

1. Continue to work in the open file or open **E6-12** from the Data CD.

2. Switch to the Stock Prices sheet.

3. Use nonadjacent selection to select the ranges **A5:A10** and **C5:F10.**

4. Click the **Chart Wizard** button and create a stock chart as follows:
   Screen 1: Click **Stock** Chart Type and **Open-High-Low-Close** as the chart subtype; click **Next**.
   Screen 2: Check data series; click **Next.**
   Screen 3: Enter: `Valumart Retail Stores, Inc` as the chart title. On the Data Table tab, click **Show data table**; click **Next**.

   Screen 4: Locate the chart as an object on the Stock Prices sheet; click **Finish.**

5. Place the chart in the range **A12:H35.**

6. Create a Volume-Open-High-Low-Close chart using all the data in the range **A5:F10.** In Step 2, change the data so that the series is arranged by columns. Enter an appropriate chart title and place it on a new chart sheet.

7. Move the Chart1 sheet so that it is the third sheet.

8. Save the file **E6-12.** Close the file.

REHEARSAL

TASK 2

GOAL
To create diagrams and charts to demonstrate and analyze investment portfolio performance for stocks and fund investments

SETTING THE STAGE/WRAPUP
File name: **6.2portfolio**

WHAT YOU NEED TO KNOW

▶ Individuals who invest in stocks and mutual funds, and businesses whose stocks are traded publicly, are interested in tracking the performance of their stocks. The stocks or investments that people or businesses own are said to be in an investment *portfolio*.

▶ The performance of a stock can be compared to the Standard & Poor's (S&P) 500 index and/or to the performance of other stocks in the same industry or sector. The sector average shows the growth of the stocks in that industry. The *S&P 500* is a market index, made up of 500 blue-chip stocks, that is used to predict the general trend of U.S. stocks. If the S&P 500 index increases, it is generally a sign that the market is in a positive mode.

▶ In this Rehearsal activity, you will create and format charts and diagrams to present investment options to Alivea James, the president of In-Shape Fitness Centers. The workbook will consist of a diagram to show the company's investment goals, an analysis of stock funds in the health sector, and a chart to track the prices for a specific stock she is interested in purchasing.

▼ DIRECTIONS

1. Open **6.2portfolio** from the Data CD.

2. On the **Portfolio** sheet, create a pyramid diagram to display the company's investment objectives.
   a. Enter the text in the diagram as shown in Illustration A.
   b. Use the AutoFormat button on the diagram bar to select the **3-D color diagram** style.
   c. On the Page Setup dialog box on the Margins tab, center the worksheet vertically and horizontally.

3. On the **Fund Analysis** sheet, create a bar chart to show the comparison between both health funds, the sector average, and the S&P 500 average.
   a. Use a bar chart and select the clustered bar with a **3-D visual effect** style.
   b. In Step 2, select **columns** as the orientation for the data series.
   c. Chart title: `Investment Returns for Health Funds`
   d. X-axis title: `Years Held`
   e. Place on the Fund Analysis sheet.

4. Place the chart under the worksheet and size it appropriately.

5. Format both axis labels and the legend to **8 point** font.

6. Create the following graphics as shown in Illustration B on page 176:
   a. Arrow to point to TR Health value. Format color to match TR Health bar.
   b. Text box with text as shown.
   c. Establish an Internet connection and find a stock market graphic from Office Online.

7. Format the worksheet and place and size the graphics.

Continued on next page

8. On the **Stock Analysis** sheet for Jackson Laboratories, create a Volume-Open-High-Low-Close chart with a data table. Be sure to plot the data by columns.

9. Place and modify the chart as needed to view data clearly, including formatting the data table and axis labels for **8 point** font.

10. Search for clip art in Medical, Health, or Science categories, and enter the graphics, as shown in Illustration C on page 177.

11. Use fill color to shade the background of all sheets, charts, and chart borders. Format titles and headings to improve their appearance.

12. Print one copy of each worksheet.

13. Save the file **6.2portfolio.** Close the file.

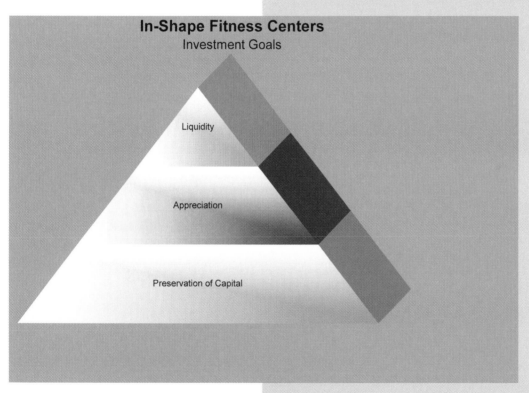

Illustration A

Investment Returns over Years Held
Health Funds compared to Health Sector and S & P 500

Years	TR Health	FD Health	Sector	S & P 500
One	21.88%	10.24%	20.27%	-0.90%
Three	17.97%	12.20%	17.89%	13.15%
Five	16.92%	14.53%	12.42%	18.36%
Ten	19.97%	15.75%	14.62%	17.37%

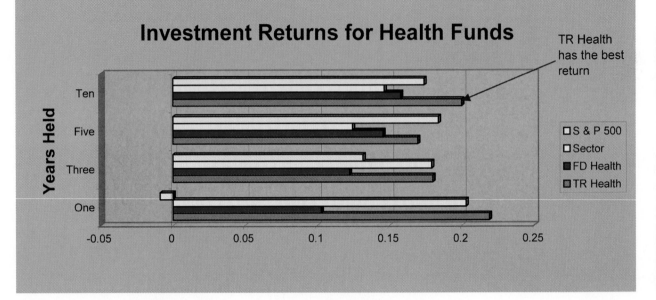

Illustration B

JACKSON LABORATORIES
Stock Prices for the week of June 12

DATES	VOLUME	OPEN	HIGH	LOW	CLOSE
6/12	143567	56.25	58.75	55.85	57.67
6/13	158764	57.67	59.60	57.25	59.60
6/14	149870	59.60	59.60	57.65	57.80
6/15	154334	58.20	60.00	58.20	59.75
6/16	153235	59.75	60.75	59.25	60.25

market-wide downturn

JACKSON LABORATORIES

	6/12	6/13	6/14	6/15	6/16
■VOLUME	143567	158764	149870	154334	153235
OPEN	56.25	57.67	59.6	58.2	59.75
HIGH	58.75	59.6	59.6	60	60.75
LOW	55.85	57.25	57.65	58.2	59.25
CLOSE	57.67	59.6	57.8	59.75	60.25

Illustration C

Cues for Reference

Create Diagrams
1. Click **View, Toolbars,** and **Drawing.**
2. Click **Insert Diagram** or **Organization Chart** button.
3. Select diagram type.
4. Click **OK.**
5. Add appropriate text.
6. Drag to size.

Modify Diagrams
- Right-click diagram element, select Format Diagram or Format Autoshape, and use the dialog box to make settings.

   or

1. Click the **AutoFormat** button on the Diagram or Organization Chart toolbar.
2. Select the diagram style.
3. Click **OK.**

Create Graphics
1. Click **View, Toolbars,** and **Drawing.**
2. Click desired graphic button.
3. Drag to size.

Modify Graphics
1. Right-click graphic.
2. Click **Format** (graphic name).
3. Select formatting changes.
4. Click **OK.**

Size and Place Graphics
1. Click graphic.
2. Use handles to drag to size.
3. Place mouse pointer on graphic until it becomes a four-headed arrow, and drag to location.

Insert Pictures
1. Click **Insert, Pictures, Clip Art.**
2. In task pane, enter search criteria.
3. Click **Go.**
4. Locate required graphic.
5. Click down arrow and click **Insert.**
6. Size and place graphic.

Download Pictures
1. Establish your Internet connection, if necessary.
2. Click **Insert, Pictures, Clip Art.**
3. In task pane, click **Clip art on Office Online.**
   Office XP: In task pane, click **Clips Online.**
4. Enter search criteria. Click **Go.**
5. Click selection box on desired clip.
6. Click **Download 1 item, Download Now.**
7. Right-click clip art in your task pane and click **Insert.**

PERFORMANCE

SETTING THE STAGE/WRAPUP

Act I File name: **6p1.income**
Act II File name: **6p2.expense**
Act III File name: **6p3.stock**

WHAT YOU NEED TO KNOW

Act I

You work in the Finance Department of the Air Land Sea Travel Group. Your department has been asked to create charts for a branch manager meeting about the income and profit figures for the quarter.

Follow these guidelines:

* Open **6p1.income,** and use the Optional Analysis sheet for the chart data.

* Create a column chart on a chart sheet to compare Total Income and Net Income. Format the chart titles, axis labels, and tab name so that the data is easy to read.

* Copy the column chart sheet and do the following:

  * Change the type to a bar chart and the sheet name to **Bar Chart.**

  * On the Source Data step, change the orientation of data from columns to rows to get a different perspective for the bar chart, as shown in the illustration on the next page.

  * Format the data series to display data labels for values.

* Create a pie chart for Total Income and one for Net Income data and place both on the Optional Analysis sheet. Use percentages as labels on the pie sections, and color the charts and chart borders to match the worksheet.

* Add graphics, if necessary, to point out important information, or add the company logo to the charts or worksheet. Download a travel graphic, if possible, to add to the blank area on the bar chart.

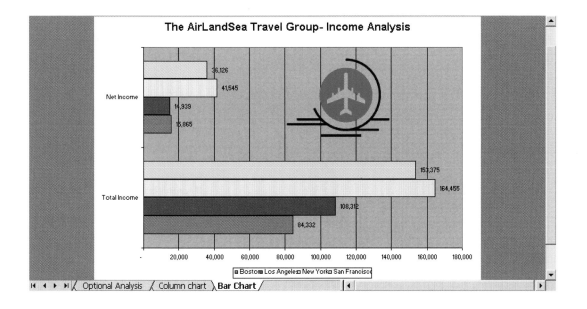

The AirLandSea Travel Group- Income Analysis

* Print the charts and the Optional Analysis sheet.

* Save your work.

Act II

Odyssey Travel Gear has prepared income statements for June 30 and December 31, 2004, by combining data from all its stores. The president is interested in reducing expenses and has asked you to prepare charts to analyze and compare the expenses for the stores for each semiannual report.

Follow these guidelines:

* Open **6p2.expense.** You will use the December 31 and June 30 sheets for your chart data.

* On the December 31 sheet: Create a line chart of the December 31 expense data and place it on the sheet. Use a nonadjacent selection of data, including titles in the range A5:F5 and expense data in the range A12:F14. Format the axis label and legend fonts. Add a travel graphic or logo to the chart. Copy the line chart and place it below the original chart. Change the type to a bar chart, so that there are two charts on the worksheet.

* Repeat this analysis for the June 30 sheet.

* Insert a new sheet and name it: **Expense Dollar**. Create two pie charts to show the total expense dollar for December 31 and June 30, as shown in the illustration on the next page. For each pie chart, select the Expenses labels in Column A and the Totals in Column G and place the pie charts on the Expense Dollar sheet. Be sure to indicate the date in the chart title and add percentage labels.

* Use drawing objects to point out the area of increased expenses and add other graphics, if necessary. Color the background and borders of the pie charts.

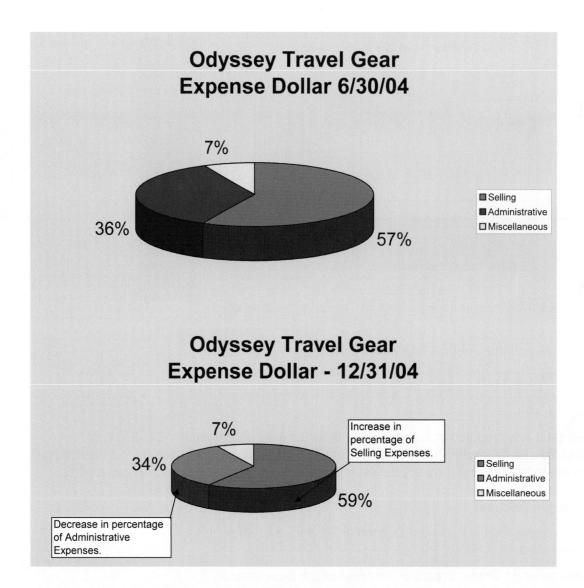

Odyssey Travel Gear
Expense Dollar 6/30/04

7%

36%

57%

■ Selling
■ Administrative
□ Miscellaneous

Odyssey Travel Gear
Expense Dollar - 12/31/04

7%

Increase in
percentage of
Selling Expenses.

34%

59%

■ Selling
■ Administrative
□ Miscellaneous

Decrease in percentage
of Administrative
Expenses.

✦ Print the sheets that contain charts and save and close the file.

Act III

Trilogy Productions is a public corporation whose stock is traded daily on the stock exchange. The management of the company tracks the open, high, low, and close prices of the stock and the volume of shares traded each day. Management also wants to compare the investment value of owning a share in the company to the average return of other companies in their sector, and to the general market or to the S&P 500. The company is in the Media or Entertainment sector.

You have been asked to prepare charts from the stock data provided for the next meeting of the board of directors. Also, you will research the Media sector on the Internet.

Follow these guidelines:

✴ Use the file **6p3.stock.**

✴ On the Investment Analysis sheet, create a column chart to compare the investment growth of Trilogy stock as compared to that of the S&P 500 and the Media sector. Begin your data selection in Cell A6.

✴ Create a line chart of the prices for 2000–2004 and place it on a separate chart sheet named Price History Chart. Use a data table to show the stock prices.

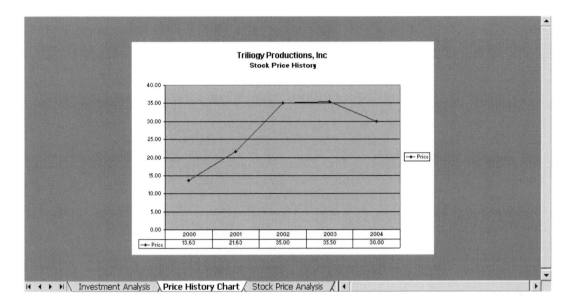

✴ On the Stock Price Analysis sheet, create an Open-High-Low-Close chart. Also use the data to create a Volume-Open-High-Low-Close chart on a separate sheet named Stock Price Chart 11-15.

✴ Format charts and font sizes on titles and axis labels so that they present well. Add a company logo to the charts and/or worksheets. Add drawing objects to point out the increase in the stock price on 11/17 because of a favorable announcement about a new production.

✴ Research the Media, or Media and Entertainment, sector and print a company capsule on one or more media companies, such as Dreamworks, Disney, or Pixar. Also, compare the annual revenue of several such companies on a worksheet or in a report.

✴ You can use a search engine to look up the sector or find it on the www.hooversonline.com Web site. Their home page provides links to the most frequently viewed companies by industry or sector. Select the sector and complete your research.

✴ Print a copy of all worksheets in the file. Save your work.

Integration/Excel and the Web

In this lesson, you will learn to use Excel features to integrate worksheets, charts, and Internet elements into Word documents. You will create a benefit statement, a letter, a travel guide, a quarterly report, and use Outlook features to make apointments and meeting arrangements.

Upon completion of this lesson, you should have mastered the following skill sets:

* Understand integration basics
* Copy and paste data between applications
* Embed worksheets or charts
  * Edit an embedded object
* Insert a worksheet in Word
* Link data between applications
  * Edit a linked object
* Display and use the Web toolbar
  * Paste Web data

* Use Smart Tags to find stock information
* Convert files to alternative file types
* Use Outlook features with Excel
* Create and modify appointments in Outlook
* Create and respond to meeting requests.

Terms
Software-related
  Integration
  Source file
  Destination file
  Embedded file
  Linked file
  Appointments
  Events
  Meetings
Document-related
  Benefits

GOALS
To create documents containing worksheets and charts
To practice using the following skill sets:
- Understand integration basics
- Copy and paste data between applications
- Drag and drop between applications
- Embed worksheets and charts
  - Edit an embedded object
- Insert a worksheet in Word

EXCEL

WHAT YOU NEED TO KNOW

Understand Integration Basics

▶ *Integration* is the sharing or combining of data between Office applications. The source file provides the data, and the destination file receives the data. For example, an Excel chart or worksheet (the *source file*) can provide supporting or visual documentation of materials for a Word document (the *destination file*), as shown in Figure 7.1. You can paste, embed, or link data into the destination file; the choice depends on the features you require for the file.

	A	B	C	D	E	F	G
1	Four Corners Realty Company						
2	Multiple Listing Service						
3	Type	Sq. Ft.	Bedrooms	Baths	View	Maintenance	Price
4	Condo	1200	2	2	Intracoastal	325	145,999
5	Condo	1050	2	1 1/2	Ocean	390	142,900
6	Condo	1400	2	2	No	285	139,900
7	Condo	1000	2	1 1/2	Ocean	385	143,999
8	Condo	1350	2	2	Intracoastal	325	146,545
9							

(Source file)

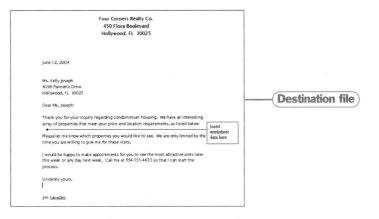

(Destination file)

Four Corners Realty Co.
450 Flora Boulevard
Hollywood, FL 30025

June 12, 2004

Ms. Kelly Joseph
4098 Palmetto Drive
Hollywood, FL 30025

Dear Ms. Joseph:

Thank you for your inquiry regarding condominium housing. We have an interesting array of properties that meet your price and location requirements, as listed below:

Insert worksheet data here

Please let me know which properties you would like to see. We are only limited by the time you are willing to give me for these visits.

I would be happy to make appointments for you to see the most attractive units later this week or any day next week. Call me at 954-555-4433 so that I can start the process.

Sincerely yours,

Jim Savadeo

Figure 7.1 Source and destination files

Copy and Paste Data Between Applications

▶ To copy and paste data between applications, the source and destination files should both be open. You can open either file in its application and then click Start to open the second application. Use the taskbar buttons to switch between applications, as shown in Figure 7.2.

Figure 7.2 Taskbar application buttons

▶ To paste Excel data into a Word document, go to the Excel file and copy the data you need from the worksheet. Then, switch to the Word document and paste it to the location you want in the document.

▶ You can edit a worksheet that you paste into a Word document. However, there is no connection to the original worksheet or to Excel, and you cannot view or change the formulas. Use this method only when updated or linked data is not necessary or when formulas do not need editing.

T R Y *it* O U T *E7-1*

1. In Excel, open **E7-1.xls** from the Data CD.

2. Click **Start, All Programs, Microsoft Office, Microsoft Office Word 2003,** and open **E7-1WD.doc** from the Data CD.

3. Switch to the Excel source file using the taskbar button.

4. Select the worksheet data in the Excel file, **A1:G8**.

5. Click the **Copy** button.

6. Switch to the Word destination file using the taskbar button.

7. Place the insertion point between the first and second paragraphs of the letter, as shown in Figure 7.1.

8. Click the **Paste** button. The worksheet is integrated into the Word document.

9. Change the price of the first condo to: 144,999.

10. Switch back to the Excel file and notice that the change did not affect the worksheet.

11. Close the files without saving them.

Drag-and-Drop Data Between Applications

▶ You can also use the drag-and-drop technique to copy and paste the data if you make both the source and destination documents visible using Window options.

▶ To see both files, right-click the taskbar to display the shortcut menu, as shown in Figure 7.3. Click Tile Windows Vertically; both files become visible on the screen, arranged vertically.

▶ To drag-and-drop the data between files, select the data, point the mouse at the selection until you see the four-headed selection arrow, and press and hold the Ctrl key to copy (rather than move) the data.

Figure 7.3 Taskbar shortcut menu

1. Open **E7-2.xls** and **E7-2WD.doc** from the Data CD.

2. Right-click the **taskbar** and click **Tile Windows Vertically** from the shortcut menu.

3. In the Excel source file, select the worksheet data.

4. Point the mouse at the edge of the selection until the pointer becomes a four-headed selection arrow, and press and hold the **Ctrl** key.

5. Drag-and-drop the worksheet data in the space between the first and second paragraphs of the Word document.

6. If necessary, insert a blank line above and below the worksheet in the document.

7. Double-click on the worksheet in the Word document to change the price of the first condo to **144,999**.

8. Notice that the change did not affect the worksheet.

9. Save and close the files.

Embed Worksheets or Charts

▶ An _embedded file_ is pasted in a destination file as an object that becomes part of the file and that can be edited in its source application. Therefore, when you double-click an embedded Excel file, you can edit it in Excel mode.

▶ To embed a worksheet, copy the worksheet in Excel, and in the Word application, click Edit, Paste Special, and click Microsoft Office Excel Worksheet Object. Notice the source file name in the Paste Special dialog box, shown in Figure 7.4, and the Result text in both Figures 7.4 and 7.5.

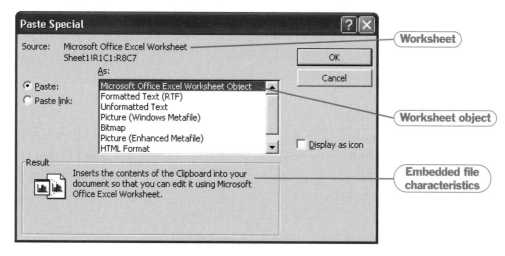

Figure 7.4 Paste Special dialog box for worksheet

▶ To embed a chart, first copy the chart in Excel, then insert the chart in the desired Word document by clicking Edit, Paste Special in the Word application. When the Paste Special dialog box opens, as shown in Figure 7.5, select Microsoft Office Excel Chart Object and click OK.

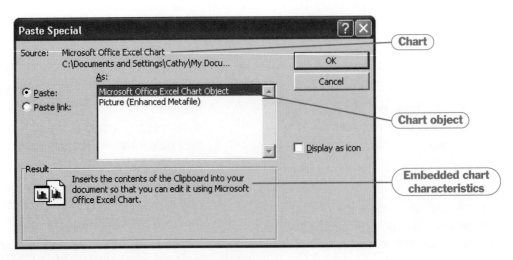

Figure 7.5 Paste Special dialog box for chart

TRY *it* OUT E7-3

1. Open **E7-3WD.doc** and **E7-3.xls** from the Data CD in the appropriate applications.

2. On the Excel worksheet, copy the worksheet in the range **B1:D10.**

3. Switch to the Word document and place the insertion point below the last line of text.

4. Click **Edit, Paste Special**, and select **Microsoft Office Excel Worksheet Object.**

5. Click **OK** and the file is embedded.

6. Switch to the Excel worksheet and copy the chart.

7. Switch to the Word document and place the insertion point below the embedded worksheet.

8. Click **Edit, Paste Special,** and check that **Microsoft Office Excel Chart Object** is selected.

9. Click **OK** and the chart is embedded.

10. Do not close the files.

Edit an Embedded Object

▶ To edit an embedded worksheet or chart, double-click it. You can then edit the file in Excel mode with Excel menus and toolbars. However, your edits change only the destination (Word) file, not the source (Excel) file.

TRY *it* OUT E7-4

1. Continue to work in the open files or open **E7-4.xls** and **E7-4WD.doc** in the appropriate application.

2. Double-click the embedded worksheet.

3. Format the values in the ranges **B4:B5** and **C8:C10** for currency.

4. Click on the document page to leave **Excel** Edit mode. (Notice the edits.)

5. Switch to the Excel file and notice that the source file did not change.

6. Save the files. Close both files.

Insert a Worksheet in Word

▶ On the Standard toolbar in Word, there is an Insert Microsoft Excel Worksheet button that allows you to create a new embedded Excel worksheet. When you click this button, you can select the number of cells for the width and length of the new worksheet, as shown in Figure 7.6. You will be in Excel mode, with Excel menus, and can then create a worksheet with the number of rows and columns you specified.

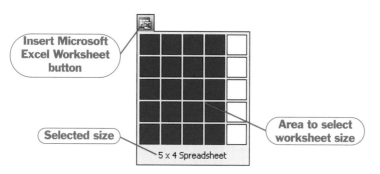

Figure 7.6 Insert Microsoft Excel Worksheet button

TRY it OUT E7-5

1. In Word, open **E7-5WD.doc** from the Data CD.

2. In the space under the first paragraph, click the **Insert Microsoft Excel Worksheet** button.

3. Select an Excel worksheet that is four cells wide by five cells high.

4. Enter the following data:

REIMBURSEMENT CALCULATION			
Dental bill	$350		
First	$100	100%	$100
100–500	$250	80%	
Reimbursement			

5. Enter a formula in **Cell D4** to calculate 80% of 250.

6. Enter a formula in **Cell D5** to add the contents of the range **D3:D4.**

7. Format cells D4 and D5 for currency with no decimals.

8. Adjust column width as necessary.

9. Click the Word document page.

10. Save and close the file.

REHEARSAL

TASK 1

GOAL

To create correspondence and a benefits program document that includes worksheets and a chart

SETTING THE STAGE/WRAPUP

Margins: 1" left and right
Start line: At 2.5"
File names: **7.1benefits.doc**
            7.1rates.xls
            7.1calcmemo.doc

WHAT YOU NEED TO KNOW

▶ New employees are often given an employee manual containing company procedures, policies, and benefits. *Benefits* are medical, dental, life insurance, and other plans that the employer makes available to employees. The employer may provide the benefits or the employee may pay a group rate premium for the policies.

▶ When you integrate Excel worksheets and charts into a Word document, you can size the data and move the margins to align worksheets to the center of the page.

▶ In this Rehearsal activity, you will integrate worksheets and charts from an Excel workbook to enhance the Sutton Investment Group Benefits Program, which is contained in a Word document.

▼ DIRECTIONS

1. Open **7.1benefits.doc** and **7.1rates.xls** from the Data CD in the appropriate application.

2. On Page 4 of the Benefits Program, at the end of the Dental section, enter the following text, as illustrated on page 190: DENTAL PLAN RATES AND BENEFITS.

3. Use Format Painter to copy the format from the paragraph headers to the new text. Format the new text in **Heading 2** style.

4. Switch to the Excel worksheet to copy the data on the Dental sheet and paste it to the Benefits Program.

5. Move the margin manually so that the worksheet is centered horizontally.

6. On the worksheet, use Find and Replace to change the word "Covered" to: 100%.

7. Switch to the Education sheet in the Excel workbook.

8. Copy the worksheet in the range **A1:F22** and use Paste Special to embed the data on Page 6 of the Benefits Program, the last page.

9. Double-click the worksheet in the Word document and edit the title as illustrated; using the **Forte** font, **18 point.** Format the subtitle as **Forte 10pt.**

10. Change the annual contribution by employee to **$1,200**, as illustrated. (Notice the changes in the growth data.)

11. Switch to the Education sheet in the Excel workbook.

12. Select the chart, and use Copy and Paste Special to embed the chart under the worksheet on the last page of the Benefits Program; center the chart on the page.

13. Print a copy of the Benefits Program.

Continued on next page

14. Save both files. Close both files.

15. Open **7.1calcmemo.doc** from the Data CD, as shown on page 191.

16. Insert a worksheet that is 4 cells wide by 5 cells long two lines below the last line of the memo. Enter the following data:

	BILLED	COVERAGE	PAYMENT
Exam	$80	100%	
X-Rays	$120	100%	
Oral Surgeon	$950	75%	
Reimbursement			

17. Calculate the payment for each item and the total reimbursement.

18. Print a copy of the memorandum.

19. Save the file **7.1calcmemo.doc.** Close the file.

Dental

As you read this booklet describing your dental coverage options through the Sutton Investment Group Benefits Program, you should ask yourself when you want from your dental coverage:

1. Do you want the freedom to choose any dentist regardless of cost?

2. Do you want to have lower costs in exchange for receiving dental care from a limited selection of dentists?

3. Would you rather have no dental coverage at all?

WHO IS ELIGIBLE FOR DENTAL BENEFITS?

Regular employees on the domestic payroll of Sutton Investment Group, who have completed at least one calendar month of service as a regular employee and who work at least 20 hours each week are eligible to participate in the benefit options available through Sutton Investment Group Benefits.

You can also enroll your eligible dependents for Medical, Dental and Life Insurance coverage. For Sutton Investment Group Benefits, your eligible dependents are your:

✓ Spouse, and
✓ Unmarried children who are under age 19 (or age 23 if they are full-time students).

Children include natural and legally adopted children, stepchildren living in your home and any other child who is supported solely by you and living in your home. Coverage may be continued beyond age 23 under certain circumstances.

Dependents are not eligible for any benefits under the Benefits Program if they are in military service and may not be eligible if they live permanently outside the United States and Canada.

TRADITIONAL DENTAL PLAN

If you answered, "yes" to the first question, you may want to elect the Traditional Dental Plan. Under the Traditional Dental Plan, you have the freedom to choose any licensed dentist. You also have the option of utilizing the Preferred Dentist Program offered with the Traditional Dental Plan to help control Plan expenses and help lower your out-of-pocket costs.

Page 3

PLEASE NOTE THE FOLLOWING:

This brochure is not a complete description of the Dental Plan offered through Sutton Investment Group Benefits Program. This is only a summary and is not a substitute for the official Plan documents.

The provisions of the official Plan documents and of applicable law will govern in the event of any inconsistency between those provisions and the provisions of this brochure.

Dental Plan Rates and Benefits

Sutton Investment Group
Dental Plan Monthly Premium

Type of Coverage	Employee	Each Dependent
Traditional Dental Plan	27	22
Preferred Dentist Plan	20	15

Dental Plan Benefits

Service	
Examination	100%
X-Rays	100%
Cleaning	100%
Restorative	80%
Endodontists	75%
Oral surgeons	75%
Periodontics	60%
Orthodontics	50%

Page 4

Education

EDUCATION INCENTIVE PLAN

The Sutton Investment Group's Benefits Program will help you pay for your children's education. The Education Incentive Plan helps you plan ahead for the day tuition bills begin to arrive.

WHO IS ELIGIBLE FOR EDUCATION BENEFITS?

Regular employees on the domestic payroll of Sutton Investment Group, who have completed at least one calendar month of service as a regular employee and who work at least 20 hours each week are eligible to participate in the benefit options available through Sutton Investment Group Benefits.

The Education Incentive Plan is designed to help you save from $5,000 to $40,000 (over a five-to-fifteen year period) toward the education costs you anticipate for each of your dependent children. You may choose to set aside an amount needed to reach your savings goal for one or more dependent children in the selected time period as follows:

✓ The maximum goal is $40,000 per child; the minimum is $5,000.

✓ You may have a maximum of four plan accounts per child.

✓ The Company contributes 15% of the amount of your payroll toward Education Benefits.

The funds will accumulate over a period of five to fifteen years, but not beyond your child's 25th birthday. When a plan reaches the level of money you desire, the funds are paid to you. You can request that the account be cancelled and paid out earlier.

HOW TO GET THE MOST OUT OF THE EDUCATION PLAN

The matching contributions from Sutton Investment Group are reported as ordinary income on your W-2 tax form. That means that any money you earn through our investment, are subject to taxes until all the proceeds are paid out to you.

Your savings and the company matching contributions are invested in stocks and bonds. The full amount of your account will automatically be paid to you upon cancellation of this plan.

Page 5

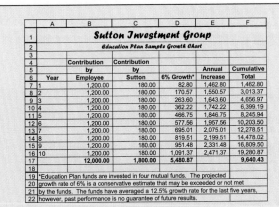

	A	B	C	D	E	F
1			Sutton Investment Group			
2			Education Plan Sample Growth Chart			
3						
4		Contribution	Contribution			
5		by	by		Annual	Cumulative
6	Year	Employee	Sutton	6% Growth*	Increase	Total
7	1	1,200.00	180.00	82.80	1,462.80	1,462.80
8	2	1,200.00	180.00	170.57	1,550.57	3,013.37
9	3	1,200.00	180.00	263.60	1,643.60	4,656.97
10	4	1,200.00	180.00	362.22	1,742.22	6,399.19
11	5	1,200.00	180.00	466.75	1,846.75	8,245.94
12	6	1,200.00	180.00	577.56	1,957.56	10,203.50
13	7	1,200.00	180.00	695.01	2,075.01	12,278.51
14	8	1,200.00	180.00	819.51	2,199.51	14,478.02
15	9	1,200.00	180.00	951.48	2,331.48	16,809.50
16	10	1,200.00	180.00	1,091.37	2,471.37	19,280.87
17		12,000.00	1,800.00	5,480.87		9,640.43
18						
19	*Education Plan funds are invested in four mutual funds. The projected					
20	growth rate of 6% is a conservative estimate that may be exceeded or not met					
21	by the funds. The funds have averaged a 12.5% growth rate for the last five years,					
22	however, past performance is no guarantee of future results.					

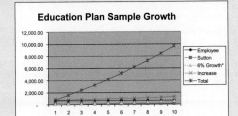

Education Plan Sample Growth

Page 6

Sutton Investment Group

MEMORANDUM

To: Michael Jasko, Brokerage Department

From: Lynn Goodwin, Human Resources

Date: November 15, 2004

Re: Dental coverage

In response to your call regarding the coverage for your dental bills listed below, please note the calculations that will be applied by our Dental Plan administrators. You should be receiving a check shortly.

Dental Bill as per your telephone call:
Exam $ 80
X-Rays $120
Oral Surgeon $950

Insert worksheet here

Cues for Reference

Open Office Files from Multiple Applications
1. Start the first application.
2. Open the file.
3. Click **Start, All Programs, Microsoft Office** and the name of the second application.
4. Open the file.

Office XP:
1. Click Start, Open Office Document.
2. Click the file to open. The second application opens automatically.

Switch Between Applications and Files
- Click the **File** button on the Taskbar.

Copy Files Between Applications
1. In the first application, select the data you want to copy.
2. Click the **Copy** button.

3. Click the **File** button on the taskbar to switch between files and applications.
4. Place the insertion point in the location you want.
5. Click the **Paste** button.

Embed a Worksheet/Chart in a Word Document
1. In Excel, select the worksheet/ chart you want to embed.
2. Click the **Copy** button.
3. Click the **File** button on the taskbar to switch between files and applications.
4. Place the insertion point in the location you want.
5. Click **Edit, Paste Special.**
6. Click **Microsoft Office Excel Worksheet Object** or **Microsoft Office Excel Chart Object.**
7. Click **OK.**

Edit an Embedded Worksheet/Chart
- Double-click worksheet/chart to work in Excel mode.

Insert a Worksheet in Word
1. In Word, click the **Insert Microsoft Excel Worksheet** button.
2. Select the number of cells for the width and length of the worksheet.
3. Release the mouse and make worksheet entries in the worksheet.

GOALS

To create a letter with a linked worksheet with Internet updates

To practice using the following skill sets:

- ✴ Link data between applications
  - ✴ Edit or format a linked object
- ✴ Display and use the Web toolbar
  - ✴ Paste Web data
- ✴ Use Smart Tags to find stock information
- ✴ Convert files to alternative file types
- ✴ Use Outlook features with Excel
- ✴ Create and modify appointments in Outlook
- ✴ Create and respond to meeting requests.

WHAT YOU NEED TO KNOW

Link Data Between Applications

▶ In Lesson 5, you used the Paste Link feature to link data between different workbooks or worksheets. You can also use paste link between different applications to create a *linked file,* so that if the source data changes, it will change in the destination document as well. The Link feature differs from embedding and copying, because a link is a shortcut to the source file; therefore, the data is not actually located in the destination file.

▶ There are three advantages to linking integrated data:

- When you double-click a linked Excel worksheet in a Word destination file, you are brought into Excel to make edits and view formulas.

- Any change you make to the worksheet in either the source or destination documents will appear in both places.

- The destination file is smaller in size than a copied or embedded file because the data remains stored in the source file.

▶ To paste link data between applications, copy the data from the source file, switch to the destination file, click Edit, Paste Special, select the object type, and the Paste link button from the dialog box, as shown in Figure 7.7. You can use this method to link worksheet or chart data to another application.

Paste link selected

Linked file characteristics

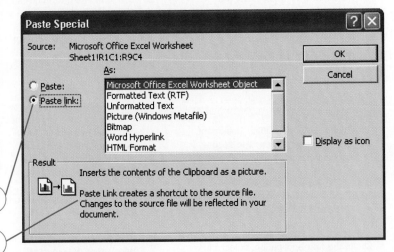

Figure 7.7 Paste Special dialog box with Paste link selected

TRY*it*OUT *E7-6*

1. Open **E7-6WD.doc** and **E7-6.xls** from the Data CD in the appropriate applications.

2. On **E7-6,** the worksheet, select and copy the data in the range **A1:D9.**

3. Switch to **E7-6WD,** the document, and place the insertion point below the last line of text.

4. Click **Edit, Paste Special,** and click **Microsoft Office Excel Worksheet Object.**

5. Click **Paste link** and **OK.** (The worksheet is linked to the document.)

6. Switch to the worksheet and select and copy the chart.

7. Place the insertion point below the linked worksheet.

8. Click **Edit, Paste Special,** and click **Microsoft Office Excel Chart Object.**

9. Click **Paste Link** and **OK.** (The chart is linked to the document.)

10. Size the chart so that it fits on the page.

11. Do not close the files.

Edit or Format a Linked Object

▶ To edit a linked Excel object in a destination file, double-click the object. You will be in Excel, in the source file, and able to use Excel menus to make changes. All changes you make are saved to the original source file and, therefore, automatically update in both locations. If you edit information in the source file, it also automatically updates in the linked location.

▶ You can format an object by selecting it and using the appropriate format buttons on the toolbar, or by right-clicking it and using the Format Object dialog box.

TRY*it*OUT *E7-7*

1. Continue to work in the open files or open **E7-7WD.doc** and **E7-7.xls** in the appropriate applications.

2. In the Word file double-click the worksheet data.

3. In Excel mode, select the graphic and delete it.

4. Switch to the Word document, using the taskbar button.

5. Right-click the worksheet and click the **Update link** option, if necessary, to view the edit.

6. Switch to the Excel workbook and change the value in **Cell B9** to **33.54%.** Notice the change in the chart.

7. Switch to the Word document, repeat Step 5, and notice the updates.

8. Center the worksheet and chart horizontally. Select each and click the **Center** alignment button.

9. Save both files as **E7-7WD.doc** and **E7-7.xls.** Close both files.

Display and Use the Web Toolbar

▶ The Internet provides access to countless Web sites, many of which contain information you can use to enhance your presentation, provide documentation, or provide current data for worksheets and other Office applications.

► Every Office application has a Web toolbar that allows you to use Internet features seamlessly with your application. Click View, Toolbars, and Web to display the toolbar, as shown in Figure 7.8. You must have an Internet Service Provider (ISP) to use the Web toolbar.

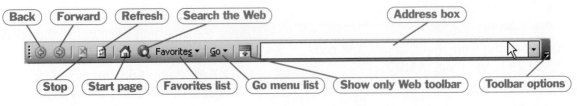

Figure 7.8 Web toolbar

► To locate information on the Web, you may use the Search button and search engines on the Web or enter the address of a known site. When you are online and click the Search button, a screen displays, similar to that shown in Figure 7.9. You can select an area to search or enter a text string in the Search box.

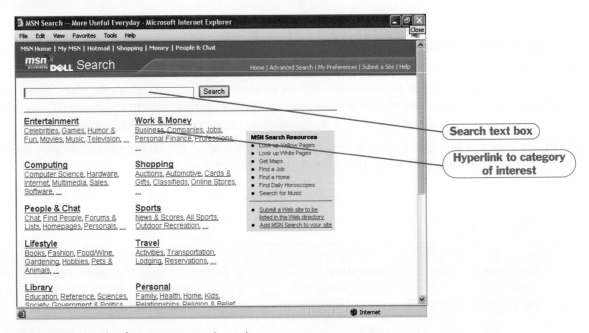

Figure 7.9 Sample of an Internet search window

TRY*it* OUT E7-8

1. Open **E7-8** from the Data CD.

2. Click **View, Toolbars,** and **Web.**

3. Click the **Search the Web** button on the Web toolbar. (Your Internet connection is established, and a search window displays.)

4. Enter "currency rates" in the Search box. Click **Search.**

5. Select the **moneycentral.msn.com** site titled World Currency Rates.

   Note: If you knew this address, you would enter it in the address box on the Web toolbar to go there directly.

6. View the currency rates Web site.

7. Continue to work on this Web site in the next Try*it*Out.

Paste Web Data

▶ You can copy Web data using Edit, Copy while in the Web browser. Sometimes you must copy an entire block of data even though you only need a portion of it. When you switch back to Excel, you can click Paste and use the Paste Options button to select one of three options: Keep Source Formatting, Match Destination Formatting, or Create Refreshable Web Query, as shown in Figure 7.10. You can delete any unnecessary data once it is in Excel.

Figure 7.10 Paste options for Web paste

TRY it OUT *E7-9*

1. Continue to work in **E7-8** and on a currency rate Web site or on moneycentral.msn.com.

2. On the Web site, select the table of currency rates provided, click **Edit, Copy,** or right-click and click **Copy.**

3. Switch to Excel and paste the table to the bottom of E7-8.

4. Click the **Paste Options** button on the screen and click **Match Destination Formatting.**

5. Move the data from the Per US$ column to the appropriate currency listed on the worksheet.

6. Replace the contents of Cell D4 with today's date (press Ctrl+;).

7. Delete the currency table from the bottom of the worksheet.

8. Save the file as **E7-9.** Close the file. *Note:* Solution file will vary since rates change daily.

Use Smart Tags with the Internet

▶ Smart tags for financial symbols utilize the Internet to provide updated information to your worksheet. As noted in Lesson 2, if Smart Tags do not display on your computer, click Tools, AutoCorrect options, and then on the Smart Tags tab, click Label data with smart tags and check Financial Symbol, if it is not already selected.

▶ When you enter a stock symbol, the Smart tag options button provides Internet research options for that company, as shown in Figure 7.11. You can use this feature just to view stock quotes, company reports, or recent news, or you can insert a refreshable stock price. This price will update in the file as long as you are online. The refreshable stock price provides a considerable amount of information and should be placed on a separate sheet.

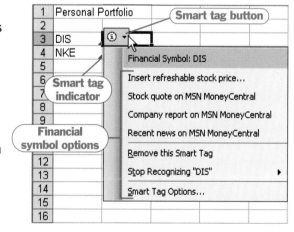

Figure 7.11 Smart tag options for financial symbols

1. While online, open **E7-10** from the Data CD.

2. Click the **Smart tag options** arrow for the **DIS** (Disney) financial symbol.

3. Select **Stock quote on MSN MoneyCentral.**

4. View the current quote and close the window.

5. Click the **Smart tag options** arrow for the **NKE** (Nike) financial symbol.

6. Select **Company report on MSN MoneyCentral.**

7. View the report and close the window.

8. Click the **Smart tag options** arrow for **DIS.**

9. Select **Insert refreshable stock price** and click **OK** to place data on a new sheet.

10. Rename the sheet **Disney.**

11. Repeat the procedure for the **NKE** symbol.

12. Save the file as **E7-10.** Close the file. You may wish to open the file on another day, and click the **Refresh Data** button on the External Data toolbar, to view the refreshed data.

Convert Files to Alternative File Types

▶ Excel generally saves files using the .xls format. However, you can save worksheets using other file formats for data transportability, including various versions of Excel, Lotus and Quattro Pro, and text formats, by selecting the file type in the Save As dialog box.

▶ When you save a file in a text format, you will be warned that Excel formats and features will not be preserved and that only the active sheet is saved. You can save in text formats such as .txt (tab separated values) or .csv (comma separated values), as shown in Figure 7.12. Columnar data will be separated either by tabs or commas, depending on your choice. Each row of data will end in a carriage return.

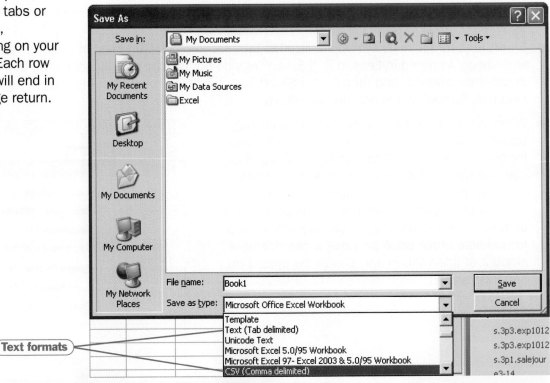

Figure 7.12 Save As dialog box

1. Open **E7-11** from the Data CD.

2. Save the file as a Text (Tab delimited) file, **E7-11txt.**

3. Click **OK** at the warning that only the active sheet will be saved.

4. Click **Yes** to acknowledge that Excel formats will be lost.

5. Save the file as a CSV (Comma delimited) file, **E7-11csv.**

6. Click **OK** and **Yes** to bypass the two warning messages.

7. Close the file.

8. In Word, open **E7-11txt.** Note the tab separated values.

9. In Word, open **E7-11csv.** Note the comma separated values.

10. Close the Word files.

Use Outlook Features with Excel

▶ If you are using Outlook as your communications software, you can use its features to help you work with Excel. Refer to Appendix I for an introduction to Outlook.

▶ There are many ways to use Outlook with Excel worksheets or tasks, such as:

- Send worksheets via e-mail to anyone in your Contacts list.
- Use the calendar or task feature to schedule preparation or review of financial reports.
- Use the journal to document decisions or record interactions made with someone on your contacts list.
- Distribute reports to members of your committee or staff via e-mail.
- Use the calendar and/or journal to document dates and times for billing clients for your time.

▶ If you wish to send a file from Excel, click File, Send to, and Mail Recipient. Then, you can click the To button to select the recipient from your contacts list, as shown in Figure 7.13.

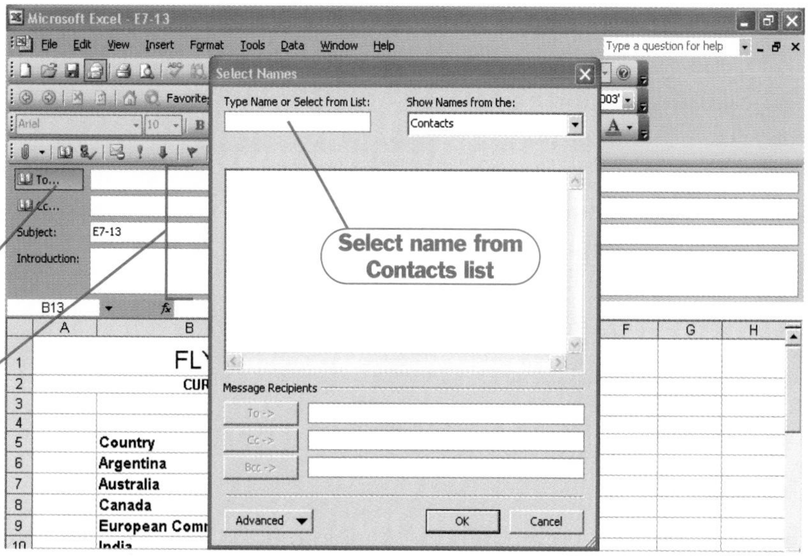

Figure 7.13 Select Names dialog box and e-mail screen in Excel

1. Open Outlook and your Internet connection. In Excel, open **E7-12**

2. Click **File, Send to,** then **Mail Recipient.**

3. Click the **To** button and select a contact from your Outlook address book. (If you have no contact entries, click **Cancel** and enter an e-mail address in the To box.)

4. Note that the file name is the Subject.

5. In the Introduction box enter **These are the current currency rates.** *Note: Outlook Express users will not get an Introduction box.*

6. Click the **Send** button.

7. Switch to Outlook.

Create and Modify Appointments and Events in Outlook

Create New Appointments and Events

▶ *Appointments* are activities that you schedule in your calendar that do not involve inviting other people or reserving resources. *Events* are activities that last 24 hours or longer such as trade shows, seminars, or vacations. In Calendar view, to add an appointment or an event, click New on the Standard toolbar, as shown in Figure 7.14, or double-click the day (or hour) on the calendar, as shown in Figure 7.15.

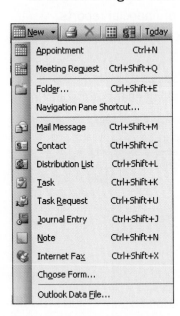

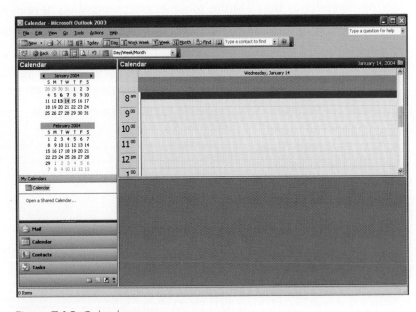

Figure 7.14 New button options in Outlook

Figure 7.15 Calendar view

▶ Input the information into the Appointment dialog window that displays, as shown in Figure 7.16. You can set a reminder to occur at a specified interval before an appointment or event. Reminders pop up on your screen at the designated time when Outlook is running, even if it is not your active application. When a calendar item has a reminder setting, a bell symbol appears in the daily and weekly calendar views.

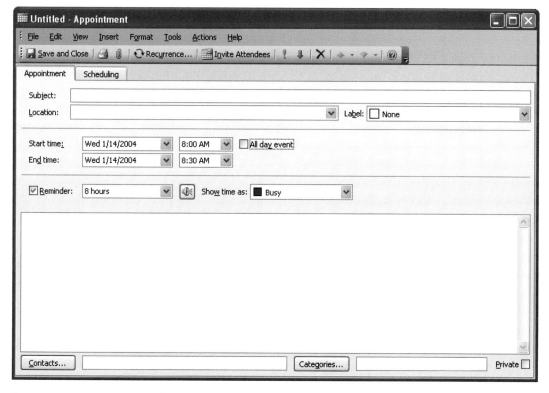

Figure 7.16 Appointment dialog window

▶ The Show time as window is used to insert an identifying colored bar on the left side of an appointment or event in the 1-day and 5-days views: Busy–blue, Free–clear, Tentative–blue/white striped, Out of Office–purple.

▶ You can make an appointment or event private so that it is hidden from others who may share your calendar from their own networked computers by clicking the Private box in the lower-right corner of the screen. The sharing computers will only see that the time has been blocked out but you will have the details. A key symbol appears next to private appointments or events in the daily and weekly calendar views on your computer.

T R Y i t O U T *E7-13*

1. In Outlook, click the **Calendar View** button.

2. Click the **New** button on the Standard toolbar.

3. Enter: `Lunch with Marilyn Ellis` in the Subject box in the Appointment Window.

4. In the Location box, enter: `ALS Travel Group executive dining room`.

5. Select next Thursday's date, using the **Start Time** down arrow to display the Calendar.

6. Set **12:00 PM** for a Start time. If the Start Time and End Time Hour boxes are not visible, click on **All day event** to deselect that option.

7. In the End Time location, set the same date and select **1:00 PM** for the time.

8. In the Notes section (the large text box) in the lower portion of the Appointment Dialog Box, enter: `Bring employee list`.

Continued on next page

9. Click **Reminder** to set the feature and select 2 hours. A reminder will display at 10 a.m. that day.

10. Click the list arrrow for the **Show time as** setting. Select **Out of Office.**

11. Click on the **Private** box in the lower right corner of the screen.

12. Click on **Save and Close** on the Appointment dialog box toolbar.

13. Click on the **5 Work Week** button and select the appropriate week from the calendar displayed at the left to view your settings.

Create Recurring Appointments with Labels

▶ If the appointment or event will be one of a recurring series, click the Recurrence button on the tool bar of the Appointment dialog window. Settings for pattern and range of the appointment can then be set on the Appointment Recurrence dialog box, as shown in Figure 7.17. The recurring symbol will appear next to any recurring appointments or events.

▶ In the Appointment dialog box you can label an appointment according to several categories, including Business, Personal, Must Attend, Vacation, and Travel Required, by selecting from the items on the drop-down list, as shown in Figure 7.18. This feature displays the appointment in a distinct color; for example, the Business label displays your appointment with a blue highlight; the Personal label appears in green.

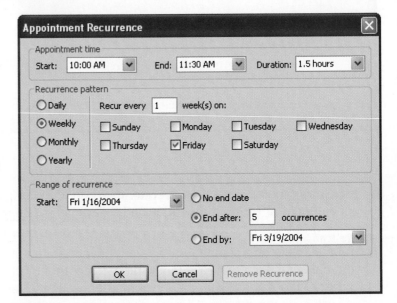

Figure 7.17 Appointment Recurrence dialog box

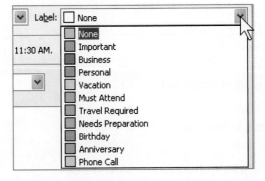

Figure 7.18 Label settings on Appointment window

You should be in Calendar View in Outlook.

1. On the Calendar, double-click on next Friday's date, or click **New, Appointment.**

2. Enter: `Training Session` in the Subject box in the Appointment Window.

3. In the Location box, enter: `Conference room`.

4. Note that the Start time date is set. Set **10:00 AM** as the Start time. *Note: Click on **All day event** to deselect that option if the time options are not available.*

5. In the End time location, select **11:30 PM** for the time.

6. In the Notes section in the lower portion of the Appointment dialog box, enter: `Salesmanship Course`.

7. Click **Reminder** to set the feature and select **1 hour**.

8. Click the **Recurrence** button on the toolbar.

9. Make settings for a weekly pattern on Friday that ends after 5 occurrences, as shown in Figure 7.17. Click **OK.**

10. Click the list arrow for Label on the Appointment window and select **Must Attend.**

11. Click on **Save and Close** on the Appointment dialog box toolbar.

12. Click on the **5 Work Week** and the **31 Month** buttons, changing the selected weeks as necessary to view your settings.

Modify or Delete Appointments and Events and Set Level of Importance

▶ You can double-click an appointment or event in any Calendar view to open its Appointment dialog window for purposes of viewing details or changing information. Edit the appointment or event information as desired. To delete a calendar item, right-click it and select Delete from the shortcut menu.

▶ When an appointment is created, it has a neutral level of importance. Use the Appointment window toolbar to change the level of importance of an appointment or event to either High or Low.

You should be in Calendar View in Outlook.

1. Click on the Thursday luncheon date on the Calendar.

2. Double click **Lunch with Marilyn Ellis** on the Calendar.

3. Select the text **ALS Travel Group executive dining room** in the Location box and enter: `The Trolley Restaurant`.

4. Use the drop-down list in the Start time box to change the appointment to **12:30,** ending at **1:30.**

5. Click the **Importance: High** button on the toolbar.

6. Click **Business** in the Label box.

7. Click **Save and Close** on the toolbar.

8. Click Thursday's date in the Calendar window to display the rescheduled appointment.

Create and Respond to Meeting Requests

▶ *Meetings* are appointments to which you invite others and/or reserve resources. To add a meeting to your calendar and send requests to others to attend, click the list arrow to the right of the New button and select Meeting Request from the options that display. (See Figure 7.19.)

▶ The Meeting dialog window that displays, as shown in Figure 7.20, is very similar in appearance to the Appointment dialog window. However, the Meeting dialog window has a To... box for listing the e-mail addresses of persons you are inviting. When you click the To button, the Contacts in your Address book display so that you can select participants. When you click the Send button on the toolbar, the completed meeting request is sent to the invitees.

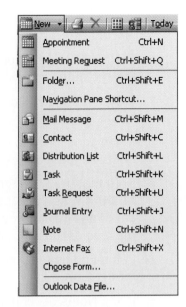

Figure 7.19 New button list options

Send button

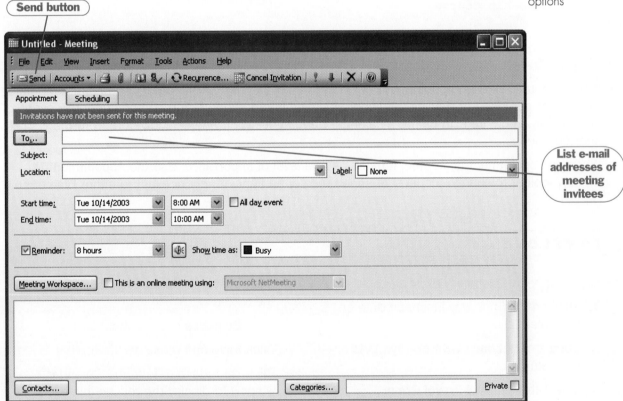

List e-mail addresses of meeting invitees

Figure 7.20 Meeting dialog window

You should be in Calendar View in Outlook.

1. Click the list arrow to the right of the **New** button and select **Meeting Request.**

2. Click the **To...** button.

3. Select a participant from your Contacts list and click **Required.**

4. Select a second participant from your Contacts list and click **Required.** Click **OK.**

5. In the Subject box, enter: `Meet with Tom Bukata`.

6. In the Location box, enter: `Trilogy Productions, New York Office`.

7. Click tomorrow's date and **2:30 PM** for the Start time.

8. Click tomorrow's date and **3:30 PM** for the End time.

9. Set a three-hour reminder.

10. In the Notes section, enter `Presentation of communications proposal.`

11. Click **File, Close;** click **Yes** when asked if you want to save changes. The meeting request is saved in the calendar.

12. Click **No** when asked if you want to send.

Respond to Meeting Requests

▶ When one of your invitees receives a meeting request from you, it will appear as an e-mail, as shown in Figure 7.21. He or she can Accept, Tentatively accept, Decline, or Propose a new Time using the buttons on the Meeting toolbar. The response will be sent back to your e-mail address.

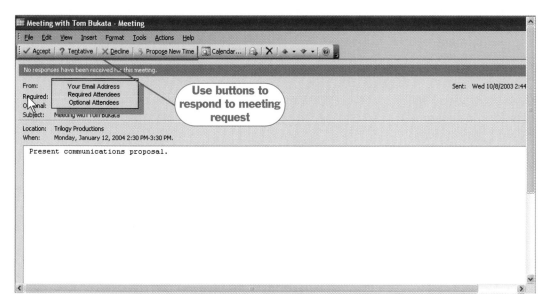

Figure 7.21 Meeting Request response dialog window

REHEARSAL

TASK 2

 GOALS
To create a letter with a linked worksheet with Internet updates
To schedule an appointment and to e-mail a worksheet

SETTING THE STAGE/WRAPUP

Margins:	Default
Start line:	At 1"
File names:	7.2stocks.xls
	7.2broker.doc

WHAT YOU NEED TO KNOW

▶ Investment or brokerage firms can manage your stock or equity holdings. Most brokerage firms now also have online brokerage Web sites so that you can buy or sell stocks directly in your account.

▶ Stocks represent your ownership certificates in publicly traded companies. The current prices of stocks vary with the economy and market conditions, and can be obtained on your investment firm's Web site or on other "quote" sites.

▶ In this Rehearsal activity, you will work on projects for Mr. Calarco, as follows: update his portfolio worksheet with current stock prices from the Internet, integrate the worksheet into a letter to the Sutton Investment Group, save the worksheet as a text file, use the information in an e-mail, and schedule a meeting with Mr. Roxbury.

▼ DIRECTIONS

1. Open **7.2stocks.xls** from the Data CD and view the names and symbols of the stocks in the portfolio.

2. Verify that the Web toolbar is displayed and search for a site that shows stock quotes, or go to www.stockquotes.com or www.moneycentral.msn.com.

3. Use the stock symbol from the worksheet and look up each current market price. Copy and paste each price to the Excel worksheet, matching the destination format.

4. Enter a formula, multiplying market price by shares owned, to find the market value of the shares in **Column G,** as shown in Illustration A.

5. Find the total market value and correct number formats, if necessary.

6. Open **7.2broker.doc** from the Data CD.

7. Copy and paste link the Excel worksheet from **7.2stocks.xls** to the Word letter after the second paragraph, as shown in Illustration B.

8. Switch back to the Excel worksheet and check the formula for the cost total in **Column E.**

9. Edit and correct the formula.

10. Switch back to the Word document to check if the changes updated to the linked file. Right-click the linked file and update, if necessary.

11. Print a copy of the letter.

12. Save both files. Close **7.2broker.doc**.

13. Save the Excel file as a .csv (comma separated values) file and name it **7.2stockcsv.** Close the file and Excel.

14. In Word, open the **7.2stockcsv** file.

Continued on next page

15. Delete the rows of text above and below the names of the stocks and the values to the right of the number of shares, and insert the text as shown in Illustration C.

16. Send the document by e-mail to Mr. Calarco's original stock broker. Use an address provided by your instructor or from your Contacts list. Change the subject to **Account transfer.**

17. Close and save the Word file.

18. In Outlook, create an appointment with Mr. Roxbury of Sutton Investment Group for one week from today at 4:30 p.m. in his office.

19. Close all files.

JAMES CALARCO
Investment Record

COMPANY NAME	SYMBOL	SHARES	DATE BOUGHT	COST	MARKET PRICE	MARKET VALUE
Nike Inc	NKE	300	09/30/02	12,345.32		
MicroSoft	MSFT	200	06/04/02	5,342.54		
Bank of America	BAC	200	10/14/03	16,342.32		
J P Morgan Chase	JPM	100	11/25/03	3,632.98		
Intel	INTC	100	07/07/04	3,132.89		
TOTALS				**28,450.73**		

Find current market prices for stocks on the Internet

Enter formulas to find total market value for each stock

Illustration A

Check formula   Find totals

James Calarco
460 West End Avenue
New York, NY 10023
Phone: 212-555-3432

March 5, 2005

Mr. Marcus Roxbury
Sutton Investment Group
34562 Corona Street
Los Angeles, CA 90001

Dear Mr. Roxbury:

I am interested in transferring my portfolio of investments to your firm as I am dissatisfied with my current brokerage firm. After our telephone conversation and my visit, I feel that your company can provide me with the service I require.

A list of my investments with the current market value is provided below:

Please send me the necessary forms. I look forward to hearing from you.

Sincerely yours,

James Calarco

Paste link worksheet here

Illustration B

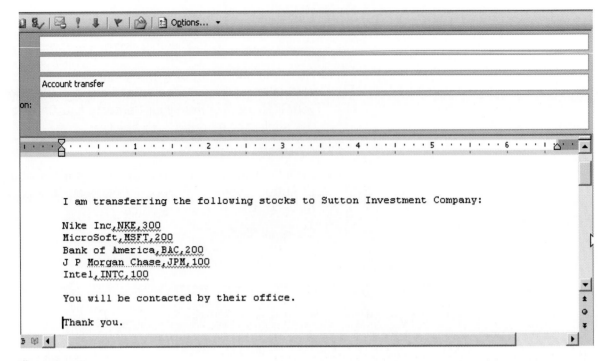

Account transfer

on:

I am transferring the following stocks to Sutton Investment Company:

Nike Inc,NKE,300
MicroSoft,MSFT,200
Bank of America,BAC,200
J P Morgan Chase,JPM,100
Intel,INTC,100

You will be contacted by their office.

Thank you.

Illustration C

View Web Toolbar
- Click **View, Toolbars,** and **Web.**

Paste Link Between Applications
1. Open files you want to link.
2. In source file, select data to link.
3. Click the **Copy** button.
4. Switch to desination file.
5. Click **Edit, Paste Special.**
6. Click **Paste Link** and select object to link.
7. Click **OK.**

Edit a Linked File
- Edit data in either the source or destination files. (The data will change in both locations.)

Copy and Paste from the Web
1. Locate data you need from Web site.
2. Select data.

3. Click **Edit, Copy,** or right-click and choose **Copy** option, or click **Copy** button.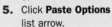
4. Switch back to Excel.
5. Click **Paste** button.
   or
5. Click **Paste Options** list arrow.
6. Select appropriate Paste option.

Save Excel File as a Text File
1. Click **File, Save As.**
2. Click the list arrow in the Save as type box.
3. Select the .txt or .csv format.
4. Click **Save.**

E-mail Word or Excel files
1. Click **File, Send to, Mail Recipient.**
2. Select a contact from the Address book in the To box or enter an address.

3. Change the subject line, if necessary.
4. Type introductory comments, if necessary.
5. Click the **Send** button.

Schedule an Appointment
1. Click **File, New,** and **Appointment.**
   or
   Click **Actions, New Appointment.**
2. Enter subject in Subject box.
3. Enter location in Location box.
4. Click the arrow to open the Start time calendar.
5. Set Date.
6. Set Start time.
7. Set End time.
8. Set Categories, Notes, or Recurrence as necessary.
9. Click the **Save and Close** button.

PERFORMANCE

SETTING THE STAGE/WRAPUP

Act I File names: 7p1.travel guide.doc
7p1.tips.doc

Act II File names: 7p2.income.xls
7p2.quarterly.doc

EXCEL

WHAT YOU NEED TO KNOW

Act I

You work in the Marketing Department of the Air Land Sea Travel Group. Your company has developed Travel Guide 2005, a handbook that contains practical information for the traveler. Your supervisor would like to add several pages on currency conversion tips, including information about the euro and the latest exchange rates for a list of currencies.

Follow these guidelines:

* Open **7p1.tips.doc, 7p1.currency.xls,** and **7p1.travel guide.doc** from the Data CD.

* In **7p1.currency.xls:**

  * Enter today's date in Cell B2.

  * Find what one unit of the currency in Column A is in U.S. dollars for each item. You may find currency converters using a search engine or you can go to www.moneycentral.msn.com and use their conversion feature. Enter the information in Column B.

* In **7p1.tips.doc:**

  * Use Office Online to insert a clip art object in the second paragraph representing "foreign currency."

  * Integrate the worksheet data from **7p1.currency.xls** into the location above the "What is the EURO" paragraph.

  * Select the entire document and copy and paste it to **7p1.travel guide.doc,** immediately before the References page. Center the linked sheet.

* In **7p1.travel guide.doc,** check that the new information copied correctly and that the pagination is appropriate. (The References material can be placed at the bottom of the 7p1.tips text.)

* Save all files and print a copy of the new guide.

Act II

You work in the Accounting Department of the Air Land Sea Travel Group. Your department has developed an income workbook for the second quarter consisting of income statements for all offices, a consolidated income statement, an income analysis, and two charts.

The chief financial officer, Tyler Willem, has prepared a document explaining the quarterly results and would like the worksheet data integrated into one report. The report will be sent electronically to all managers, officers, and interested parties, and a printed copy will be kept on file. Tasks will be entered into Outlook and a meeting will be scheduled to review these reports.

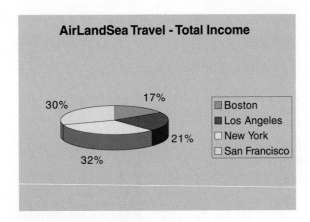

Follow these guidelines:

✻ Open **7p2.income.xls** and **7p2.quarterly.doc** from the Data CD.

✻ Link the worksheets and chart data where appropriate, as indicated in the document.

- Remove the parenthetical insert instructions from the document.

- Remove the text box and arrow from the Net Income pie chart.

- Create a hyperlink with appropriate text to the worksheet.

- Adjust the size of the objects so that the pages do not have large blank areas, and center the objects horizontally on the page.

✻ Research the current outlook for the travel industry on the Internet. Summarize your findings in several sentences. (If you quote or copy data from a Web site, be sure to indicate your source.)

✻ Write an e-mail, addressed to managers and officers, that includes the following:

- Announce that the quarterly report and income data are attached.

- Report on the current outlook for the travel industry, as per your research.

- Attach the quarterly report and income files to the e-mail.

✻ In Outlook, schedule a conference call with the staff in the store for 4:00 p.m. EST two days from today. Send an e-mail to the store informing them of the conference call meeting.

✻ Print a copy of the quarterly report. Save and close all files.

PERFORMING WITH EXCEL
ADVANCED UNIT

Budgets and Templates

In this lesson, you will learn to use Excel features to combine information across worksheets and workbooks, including consolidating, sharing, and merging workbooks. You will also learn to create and edit a workbook template to display a budget.

Upon completion of this lesson, you should have mastered the following skill sets:

* Create a workspace consisting of two or more workbooks
* Consolidate data from two or more worksheets
* Define and modify workbook properties
* Create a workbook template
* Create a new workbook based on a user-created template
* Change the default file location for templates
* Edit a workbook template
* Create a shared workbook
* Track, accept, and reject changes in workbooks
* Merge workbooks

Terms
Software-related
Workspace
Data consolidation
Properties
Template
Shared workbook
Track changes
Merged workbook
Document-related
Consolidated budget
Quarterly budget
Divisional sales report

TRYOUT

GOALS

To create a consolidated budget with specific properties

To practice using the following skill sets:

⚹ Create a workspace consisting of two or more workbooks

⚹ Consolidate data from two or more worksheets

⚹ Define and modify workbook properties

TASK 1

EXCEL

WHAT YOU NEED TO KNOW

About Advanced Excel

▶ Excel is a powerful spreadsheet tool that you can use to analyze, chart, and manage data for personal, business, and financial purposes. Using Excel, you can produce worksheets, charts, and databases, as well as publish data to the Web.

▶ Advanced Excel allows you to build on your basic knowledge of Excel to conduct analyses of financial data, manage and share data with other users, and customize records and reports.

▶ As discussed in Introductory Excel, the default Excel screen shows the most frequently used toolbar buttons from the Standard and Formatting toolbars on one row. To correlate your screen with the illustrations in this text, display both toolbars fully, as shown in Figure 8.1, by clicking the Toolbar Options arrow and selecting the Show Buttons on Two Rows option.

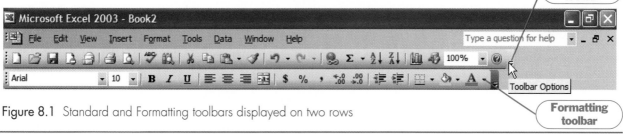

Figure 8.1 Standard and Formatting toolbars displayed on two rows

Create a Workspace Consisting of Two or More Workbooks

▶ A convenient way to access two or more workbooks on the same screen is to create a workspace. A *workspace* is a shared location in which you store several workbooks.

▶ To create a workspace, first open each workbook. Size and place the workbooks so that they are displayed in the position you want.

▶ Click File, Save Workspace, as shown in Figure 8.2. Enter the name of the workspace in the Save Workspace dialog box.

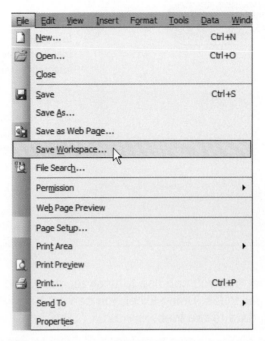

Figure 8.2 Save Workspace

▶ You can close each workbook individually, or you can press the Shift key while you click File, Close All to close them simultaneously.

▶ When you open the workspace, all of the workbooks in it are available on your screen. They appear in the same format in which you saved them. A workspace file is identified in the Open dialog box by the file type, "Microsoft Office Excel Workspace" with an .xlw extension, and by an enhanced file icon. If you make any changes to the individual workbooks, the changes should be saved.

TRY*it*OUT *e8-1*

1. Open **E8-1A** from the Data CD.

2. Open **E8-1B** from the Data CD.

3. Arrange the files on your screen by clicking **Window, Arrange.** Select **Horizontal.** Click **OK.**

4. Click **File, Save Workspace.** Name the workspace: **E8-1budws.**

5. Select a location in which to save the workspace. Click **Save.**

6. Press the **Shift** key and click **File, Close All.**

7. Open the workspace by clicking the **Open** button, then click the name of the workspace. Click **Open.**

8. Click **Window** on the menu bar. Then click **Arrange, Vertical.** Click **OK.**

9. Format column C in each worksheet for Currency with no decimal places.

10. Click **File, Save Workspace** and accept the same workspace file name. Click **Save.**

11. Click **Yes** to replace the existing workspace file.

12. Click **Yes to All** to save workbook changes.

13. Press the **Shift** key and click **File, Close All** to close both files.

Consolidate Data from Two or More Worksheets

▶ *Data consolidation* is a way to combine the information from different workbooks or worksheets and store it in another workbook or worksheet. This function is useful when different departments or companies have budgets, financial statements, or other business documents that contain data to be combined or summarized.

▶ If you are consolidating data from different workbooks, you can make the workbooks more accessible and easier to work on by creating a workspace that contains them.

▶ To consolidate data:

- Open all workbooks with the data you want to consolidate. If several worksheets are contained in one workbook, open that file.

- Create a new workbook (or worksheet) that contains the labels for the consolidated data. Copy and paste the data from one of the worksheets to the consolidated worksheet.

- Select a cell for the destination of the consolidated numeric data. The data is filled in starting from that location.

- Click Data, Consolidate. The Consolidate dialog box opens, as shown in Figure 8.3.

▶ The Function drop-down list contains several operations including Sum, Count, Product, and statistical functions such as Average. Select the function from the list that should be applied during the consolidation process.

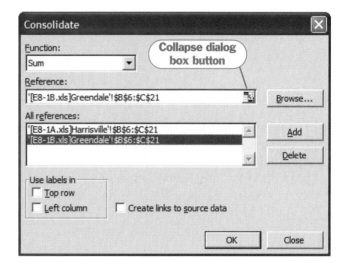

▶ You can enter the cell references to consolidate in the Reference box. Or, click the Collapse Dialog Box button, as shown in Figure 8.3, go to the first worksheet, and select the cells containing the data you want to consolidate. Click the Expand Dialog Box button, as shown in Figure 8.4, to return to the dialog box.

Figure 8.3 Consolidate dialog box

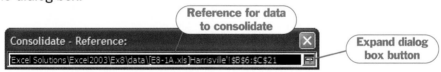

Figure 8.4 Consolidate - Reference box

▶ Continue to select all of the data you want to combine, moving across worksheets or workbooks and clicking Add for each range of cells you select. When you have completed the data selection, the All references box in the Consolidate dialog box lists the data that you combined. If there are any errors in this list, select the incorrect reference and click Delete.

▶ Notice that the Consolidate dialog box provides the option to create links to the source workbooks and to use labels as the consolidating criteria.

1. Open **E8-2budws,** a workspace file, from the Data CD.

2. Click the **New** workbook button and save the workbook as **E8-2cons.**

3. Use the taskbar to return to **E8-1A** and select the range **A5:A21.**

4. Copy the data and paste to **E8-2cons,** starting at Cell A5. Adjust column width.

5. In **E8-2cons,** click **Cell B6.**

6. Click **Data, Consolidate.** In the Consolidate dialog box, leave the Function as Sum.

7. Click the **Collapse Dialog Box** button.

8. Go to the file **E8-1A** and select the range **B6:C21.**

9. Click the **Expand Dialog Box** button. Click **Add.**

10. Repeat Steps 7, 8, and 9 for the **E8-1B** file.

11. Click **OK.** *Note that the data from both worksheets are consolidated in the new workbook. You may have to adjust column widths.*

12. Copy the headings in Rows 1:3 from the **E8-1A** worksheet to the top of **E8-2cons.** Change Row 2 to: `Budget: Consolidated.`

13. Save and close all files.

Define and Modify Workbook Properties

▶ File or workbook *properties* are facts about a file that provide identification or information for using, sorting, or organizing the file. Some properties include statistics that are automatically updated by the Office application, while others are preset and require text input. You can display the Properties dialog box while in a workbook by clicking File, Properties. The dialog box contains five tabs which display or provide settings for various types of properties. On the Summary tab, shown in Figure 8.5, you can enter text to summarize workbook contents. The Keywords property allows you to enter keywords that you can later use for search purposes.

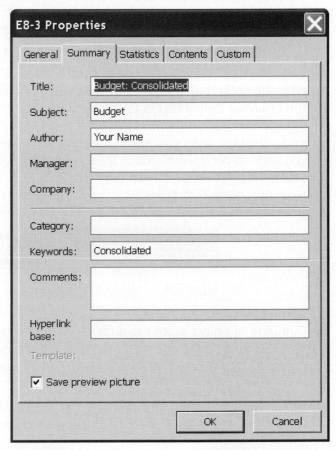

Figure 8.5 Properties dialog box, Summary tab

► Custom properties provide additional information for routing, identification, or sorting purposes. Custom property data can be text, numbers, dates, or yes/no values. You can create a name for the property or use one from the list. The data type must be selected and then the property value entered. When you click Add, the property will appear in the Properties section on the Custom tab, as shown in Figure 8.6.

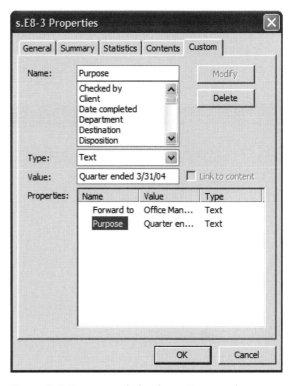

Figure 8.6 Properties dialog box, Custom tab

TRY *it* OUT e8-3

1. Open **E8-3** from the Data CD.

2. Click **File, Properties** and select the **Summary** tab, if necessary.

3. Enter the Title, Subject, and Keywords data as illustrated in Figure 8.5. Enter your name as author, if it is not already there.

4. Select the **Custom** tab in the Properties dialog box.

5. In the **Name** box, select **Forward to.**

6. In the **Type** box, select **Text** as the Value type, if necessary.

7. In the **Value** box, enter `Office Managers`. Click **Add.**

8. Set a custom property for **Purpose,** with a Text value of `Quarter 3/31/03`.

9. Click **Add** and click **OK.**

10. Save and close the file.

▶ You can view properties for an open file using File, Properties. However, if you are looking for a file with specific properties, you can view the properties in the Open dialog box by clicking the Views button and selecting Properties. As shown in Figure 8.7, the property data on the right of the dialog box describes the file so that you can locate the information you need.

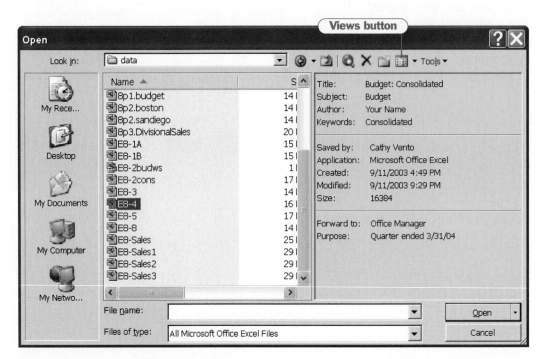

Figure 8.7 Open dialog box, Properties view

▶ Properties may be modified by editing entries. Click Modify on on the Custom tab of the Properties dialog box to make changes. You can delete a Custom property by selecting the property and clicking the Delete button.

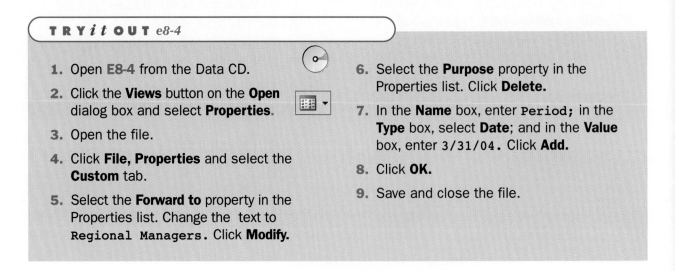

TRY it OUT e8-4

1. Open **E8-4** from the Data CD.

2. Click the **Views** button on the **Open** dialog box and select **Properties**.

3. Open the file.

4. Click **File, Properties** and select the **Custom** tab.

5. Select the **Forward to** property in the Properties list. Change the text to **Regional Managers**. Click **Modify.**

6. Select the **Purpose** property in the Properties list. Click **Delete.**

7. In the **Name** box, enter **Period;** in the **Type** box, select **Date**; and in the **Value** box, enter **3/31/04**. Click **Add.**

8. Click **OK.**

9. Save and close the file.

REHEARSAL

TASK 1

GOAL
To create a consolidated budget with specific properties

SETTING THE STAGE/WRAPUP
File names: 8.1Sutton1
8.1Sutton2
8.1CBws
8.1SuttonCB

WHAT YOU NEED TO KNOW

▶ Consolidated financial statements combine corresponding financial information from two or more sources, such as departments within a company or within affiliated companies owned by a larger corporation. A *consolidated budget* combines the planned or actual income and expenses from several departments or companies.

▶ A *quarterly budget* is prepared four times a year to reflect income and expense activity up to the end of each three-month period. These statements are usually dated the last day of March, June, September, and December. Quarterly budgets are often used to compare proposed income and expenditures with actual income and expenditures.

▶ In this Rehearsal activity, you will create a consolidated quarterly budget to show the accumulated activity for two departments that are part of the Sutton Investment Group. You will combine departmental data for the proposed and actual budgets for the second quarter and set worksheet properties.

DIRECTIONS

1. Open **8.1Sutton1** and **8.1Sutton2** from the Data CD.

2. Enter formulas to calculate the Total Expenses and the Net Income for the Budget and Actual columns on both worksheets, as shown in Illustration A on the next page.

3. Size and position the two files according to your preference.

4. Save a workspace for these two files as **8.1CBws** and, when prompted, save **8.1Sutton1** and **8.1Sutton2.**

5. Copy the headings in Rows 1:4 from one of the files to a new workbook.

6. Copy the labels in Column A from one of the files to the new workbook.

7. Consolidate the data from each of the two departments for the columns labeled Budget and Actual.

8. Edit titles on the new sheet reflecting that it is a consolidated budget for the second quarter. Include the company name, report title, and quarter ending date.

9. Add border rulings, as necessary, as shown in Illustration B on the next page.

10. Set the following properties for the consolidated worksheet.
    a. Summary properties: Enter the title (business name), subject, and your name; use Budget as the category and Consolidated Budget as the keywords.
    b. Custom properties: Department: Mutual Funds and Securities; Forward to: Managers and Acctg. Depts.

11. Print a copy of the consolidated budget.

12. Save the file as **8.1SuttonCB** and close all files.

Sutton Investment Group
Mutual Funds Division
For Quarter Ended June 30, 2004

	Budget	Actual
Revenue		
Net Sales/Fees	120,000	132,450
Expenses:		
Advertising	4,500	3,475
Depreciation	7,500	7,500
Interest	13,000	13,909
Miscellaneous Expenses	600	625
Rent	10,500	10,500
Salaries/Commissions	60,000	65,090
Supplies	2,300	2,532
Travel	5,000	5,200
Total Expenses		
Net Income		

Enter formulas to calculate Total Expenses and Net Income on both department worksheets

Illustration A

Sutton Investment Group
Consolidated Budget
For Quarter Ended June 30, 2004

Edit label for Consolidated Budget

	Budget	Actual
Revenue		
Net Sales/Fees		
Expenses:		
Advertising		
Depreciation		
Interest		
Miscellaneous Expenses		
Rent		
Salaries/Commissions		
Supplies		
Travel		
Total Expenses		
Net Income		

Consolidate data from department worksheets to obtain combined values

Copy and paste labels from one of the departmental budgets

Illustration B

Cues for Reference

Create a Workspace
1. Open each workbook.
2. Size and position each workbook on screen.
3. Click **File, Save Workspace.**
4. Enter name of new workspace and click **Save.**

Consolidate Data
1. Open a new workbook.
2. Copy and paste, or enter, any labels you want in new workbook.
3. Select cell where consolidated data will begin.
4. Click **Data, Consolidate.**
5. Select function you want to use.
6. Select references for each worksheet from which you are consolidating data using the Collapse and Expand Dialog Box buttons.
7. Click **Add** after each one.
8. Click **OK.**

TRYOUT

GOALS

To create, edit, and use a budget template
To practice using the following skill sets:
- ✳ Create a workbook template
- ✳ Create a new workbook based on a user-created template
- ✳ Change the default file location for templates
- ✳ Edit a workbook template

TASK 2

WHAT YOU NEED TO KNOW

Create a Workbook Template

▶ A *template* is a workbook that has settings such as fonts, formatting styles, graphics, formulas, and labels, but no data. It serves as an outline or guide into which you can enter data. A template is convenient to use when a business utilizes the same forms, documents, or reports repeatedly. Templates also facilitate data consolidation because worksheet data is always in the same position on template-developed forms.

▶ You have already learned that Excel provides some standard templates, both in the Templates folder and on the Microsoft Office Online Web site. In this section you will learn how to create your own templates.

▶ To create a template, enter all of the data and formats you want to appear on the worksheet, including labels, constant values, fonts, borders, and formulas. When you enter a formula without data, it will result in zeros, an error message, or a dash, until you enter data.

▶ When the file is completed, click File, Save As. In the Save As dialog box, as shown in Figure 8.8, name the file and select Template from the Save as type drop-down list. Although saved templates are located, by default, in the Templates folder, you can change the file location. *Note: Templates have the file extension .xlt.*

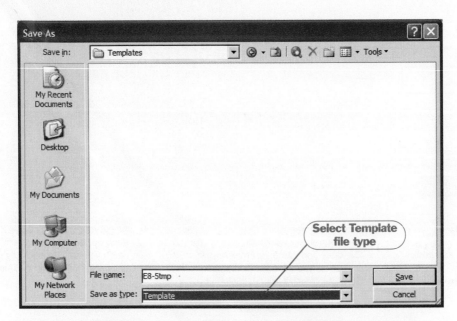

Figure 8.8 Save As dialog box

1. Open **E8-5** from the Data CD.

2. Format **Cells A5:E8** so that the labels are Bold and the cell background color is Gray-25%.

3. Note that some formulas have already been entered.

4. Enter formulas in Cells **B15:D15** to find Gross Profit. *Hint: Net Sales – Cost of Goods Sold.*

5. Enter formulas in Cells **B21:D21** to find Total Expenses.

6. Format **Columns B, C,** and **D** for commas with no decimal places.

7. Format **Column E** for percentage with two decimal places.

8. Click **File, Save As.** Name the file: **E8-5tmp.**

9. Select **Template** as the file type.

10. Click **Save** and close the file.

Create a New Workbook Based on a User-Created Template

▶ Once you have created a template, you can use it to create workbooks containing data. When you want to use your template, click File, New. Select the On my computer link in the task pane. Your saved template should appear in the General tab, as shown in Figure 8.9. Double-click the template file to open it.

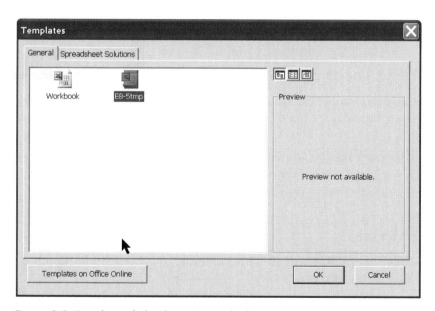

Figure 8.9 Templates dialog box, General tab

▶ When you open a template file, Excel adds a 1 to the file name so that if you save the file, it does not overwrite the template. Once the template is open, enter the data and save the file as an Excel workbook with a new name (.xls file extension). When you close the newly named file created from the template, the template stays in its original form.

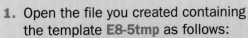

1. Open the file you created containing the template **E8-5tmp** as follows:
   a. Click **File, New,** and click the **On my computer** link in the task pane.
   b. Double-click the file name **E8-5tmp** in the General tab. Notice that the file opens as **E8-5tmp1.**

   or, open **E8-5tmp** from the Templates folder on the Data CD.

2. Enter the following in **Cell D3**: 9/30/2004 and format date, if necessary.

3. Enter the following data in the appropriate cells as follows:

	Budget	Actual
Net Sales	10000	11000
Cost of Goods Sold	5000	5400
Advertising/ Promotions	500	600
Salaries/Wages	3000	3100
Supplies	400	500
Taxes	300	400

4. Click **File, Save As** and select an appropriate folder in the Save in box.

5. Save the file as: **E8-6.** Close the file.

6. Open **E8-5tmp** using the procedure in Step 1 and notice that the template is intact.

7. Do not close the file.

Change the Default File Location for Templates

▶ By default, templates are located in the Templates folder, as shown in Figure 8.9. However, you can select a different folder manually by changing the Save in folder on the Save As dialog box, shown in Figure 8.8.

▶ You can create a new folder within your working folder for templates and save templates to that folder. To open a template from your new folder, switch to that folder, and set the Files of type box to Templates or All Microsoft Office Excel Files.

Edit a Workbook Template

▶ To edit a workbook template, open the template file and make any changes in the style, formatting, labels, or graphics that are necessary.

▶ If you want to replace the original template, save as a Template file type with its original file name. If you want to save your revisions as a new file, assign a new name and save it as a Template file type.

1. Continue to work in the template **E8-5tmp** or open **E8-7tmp** from the Templates folder on the Data CD.

2. Insert a row below **Row 18.** Enter `Rent`.

3. Use the fill handle to bring formulas down in columns D and E.

4. Click **File, Save As.** Navigate to where you want to save your templates.

5. On the Save As dialog box, click the **Create New Folder** button.

6. When the New Folder dialog box apears, name it **My Templates** and click **OK.**

7. Select **Template** in the **Save as type** box.

8. Click the **Save in** list arrow and locate the new folder.

9. Save the file as a template, **E8-7tmp.**

10. Close the file. Click **File, Open** and navigate to the My Templates folder to open the template and view the saved changes. *Note: Be sure that the Files of type setting is for All Microsoft Office Excel Files or for Templates in that folder.*

11. Close the file.

REHEARSAL Again

TASK 2

GOAL
To create, edit, and use a budget template

SETTING THE STAGE/WRAPUP
File names: 8.2FC
8.2FCQB (template)
8.2QBGreendale
8.2QBFrankford
8.2QBCons

WHAT YOU NEED TO KNOW

▶ Companies budget for a financial quarter in advance. To analyze for trends, they later compare the actual figures to the budgeted values to determine the percent of increase/decrease.

▶ Formulas in templates with blank data cells will result in zeros, an error message, or a dash, until you enter data.

▶ In this Rehearsal activity, you will create and edit a template for a quarterly budget form for the branches of the Four Corners Realty Company. You will use the template to create a budget for two branches and then create a regional consolidatated budget.

▼ DIRECTIONS

1. Open **8.2FC** from the Data CD. Use the illustration on the next page as a guide.

2. Merge and center the title in **Row 1** over the range **A1:E1.**

3. Format **Columns B, C,** and **D** to use the Accounting format for numbers, and **Column E** to use Percentage format with two decimal places, as shown in the illustration on the next page. *Hint: Click **Format, Cells,** click the **Number** tab, and select the appropriate format.*

4. Insert the formulas to compute **Total Expenses, Net Income, Increase/Decrease,** and **%Increase/Decrease,** as follows:
   a. In **Cell B20,** enter a formula to find the **Total Expenses** and use the fill handle to drag this formula to **Cell C20.**
   b. In **Cell B22,** enter a formula to find the **Net Income** and use the fill handle to drag this formula to **Cell C22.**
   c. In **Cell D7,** enter a formula to find the **Increase/Decrease** of the Actual over the budgeted items *(Hint: C7-B7* and use the fill handle to drag this formula down **Column D,** through **Cell D22.**
   d. In **Cell E7,** enter a formula to find the percent Increase/Decrease *(Hint: D7/B7)* and use the fill handle to drag this formula down **Column E,** through **Cell E22.**
   e. Clear the formulas from **Rows 8, 9,** and **21.**
   f. Adjust lines and borders, if necessary.

5. Save it as a **Template** file type and name it: **8.2FCQB.**

6. Close the file.

7. Open the template file **8.2FCQB** from the Templates folder on the Data CD.

Continued

8. You will create two separate budgets for the Greendale and Frankford Offices for the quarter ending June 30, 2004. Prepare the Greendale budget first using the **8.2FCQB** template. Save it as a workbook, **8.2QBGreendale.** Then, open the template, **8.2FCQB**, and prepare the Frankford budget. Save it as a workbook, **8.2QBFrankford.**

    a. Enter the Office name in **Cell D2.**

    b. Enter the quarter ended date in **Cell B3.**

    c. Enter the following data for the **Budget** and **Actual** columns:

| | Greendale | | Frankford | |
	Budget	Actual	Budget	Actual
Net Sales	100,000	120,000	86,000	88,000
Advertising	6,000	6,500	3,500	3,400
Depreciation	1,000	1,000	800	800
Insurance	700	700	575	575
Legal/Accounting	6,000	7,000	4,000	4,150
Miscellaneous Expenses	500	700	425	400
Rent	8,200	8,200	6,000	6,000
Repairs/Maintenance	600	750	500	450
Salaries/Commissions	50,000	60,000	43,000	44,000
Supplies	500	600	350	340
Utilities	800	850	675	700

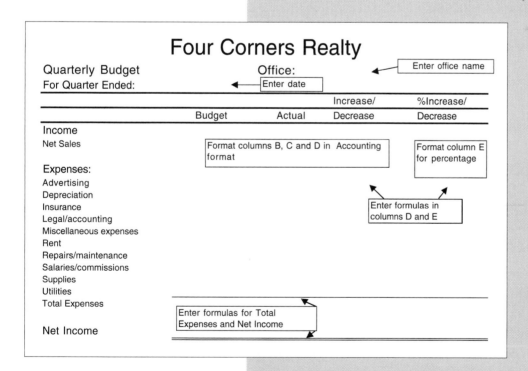

9. Open the **8.2FCQB** template and use the fill color button to shade the range **A1:E3** to **Pale Blue.**

10. Save the revised template: **8.2FCQB.**

11. Create a consolidated budget including data from Cells B7:C19 from the budgets for both offices.
    a. The template and the Greendale and Frankford budgets should be open.
    b. On the template, enter Consolidated in **Cell D2** and enter the quarter ended date in **Cell B3.**
    c. Consolidate the data from both budgets onto the template.
    d. Save the file as a workbook, **8.2QBcons.**
    e. Print a copy of the consolidated budget.

12. Close and save all files

TRYOUT

TASK 3

GOALS

To create a divisional sales report using shared and merged workbooks
To practice using the following skill sets:
* Create a shared workbook
* Track, accept, and reject changes in workbooks
    * Track changes
    * Accept and reject changes
* Merge workbooks

WHAT YOU NEED TO KNOW

Create a Shared Workbook

▶ There may be instances in which you want more than one user to work on the same file in order to add or modify data. For example, several people may have responsibility for adding data to files containing budgets, sales reports, or inventories.

▶ Excel has a feature that allows you to create a *shared workbook,* a workbook that a number of users can edit. When you create a shared workbook, changes made by each user are marked with a comment. You can review these changes and decide whether to accept or reject them. Later, all of the modifications you accept can be put together in the form of a merged workbook, a workbook that incorporates the selected changes made by various users of the file.

▶ To create a shared workbook, click Tools, Share Workbook. The Share Workbook dialog box opens, as shown in Figure 8.10. In the Editing tab, check the box: Allow changes by more than one user at the same time. If you are finished at this point, click OK.

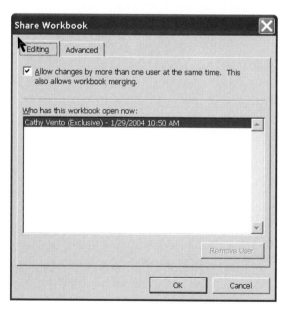

Figure 8.10 Share Workbook dialog box — Editing tab

► In the Advanced tab, as shown in Figure 8.11, you can select how long you will track changes, how frequently the file will be updated, and what to do when suggested changes conflict with each other. When you have made your selections, click OK.

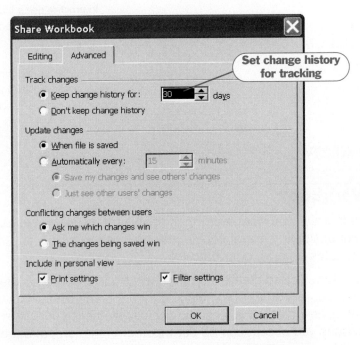

Figure 8.11 Share Workbook dialog box — Advanced tab

► A good way to avoid confusion when you create a shared workbook is to keep a copy of the original workbook in a separate file, which is not open to changes. Any users who make changes must start with the shared workbook and save their modified files from it with a new name. When you are ready to merge workbooks, work with the original workbook and the modified workbooks saved from this workbook. If a user saves the modifications without renaming the file, you will still have a copy of the original workbook.

TRY it OUT *e8-8*

1. Open the file **E8-8** from the Data CD.

2. Save the file as **E8-Sales** in your Solutions folder.

3. Click **Tools, Share Workbook.**

4. In the Editing tab, check the box labeled **Allow changes by more than one user at the same time.**

5. In the Advanced tab, select **Keep change history for** and change to 15 **days.**

6. Click **OK.** Click **OK** at prompt to save file.

7. Close the file. *Note: To maintain a single shared file, hereafter you will use the E8-Sales file from the Data CD .*

8. Have another user open **E8-Sales,** from the Data CD, and change **Cell D9** to: $500,000. If this is not possible, do it yourself.

9. Save the file as **E8-Sales1** and close the file.

Track, Accept, and Reject Changes in Workbooks

Track Changes

▶ When multiple users are working on a file, you will probably want to monitor the changes made—who made the change, and the date and time each person did so. Excel has a feature that permits you to *track changes,* which allows you to view the modifications made to a file by each user.

▶ To track changes in a file, click Tools, select Track Changes, and click Highlight Changes. The Highlight Changes dialog box opens, as shown in Figure 8.12.

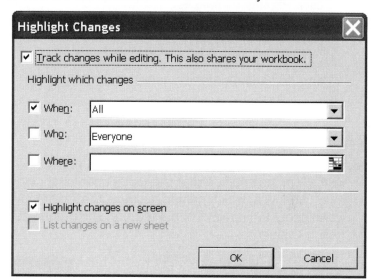

Figure 8.12 Highlight Changes dialog box

- Check the box labeled Track changes while editing.

- Check the box labeled When to select which changes you want to review.

- Check the box labeled Who to select a specific person's changes or leave blank to show everyone's changes except your own.

- Check the box labeled Where if you want to select a specific range of cells for tracking changes. Otherwise, the whole worksheet will be tracked.

- Check the box labeled Highlight changes on screen if you want to view the changes as you enter them.

- The List Changes on a new sheet box is dimmed and only available after the workbook is saved as a shared workbook. It provides a history of changes on a separate history worksheet.

- Click OK.

▶ Excel then displays a message that the action will save the workbook. Click OK. The title bar will show the file name with [Shared] added to it.

▶ Once you have enabled Track Changes, any cell you modify will contain a dark triangle in the upper-left corner. When you move the mouse over the cell, a comment appears indicating who made the change and when. The comment also gives the original data contained in the cell. Figure 8.13 shows an example of a comment.

	A	B	C	D	E	F	G	H	I
1									
2			Four Corners Realty						
3			Sales Report						
4									
5	Region	Quarter1	Quarter2	Quarter3	Quarter4				
6	North	$ 400,000.00	$ 500,000.00	$ 450,000.00	$ 800,000.00				
7	East	$ 600,000.00	$ 700,000.00	$ 800,000.00	$ 900,000.00				
8	South	$ 500,000.00	$ 700,000.00	$ 650,000.00	$ 850,000.00				
9	West	$ 800,000.00	$ 650,000.00	$ 600,000.00	$ 800,000.00				
10									
11	Total	$2,300,000.00	$2,550,000.00	$2,500,000.00	$3,350,000.00				
12									

Cathy Vento, 1/29/2004 5:02 PM: Changed cell E9 from ' $850,000.00 ' to ' $800,000.00 '.

Figure 8.13 Example of comment when tracking changes

1. Open **E8-Sales** from the Data CD.

2. Save the file as **E8-Sales2.**

3. Click **Tools,** select **Track Changes,** and click **Highlight Changes.**

4. In the **Highlight Changes** dialog box, check the box **Track changes while editing.** Leave the box labeled **When** checked and the default selection as

Since I last saved. Check the box **Highlight changes on screen.**

5. Click **OK.** Click **OK** if a message appears.

6. Change **Cell E9** to: **$800,000.** Press **Enter.** Place the mouse over the cell to view the comment.

7. Save and close the file.

Accept and Reject Changes

▶ Once modifications have been made to a file by any user, you can accept changes. In other words, you can decide that the modifications should stay on the worksheet. You can also reject changes, which means deciding that the modifications should not be made to the worksheet. To implement this feature, click Tools, select Track Changes, and click Accept or Reject Changes.

▶ The Select Changes to Accept or Reject dialog box opens, as shown in Figure 8.14. You can decide to review changes by time, user, or location on the worksheet. Check any of the relevant boxes labeled When, Who, or Where. Each contains a drop-down menu from which you can make a selection. Click OK.

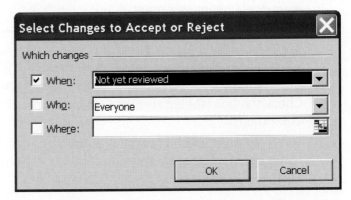

Figure 8.14 Select Changes to Accept or Reject dialog box

▶ The Accept or Reject Changes dialog box opens, as shown in Figure 8.15. Each change made to the worksheet appears, one at a time. You can click Accept or Reject for each change. If you want to accept or reject all of the changes, click Accept All or Reject All.

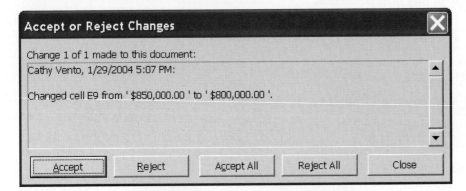

Figure 8.15 Accept or Reject Changes dialog box

1. Open the file **E8-Sales2** that you saved in the previous Try it Out.

2. Click **Tools,** select **Track Changes,** and click **Accept or Reject Changes.**

3. In the Select Changes to Accept or Reject dialog box, leave the **When** box checked

and the selection as **Not yet reviewed.** Click **OK.**

4. In the Accept or Reject Changes dialog box, click **Accept.**

5. Save and close the file.

Merge Workbooks

▶ As you learned earlier in this lesson, if several different users have made changes to a file, you will likely want to create a single, or merged, workbook that contains all of the changes.

▶ A *merged workbook* must be created from files saved from the same original shared workbook. Thus, you must first designate the workbook as a shared workbook. All users must start with this workbook and save their modified files from it.

▶ To create a merged workbook, first open the original shared workbook. Click Tools, Compare and Merge Workbooks. When prompted by Excel to save the file, click OK.

▶ The Select Files to Merge Into Current Workbook dialog box opens, as shown in Figure 8.16. Select the file that contains modifications and click OK. If there are additional files you want to merge into the workbook, click Tools, Compare and Merge Workbooks again. Repeat the instructions in this step as many times as necessary.

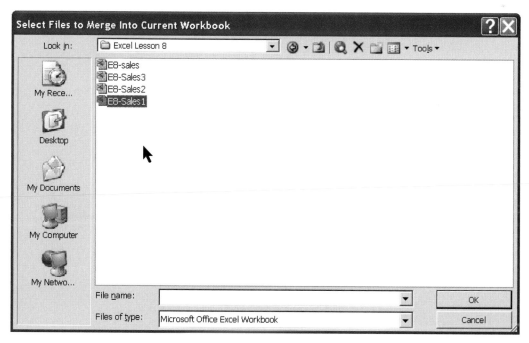

Figure 8.16 Select Files to Merge Into Current Workbook dialog box

1. Open **E8-Sales** from the Data CD.

2. Change the data in **Cell E6** to: $700,000.

3. Save the file as **E8-Sales3**. Close the file.

4. Open **E8-Sales** again. Notice the value in D9.

5. Click **Tools, Compare and Merge Workbooks**. In the **Select Files to Merge Into Current Workbook** dialog box, select the file **E8-Sales1** and click **OK**. *Note: All the merged files must have been created from the same shared workbook, otherwise an error message will appear.*

6. Notice the change in the D9 value.

7. Repeat Step 5 two times, selecting the files **E8-Sales2** and **E8-Sales3** on successive passes through the process.

8. Notice the changes to the column E total.

9. Save the file as **E8-Salesmerged** and close it.

REHEARSAL

TASK 3

GOAL
To create a divisional sales report using shared and merged workbooks

SETTING THE STAGE/WRAPUP
File names: 8.3DivisionalSales
8.3cactus
8.3moreland
8.3pueblo
8.3DivSalesRept
8.3DivCactus
8.3DivMoreland
8.3DivPueblo
8.3DivSalesFinal

WHAT YOU NEED TO KNOW

▶ Companies with several branches or divisions often need to prepare a *divisional sales report,* a summary of the sales figures for each segment of the company. Because many divisions are feeding data into one report, the ability to share and merge workbooks is very useful for this task.

▶ In this Rehearsal activity, you will prepare a divisional sales report for In-Shape Fitness Centers. Five branches are reviewing a workbook that contains their revenues for a company quarterly report. Some of the sales data needs to be changed for several branches because they incorrectly recorded gift memberships in the fourth quarter. You will create a shared workbook, track changes made by different users, make corrections and save copies of the shared workbook, and create a merged workbook from the files saved by several users. You will be making all the changes in this problem, but in practice each corrected worksheet would be saved by users from each branch.

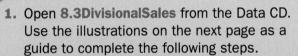

DIRECTIONS

1. Open **8.3DivisionalSales** from the Data CD. Use the illustrations on the next page as a guide to complete the following steps.

2. Enter formulas to complete the Quarterly and Location totals for the year, as shown in Illustration A.

3. Save the file as **8.3DivSalesRept.**

4. Use this file to create a shared workbook.

5. The three branches that had to make changes are Cactus, Moreland, and Pueblo. Assume that the following steps were performed by users at each branch:

   a. Open the **8.3cactus** worksheet. Notice that the fourth quarter sales, as shown in Illustration B, have been corrected and are different from sales listed on the Divisional Sales Report.

   b. Arrange both worksheets on the screen horizontally. Compare the fourth quarter sales from the updated Cactus report with the Divisional Sales report.

   c. Switch to the **8.3DivSalesRept.**

   d. Turn on tracking for changes made to this worksheet.

   e. Change the fourth quarter sales data for the Cactus branch, as per the **8.3cactus** file. Accept this change.

   f. Save the file as **8.3DivCactus.**

   g. Close all files.

Continued

6. Reopen the **8.3DivSalesRept** file. Repeat Steps 5 a-g, making the correction for the fourth quarter found in the **8.3moreland** file, found on the Data CD. Name the corrected report **8.3DivMoreland.** Close both files.

7. Reopen the **8.3DivSalesRept** file. Repeat Steps 5 a-g, making the correction for the fourth quarter found in the **8.3pueblo** file, found on the Data CD. Name the corrected report **8.3DivPueblo.** Close both files.

8. Reopen the **8.3DivSalesRept** file, your original shared file.

9. Merge the three edited files, **8.3DivCactus, 8.3DivMoreland,** and **8.3DivPueblo.**

10. Save the merged file as **8.3DivSalesFinal.**

11. Print a copy.

12. Close the file.

	A	B	C	D	E	F	G
1							
2				*In-Shape Fitness Centers*			
3				*Divisional Sales Report (2005)*			
4							
5	Location		Q1	Q2	Q3	Q4	Total
6	Cactus Drive		$ 50,000	$ 75,000	$ 60,000	$ 70,000	
7	Pueblo Street		$ 75,000	$ 100,000	$ 110,000	$ 105,000	
8	Main Avenue		$ 100,000	$ 110,000	$ 125,000	$ 130,000	
9	Pima Street		$ 150,000	$ 160,000	$ 130,000	$ 155,000	
10	Moreland Street		$ 60,000	$ 75,000	$ 130,000	$ 55,000	
11							
12	Total					Find Quarterly and Location Totals	
13							

Illustration A

	A	B	C	D	E	F	G	H	I	J
1				*In-Shape Fitness Centers*						
2				*Cactus Drive Sales Report (2005)*						
3								This is the corrected		
4	Sales		Q1	Q2	Q3	Q4		sales report from the		
5								Cactus branch		
6	Memberships		$36,100	$56,570	$43,250	$42,750				
7	Classes		$ 5,000	$ 7,430	$ 6,000	$ 7,000				
8	Café		$ 8,900	$11,000	$10,750	$11,750				
9										
10	Total		$50,000	$75,000	$60,000	$61,500				
11										
12				Corrected fourth quarter						
13				sales; change fourth quarter						
14				sales on the Divisional Sales						
15				Report to this number						
16										

Illustration B

Create a Shared Workbook
1. Click **Tools, Share Workbook.**
2. In **Editing** tab, check **Allow changes by more than one user at the same time.**
3. In **Advanced** tab, make any changes you want in length of time changes are tracked, frequency of file updates, and what to do with conflicting changes.
4. Click **OK.**

Track Changes
1. Click **Tools,** select **Track Changes,** and click **Highlight Changes.**
2. In **Highlight Changes** dialog box, check **Track changes while editing.** Make any other selections you want for which changes you will review. Check **Highlight changes on screen** to see changes as you enter them.
3. Click **OK.**

Accept or Reject Changes
1. Click **Tools,** select **Track Changes,** and click **Accept or Reject Changes.**
2. In **Select Changes to Accept or Reject** dialog box, decide whether to review changes by time, user, or location on worksheet. Click **OK.**

3. In **Accept or Reject Changes** dialog box, as each change appears, click **Accept** or **Reject.** Or, click **Accept All** or **Reject All.**

Merge Workbooks
1. Click **Tools, Compare and Merge Workbooks.** Click **OK** when Excel asks you about saving the file.
2. In **Select Files to Merge Into Current Workbook** dialog box, select file to merge into open workbook. Click **OK.** Repeat for each file to merge into workbook.

PERFORMANCE

SETTING THE STAGE/WRAPUP

✶ Act I File names:
8p1.budget
8p1budtemp
8p1budgroup

✶ Act II File names:
8p2.boston
8p2.sandiego
8p2.budtemp
8p2consolbud

✶ Act III File names:
8p3.DivisionalSales
8p3.DivSales
8p3.DivSalesFairfax
8p3.DivSalesAlexandria
8p3.DivSalesFallsChurch
8p3.DivSalesFinal

EXCEL

WHAT YOU NEED TO KNOW

Act I

The Air Land Sea Travel Group would like each department in the organization to use the same quarterly budget form to facilitate financial planning.

Prepare a template for the quarterly budget, using **8p1.budget** on the Data CD as a starting point. You are also asked to prepare the budget for the Group Travel Department for the quarter ending September 30, 2004, and to revise the template.

Follow these guidelines:

✶ Format and enhance the title area in **Rows 1:4** by changing font size, and/or styles and adding color as desired. Make labels for Income, Expenses, and Net Income a bit larger than those in the rest of the budget.

✶ Enter the formulas necessary to complete the budget template.

✶ Apply the appropriate number formats to each column and adjust column width as necessary.

✶ Apply borders to the appropriate cells to follow accounting styles and to enhance the column headings.

✶ Save the form as a template in the Templates folder and name it: **8p1.budtemp.**

✶ Add a line for Supplies to the list of expenses by inserting a line on the template, in alphabetical order. Fill in formulas and check the formulas for totals. Resave the template using the same name. See the illustration of the completed template on the next page.

	A	B	C	D	E
1	Air Land Sea Travel				
2	Quarterly Budget				
3	Office:				
4	For the quarter ended:				
5				Increase/	%Increase/
6		Budget	Actual	Decrease	Decrease
7	Income				
8	Net Sales			$ -	#DIV/0!
9					
10	Expenses				
11	Advertising			$ -	#DIV/0!
12	Rent			$ -	#DIV/0!
13	Salaries			$ -	#DIV/0!
14	Supplies			$ -	#DIV/0!
15	Utilities			$ -	#DIV/0!
16	Total Expenses	$ -	$ -	$ -	#DIV/0!
17					
18	Net Income	$ -	$ -	$ -	#DIV/0!

✶ Use the template to create the Group Travel Department budget for the quarter ending September 30, 2004, by completing the title rows and using the data below:

	Budget	Actual
Net Sales	30,000	34,000
Advertising	1,200	1,425
Rent	6,000	6,000
Salaries	18,000	19,000
Supplies	500	675
Utilities	300	375

✶ Save it as a workbook and name it: **8p1.budgroup.**

✶ Print a copy of the report.

Act II

Odyssey Travel Group has budget data from its Boston and San Diego operations. They wish to create a template for this form, set file properties, complete both budgets, and consolidate the data into a consolidated budget.

Open the files **8p2.boston** and **8p2.sandiego** from the Data CD.

odyssey travel group

Follow these guidelines:

✶ Complete the formulas in the **8p2.boston** file. Find the Gross Income by subtracting Cost of Goods Sold from Net Sales. Calculate Total Expenses and Net Income. Format the file with colors, fonts, borders, and alignment features. Save the file as **8p2.boston.**

- Delete the data and office location and save the worksheet as a template, **8p2.budtemp.** Set the template properties. Include entries for Title, Author, Category (Accounting), and Keywords (Quarterly budget). Close the template.

- Reopen the template and copy the San Diego data from **8p2.sandiego** into the template and add the San Diego title. Save it as **8p2.sandiego.**

- Create a workspace with the solution files for San Diego and Boston. Save the workspace as **8p2.bud.xlw.**

- Use the template to create a worksheet for a consolidated budget. Consolidate the data from both budgets. Enter an appropriate title on the consolidated budget. Save the consolidated budget as **8p2.consolbud.** See the illustration of the completed budget below.

	A	B	C	D
1	Odyssey Travel Gear			
2	Consolidated Budget			
3	Quarterly Budget for Period Ending June 30, 2004			
4				
5	Income		Proposed	Actual
6	Net Sales		$ 200,000.00	$ 203,000.00
7				
8	Cost of Goods Sold		$ 115,000.00	$ 116,000.00
9				
10	Gross Income		$ 85,000.00	$ 87,000.00
11				
12	Expenses			
13	Advertising		$ 5,000.00	$ 4,900.00
14	Miscellaneous		$ 1,000.00	$ 1,000.00
15	Postage		$ 600.00	$ 675.00
16	Rent		$ 5,900.00	$ 5,900.00
17	Salaries		$ 44,000.00	$ 44,000.00
18	Supplies		$ 1,000.00	$ 1,120.00
19	Total Expenses		$ 57,500.00	$ 57,595.00
20				
21	Net Income		$ 27,500.00	$ 29,405.00

Act III

Green Brothers Gardening is preparing a quarterly sales report that includes data from all three of its locations. Open the file **8p3.DivisionalSales** from the Data CD as illustrated on the next page. You will create a shared workbook so that individuals at each of the three locations can review and make changes to the file. The bookkeepers at each location are reviewing their quarterly totals and have indicated that some revenues were overstated and some were understated for different quarters. They have sent supporting records for the changes they want to make. You will review the changes by tracking and accepting or rejecting the changes made by individuals. Finally, you will merge the files created by several users.

GREEN BROTHERS GARDENING

	A	B	C	D	E	F	G
1							
2				*Green Brothers Gardening*			
3				*Divisional Sales Report (2005)*			
4							
5	Location		Q1	Q2	Q3	Q4	Totals
6	Fairfax		$12,000.00	$ 17,000.00	$ 15,000.00	$ 10,000.00	
7	Falls Church		$20,000.00	$ 24,000.00	$ 24,000.00	$ 18,000.00	
8	Alexandria		$32,000.00	$ 33,000.00	$ 20,000.00	$ 28,000.00	
9							
10	TOTAL						

Data File: 8p3 Divisional Sales

Follow these guidelines:

* Total all data vertically and horizontally. Save the workbook as **8p3.DivSales.**

* Create a shared workbook for the file and save it.

* The bookkeeper in Fairfax reviews the data and believes the data for **Cell F6** should be changed to: **$9500.** Change the data in that cell. Save the file as **8p3.DivSalesFairfax.** Close the file.

* Reopen your shared file **8p3.DivSalesFairfax** and enable the Track Changes feature. Reject the change made by the bookkeeper. Save and close the file.

* The bookkeeper in Falls Church reviews the data and wants to change **Cell D7** to **$23,500** and **Cell E7** to **$24,500.** Open the file **8p3.DivSales** (your shared file) and change those data values. Save the file as **8p3.DivSalesFallsChurch.** Close the file.

* Reopen the file **8p3.DivSalesFallsChurch** and enable the Track Changes feature. Accept the changes made by the bookkeeper. Save and close the file.p

* The bookkeeper in Alexandria reviews the data and wants to change **Cell C8** to **$33,000** and **Cell D8** to **$32,500.** Open the file **8p3.DivSales** (your shared file) and change those data values. Save the file as **8p3.DivSalesAlexandria.** Close the file.

* Reopen the file **8p3.DivSalesAlexandria** and enable the Track Changes feature. Accept the change made by the bookkeeper. Save and close the file.

* Open your shared file and merge the workbooks created by the three bookkeepers.

* Save the file as **8p3.DivSalesFinal.**

LESSON 9

Data Tables

In this lesson, you will learn how to customize and audit numerical information in a data table. You will apply these skills to the creation of a sales commission analysis and a regional sales analysis. You will also learn how to name and use ranges in formulas, use the LOOKUP functions in Excel, and evaluate, validate, and watch formulas. You will use these features to create a bonus table and a currency conversion table.

Upon completion of this lesson, you should have mastered the following skill sets:

✷ Create and modify custom number formats
✷ Use conditional formats
✷ Name a range
  ✶ Modify a named range
  ✶ Use a named range reference in a formula
✷ Use Lookup and Reference functions
✷ Audit formulas
  ✶ Trace dependents
  ✶ Trace precedents
  ✶ Trace errors
✷ Watch and evaluate formulas

Terms
Software-related
  Custom number format
  Conditional formats
  Named range
  HLOOKUP
  VLOOKUP
  Dependents
  Precedents
  Tracer arrows
  Evaluate Formula
  Watch Window
Document-related
  Sales commission analysis
  Listing agent
  Selling agent
  Regional sales analysis
  Bonus table
  Currency conversion table

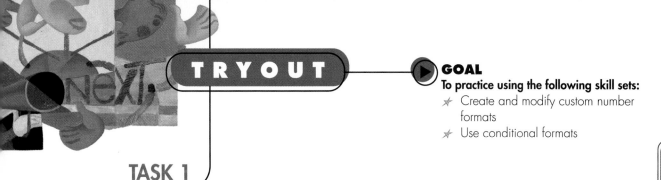

TRYOUT

GOAL
To practice using the following skill sets:
- Create and modify custom number formats
- Use conditional formats

TASK 1

WHAT YOU NEED TO KNOW

Create and Modify Custom Number Formats

▶ Excel provides several ways to display numbers in a format that suits your needs and makes the information in a worksheet clear and readable. A *custom number format* is a user-created format that specifies how Excel displays numbers within a cell. It can format the number of decimal places, the position of commas, or it can modify Excel's options for representing scientific notation, currency, percents, dates, and times.

▶ To create a custom number format, select the cells you want to format. Click Format, Cells or press the Ctrl + 1 keys. This opens the Format Cells dialog box. Click the Number tab and click Custom in the Category box, as shown in Figure 9.1.

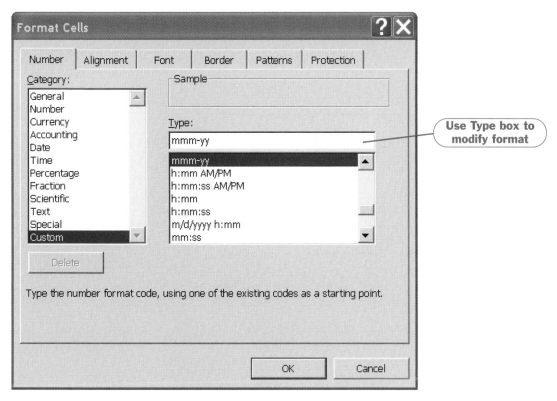

Figure 9.1 Format Cells dialog box

▶ To create a custom number format that does not appear in the dialog box, scroll down under Type and select the custom format closest to the format you want to use as a starting point. Click in the Type box and modify its contents with your own format codes. Click OK.

▶ The table below shows some of the symbols that are used in custom number formats.

NUMBER FORMAT	
Codes	Instruction
#	Display a digit in a particular decimal place; do not put in a value if the number has fewer digits
0	Display a digit in a particular decimal place; put a zero in that location if the number has fewer digits
,	Place a comma at the location to indicate thousands
.	Place a decimal point at the location
$	Place a dollar sign at the location
%	Place a percent sign at the location
E+	Put the numbers to the right in scientific notation
M or m	Months for dates and minutes for time
D or d	Days
Y or y	Years
H or h	Hours
S or s	Seconds

▶ When you create a custom number format, Excel saves it with the workbook. Your new custom number format appears at the bottom of the Type list in the Format Cells dialog box. You can delete a selected custom number format from the Type box by clicking Delete.

TRY it OUT e9-1

1. Open **E9-1** from the Data CD.

2. Select **Cells C6:C18.**

3. Click **Format, Cells,** and click the **Number** tab.

4. Select **Custom** in the Category box.

5. Select **mmm-yy** in the box under Type.

6. In the Type box, add **dd–** between the month and year symbols and add **yy** so that the entry looks like **mmm–dd–yyyy**

7. Click **OK.**

8. Leave the file open.

Use Conditional Formats

▶ *Conditional formats* allow you to apply specific formats to the content of a cell or range of cells if it meets certain criteria. Conditional formatting is a convenient way to make relevant or important data in a table stand out. For example, you might want to highlight data that exceeds or falls below a certain value in a different color or font style.

▶ To create a conditional format, click Format, Conditional Formatting. The Conditional Formatting dialog box opens, as shown in Figure 9.2.

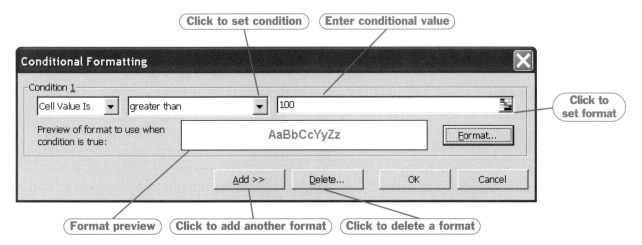

Figure 9.2 Conditional Formatting dialog box

▶ In the first box, use the drop-down list to apply the conditional formatting to either a cell or a formula. In the second box, select the relative condition you want to apply from the drop-down list; for example, between or greater than. If you select between, or not between, in the second box, then two boxes will appear to the right. Enter the parameters that the condition should be between (for example, 1 and 100) in the third and fourth boxes, respectively. If you select an absolute condition such as greater than, only one box will appear where you can enter the appropriate value. When you click the Format button in the Conditional Formatting dialog box, you can specify the formatting features you want to apply to any data that meets the conditions. The preview window shows how the data looks if the condition is true.

▶ If you want to apply another conditional format, click Add. You can apply up to three conditional formats. Click OK when you are done.

▶ To remove any conditional formats you no longer need, you need to reselect the formatted range and click Delete on the Conditional Formatting dialog box. The Delete Conditional Format dialog box opens, as shown in Figure 9.3. Check the boxes for any of the conditional formats you want to remove. Click OK when you are done.

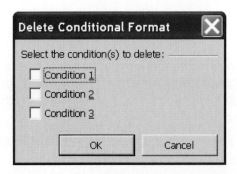

Figure 9.3 Delete Conditional Format dialog box

Note: To locate any conditional formats you have applied in a worksheet, click Edit, Go To, and Special. Click Conditional formats, click OK, and Excel highlights the cells to which you have applied conditional formatting.

TRY it OUT e9-2

1. Continue to work in the open file or open **E9-2** from the Data CD.

2. Select **Cells G6:G19.**

3. Click **Format, Conditional Formatting.**

4. In the left box, leave the selection as **Cell Value Is.** In the next box, click the list arrow and select **greater than.** In the right box, enter 100.

5. Click the **Format** button. Select **Bold** and select the color **Red.** Click **OK.**

6. Click **Add.** Condition 2 selection boxes should appear.

7. In the left box, leave the selection as **Cell Value Is.** In the next box, click the list arrow and select **less than.** In the right box, enter 50.

8. Click **Format.** Select **Bold** and select the color **Blue.**

9. Click **OK** twice. Notice the conditional formats.

10. Select **Cells G6:G19**, if necessary, and click **Format, Conditional Formatting.**

11. Click **Delete** and select Condition 2 to delete. Click **OK.**

12. Click **OK** and notice the change in formatting.

13. Close and save the file.

REHEARSAL

GOAL
To conduct a sales commission analysis

SETTING THE STAGE/WRAPUP
File name: **9.1HomeSales**

TASK 1

WHAT YOU NEED TO KNOW

▶ Some businesses pay employees with commissions, which are compensations based on a percentage of the selling price of a product or service. A business may examine employees' sales performance over a specified period of time by doing a *sales commission analysis*. The business may conduct the study to see if there are notable patterns or to identify individuals who meet, or fall below, sales goals or other criteria important to the business.

▶ A real estate broker who signs up the homeowner or "lists" the home for sale is called the *listing agent*. The real estate broker who finds a buyer for the home is called the *selling agent*. The real estate agency provides office services to the brokers. The brokers and the agency generally share a commission on a home that averages 6% of the selling price.

▶ In this Rehearsal activity, you will conduct a sales commission analysis for Four Corners Realty to calculate commissions and to identify real estate brokers to honor for exceeding quarterly sales goals. Those who had commissions in excess of $20,000 will be named to the Gold Circle and those who had commissions in excess of $10,000 will be named to the Silver Circle. In addition, you will complete an analysis of agency revenues on another sheet in the same workbook.

▼ DIRECTIONS

1. Open **9.1HomeSales** from the Data CD.

2. Format the dates in **Column C** so that they appear as d-mmm-yyyy, as shown in the sales list in Step 3 and as indicated in Illustration A on the next page.

3. Using the information in the list below, calculate a 2.5% commission for a property listing and a 2% commission for a property sale for the agents listed. The sales list shows that, in some cases, the agents receive one or both of these commissions.

Broker	Price of Home	Closing	Listing	Selling
Arnold, John	$120,000.00	15-Apr-2005	X	
Butler, Jean	$237,000.00	2-Apr-2005	X	
Freeman, Marilyn	$172,500.00	27-Apr-2005	X	X
Wreston, David	$175,000.00	11-Apr-2005		X
Arnold, John	$199,250.00	2-May-2005	X	X
Butler, Jean	$189,500.00	14-May-2005	X	
Cisco, Michael	$89,000.00	5-May-2005	X	X
Arnold, John	$240,000.00	6-Jun-2005		X
Freeman, Marilyn	$195,600.00	10-Jun-2005	X	X
Freeman, Marilyn	$187,500.00	15-Jun-2005	X	

a. Enter formulas in **Column D** to calculate a 2.5% commission on the price of each home.
b. Delete the formulas in the blank areas and where they do not apply in the Listing column, as per the monthly sales table above.
c. Enter formulas in **Column E** to calculate a 2% commission on the price of each home.
d. Delete the formulas in the blank areas and where they do not apply in the Selling column, as per the monthly sales table above.

Continued on next page

Illustration A

4. Calculate each broker's total commissions for the quarter in **Column F,** in the locations shown in the illustration.

5. Format the Total Commission column so that the data for any realtor who has more than $20,000 in commissions appears in red and bold.

6. Format the Total Commission column so that the data for any realtor who has more than $10,000 in commissions appears in blue and bold.

7. Replace any border lines that have been deleted.

8. Name the worksheet tab `Sales Commissions.`

9. Copy the worksheet to Sheet2 to begin creating an analysis of agency fees for the quarter.

10. Delete columns that are not needed and add new column headings so that your worksheet headings look like Illustration B on the next page.

11. In the **Agency Listing .5%** column in **Cell F6,** enter an IF statement to multiply the Price of Home Sold column by .5% if the value in the Listing Agent column is greater than 1; otherwise, there should be no entry. Hint: =IF(D6>1,.5%*B6, 0)

12. Copy the formula for all homes and delete any zero entries.

13. In the **Agency Sales 1%** column, enter an IF statement to multiply the Price of Home Sold column by 1% if the value in the Selling Agent column is greater than 1; otherwise, there should be no entry.

14. Copy the formula for all homes and delete any zero entries.

FOUR CORNERS REALTY (Greendale Office) Agency Commissions/Quarter Ending June 30, 2005					
Price of Home Sold	Closing Date	Listing Agent 2.5% Commission	Selling Agent 2% Commission	Agency Listing .5%	Agency Sales 1%

Illustration B

15. Total the **Agency Listing .5%** and **Agency Sales 1%** columns.

16. Format all money values for commas with two decimal places, replace any border lines that have been deleted, and delete conditional formats from this sheet.

17. Name the worksheet tab `Agency Commissions.`

18. Print a copy of both the Sales Commissions and the Agency Commissions report.

19. Save and close the file.

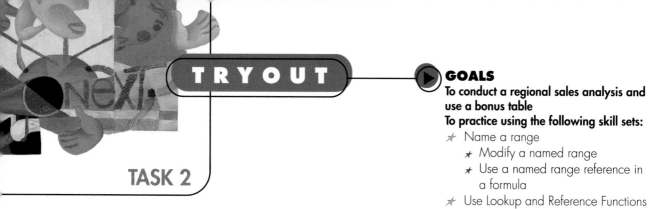

TRYOUT

GOALS

To conduct a regional sales analysis and use a bonus table

To practice using the following skill sets:

* Name a range
  * Modify a named range
  * Use a named range reference in a formula
* Use Lookup and Reference Functions

TASK 2

WHAT YOU NEED TO KNOW

Name a Range

▶ A *named range* is a label that Excel assigns to a specified range of cells. For example, the Cells A2:A10 might be named TotalSales. When they are used in formulas, named range references can make it easier to follow the logic behind a computation.

▶ To create a named range, select the cells you want to name. Click the Name Box to the left of the Insert Function button, as shown in Figure 9.4. Enter the name of the range and be sure to press the Enter key. The first character of the name of a named range must be a letter and names cannot contain spaces or cell references. Use the underscore character (_) or period (.) to designate a space. For example, Total_Sales is a valid name.

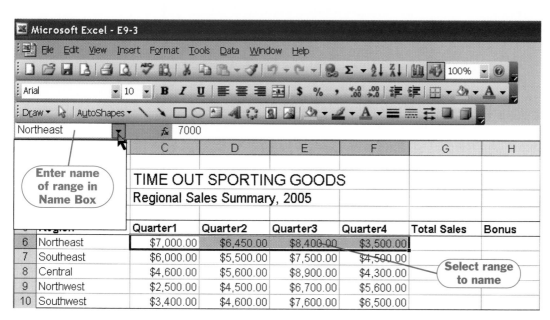

Figure 9.4 Name Box

▶ Naming ranges makes it easy to select a range. When you click the list arrow next to the Name Box, and click the name of the range you have created, Excel selects all of the cells on the worksheet to which the name refers.

1. Open **E9-3** from the Data CD.

2. Select **Cells C6:F6.**

3. Click in the **Name Box** and enter **Northeast.** Press the **Enter** key. Click a cell outside of the current selection.

4. Click the list arrow in the **Name** box. Select **Northeast.** Notice which cells Excel highlights.

5. Select the data from each of the other regions and name them appropriately.

6. Select **Cells E14:F20.**

7. Click in the **Name Box** and enter `Table.`

8. Press the **Enter** key.

9. Save the file and leave it open.

Modify a Named Range

▶ If you want to modify a named range, click Insert, select Name, and click Define. The Define Name dialog box opens, as shown in Figure 9.5. Select the name you want to modify from the list. Enter the new name under Names in workbook and click Add. To delete a name, select it from the list and click Delete.

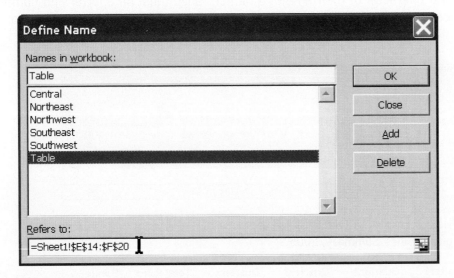

Figure 9.5 Define Name dialog box

1. Continue to work in the open file or open **E9-4** from the Data CD.

2. Click **Insert, Name** and click **Define.**

3. Select the name **Table.**

4. In the Names in workboox box, edit the name to read `Table_Bonus.`

5. Click **Add.**

6. Select the name **Table.**

7. Click **Delete.** Click **OK.**

8. Click the **Name Box** to view the list of named ranges.

9. Save the file and leave it open.

Use a Named Range Reference in a Formula

▶ You can use named ranges in the same ways that you use cell ranges. For example, when you write a formula, simply enter the name of the range that you want to include in a mathematical function. When you use a named range it is an absolute reference to that location.

▶ If you use the AutoSum button to total a named range, the range name will automatically appear in the Sum formula. If you are using the Insert Function button to perform a mathematical operation, you can enter the name of the range in the appropriate place in the dialog box.

TRY*it* OUT e9-5

1. Continue to work in the open file or open **E9-5** from the Data CD.

2. Click **Cell G6** and enter =Sum(Northeast). Press the **Enter** key.

3. Copy the formula to **Cell G7**. Notice that the name of the range does not change and the result is incorrect and the same as **G6**. Delete the results in **Cell G7**.

4. Select **Cell G7** if necessary, and click the **AutoSum** button. Excel places the correct range name in the Sum function. Press the **Enter** key to accept the formula.

5. Repeat Step 2 for each cell in the Total Sales column.

6. Leave the file open.

Use Lookup and Reference Functions

▶ Excel provides two LOOKUP functions, HLOOKUP and VLOOKUP, that check data values against a table and enter a resulting data point in a specified location on a worksheet. Some examples of the ways you can use these functions include looking up taxes to create a payroll, locating postage rates to complete a bill of sale, or finding bonuses based on sales figures for sales personnel.

▶ Use *HLOOKUP* (Horizontal LOOKUP) when the data you are looking up is arranged in rows.

▶ Use *VLOOKUP* (Vertical LOOKUP) when the data you are looking up is arranged in columns.

▶ To use the LOOKUP functions, you must first create the table containing the data you are looking up. This table must appear in a separate location on the worksheet or on a separate worksheet.

▶ When you click the Insert Function button, the Insert Function dialog box opens, as shown in Figure 9.6. Click the list box arrow of the Or select a category box, scroll down and click Lookup & Reference. In the Select a function box, click the list arrow and click either HLOOKUP or VLOOKUP, depending on how you have arranged your lookup table. Click OK.

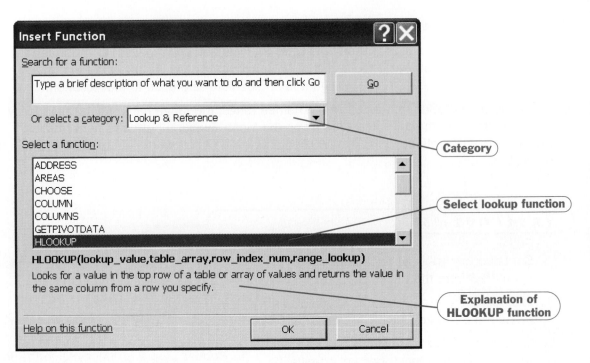

Figure 9.6 Insert Function dialog box

▶ The Function Arguments dialog box opens, as shown in Figure 9.7. Lookup_value refers to the number to be found on the lookup table. Table_array refers to the lookup table that contains the values against which Excel checks. Col_index_num refers to the column number in the lookup table that contains the data you want to enter in your worksheet.

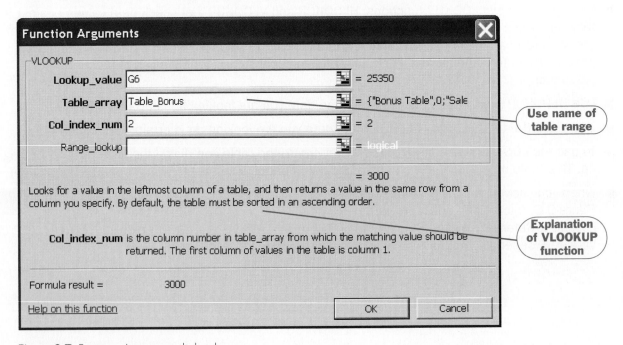

Figure 9.7 Function Arguments dialog box

► Notice the labeled worksheet in Figure 9.8 that shows all the parts of the formula shown in Figure 9-7 and on the formula bar. When you have entered all of these values, click OK. The lookup table should be in a named range to enter the name in the Table_array area and to make the table range an absolute reference so that the range does not change when the formula is copied.

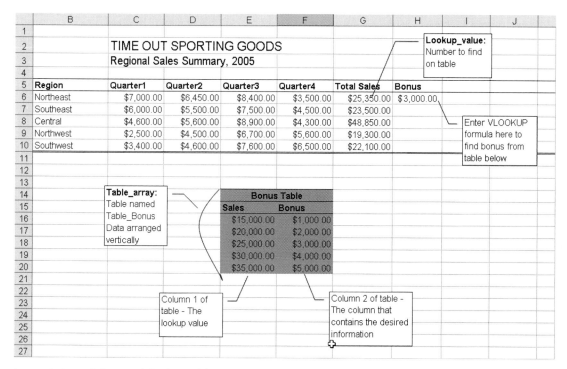

Figure 9.8 Worksheet with lookup table

TRY*it* OUT e9-6

Note: You will enter a lookup formula to enter the appropriate bonus based on the sales made for the quarter.

1. Continue to work in the open file or open **E9-6** from the Data CD.

2. Click **Cell H6.**

3. Click the **Insert Function** button. *fx*

4. In the second box, select **Lookup & Reference.**

5. In the third box, select **VLOOKUP,** since data is arranged in the Bonus_Table vertically. Click **OK.**

6. In the Function Arguments dialog box, click in the box **Lookup_value** and enter **G6** (or you can click that cell in the worksheet) to LOOKUP the sales on the table.

7. Click in the box **Table_array** and enter **Table_Bonus** to direct Excel to the range of the data table, or you can collapse the dialog box, select the table, and expand the dialog box.

8. Click in the box **Col_index_num** and enter **2**. This is because you want the bonus data that is in Column 2 of the Bonus Table.

9. Click **OK.** Check that the correct bonus was entered.

10. Copy the lookup formula to the other cells in the column. (Table_Bonus stays in each formula as a constant.) Replace the border in H10.

11. Print, save, and close the file.

REHEARSAL Again

TASK 2

GOAL
To conduct a regional sales analysis and use a bonus table

SETTING THE STAGE/WRAPUP

File names: 9.2ne
               9.2se
               9.2nw
               9.2sw
               9.2SuttonSales
               9.2regionws

WHAT YOU NEED TO KNOW

▶ Businesses that sell products or services often have regional sales offices that provide services for different parts of the country or the world. The company may want to conduct a *regional sales analysis* to determine their sales figures for different areas of their sales territory. This analysis might be useful in planning where to promote particular products or services, or where to allocate sales efforts.

▶ Businesses that sell products or services might also want to reward employees who meet or exceed certain sales goals. You can create a *bonus table* to define the extra money awarded to sales personnel, based on their performance.

▶ Companies that are reporting large amounts of money often round the values to thousands rather than showing all the detail. For example, $564,678 expressed in thousands would be shown as 565, with a notation that values are in thousands.

▶ In this Rehearsal activity, you will conduct a regional sales analysis for the Sutton Investment Group. You will create a workspace and paste link the data from four regional reports into one report. You will create and apply a bonus table that allocates rewards to high-performing regional offices. The corporate officers have decided to let each regional office distribute the bonuses as they deem appropriate.

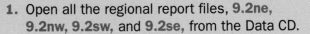

DIRECTIONS

1. Open all the regional report files, **9.2ne, 9.2nw, 9.2sw,** and **9.2se,** from the Data CD.

2. Notice that the numbers are expressed in thousands.

3. Find the totals for each region in **Row 9** of the individual worksheets.

4. Include a single line above and double lines below the totals.

5. Arrange the worksheets on the screen so that the totals are visible and save them as a workspace, **9.2regionws.** (Try a tiled arrangement.)

6. Open **9.2SuttonSales** from the Data CD.

7. Copy and paste link the totals from each report to the appropriate location on the Regional Summary report. *(Hint: Copy the totals from a region, place the insertion point in an appropriate location on the summary, click **Edit, Paste Special,** and **Paste Link.** Be careful to place the totals on the correct line.)*

8. Close the individual regional reports.

9. On the summary report shown on the next page, name the range for each region.

10. Calculate the Total Sales for each region by entering =Sum(named range reference).

11. Format values for commas with no decimal places.

Continued on next page

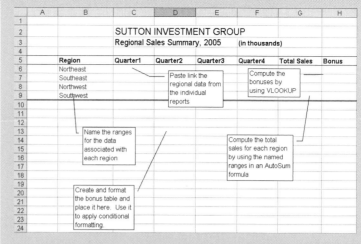

The table above shows a spreadsheet with the following layout:

	A	B	C	D	E	F	G	H
1								
2			SUTTON INVESTMENT GROUP					
3			Regional Sales Summary, 2005		(in thousands)			
4								
5		Region	Quarter1	Quarter2	Quarter3	Quarter4	Total Sales	Bonus
6		Northeast						
7		Southeast						
8		Northwest						
9		Southwest						

Callouts:
- Paste link the regional data from the individual reports
- Compute the bonuses by using VLOOKUP
- Name the ranges for the data associated with each region
- Compute the total sales for each region by using the named ranges in an AutoSum formula
- Create and format the bonus table and place it here. Use it to apply conditional formatting.

12. Create a bonus table starting in **Cell E12.** List the bonuses as follows:

SALES	
(thousands)	*Bonus*
3,000	$50,000
4,000	$60,000
5,000	$70,000
6,000	$80,000
7,000	$90,000
8,000	$100,000
9,000	$110,000
10,000	$120,000

13. Format the Sales numbers for commas, the Bonus values for currency, and both for no decimal places.

14. Format the bonus table in **Light Green** to set it apart from the other data in the table.

15. Name the range of cells that contains the bonus table **Bonus_Table.**

16. Find the bonus amounts for each sales region by using VLOOKUP.

Note: Once you obtain the value for the first cell in the bonus column, you can use the fill-handle to fill in the rest of the values in that column.

17. Correct borders, if necessary.

18. Apply conditional formatting to **Column G** so that the sales figures in any region that exceed 9,000 (nine million dollars), are highlighted in **Blue.** Highlight any region where total sales fell below 4,000 (four million dollars), in **Red.** *(Hint: Select the values from the Bonus_Table.)*

19. Print and save the **9.2SuttonSales** file and close it.

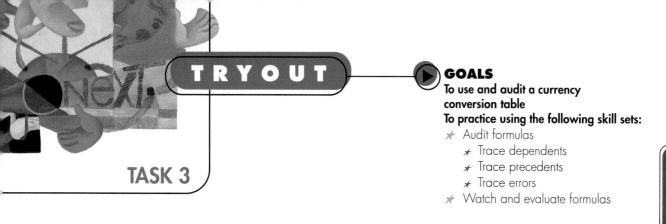

TRYOUT

TASK 3

GOALS
To use and audit a currency
conversion table
To practice using the following skill sets:
✴ Audit formulas
  ✴ Trace dependents
  ✴ Trace precedents
  ✴ Trace errors
✴ Watch and evaluate formulas

EXCEL

WHAT YOU NEED TO KNOW

Audit Formulas

▶ If you have an error in a formula, you can trace the cells that are connected to the formula to try to resolve the error. This procedure is especially helpful when you are using a worksheet created by someone else.

▶ Excel provides several new features to assist you as you track down errors in formulas. These include the Evaluate Formula function and Formula Auditing mode.

Trace Dependents

▶ *Dependents* are cells containing formulas that reference the cell you are auditing. If you click a cell, you can see all of the other cells that use it in a formula. To locate dependents, first click the cell you are auditing, then click Tools, select Formula Auditing, and click Trace Dependents, as shown in Figure 9.9.

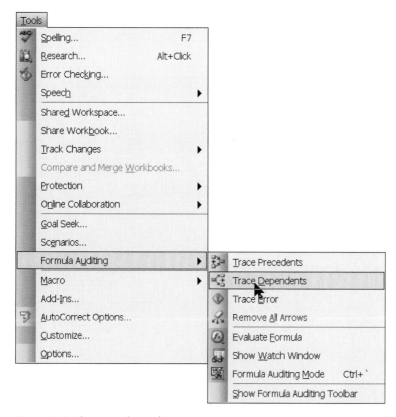

Figure 9.9 The Formula Auditing menu

► Excel draws *tracer arrows* to each cell in which a formula includes that specific cell, as shown in Figure 9.10.

	A	B	C	D	E	F	G
1							
2				TIME OUT SPORTING GOODS			
3			Item:			Duffle bag	
4			Current price per item:			$ 12.95	
5							
6				CONVERSION FACTOR			GROSS SALES
7	COUNTRY		CURRENCY	Per US$	FOREIGN PRICE PER ITEM	# ITEMS SOLD	(Foreign Currency)
8	Brazil		Real	2.951	38.22	50	1910.7725
9	Canada		Dollar	1.3273	17.19	100	1718.8535
10	European Union		Euro	0.787	10.19	25	254.79125
11	Japan		Yen	107.05	1386.30	30	41588.925
12	Mexico		Peso	10.975	142.13	45	6395.68125
13	Switzerland		Franc	1.2413	16.07	50	803.74175
14							

Figure 9.10 Example of tracing dependents

► Another way to trace dependents is to use the Formula Auditing toolbar, as shown in Figure 9.11. Click Tools, select Formula Auditing, and click Show Formula Auditing Toolbar. Click the Trace Dependents button to locate a cell's dependents. The next button to the right, the Remove Dependent Arrows button, removes the dependent arrows.

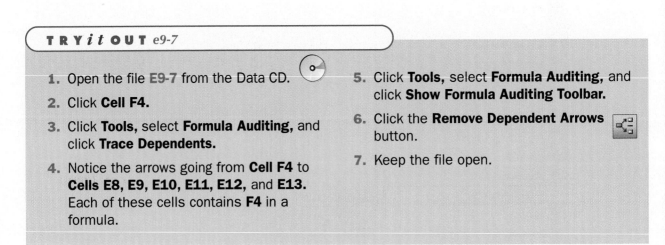

Figure 9.11 The Formula Auditing toolbar

T R Y *it* O U T *e9-7*

1. Open the file **E9-7** from the Data CD.

2. Click **Cell F4.**

3. Click **Tools,** select **Formula Auditing,** and click **Trace Dependents.**

4. Notice the arrows going from **Cell F4** to **Cells E8, E9, E10, E11, E12,** and **E13.** Each of these cells contains **F4** in a formula.

5. Click **Tools,** select **Formula Auditing,** and click **Show Formula Auditing Toolbar.**

6. Click the **Remove Dependent Arrows** button.

7. Keep the file open.

Trace Precedents

▶ *Precedents* are cells that are referenced in a formula selected for audit. If you click a cell containing a formula, you can trace all of the cells that contribute to that formula.

▶ To locate precedents, first click the cell containing the formula you want to audit, then click Tools, select Formula Auditing, and click Trace Precedents. Excel draws tracer arrows to the audited cell from each cell that contributes to the formula, as shown in Figure 9.12.

	A	B	C	D	E	F	G
1							
2				TIME OUT SPORTING GOODS			
3			Item:			Duffle bag	
4			Current price per item:			$ 12.95	
5							
6				CONVERSION FACTOR			GROSS SALES
7	COUNTRY		CURRENCY	Per US$	FOREIGN PRICE PER ITEM	# ITEMS SOLD	(Foreign Currency)
8	Brazil		Real	2.951	38.22	50	1910.7725
9	Canada		Dollar	1.3273	17.19	100	1718.8535
10	European Union		Euro	0.787	10.19	25	254.79125
11	Japan		Yen	107.05	1386.30	30	41588.925
12	Mexico		Peso	10.975	142.13	45	6395.68125
13	Switzerland		Franc	1.2413	16.07	50	803.74175
14							

Figure 9.12 Example of tracing precedents

▶ Another way to trace precedents is to use the Formula Auditing toolbar discussed above. Click the Trace Precedents button. To remove precedent arrows, click the button to its right, the Remove Precedent Arrows button, or you can click Remove all arrows to remove any auditing arrows.

TRY it OUT e9-8

1. Continue to work in the open file or open **E9-8** from the Data CD.

2. Click **Cell E12.**

3. Click **Tools,** select **Formula Auditing,** and click **Trace Precedents.**

4. Notice the arrows going from **Cells D12** and **F4** to **Cell E12.** These cells are referenced in the formula in **E12,** shown on the formula bar.

5. Click **Tools,** select **Formula Auditing,** and click **Show Formula Auditing Toolbar,** if necessary to display the toolbar.

6. Click the **Remove Precedent Arrows** button.

7. Close and save the file.

Trace Errors

▶ If you enter a formula and you get one of Excel's error messages, such as #VALUE!, #NAME?, or #DIV/0!, you can begin to resolve the error by using the Trace Error function on the Formula Auditing menu. Click the cell with the error and click Tools, select Formula Auditing, and click Trace Error. Excel draws lines from all of the cells that are referenced in the formula. Red lines are drawn from the cells in which there are errors, as shown in Figure 9.13.

▶ A Trace Error button is also available on the Formula Auditing toolbar. Clicking it produces the lines to referenced cells described above.

▶ When a cell contains an error, it will have a small triangle in the top left corner. When you click the cell with the error, an Error button appears with several options to help you resolve the problem in your formula. These options vary with the type of error in the cell. The options might include a link to the Help file, the Trace Error button, or the option to ignore the error, as shown in Figure 9.13

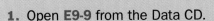

	A	B	C	D	E	F	G
1							
2				TIME OUT SPORTING GOODS			
3			Item:			Duffle bag	
4			Current price per item:			$ 12.95	
5							
6				CONVERSION FACTOR			GROSS SALES
7	COUNTRY		CURRENCY	Per US$	FOREIGN PRICE PER ITEM	# ITEMS SOLD	(Foreign Currency)
8	Brazil		Real	2.951	38.22	50	1910.7725
9	Canada		Dollar	1.3273	17.19	100	1718.8535
10	European Union		Euro	0.787	10.19	25	254.79125
11	Japan		Yen	1	#VALUE!	30	#VALUE!
12	Mexico		Peso	1		45	6395.68125
13	Switzerland		Franc			50	803.74175
14			**Error button and options**		Error in Value		
15					Help on this error		**Red line points to cell with error**
16					Show Calculation Steps...		
17					Ignore Error		
18					Edit in Formula Bar		
19					Error Checking Options...		
20					Show Formula Auditing Toolbar		
21							

Figure 9.13 Example of Tracing Errors

TRY it OUT e9-9

1. Open **E9-9** from the Data CD.

2. Click **Cell G11.**

3. Click **Tools,** select **Formula Auditing,** and click **Trace Error.**

4. The lines point from the cells that contribute to the formula. The red line indicates that **Cell E11** contains an error.

5. Click the list arrow on the Error button to view options.

6. Click **Help on this error** and view the possible causes and solutions.

7. Click the **Close** button.

8. Edit the formula in **Cell E11** so that it reads =F4*D11.

9. Keep the file open.

Watch and Evaluate Formulas

▶ A new function in Excel is *Evaluate Formula.* This function allows you to see the step-by-step calculations that a formula performs. Often, observing this step-by-step procedure can help you track down an error. To use this function, click the cell you are auditing and click Tools, select Formula Auditing, and click Evaluate Formula. The Evaluate Formula dialog box opens, as shown in Figure 9.14. Click Evaluate. Excel conducts the first step of the computation. Each time you click Evaluate, Excel executes the next step in the computation. When you have finished looking at the steps, click Close.

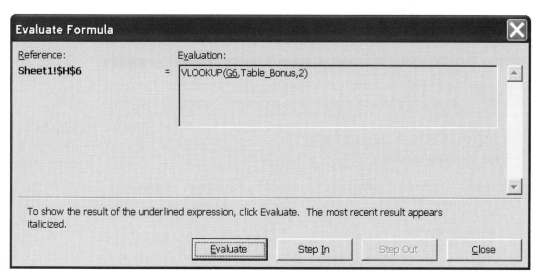

Figure 9.14 Evaluate Formula dialog box

▶ You can also access the Evaluate Formula function by clicking the Evaluate Formula button on the Formula Auditing toolbar.

▶ If you wish to watch a certain formula in a worksheet, you can add a *Watch Window* to your screen and place it below the toolbars. As shown in Figure 9.15, the workbook name, sheet, cell, value, and formula are displayed in the window.

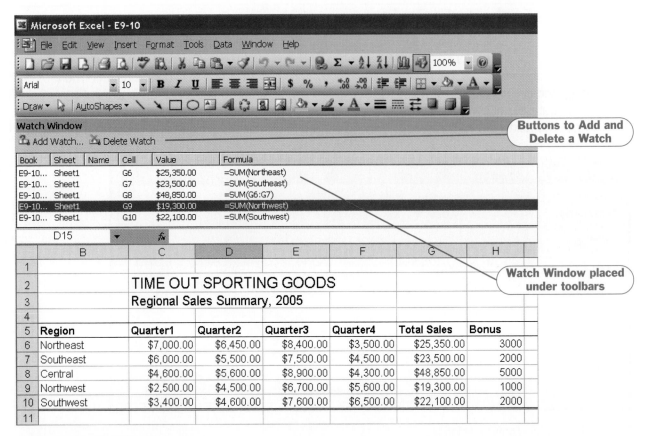

Figure 9.15 Watch Window

▶ To create a Watch Window, select the cell or range of cells to be watched, and click Tools, select Formula Auditing, and click Show Watch Window. Click the Add Watch button and click Add, as shown in Figure 9.16. The information will be displayed for the selection. You can move the Watch Window so that it appears under your toolbars. To delete a watch, select the cell information in the Watch Window, and click the Delete Watch button. This window will remain on the screen when you close the file. You can hide the window by clicking Tools, Formula Auditing, and Hide Watch Window

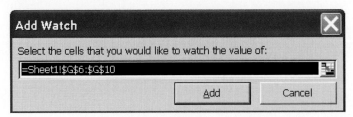

Figure 9.16 Add Watch dialog box

EXCEL

1. Continue to work in the open file or open **E9-10** from the Data CD.

2. Click **Cell H8.**

3. Click **Tools,** select **Formula Auditing,** and click **Evaluate Formula.**

4. Click **Evaluate** three times. Notice the result in the Evaluation box each time you click.

5. Click **Close.**

6. Click **Tools,** select **Formula Auditing,** and click **Show Watch Window.**

7. Notice the Watch Window that appears. Select the range **G6:G10.**

8. Click the **Add Watch** button and note the selected range in the dialog box. Click **Add.**

9. Move the Watch Window under your toolbars.

10. Select the **G9** watch and click the **Delete Watch** button.

11. Delete the remaining watch cells as per the directions in Step 10.

12. Click **Tools,** select **Formula Auditing,** and click **Hide Watch Window.**

13. Close the file. Do not save.

REHEARSAL

TASK 3

 GOAL
To use and audit a currency
conversion table

SETTING THE STAGE/WRAPUP
File name: **9.3WatchSales**

WHAT YOU NEED TO KNOW

▶ For companies that engage in
international business, it is
important to use a *currency
conversion table* that identifies
the current exchange rate for U.S.
dollars. The table can contain the
U.S. dollar value of the foreign
currency, the foreign currency
equivalent of a U.S. dollar, or
both. It can also contain
computations based on these
exchange rates.

▶ A good source for daily foreign
currency exchange rates is:
http://moneycentral.msn.com/investor/
market/rates.asp.

▶ In this Rehearsal activity, you will
work with a currency conversion
table for another product that the
Time Out Sporting Goods
Company sells on the world
market. The table contains
several errors. You will locate the
sources of the errors, using the
auditing tools you learned about,
and correct those errors.

▼ DIRECTIONS

1. Open the file **9.3watchsales** from the Data CD.

2. Audit the errors in **Column F** illustrated on the
   next page. Trace the precedents and/or dependents
   in the cells that have errors.

3. Locate the cells that contain the source of the
   errors and correct them.

4. Remove all tracer arrows.

5. Name the value in F4 (Current_price). Using the
   Number of Items Sold, calculate the **Gross Sales in
   US $** for each country using the name for Current
   price per item.

6. Copy the formula for each country.

7. Total the **Gross Sales (US $)** column.

8. Format the **Foreign Price Per Item** and **Gross Sales
   (Foreign Currency)** columns in Comma format.

9. Select **Cell G8** and evaluate the formula.

10. Display a Watch Window and add a watch for the
    formula in **Cell G11.** We are watching falling sales in
    the Japanese market.

11. Print a copy of the file.

12. Save the file.

13. Delete the watch for **Cell G11** and hide the
    Watch Window.

14. Close the file.

TIME OUT SPORTING GOODS

	A	B	C	D	E	F	G
1							
2			**TIME OUT SPORTING GOODS**				
3		Item:				**Sports Watch**	Name the value in this cell
4		Current price per item:				$ 79.99	
5							
6			CONVERSION FACTOR	FOREIGN PRICE	NUMBER OF	GROSS SALES	GROSS SALES
7	COUNTRY	CURRENCY	(Per US$)	PER ITEM	ITEMS SOLD	(Foreign Currency)	(US $)
8	Brazil	Real	2.951	236.05	75	17703.78675	
9	Canada	Dollar	1.3273	106.17	125	13271.34088	
10	European Union	Euro	0.787	62.95	75	4721.40975	
11	Japan	Yen	107.05	#DIV/0!	50	#DIV/0!	
12	Mexico	Peso	10.975	#VALUE!	100	#VALUE!	
13	Switzerland	Franc	1.2413	99.29	130	12907.90631	
14							
15						Total	
16							
17							
18							
19							
20							
21							

Locate the sources of the errors on this worksheet starting with this column

Calculate the sales in US dollars and total the column

EXCEL

Cues for Reference

Audit a Formula
1. Trace dependents by clicking **Tools, Formula Auditing,** and selecting **Trace Dependents,** or use the Formula Auditing toolbar.
2. Trace precedents by clicking **Tools, Formula Auditing,** and selecting **Trace Precedents,** or use the Formula Auditing toolbar.

Locate and Resolve Errors in Formulas
1. Click **Tools, Formula Auditing,** and select **Trace Error,** or use the Formula Auditing toolbar.

2. To see step-by-step computations in a formula, click **Tools, Formula Auditing,** and select **Evaluate Formula,** or use the Formula Auditing toolbar.

Watch Formulas
1. Click **Tools, Formula Auditing,** and select **Show Watch Window.**
2. Select the cell or range to be watched.
3. Click the **Add Watch** button.
4. Click **Add**.

Delete a Watch
1. Select watch cell information.
2. Click **Delete Watch** button.

Hide Watch Window
Click **Tools, Formula Auditing,** and select **Hide Watch Window.**

PERFORMANCE

▶ SETTING THE
STAGE/WRAPUP

✴ Act I File name:
     9p1.OTGBonus
✴ Act II File name:
     9p2.India,
     9p2.Japan,
     9p2.Korea,
     9p2.LastDragon-
     Expenses

WHAT YOU NEED TO KNOW

Act I

The Odyssey Travel Gear Company would like to conduct a sales commission analysis in order to give its top salespeople end-of-the-year bonuses. The figures from this analysis will be used to calculate the total sales staff compensation for the year.

Open the file **9p1.OTGBonus** from the Data CD. The quarterly commissions figures for the sales staff appear in the table.

The bonus amount for each level of total commissions is given below:

Commissions	Bonus
$0	$0
$15,000	$1,000
$20,000	$2,000
$25,000	$3,000
$30,000	$4,000
$40,000	$5,000

Compute the bonus (if any) that each salesperson should receive. Format any total commissions figures for individual salespeople that exceed $25,000 in bold and red, and any total sales figures that exceed $15,000 in bold and green.

Copy the Total Commissions and Bonus data to the Sales Staff Compensation sheet, using Paste Special Values and number formats, and calculate the total compensation including the Base Salary, as shown in the illustration.

	A	B	C	D	E
1					
2			ODYSSEY TRAVEL GEAR		
3			Sales Staff Compensation		
4			2005		
5	Salesperson	Base Salary	Total Commissions	Bonus	Total Compensation
6	Adrich	$11000			
7	Burdoon	$11000			
8	Jannell	$12000			
9	Smith	$10000			
10	Winters	$11000			
11	Total				
12					

Follow these guidelines:

- ✶ Find Quarterly and Salesperson totals and, whenever possible, name the ranges that you will use in formulas.

- ✶ Format all currency figures in a custom number format in which there is a dollar sign but no comma to indicate thousands.

- ✶ When you create the bonus table, put it in a separate place on the worksheet, format it in pale grey, and name the range.

- ✶ Use the correct LOOKUP function to derive the bonus figures.

- ✶ Copy the Total Commissions and Bonus data to the Sales Staff Compensation worksheet using Paste Special Values and number formats.

- ✶ Calculate the Total Compensation column and complete the final total line.

- ✶ Enhance the appearance of both worksheets by changing alignments and by using color and border formats.

- ✶ Save and print the workbook.

Act II

Although most of the film was shot in Hollywood, Trilogy Productions has just finished filming scenes from "The Last Dragon" in several foreign locations, including Japan, India, and Korea. The production teams from each country have submitted expense workbooks to the accounting office. The information now needs to be combined and converted to U.S. currency.

Open the files **9p2.India, 9p2.Japan,** and **9p2.Korea** from the Data CD. The workbooks include the currency conversion factors to convert the figures to U.S. dollars, as well as the computations to translate the figures to U.S. dollars. However, each workbook contains errors.

Use Excel's formula auditing tools to locate the sources of the errors. Make all necessary corrections and remove all tracer arrows. Then consolidate the data from each of the three workbooks into a new workbook.

Follow these guidelines:

- Start tracing errors in cells that contain totals, for example, **Cell F15** in each of the three workbooks.

- Correct all errors and save each workbook.

- Use the Internet to research the current conversion rates for these workbooks. Enter the date of your research on the report and change the rates as necessary. A good source for daily foreign currency exchange rates is: http://moneycentral.msn.com/investor/market/rates.asp.

- Save the workbooks.

- Create a new worksheet for consolidated expenses and create headings and labels as shown in the illustration below. Save the workbook as **9p2.LastDragon.**

- Create a workspace with the new workbook and the three expense workbooks. Name the workspace **9p2dragon.**

- Select the range **C9:C14**, or the Total Expenses (U.S. Dollars) column, in the new workbook and add the US Expense data in the range **F8:F13** from each workbook to the new location.

- Compute the consolidated total expenses in U.S. dollars for all three countries.

- Enter today's date.

- Format the Consolidated Expenses worksheet, including colors and borders, to make it look attractive.

- Save the new workbook and print the file.

TRILOGY PRODUCTIONS
Expenses: Foreign Locations for "The Last Dragon"
Consolidated Expenses

Date:

Expenses	Total Expenses (US Dollars)
Film	
Food	
Miscellaneous	
Payroll	
Props	
Supplies	
Total	

Accounting Records

In this lesson, you will learn to customize Excel toolbars, menus, and default settings so that you can create accounting records more efficiently for accounts receivable, which are records for customers who owe you money. You will also learn to create a depreciation schedule and protect it by using passwords and protections. A series of commands will be saved as a macro to make repetitive tasks easier to complete.

Upon completion of this lesson, you should have mastered the following skill sets:

- ✶ Customize toolbars and menus
  - ✶ Add custom menus
  - ✶ Delete custom menus
  - ✶ Add and remove buttons from toolbars
- ✶ Modify Excel Default Settings
  - ✶ Modify default font
  - ✶ Set default number of worksheets
- ✶ Modify passwords, protections, and properties
  - ✶ Protect individual worksheets
  - ✶ Use passwords for protection
- ✶ Add cell protection
- ✶ Protect workbooks
- ✶ Create, edit, and run macros
  - ✶ Create macros
  - ✶ Use relative reference macros
  - ✶ Set macro settings
  - ✶ Run macros
  - ✶ Edit macros using the Visual Basic Editor
  - ✶ Delete a macro
  - ✶ Use digital signature for macro projects

Terms
Software-related
Custom menu
Protection
Password
Locked cells
Macro
Visual Basic Editor
Document-related
Accounts receivable
Accounts receivable aging report
Depreciation schedule
Straight-line depreciation

TRYOUT

TASK 1

GOALS

To prepare custom toolbars and menus for an accounts receivable aging report and to change default settings

To practice using the following skill sets:

* Customize toolbars and menus
    * Add custom menus
    * Delete custom menus
    * Add and remove buttons from toolbars
* Modify Excel Default Settings
    * Modify default font
    * Set default number of worksheets

EXCEL

WHAT YOU NEED TO KNOW

Customize Toolbars and Menus

▶ When you repeat the same tasks in Excel, you may find it useful to create your own customized drop-down menu that contains the buttons and commands you use frequently. Or, you can modify one of the preexisting toolbars in Excel so that it contains the buttons that you use most often.

Add Custom Menus

▶ A *custom menu* is a set of buttons and commands Excel groups into a user-created drop-down menu. You can take buttons and commands from anywhere in Excel and place them all in one convenient location with its own name.

▶ To create a custom menu, click Tools, Customize. The Customize dialog box opens, and when you click the Commands tab, it displays as shown in Figure 10.1. Scroll down the Categories box and select New Menu. In the Commands box, click New Menu and drag it to the toolbar on which you want the custom menu to appear. A bar, shaped like the letter "I," indicates where Excel will place the menu.

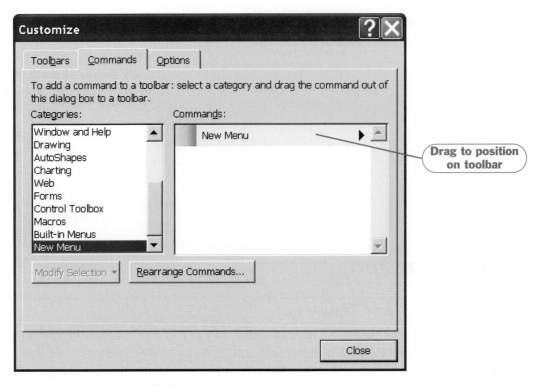

Figure 10.1 Customize dialog box

▶ To name your menu, keep the Customize dialog box open and right-click New Menu on the main menu toolbar. On the shortcut menu that appears, select New Menu in the Name box and enter the name of your menu, as shown in Figure 10.2. Press the Enter key.

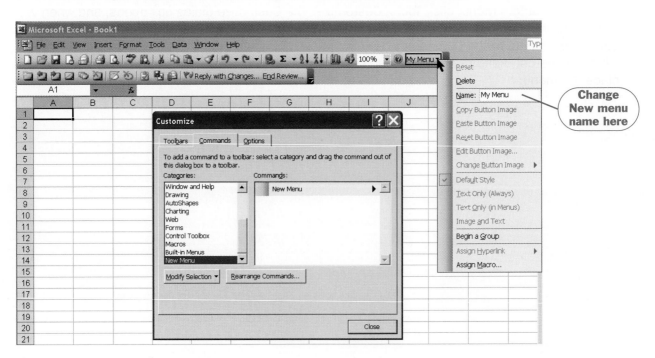

Figure 10.2 Enter name of new menu

▶ To add commands to the custom menu, click the menu name you have created. A box that holds the drop-down menu items appears. Go to the Customize dialog box and click the category that contains the command you want to put on your custom menu. Drag the command from the Commands box to the empty box for your custom menu, as shown in Figure 10.3. When you are done, close the Customize dialog box.

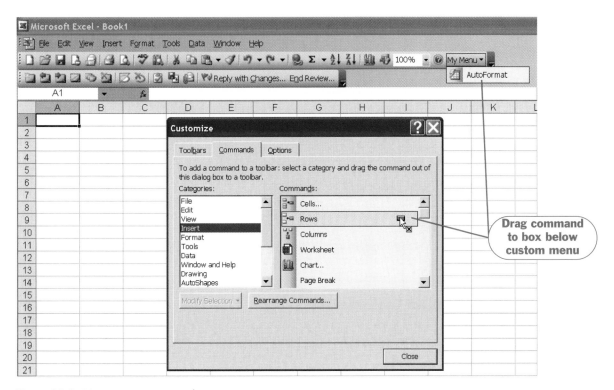

Figure 10.3 Move menu commands to custom menu

TRY it OUT e10-1

1. Open a new worksheet.

2. Click **Tools, Customize,** and the **Commands** tab.

3. Scroll down the Categories box and click **New Menu.**

4. In the Commands box, click and drag **New Menu** to the Standard toolbar.

5. Right-click **New Menu** on the Standard toolbar, select the Name box, and enter the following: My Menu. Press the **Enter** key.

6. Click **My Menu** so that you see a blank box under it.

7. In Categories, scroll up and click **Format.**

8. In Commands, scroll down to click and drag **AutoFormat** to the blank box under **My Menu.**

9. Repeat Step 6, if box is not in view.

10. In Categories, click **Insert.**

11. In Commands, click and drag **Rows** to the box under **My Menu.**

12. Click **Close** in the Customize dialog box.

13. Click the list arrow next to **My Menu** to see the commands on your customized menu.

14. Do not close the worksheet.

Delete Custom Menus

▶ To delete a command from your custom menu, open the Customize dialog box by clicking Tools, Customize. Click the new menu and the command you want to delete. Drag the command you want to delete off the menu and then close the Customize dialog box.

▶ To delete the entire custom menu from a toolbar, open the Customize dialog box by clicking Tools, Customize. Click and drag the custom menu off the toolbar.

T R Y *it* **O U T** *e10-2*

Note: Continue to work on the sheet for which you have created the custom menu, My Menu.

1. Click **Tools, Customize,** and the **Commands** tab.

2. Click the list arrow next to **My Menu** on the toolbar.

3. Click and drag **Rows** off the toolbar.

4. Click the list arrow next to **My Menu**, if necessary. Notice that the Rows command is gone.

5. Click and drag **My Menu** off the toolbar.

6. Close the Customize dialog box.

7. Do not close the worksheet.

Add and Remove Buttons from Toolbars

▶ Excel toolbars are flexible in layout. You can add, remove, or rearrange buttons on Excel's preset toolbars to suit the tasks you perform frequently.

▶ There are several ways to add buttons to toolbars:

- When toolbars are arranged side by side, some of the buttons on each toolbar are not visible. When you click the Toolbar Options arrow at the end of the toolbar, you can view those buttons and click the button you want to use. The button appears on the toolbar for future use.

- You can also click the Toolbar Options arrow and then click Add or Remove Buttons, as shown in Figure 10.4. Check off the buttons you want on the toolbar.

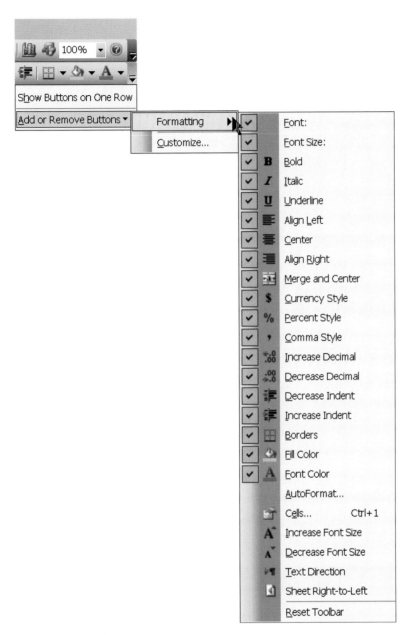

Figure 10.4 Toolbar options arrow

- If you want to add buttons from another toolbar, click Tools, Customize, and the Commands tab. Locate the menu that contains the command you want in the Categories box. Find the button you want in the Commands box. Click and drag it to the toolbar on which you want it to appear. When you are done, close the Customize dialog box.

▶ There are several ways to remove buttons from toolbars:

- Open the Customize dialog box by clicking Tools, Customize, and the Commands tab. Click the button you want to remove and drag it off the toolbar. Close the Customize dialog box.

- Hold down the Alt key. Click and drag the button off the toolbar.

- Click the Toolbar Options arrow at the end of the toolbar. Click Add or Remove Buttons, as shown in Figure 10.4, and then uncheck the buttons you do not want on the toolbar menu.

▶ If you want a toolbar to revert to its original settings, click Tools, Customize, and the Toolbars tab. Click the Reset button. Close the Customize dialog box.

Note: Continue to work on the blank worksheet.

1. Click **Tools, Customize,** and the **Commands** tab.

2. Click **Format** in the Categories box.

3. Scroll down to click **Double Underline** in the Commands box and drag it to the formatting toolbar.

4. Close the **Customize** dialog box.

5. Click the **Toolbar Options** arrow on the Formatting toolbar.

6. Select **Add or Remove Buttons** and select **Formatting**.

7. Click the **Increase Font Size** button on the list of commands.

8. Click on any blank cell and view the worksheet.

9. Click the **Toolbar Options** arrow, select **Add or Remove Buttons,** and select **Formatting.**

10. Click **Reset toolbar.** Click **OK** to confirm changes.

11. Close and do not save the worksheet.

Modify Excel Default Settings

▶ Companies and individuals may wish to change default fonts, printer settings, column width, row height, chart type, and other features to create a style for all publications and materials. If the defaults are modified, the user will not have to repeatedly change to the desired settings.

Modify Default Font

▶ When you change the default font, the worksheet will always appear in that font unless the font is reformatted. After the default font is changed, you must restart Excel to begin using it as the default.

▶ To change the default font, which is Arial, click Tools, select Options, and then click the General tab, as shown in Figure 10.5. Select a font and its size, then click OK.

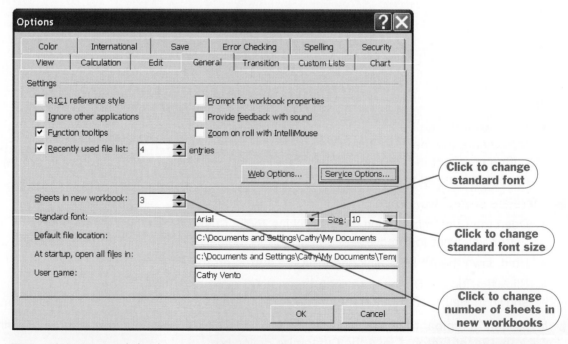

Figure 10.5 Options dialog box, General Tab

Set Default Number of Worksheets

▶ Workbooks open with three worksheets as the default setting. If you find that you always have to add worksheets because you are doing monthly or quarterly workbooks, you may wish to change the default number of worksheets that are included in a workbook.

▶ To change the default number of worksheets, click Tools, select Options, and then click the General tab. As shown in Figure 10.5, change the number in the Sheets in new workbook box.

▶ When you restart Excel to apply the new default settings, all new worksheets will be created with the new font and/or sheet settings. If you want old worksheets to match the new format, you can change the format manually or copy the worksheet into a new blank workbook and select Match Destination Formatting from the Paste Options Smart Tag, as shown in Figure 10.6

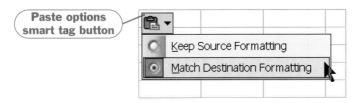

Figure 10.6 Paste Options Smart Tag

TRY it OUT e10-4

1. Open the file **E10-4** from the Data CD. Notice the font, font size settings, and number of sheets in the workbook.

2. Click **Tools,** select **Options**, and then click the **General** tab.

3. Change the font setting to **Century Gothic** and the font size to **12** point.

4. Change the Sheets in new workbook setting to **12.**

5. Click **OK.**

6. You will get a message to restart Excel for the changes to take effect. Click **OK.**

7. Exit Excel. Do not save the file.

8. Start Excel. Notice the font, font size settings, and the number of sheets in the workbook.

9. Open the file **E10-4** from the Data CD. Notice that files saved with the old settings do not change.

10. Copy the entire worksheet and open a blank workbook.

11. Paste the worksheet in A1 and click **Match Destination Formatting** from the Smart Tag Paste Options list. The workbook will paste with new font settings.

12. Reset the worksheet defaults to **Arial 10** with **3** sheets in each workbook, as per Steps 2, 3, 4, and 5 above.

13. Exit Excel, do not save the files.

14. Restart Excel to have the settings take effect.

EXCEL

REHEARSAL

TASK 1

▶ **GOAL**
To change default settings, and to create a custom menu and toolbar buttons to use with an accounts receivable aging report

SETTING THE STAGE/WRAPUP
File name: **10.1ARAging**

WHAT YOU NEED TO KNOW

▶ *Accounts receivable* are assets of a business and represent customers who owe the business money. Customers who are sold services or merchandise on credit are required to pay the bill within the time specified on the invoice. Accounts are reviewed monthly to determine which invoices are outstanding or unpaid.

▶ An *accounts receivable aging report* provides an analysis of how many days payments from customers are overdue. Many businesses expect payment within 30 days of the purchase or transaction. Based on the analysis, a company can identify delinquent customers, or may assess finance charges or late fees. These charges may vary, depending on the number of days an account is overdue, and are imposed to enforce payment.

▶ In this Rehearsal activity, you will prepare a workbook that you will use later in this lesson to create an accounts receivable aging report for Occasions Event Planning. Occasions Event Planning usually collects payment on the day of the planned event. However, if they are not paid at that time, they expect full payment for their services within 10 days of the invoice. You will change default font settings, create a custom menu, and add specific buttons to one of the toolbars in Excel to make the task easier and more efficient.

▼ DIRECTIONS

1. Change the default font settings for workbooks to Verdana, 10 point or another font on your system.

2. Exit Excel and restart to implement the settings.

3. Open **10.1ARAging** from the Data CD.

4. Copy the entire worksheet and paste it into a new worksheet, matching the destination settings. The worksheet should now have the new default settings. Adjust column widths as necessary.

5. Create a custom menu called **AgingRpt,** as shown in the illustration on the next page, that contains the following commands:
   Format, Apply Outline Borders
   Format, Fill Color
   Insert, Page Break
   File, Page Setup
   Tools, Trace Error

6. Add the following buttons to the Standard toolbar:
   Insert, Rows
   Insert, Columns
   Edit, Delete Rows
   Tools, Macros
   Tools, Record New Macro
   Data, AutoFilter

7. Remove the **AutoFilter** button from the toolbar.

8. Group the June and July sheets.
   a. Use the custom menu command to apply a **light purple** fill color to **Cells A7:H8** on the first sheet (June) of the workbook.
   b. Use the custom menu command to apply an **outline border** to **Cells A7:H8.**
   c. Use the custom toolbar button to insert a column between the **CUSTOMER** and **DAYS UNPAID** columns.
   d. Enter DUE DATE as the new column heading in **Cell D8.**
   e. Ungroup the sheets.

Continued on next page

9. Invoice 139 on the first sheet (June) has been paid. Delete **Row 13** from the report using the **Delete Rows** button you placed on the toolbar.

10. Calculate the **DUE DATE** for all invoices on both sheets, by adding 10 days to the INVOICE DATE, which are the terms of payment given to all customers. The DUE DATE results should be in Date format.

11. Save the **10.1ARAging** file.

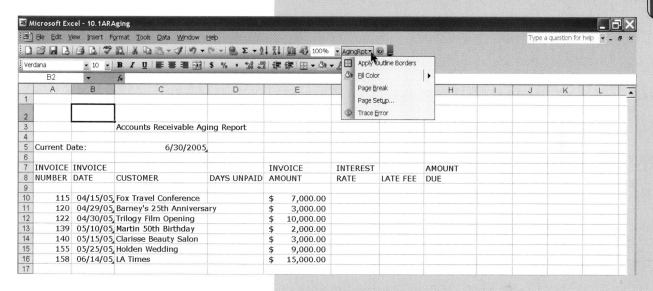

Add a Custom Menu

1. Click **Tools, Customize,** and **Commands** tab.
2. In Categories box, select **New Menu.**
3. In Commands box, click **New Menu** and drag it to toolbar on which you want menu to appear.
4. Right-click **New Menu** on toolbar. Enter a name for menu in Name box. Press **Enter.**
5. Click name of custom menu so that empty box appears.
6. Locate commands you want by looking first in Categories box, then in Commands box.
7. Click and drag commands from Commands box to Custom Menu box you created.

8. Close Customize dialog box.
9. Save and close file.

Add a Button to a Toolbar

1. Click **Tools, Customize,** and **Commands** tab.
2. Locate button you want by looking first in Categories box, then in Commands box.
3. Click and drag button from Commands box to toolbar on which you want it to appear.
4. Close Customize dialog box.

Remove a Button from a Toolbar

1. Hold down **Alt.**
2. Click and drag button you are removing off toolbar.

Modify Excel Default Font Settings

1. Click **Tools, Options,** and **General** tab.
2. Click **Standard Font** list arrow and change font style.
3. Click **Standard Font Size** list arrow and change font size.
4. Click **OK.**
5. Exit and restart Excel to implement settings.

Modify Excel Default Number of Worksheets

1. Click **Tools, Options,** and **General** tab.
2. Use increment arrows to change Sheets in new workbook setting.
3. Click **OK.**
4. Exit and restart Excel to implement settings.

▶ GOALS
To create and protect a depreciation schedule
To practice using the following skill sets:
⚹ Modify passwords, protections, and properties
⚹ Protect individual worksheets
⚹ Use passwords for protection
⚹ Add cell protection
⚹ Protect workbooks

WHAT YOU NEED TO KNOW

Modify Passwords and Protections

▶ As you learned in Lesson 8, Excel provides several features that allow multiple users to work on the same files; however, you may not want them to make changes to the data, formulas, or formatting in the file. For example, you may wish that they add their data to a budget sheet but that other data and formulas are not changed.

▶ Excel allows you to add protection to specific cells, worksheets, or an entire workbook. *Protection* means that another user can read the data, but cannot make any changes to it until that protection is removed or unless a password is used. A *password* is a sequence of letters and/or numbers that a user must enter before access to a worksheet or workbook is allowed.

Protect Individual Worksheets

▶ One way to restrict access to an Excel file is to add protection to a worksheet. By doing so, you allow other users to open the workbook, but prevent them from making specified changes to that worksheet.

▶ To protect a worksheet, click Tools, select Protection, and click Protect Sheet. The Protect Sheet dialog box opens, as shown in Figure 10.7

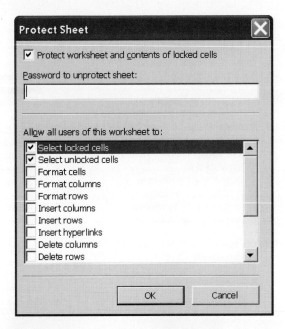

Figure 10.7 Protect Sheet dialog box

▶ The top box, labeled Protect worksheet and contents of locked cells, should be checked. The Allow all users of this worksheet to section lists commands to which you can regulate access. If you clear all of the boxes, users will not be able to do anything on the worksheet, including selecting a cell. Checking a box allows the user to perform that function. For example, in Figure 10.7, users are only allowed to select locked and unlocked cells, not to change them.

▶ Once you have added protection to a worksheet, any user attempting to make a change to a locked cell will see the message shown in Figure 10.8.

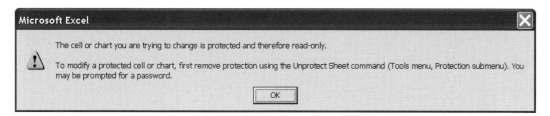

Figure 10.8 Protection warning box

▶ To cancel protection of the worksheet, click Tools, select Protection, and click Unprotect Sheet.

T R Y *it* **O U T** *e10-5*

1. Open the file **E10-5** from the Data CD.

2. Click **Tools,** select **Protection,** and click **Protect Sheet.**

3. In the Protect Sheet dialog box, make sure the box **Protect worksheet and contents of locked cells** is checked. Leave the Password field blank. In the box labeled Allow all users of this worksheet to, leave **Select locked cells** and **Select unlocked cells** checked. Click **OK.**

4. Click **Cell D10** and try to change the value to **3000.**

5. Click **OK** when you get the Microsoft Excel warning message.

6. Click **Tools,** select **Protection,** and click **Unprotect Sheet.**

7. Change **Cell D10** to **3000.**

8. Keep the file open.

Use Passwords for Protection

▶ You can add a password in the Protect Sheet dialog box to allow only designated users to make changes to the worksheet. The password is optional, but if you do not add a password, any user can remove protection from a worksheet as we just did. Once you have added a password, you and any other user must use it to access the worksheet.

▶ Enter the password you have selected in the box labeled Password to unprotect sheet. Click OK. Reenter the password in the Confirm Password dialog box that follows, as shown in Figure 10.9, and click OK.

Figure 10.9 Confirm Password dialog box

▶ IMPORTANT: If you lose or forget the password, you cannot make changes on the worksheet. Passwords can be up to 255 characters long and include letters, numbers, symbols, and spaces. Passwords are case sensitive, so pay attention to whether you are using uppercase or lowercase characters.

▶ Users who enter the password can remove protection from the sheet and then make changes on it. Click Tools, select Protection, and click Unprotect Sheet. The Unprotect Sheet dialog box opens, as shown in Figure 10.10. Enter the password and click OK. You can now make changes to the worksheet.

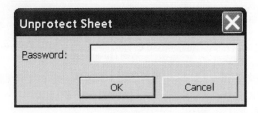

Figure 10.10 Unprotect Sheet dialog box

▶ To change a password for a protected sheet, you need the original password to unprotect the sheet and then to reprotect it with a new password. Click Tools, select Protection, and click Unprotect Sheet. Enter the current password in the Unprotect Sheet dialog box and click OK. Then click Tools, select Protection, click Protect Sheet, and enter the new password in the box labeled Password to unprotect sheet. Reenter the password in the Confirm Password dialog box and click OK. You will now need to use the new password to access the worksheet.

1. Continue to work in the open file or open **E10-6** from the Data CD.

2. Click **Tools,** select **Protection,** and click **Protect Sheet.**

3. In the Protect Sheet dialog box, leave all of the default values; this time, however, enter BUDGET in the box labeled Password to unprotect sheet. Click **OK.**

4. In the Confirm Password dialog box, reenter BUDGET.

5. Click **OK.**

6. Try to change **Cell D12** to 600.

7. Click **OK** when you get the warning message.

8. Click **Tools,** select **Protection,** and click **Unprotect Sheet.**

9. In the Unprotect Sheet dialog box, enter the password BUDGET.

10. Click **OK.**

11. Change **Cell D12** to 600.

12. Click **Tools,** select **Protection,** and click **Protect Sheet.**

13. Enter BUDGET2 in the box labeled Password to unprotect sheet. Click **OK.**

14. In the Confirm Password dialog box, reenter BUDGET2 and click **OK.** You have changed the password.

15. Close the file. Do not save.

Add Cell Protection

▶ In some situations, you may want other users to be able to use a worksheet, but you also want to restrict their access to certain cells on the worksheet. In other words, you want to create protected cells, or *locked cells.* This feature is useful when you create a worksheet and want to protect labels and formulas. You can unlock only the cells where another employee can add current data.

▶ By default, all cells in a workbook are locked, but the locked status becomes enabled only when you protect a worksheet. Therefore, to add cell protection to some portions of a worksheet only, you have to first unlock the cells you are allowing others to access and then protect the worksheet. The protection will enable locked cells for all cells except the unlocked ranges.

▶ To unlock specific cells on a worksheet, select the range of cells you want to unlock. Click Format, Cells to open the Format Cells dialog box, as shown in Figure 10.11. Click the Protection tab and clear the Locked box.

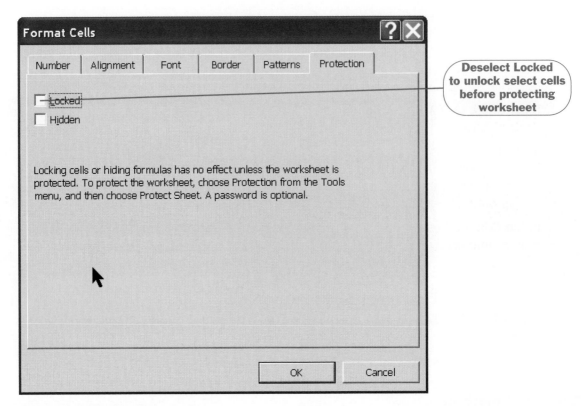

Figure 10.11 Format Cells dialog box

▶ Next, protect the worksheet. Click Tools, select Protection, and click Protect Sheet. Now, other users can make changes only to the cells you unlocked. You can add a password so that designated users can make changes in the locked cells.

T R Y *it* O U T *e10-7*

1. Open the file **E10-7** from the Data CD.

2. Select **Cells D7:D22,** the range to unlock.

3. Click **Format, Cells,** and the **Protection** tab. Clear the **Locked** box. Click **OK.**

4. Click **Tools,** select **Protection,** and click **Protect Sheet.** Leave the default values and click **OK.**

5. Try to change the value in **Cell C10** to 2000. The warning message appears because the cell is locked.

6. Change the value in **Cell D10** to 2000. This cell has been unlocked and you can change it.

7. Close the file. Do not save.

Protect Workbooks

▶ In some cases, you may want to protect an entire workbook so that users cannot add or delete sheets, rename sheets, or otherwise change the overall structure of a workbook. If you have not added worksheet protection, however, others can make changes to the data on a sheet. To protect a workbook, click Tools, select Protection, and click Protect Workbook. As with protecting a worksheet, you have the option of adding a password to allow designated users to remove workbook protection.

▶ In the Protect Workbook dialog box, as shown in Figure 10.12, check Structure if you want to prevent others from moving, adding, deleting, renaming, or copying sheets. Check Windows if you want to prevent others from changing the size or position of the windows when the workbook is opened. Add a password if you want to let designated individuals remove workbook protection. Click OK.

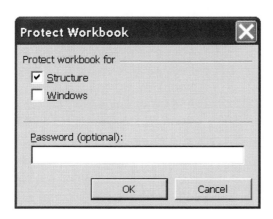

Figure 10.12 Protect Workbook dialog box

▶ To remove protection from a workbook, click Tools, select Protection, and click Unprotect Workbook. Enter the password, if you are prompted to do so. Click OK.

TRY it OUT e10-8

1. Open **E10-8** from the Data CD.

2. Click **Tools,** select **Protection,** and click **Protect Workbook.**

3. In the Protect Workbook dialog box, make sure the box for **Structure** is checked. Click **OK.**

4. Double-click the tab for **Sheet 1** to try to change its name. Click **OK** in response to the error message.

5. Try to move Sheet 1 to follow Sheet 2 by clicking and dragging the tab for **Sheet 1** to the right.

6. Change the value in **Cell C10** to 2000. (Worksheets must be protected individually.)

7. Close the file. Do not save.

EXCEL

REHEARSAL

GOAL
To add cell, worksheet, and workbook protection to a depreciation schedule

SETTING THE STAGE/WRAPUP
File name: **10.2Depreciation**

TASK 2

WHAT YOU NEED TO KNOW

▶ Businesses can obtain tax deductions for machinery, buildings, and equipment that are used to produce income. However, the deduction for the cost of such items must extend over the "estimated useful life" of each asset. A *depreciation schedule* is an accounting record that shows the cost of an asset spread over its estimated useful life.

▶ There are several methods of determining the depreciation of a business's assets. The most common way is called *straight-line depreciation.* This method assumes that the worth of an asset is spread equally over its estimated useful life. Thus, the annual amount of depreciation is calculated by subtracting its value at the end of its useful life (that is, its residual value) from its initial cost, and then dividing by the length of its useful life. For example, to calculate depreciation on a desk costing $1500 with a residual or scrap value of $500, divide the difference of $1000 by the useful life of the desk. For a five-year life, the annual depreciation is $200. Expressed as a formula, depreciation is calculated as follows:

Depreciation = (Initial Cost – Residual Value)/Estimated Useful Life

DIRECTIONS

Note: Follow the guidelines in the illustrations on the next page as you conduct the steps below.

1. Open **10.2Depreciation** from the Data CD. Work on the sheet labeled **2004,** as shown in Illustration A on the next page. *Note: Notice that the month (M) and day (D) of the asset purchase are entered in Columns C and D, using the MONTH and DAY function. (See formula bar in Illustration A.)*

2. In **Cell H7,** enter the formula for Annual Depreciation using the straight-line depreciation method described in the What You Need to Know section at left. *(Hint: =(Cost-Residual Value)/Life)*

3. In **Cell I7,** enter a formula to calculate 2004 Months, the months the company has owned the asset, using the half-month method. As explained, to calculate the months owned, you must determine if the asset was purchased after the fifteenth of the month. Hint: Use an IF statement with the D (date) and M (month) column data. =IF(D>15,12-M,12-(M-1))

4. In **Cell J7**, enter a formula to calculate 2004 Depreciation. Hint: The annual depreciation must be prorated by dividing the annual depreciation by 12 and multiplying by the 2004 Months. =(Annual Depreciation/12)*2004 months

5. Copy all formulas in **Cells H7:J7** to fill in the range **H11:J11.**

6. Total the **2004 Depreciation.**

7. Protect the worksheet. Do not use a password. Try to change the cost of the telephone system to **$6000.**

8. Copy the data on **Sheet 2004,** in the range **A7:J11,** to the sheet labeled **2005.** Adjust column width, if necessary.

Continued on next pages

- To compute the amount of money you should record for depreciation, calculate depreciation for the time that the asset is owned, using the half-month method. The annual depreciation amount is prorated using the following rules:
  - If equipment is purchased between the first and the fifteenth day of a month, depreciation is calculated for the entire month.
  - If equipment is purchased between the sixteenth day and the end of the month, depreciation is not calculated until the next month.
- In this Rehearsal activity, you will work on a depreciation schedule for assets owned by Occasions Event Planning. You will protect cells, a worksheet, and the workbook, and create a password to allow only certain users to make changes to various portions of the workbook. Protection of the data in this workbook is important since the data must be used for tax returns over a period of years. Inadvertent changes by unauthorized users can have serious consequences for the accuracy of a company's tax records.

| C7 | | | f_x | =MONTH(B7) | | | | | | |

	A	B	C	D	E	F	G	H	I	J
1		**Occasions Event Planning**								
2		**Depreciation Schedule - 2004**								
3		Straight-Line Method								
4										
5		Date				Asset	Residual	Annual	2004	2004
6	Asset	Purchased	M	D	Cost	Life	Value	Depreciation	Months	Depreciation
7	2002 White Van	2/10/2004	2	10	$21,000.00	5	$ 8,000.00			
8	Computer	3/21/2004	3	21	$ 2,800.00	3	$ 500.00			
9	Desk	3/24/2004	3	24	$ 1,500.00	5	$ 500.00			
10	Printer	3/24/2004	3	24	$ 800.00	5	$ 200.00			
11	Telephone System	6/12/2004	6	12	$ 5,000.00	5	$ 1,000.00	Enter formulas and protect cells		
12										
13	**Total**									

Illustration A

9. Copy the **2005 Purchases** sheet data to the appropriate columns on the **2005** sheet, as shown in Illustrations B and C. *Note that the M and D columns are not on the Purchases sheet.*

10. Fill in the formulas for **Columns C, D, H, I,** and **J** for the new items.

11. Total the **2005 Depreciation.** Note that the 2004 asset depreciations are incorrrect.

12. Unlock **Cells I7:I11.** Protect the worksheet.

13. Delete the **2005 Month data** for the assets purchased last year, located in **I7:I11,** and enter 12 for each item to indicate a full year of depreciation. Shade the area, as shown in Illustration C. Note the corrected depreciation.

14. Try to change the cost of an asset and note the protection.

15. Protect the workbook. Use OEP as the password. Try to delete **Sheet 2005.**

16. Use the password to unprotect the workbook.

17. To prepare for the year 2006:
    a. Insert a new sheet and label it: **2006 Purchases.**
    b. Copy the **2005 Purchases** sheet column headings to the new sheet.

18. Protect the workbook. Save and close the file.

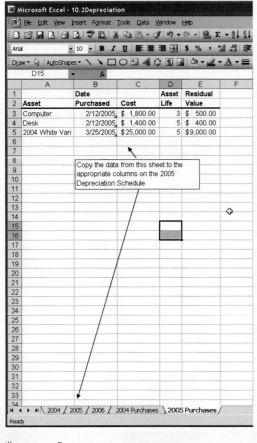

Illustration B

	A	B	C	D	E	F	G	H	I	J	K
1		**Occasions Event Planning**						After formulas are copied, shade 2004 assets and change months to 12 so that depreciation is calculated for the year			
2		**Depreciation Schedule - 2005**									
3		Straight-Line Method									
4											
5		Date				Asset	Residual	Annual	2005	2005	
6	Asset	Purchased	M	D	Cost	Life	Value	Depreciation	Months	Depreciation	
7	2002 White Van	2/10/2004	2	10	$ 21,000.00	5	$ 8,000.00	2600.00	12	$ 2,600.00	
8	Computer	3/21/2004	3	21	$ 2,800.00	3	$ 500.00	766.67	12	$ 766.67	
9	Desk	3/24/2004	3	24	$ 1,500.00	5	$ 500.00	200.00	12	$ 200.00	
10	Printer	3/24/2004	3	24	$ 800.00	5	$ 200.00	120.00	12	$ 120.00	
11	Telephone System	6/12/2004	6	12	$ 5,000.00	5	$ 1,000.00	800.00	12	$ 800.00	
12	Computer	2/12/2005	2	12	$ 1,800.00	3	$ 500.00	433.33	11	$ 397.22	
13	Desk	2/12/2005	2	12	$ 1,400.00	5	$ 400.00	200.00	11	$ 183.33	
14	2004 White Van	3/25/2005	3	25	$ 25,000.00	5	$ 9,000.00	3200.00	9	$ 2,400.00	
15											
16	Total									$ 7,467.22	
17											

Illustration C

EXCEL

Cues for Reference

Protect a Worksheet
1. Click **Tools**, select **Protection**, and click **Protect Sheet.**
2. In Protect Sheet dialog box, check **Protect worksheet and contents of locked cells.**
3. In Allow all users of this worksheet to, clear boxes for any functions you do not want other individuals to use.
4. Click **OK.**

Add a Password
1. Click **Tools**, select **Protection**, and click **Protect Sheet.**

2. In Protect Sheet dialog box, enter password in Password to unprotect sheet box. Click **OK.**
3. Reenter password in Confirm Password dialog box. Click **OK.**

Protect a Cell or Cells
1. Select cells you want to unlock. All other cells remain locked.
2. Click **Format, Cells,** and **Protection** tab.
3. Clear **Locked** box. Click **OK.**
4. Add protection to sheet following steps in Protect a Worksheet, above.

Protect a Workbook
1. Click **Tools**, select **Protection**, and click **Protect Workbook.**
2. In Protect Workbook dialog box, check whether you want to protect structure of workbook and/or size and arrangement of windows.
3. Add a password if you want.
4. Click **OK.**

Remove Protection
1. Click **Tools**, select **Protection**, and click **Unprotect Sheet.**
2. Enter password if you are prompted to do so.
3. Click **OK.**

TASK 3

GOALS
To create an accounts receivable aging
report using macros
To practice using the following skill sets:
* Create, edit, and run macros
    * Create macros
    * Use relative reference macros
    * Run macros
    * Edit macros using the Visual
      Basic Editor
    * Delete a macro
    * Use digital signature for macro
      projects

WHAT YOU NEED TO KNOW

Create, Edit, and Run Macros

▶ A *macro* is a series of actions you record to allow you to complete a task quickly and efficiently. In a macro, you can record any set of instructions that you perform over and over, such as selecting commands from a menu, formatting, and writing labels and formulas. A saved macro with your recorded commands is then readily available for use at a future time. When you are ready to use the macro, you simply use the assigned shortcut keys to run the macro and all the steps are performed.

▶ Excel records macros in the *Visual Basic Editor,* a module in Excel that uses the Visual Basic programming language. You can edit the commands that Excel records by using the syntax of Visual Basic.

Create Macros

▶ The process of creating macros involves the following general sequence of steps:

• Name the macro.

• Assign the shortcut keys for playing back the macro.

• Perform the sequence of steps you want to record in the macro.

• Stop recording the macro.

▶ To begin creating a macro, click Tools, select Macro, and click Record New Macro. The Record Macro dialog box opens, as shown in Figure 10.13. Or, you can place the Record New Macro button on your toolbar or custom menu and click it to begin creating a macro.

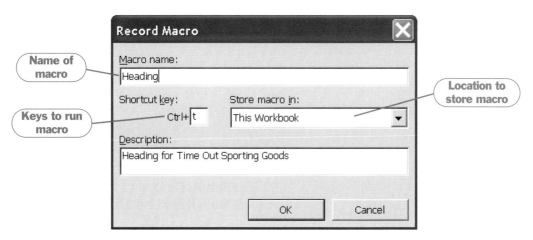

Figure 10.13 Record Macro dialog box

▶ Enter the name of the macro in the Macro name box. A macro name must start with a letter and use a name that will help you remember what the macro does. No special characters or spaces are allowed in macro names, but you can use the underscore character (_) to separate parts of a name.

▶ Select the existing text in the Description box and enter your own description of what the macro will do.

▶ Click in the Shortcut key box and enter a letter that you can use with the Ctrl key to run your macro. You should not use letters that are already assigned to perform commands with the Ctrl key; for example, Ctrl+P for Print or Ctrl+X for Cut. If you do, the macro will override these commands.

Note: You cannot use numbers or special characters as shortcut keys.

▶ Specify the location in which Excel will store the macro in the Store macro in box. You can select one of three options:

  • Select Personal Macro Workbook if you want to use the macro whenever you use Excel. Excel stores the macro in a hidden workbook that is always open. To see the hidden Personal Macro Workbook, click Window, Unhide.

  • Select This Workbook to store the macro in the current workbook only. Choose this option if you plan to use the macro only for tasks in the current workbook.

  • Select New Workbook to store the macro in a new or specified workbook. Select this option if you plan to use the macro for some workbooks, but not for all of them. You will have to open the workbook that contains the macro before you can use it.

▶ Click OK. The Status bar displays the word Recording. The Stop Recording toolbar, as shown in Figure 10.14, appears on the worksheet.

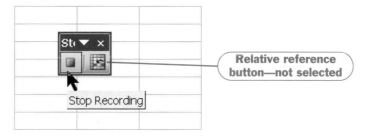

Figure 10.14 Stop Recording toolbar

▶ Enter the series of steps you want to record in the macro. Press the Enter key. Then click the Stop Recording button on the Stop Recording toolbar.

Note: Take time to plan your steps carefully since Excel will record every action you take.

T R Y _it_ O U T *e10-9*

1. Open the file **E10-9** from the Data CD.
2. Select **Cell C2.**
3. Click **Tools,** select **Macro,** and click **Record New Macro.**
4. Enter `Heading` in the Macro name box.
5. Enter `Heading for Time Out Sporting Goods` in the Description box.
6. Enter `t` in the Shortcut key box.
7. In the Store macro in box, select **This Workbook,** if not already selected.

8. Click **OK.**
9. Click **Format, Cells,** and the **Font** tab. Select **Bold Italic** and **16 pt.**
10. Click the **Alignment** tab. Select **Center** in the Horizontal box. Click **OK** to end.
11. Enter `TIME OUT SPORTING GOODS` and press the **Enter** key.
12. Click the **Stop Recording** button. Save and close the file.

Use Relative Reference Macros

▶ If the macro you create contains a range of cells, Excel records them as absolute cell references. This means that the macro plays only on those designated cells. If you want to use the macro in other cell ranges, you must click the Relative Reference button on the Stop Recording toolbar, as shown in Figure 10.14, before you record the macro. The Relative Reference button appears with a yellow border when it is active. When you record a macro with the Relative Reference button on, you can apply the macro to any cell in the worksheet.

▶ Once you have created a macro, each time you reopen the file the message shown in Figure 10.15 appears. It warns you that the file contains macros and gives you the option of disabling or enabling macros. If you want to make the macros functional, click Enable Macros. *Note: If the security for your system is set to a high level, Enable Macros will not work. See your administrator or see the information on changing security levels under Digital Signatures for Macro Projects on page 90.*

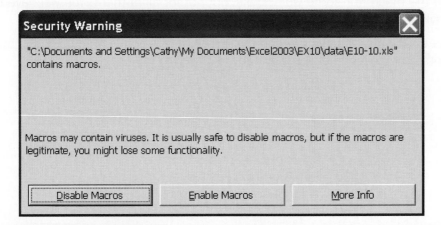

Security Warning

"C:\Documents and Settings\Cathy\My Documents\Excel2003\EX10\data\E10-10.xls" contains macros.

Macros may contain viruses. It is usually safe to disable macros, but if the macros are legitimate, you might lose some functionality.

| Disable Macros | Enable Macros | More Info |

Figure 10.15 Enabling and disabling macros

1. Open the file that you saved in the previous Try it Out or open **E10-10** from the Data CD.

2. In the dialog box that opens, click **Enable Macros.**

3. Click **Tools,** select **Macro,** and click **Record New Macro.**

4. Macro name: `Underline`
   Shortcut key: `b`
   Description: `Heavy underline`
   Store Macro in: `Personal Macro Workbook`

5. Click **OK.**

6. Click the **Relative Reference** button on the Stop Recording toolbar.

7. Select **Cells A5:G5.** Click **Format, Cells,** and the **Border** tab. Select the heavy line across the bottom of the cells. Click **OK** to end.

8. Click the **Stop Recording** button on the Stop Recording toolbar.

9. Click **Tools,** select **Macro,** and click **Record New Macro.**

10. Macro name: `Border`
    Shortcut key: `r`
    Description: `Border around column titles`
    Store macro in: `This Workbook`

11. Click **OK.**

12. Make sure the **Relative Reference** button is not depressed.

13. Select **Cells A7:G8.** Click **Format, Cells,** and the **Border** tab.

14. Select a heavy line, click the **Outline** border button, and click **OK.**

15. Click the **Stop Recording** button on the Stop Recording toolbar.

16. Keep the file open.

Run Macros

▶ To run a macro, select the cell where you want the macro to start playing. Then press the keys that you designated for the particular macro (e.g., Ctrl + letter).

▶ Another way to run a macro is to click Tools, select Macro, and click Macros. The Macro dialog box opens, as shown in Figure 10.16. Select the name of your macro from the list and click Run.

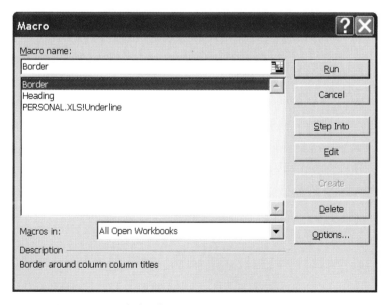

Figure 10.16 Macro dialog box

▶ You can also open the Macro dialog box by pressing the Alt + F8 keys. Then select the macro from the list and click Run. If you placed the Macros button on a toolbar or custom menu, you can click it to open the Macro dialog box. Select the macro and click Run.

T R Y *it* **O U T** *e10-11*

1. Continue to work in the open file or open E10-11 from the Data CD and enable macros.

2. On the July sheet, click **Cell C2.**

3. Press the **Ctrl + t** keys.

4. On the July sheet, click **Cell C5.**

5. Press the **Ctrl + b** keys.

6. On the July sheet, click **Cell A14.**

7. Press the **Ctrl + r** keys.

8. Keep the file open.

Edit Macros Using the Visual Basic Editor

▶ If you want to make changes in your macro, you must use the Visual Basic Editor that is located in a module attached to your worksheet.

▶ To begin editing, click Tools, select Macro, and click Macros (or click the Alt + F8 keys). Select the macro you want to edit and click Edit. The Visual Basic Editor appears, as shown in Figure 10.17. Excel lists the commands for the macro in the window. Select and reenter, delete, or add commands. The way to make changes may be obvious for some of the commands, but if you want to learn more about the syntax for programming commands, type Visual Basic Help in the question box. When you have finished making your changes, close the Visual Basic Editor.

```
E10-12.xls - Module1 (Code)

(General)                                        Heading

    Sub Heading()
    '
    ' Heading Macro
    ' Heading for Time Out Sporting Goods
    '
    ' Keyboard Shortcut: Ctrl+t
    '
        With Selection
            .HorizontalAlignment = xlCenter
            .VerticalAlignment = xlBottom
            .WrapText = False
            .Orientation = 0
            .AddIndent = False
            .IndentLevel = 0
            .ShrinkToFit = False
            .ReadingOrder = xlContext
            .MergeCells = False
        End With
        With Selection.Font
            .Name = "Arial"
            .FontStyle = "Bold Italic"        Edit FontStyle here
            .Size = 16
            .Strikethrough = False
            .Superscript = False
            .Subscript = False
            .OutlineFont = False
            .Shadow = False
            .Underline = xlUnderlineStyleNone
            .ColorIndex = xlAutomatic
        End With
        ActiveCell.FormulaR1C1 = "TIME OUT SPORTING GOODS"
        ActiveCell.Offset(11, 1).Range("A1").Select
    End Sub
```

Figure 10.17 Example of a Visual Basic module

T R Y i t O U T *e10-12*

1. Continue to work in the open file or open **E10-12** from the Data CD and enable macros.

2. Click **Tools,** select **Macro,** and click **Macros.**

3. Select the **Heading** macro. Click **Edit.**

4. Scroll down the list of commands until you see Font Style = "Bold Italic".

5. Delete "Italic". The entry should read .FontStyle = "Bold."

6. Close the Visual Basic Editor.

7. Go to Sheet 3 and click **Cell C2.**

8. Press the **Ctrl + t** keys. Keep the file open.

Delete a Macro

▶ To delete a macro stored in a workbook, click Tools, select Macro, and click Macros. Select the macro you want to remove and click Delete. If the macro is stored in the Personal notebook, you must unhide it to view and delete the macro.

1. Continue to work in the open file.

2. Click **Tools**, select **Macro**, and click **Macros**.

3. Select **Heading** and click **Delete**. Confirm the deletion, if necessary.

4. Click **Window, Unhide**.

5. Click **OK** in the Unhide dialog box.

6. Click **Tools**, select **Macro**, and click **Macros**.

7. Select **Underline** and click **Delete**.

8. Click **Window, Hide**.

9. Close the workbook. Do not save.

Digital Signatures for Macro Projects

▶ Excel 2003 provides a security feature, called digital signatures, that can verify that the macros in a file originated from the signer, are safe, and have not been altered since they were signed. A digital certificate must be installed to sign, or attach a verification to a file. You can obtain digital certification from a commercial certification authority, from your internal security administrator, or you can create your own certification using a program for that purpose. Files you certify yourself are considered unauthenticated, and will generate a Security Warning and will not be cleared by Excel except on your own computer. Digital certification is essential for persons or companies who publish software. Signed macro files remain signed until the macro codes are changed.

▶ If you have macro security set to Very High or High, you will not be able to open any files that have macros unless they are digitally signed from trusted sources. To enable unsigned macros, the security level must be set to Medium or Low. To change macro security settings, click Tools, Options and click the Security tab, as shown in Figure 10.18. Click Macro Security and note the security settings, as shown in Figure 10.19.

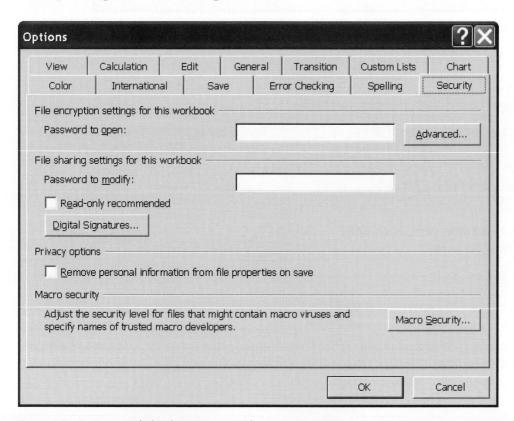

Figure 10.18 Options dialog box, Security Tab

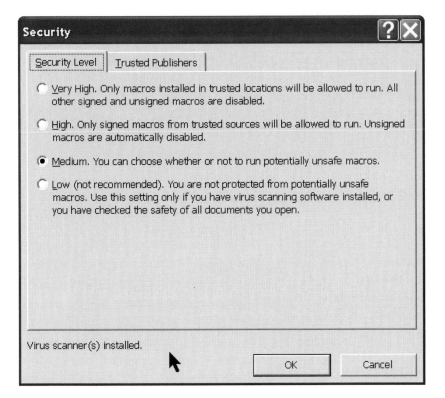

Figure 10.19 Macro Security dialog box

1. In a blank workbook, click **Tools, Options** and select the **Security** tab.

2. Click **Macro Security** and view the settings for your computer.

3. Do not change settings unless instructed by your local administrator.

4. Click **Cancel.** Click **Cancel.**

5. Click **Tools, Macro, Security** to use another method to view security settings.

6. Click **Cancel.**

REHEARSAL

TASK 3

GOAL
To create an accounts receivable aging report

SETTING THE STAGE/WRAPUP
File name: **10.3ARAging**

WHAT YOU NEED TO KNOW

▶ Customer accounts, or accounts receivable are reviewed monthly to determine which invoices are unpaid and have exceeded the terms allowed. Finance charges may be imposed to encourage payment within the terms of the sale.

▶ In this Rehearsal activity, you will:

- Create, edit, and run macros to complete the aging report for Occasions Event Planning for two months.

- Name, describe, and establish shortcut keys for the macros that relate to their purpose.

- Use the macros with the custom menus and toolbars created earlier to create an accounts receivable aging report more efficiently.

▽ DIRECTIONS

1. Open **10.3ARAging** from the Data CD or use the file you worked on in the last Rehearsal, **10.1ARAging**.

2. Add the **Record Macro** button to the AgingAR toolbar button created earlier.

3. Click **Cell C2**. Create a macro, using a name and shortcut key you provide, that does the following:
   a. Enter the heading for the report, as indicated in the illustration on the next page: `Occasions Event Planning`.
   b. Format in **Comic Sans MS**, **Bold Italic**, **18 pt**. Stop recording.

4. Go to the sheet labeled **July** and run this macro in **Cell C2**.

5. Edit the macro so that bold is removed.

6. Run the edited macro in the sheets for **June** and **July** in **Cell C2**.

7. In **Cell E10** for **June**, create a macro that does the following:
   a. Enters the formula for calculating the number of days an account is unpaid. (Hint: Subtract the DUE DATE from the Current Date, which must be an absolute cell reference.)
   b. Formats the result for **General numbers** (no decimal places). Stop recording.

8. Use the fill handle to copy the formula to the remaining invoices.

9. Go to the sheet for **July** and run this macro in **Cell E10.** Use the fill handle to fill in the remaining values for the column.

Continued on next page

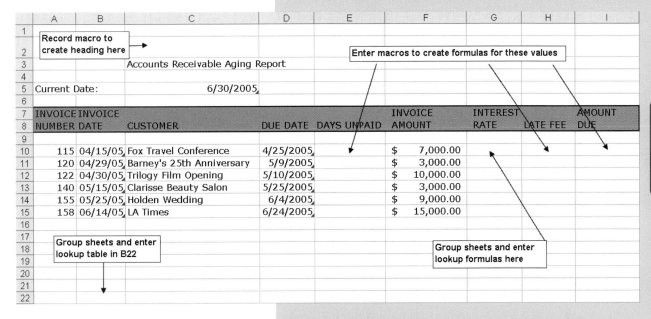

The spreadsheet shows an Accounts Receivable Aging Report with the following layout:

- Cell A2/B2 (callout): **Record macro to create heading here** (arrow pointing right)
- Row 3 (C): Accounts Receivable Aging Report
- Row 5: Current Date: (C) 6/30/2005
- Callout near E2–H2: **Enter macros to create formulas for these values**

INVOICE NUMBER	INVOICE DATE	CUSTOMER	DUE DATE	DAYS UNPAID	INVOICE AMOUNT	INTEREST RATE	LATE FEE	AMOUNT DUE
115	04/15/05	Fox Travel Conference	4/25/2005		$ 7,000.00			
120	04/29/05	Barney's 25th Anniversary	5/9/2005		$ 3,000.00			
122	04/30/05	Trilogy Film Opening	5/10/2005		$ 10,000.00			
140	05/15/05	Clarisse Beauty Salon	5/25/2005		$ 3,000.00			
155	05/25/05	Holden Wedding	6/4/2005		$ 9,000.00			
158	06/14/05	LA Times	6/24/2005		$ 15,000.00			

- Callout near rows 18–19 (A/B): **Group sheets and enter lookup table in B22** (arrow pointing down)
- Callout near rows 18–19 (G/H): **Group sheets and enter lookup formulas here**

10. Group the **June** and **July** sheets and do the following:
    a. Enter the lookup table below beginning in **Cell B22** and format the interest rate for three places.

DAYS UNPAID	INTEREST RATE
1	0.000
15	0.005
30	0.010
60	0.015
90	0.020

    b. Name the lookup table `Interest`.
    c. In **Cell G10,** enter a formula using the LOOKUP function in Excel, and the name of the table, to determine the interest rate for each customer.
    d. Format **Column G** for **Percent with one decimal place.**
    e. Use the fill handle to fill in the remaining values for the column.
    f. Ungroup the sheets.

11. In **Cell H10,** on the **June** sheet, create a macro that does the following:
    a. Enters the formula to calculate the late fee due.
    b. Formats the result for **Currency.**
    c. Fills in the remaining values for the column.

Continued on next page

EXCEL

12. In **Cell I10,** create a macro that does the following:
    a. Enters the formula for calculating the total amount due.
    b. Formats the result for **Currency.**
    c. Fills in the remaining values for the column.
    d. Adjusts column width.

13. On the **July** sheet, run the macros for the late fee and amount due in **Columns H** and **I,** respectively.

14. Print a copy of this workbook.

15. Save and close the **10.3ARAging** file.

Cues for Reference

Create a Macro
1. Click **Tools,** select **Macro,** and click **Record New Macro,** or click **Record Macro** button you have placed on toolbar.
2. In Record Macro dialog box:
    a. Enter name of macro in Macro name box.
    b. Enter a description of macro in Description box.
    c. Enter letter you will use (with Ctrl key) to enable macro in Shortcut key box.
    d. Select location in which to store macro in Store macro in box.

3. Click **OK.**
4. If macro will be used in any location on worksheet, click **Relative Reference** button.
5. Enter commands for macro and press **Enter.**
6. Click **Stop Recording** button.

Run a Macro
1. Click **Tools,** select **Macro,** and click **Macros.**
    or
   • Click **Macros** button you have placed on toolbar.
2. In Macro dialog box, click name of macro and click **Run.**

Edit a Macro
1. Click **Tools,** select **Macro,** and click **Macros.**
    or
   • Click **Macros** button you have placed on toolbar.
2. Select name of macro you want to edit. Click **Edit.**
3. Make changes to commands in Visual Basic Editor module.
4. Close Visual Basic Editor.

 SETTING THE STAGE/WRAPUP
Act I File name:
    10p1.Sales
Act II File name:
    10p2.Depreciation
Act III File name:
    10p3.Aging

WHAT YOU NEED TO KNOW

Act I

The Boston office of the Air Land Sea Travel Group is setting up a workbook for its sales to customers who have agency accounts. Since most customers use bank credit cards, the company only has a small number of sales to customers who use the agency billing system. The workbook will be used to track invoices prepared for agency account customers. Open the file **10p1.Sales** from the Data CD. You will create a custom menu and add several buttons to the Standard toolbar. You will create a macro to format dates on the worksheet. You will use these customized features to work in the sales report.

Follow these guidelines:

✳ Create a custom menu named **Sales.**

✳ Make sure the Customize dialog box is open when you are naming and adding commands to the custom menu.

✳ Add the following commands to the menu as illustrated below:
Insert, Rows
Edit, Delete Rows
Format, Currency Style
Format, Fill Color

✳ Put the following buttons on the Standard toolbar if they are not already there:
Tools, Macros
Tools, Record New Macro
Tools, Trace Error
Tools, File Search

✳ Delete the **Search** button from the Standard toolbar.

- Enter a formula to calculate Date Due, using the terms and invoice date.

- Use the customized toolbar buttons to record a macro to format dates in any column to **dd-mmm-yy** format.

- Run the macro to format all dates.

- Use the customized menu to format Amount Due for **Currency.**

- Include the following sales for the last day of the week:

INVOICE DATE	INVOICE NUMBER	TRIP DATE	CUSTOMER	TERMS-DAYS	AMOUNT
7/8/05	2442	8/15/05	Marvin Franks	30	$1500.00
7/8/05	2443	8/23/05	Lance Scully	30	$ 674.50
7/8/05	2444	7/28/05	Helen Reid	20	$ 235.65

- Use the customized menu, toolbar buttons, and macro as needed to complete all sales records.

- Print a copy of the report.

- Save your work. Close the file.

Act II

The Air Land Sea Travel Group is also preparing a depreciation schedule for all of its office equipment. Much of the data for the schedule has already been entered and must be protected so that it is not changed. Other data must be added, but only by authorized users who have a password.

Open the file **10p2.Depreciation** from the Data CD as illustrated below. You will add protection to a worksheet, to cells on a worksheet, and to a workbook. You will also create a password to allow only designated individuals to make modifications to the file.

	A	B	C	D	E	F	G	H	I
1									
2			*Air Land Sea Travel Group*						
3			*Depreciation Schedule*			2004			
4									
5									
6					Residual	Annual	2004	2004	
7	Asset	Purchased	Cost	Life	Value	Depreciation	Months	Depreciation	
8	Computer	2/1/2004	$ 2,800.00	3	$ 500.00		11		
9	Computer	2/1/2004	$ 2,800.00	3	$ 500.00				
10	Desk	2/18/2004	$ 1,500.00	5	$ 500.00				
11	Desk	2/18/2004	$ 1,500.00	5	$ 500.00				
12	Printer	2/18/2004	$ 800.00	3	$ 200.00				
13	Copier	3/5/2004	$ 10,500.00	5	$1,000.00				
14	Computer	4/20/2004	$ 2,200.00	3	$ 500.00				
15	Desk	4/21/2004	$ 1,600.00	5	$ 600.00				
16	Projector	5/10/2004	$ 5,500.00	5	$ 500.00				
17	Computer	6/20/2004	$ 1,800.00	3	$ 500.00				
18	Desk	6/20/2004	$ 1,400.00	5	$ 400.00				
19									
20									

Enter formula to calculate Straight-Line Depreciation

Enter formula to calculated prorated 2004 depreciation

Follow these guidelines:

* Start with the worksheet labeled **2004.** Use the straight-line depreciation method to enter the formula for depreciation in **Cell F8.** Notice that the formula is already entered in **Cell G8.**

* Enter a formula to calculate the 2004 Depreciation in **Cell H8.** *(Hint: Prorate the annual depreciation by dividing by 12 and multiplying by the number of months owned.)*

* Fill the formulas from **Cells F8:H8** to the range **F18:H18.** Find the Total depreciation for the year.

* Copy the information on this sheet to the Sheet **2005.** Adjust the formatting as needed. Protect the sheet labeled **2004.** Add the following password to the protection: `AirLandSea.`

* Change the entries on Sheet **2005** as follows:

    * Edit year labels to `2005.`

    * Delete the Total in H19.

    * Add the following new assets:

ASSET	PURCHASED	COST	LIFE	RESIDUAL VALUE
File Cabinets	4/12/2005	$6,350.00	5	$ 700.00
Printer	5/18/2005	$ 750.00	3	$ 150.00

    * Copy the formulas for the new items.

    * Delete the **Months** values for **2004** items, in **G8:G18,** enter `12` in **G8** and fill to **G18,** to show that the assets were owned for the entire year.

    * Total the **2005** worksheet.

    * Protect the worksheet.

* Protect the structure of the entire workbook. Use the same password as above.

* Unprotect the workbook to add a sheet labeled `Sheet 2006.` Protect the workbook again. Save and close the file.

Act III

Odyssey Travel Gear is preparing a workbook to handle its accounts receivable aging reports. Open **10p3.Aging** from the Data CD. Create macros for the corporate heading and all of the necessary formulas on the sheet labeled July. Then run the macros in the appropriate locations on the August sheet. Refer to the illustration of the July sheet on the next page to assist you with this project.

Follow these guidelines:

* The **Tools, Macros and Tools,** and **Record New Macro** buttons should be on the toolbar.

* Create a macro to enter the corporate heading that can be used in any cell. (Depress the **Relative Reference** button.)

  * In **Cell A1,** enter Odyssey Travel Gear.

  * Use **bold italic, 14 pt.**

  * Center the heading horizontally across **Columns A:I** using the **Merge and Center** button.

* Edit the macro for the corporate heading so that it appears in **18 pt.** Run the heading macro again in **Cell A2.** Delete the heading in **Cell A1** and remove the merge cells format from **Row 1.**

* In **Cell D9,** create a macro to enter the formula to calculate the due date of the invoice; format the results for dates in the **mm/dd/yy** format. (All customers are given 30 days to pay their bills; therefore, add 30 to the invoice date to find the due date.) Use the fill handle to fill in the values for all of the invoices.

* In **Cell E9,** create a macro to enter the formula computing the number of days an invoice is unpaid, i.e., the number of days past the due date. Use the **General number** format for the results. Use the fill handle to fill in the values for all of the invoices. *Hint: Use absolute reference for the date of the aging report in the formula.*

* The lookup table below should start in **Cell A20** and should be entered and named while sheets are grouped.

DAYS UNPAID	INTEREST RATE
1	0.00
30	0.01
60	0.02
90	0.03

* In **Cell G9,** use the LOOKUP function in Excel to find the interest rate for all customers using a named range for the table. Format the interest rate for Percent with one decimal place.

* In **Cell H9,** create a macro to compute the late fee for each customer. Use the fill handle to fill in the values for all of the customers.

* In **Cell I9,** create a macro to compute the total amount due for each invoice. Use the fill handle to fill in the values for all of the invoices.

* For the month of August, the following invoices are still unpaid: 265, 324, 387, and 453. In addition, there is one more invoice that has not been paid: Invoice 524, dated 7/1/02, to Bender's, for $300. Copy the data for the August aging report by copying **Columns A:G** data and then paste the data to the **August** sheet. Delete the rows for paid invoices, 200 and 432, so that only the invoices that are still unpaid are on the report. Enter the new unpaid invoice.

* Run all of the appropriate macros on the sheet for **August.**

* Print the report and save the file.

	A	B	C	D	E	F	G	H	I
1									
2				*Odyssey Travel Gear*					
3				Accounts Receivable Aging Report					
4									
5	Current Date:		31-Jul-05						
6									
7	INVOICE	INVOICE					INTEREST		AMOUNT
8	NUMBER	DATE	CUSTOMER	DUE DATE	DAYS UNPAID	AMOUNT	RATE	LATE FEE	DUE
9	200	04/30/05	Murray's Dept. Store	5/30/05		700.00			
10	265	05/02/05	Travel World	6/1/05		500.00			
11	324	05/15/05	A-Mart	6/14/05		250.00			
12	387	06/02/05	Bruni's	7/2/05		300.00			
13	432	06/15/05	Travelrama	7/15/05		200.00			
14	453	06/20/05	Webco	7/20/05		700.00			
15									
16									
17									
18									
19									
20	Days Unpaid	Interest Rate							
21	1	0							
22	30	0.01							
23	60	0.02							
24	90	0.03							
25									
26									

Data Lists

In this lesson, you will learn to use several features of Excel that allow you to manage data lists such as personnel, real estate, and inventory lists. These features include sorting a list and using subtotals, filters, group and outline criteria, data validation, and database functions.

Upon completion of this lesson, you should have mastered the following skill sets:

✴ Create and sort a list
  ✶ Create a list
  ✶ Sort a list
✴ Use subtotals with lists and ranges
✴ Define and apply filters
  ✶ AutoFilter
  ✶ Advanced Filter

✴ Add group and outline criteria to ranges
  ✶ Group data
  ✶ View and remove groups
  ✶ Outline data
✴ Use data validation
  ✶ Error messages
✴ Use database functions

Terms
Software-related
  Data list
  Record
  Field name
  Subtotal
  Filter
  Criteria range
  Data validation
  Database functions
Document-related
  Personnel list
  Real estate list
  Inventory list

TRYOUT

GOALS
To use the list, sort, and subtotal
functions in Excel on a personnel list
To practice using the following skill sets:
  * Create and sort a list
    * Create a list
    * Sort a list
  * Use subtotals with lists and ranges

TASK 1

EXCEL

WHAT YOU NEED TO KNOW

Create and Sort a List

▶ In addition to its spreadsheet functions, Excel performs many database functions. It has many features that allow you to create, manage, and obtain information from lists. Businesses can use these functions to store and analyze information about employees, customers, product inventories, and sales, to name just a few examples.

Create a List

▶ A *data list* is similar to the table object in Access, which is a columnar table of data with column headings. To create a data list, as shown in Figure 11.1, you must follow a number of conventions:

Field name

	A	B	C	D	E	F	G	H
1	LAST	FIRST	LOCATION	IDNO	HIRED	DEPT	WKSAL	ANNSAL
2	Notting	Deirdre	CT	42980	02/25/99	Sales	$ 325.60	$ 16,931.20
3	Edwards	Henry	CT	42859	03/07/98	Sales	$ 400.89	$ 20,846.28
4	Martin	Hester	NJ	43449	04/05/01	Stock	$ 450.76	$ 23,439.52
5	Wendt	Jack	NY	44689	05/24/00	Stock	$ 375.66	$ 19,534.32
6	Rogers	James	CT	42785	05/04/01	Stock	$ 348.77	$ 18,136.04
7	Brown	James	NY	44783	06/12/00	Admin	$ 495.82	$ 25,782.64
8	Bartlett	Jane	NY	44132	01/05/99	Sales	$ 362.33	$ 18,841.16
9	Selman	Jean	CT	42234	05/30/96	Admin	$ 600.45	$ 31,223.40
10	McCarthy	Joan	NY	44675	03/14/00	Sales	$ 322.79	$ 16,785.08
11	Sullivan	Karen	CT	42898	02/20/02	Sales	$ 325.00	$ 16,900.00
12	Dodge	Kiley	NJ	43212	04/16/98	Sales	$ 460.96	$ 23,969.92
13	Yaeger	Kimberly	NY	44332	04/19/99	Sales	$ 390.68	$ 20,315.36
14	Smith	Lisa	NJ	43989	05/17/99	Sales	$ 378.56	$ 19,685.12
15	Darlington	Marie	NY	44909	09/18/00	Admin	$ 450.22	$ 23,411.44
16	Fargo	Susan	CT	42345	12/02/97	Admin	$ 525.66	$ 27,334.32
17	Cuddy	Timothy	CT	42784	01/05/99	Stock	$ 390.54	$ 20,308.08
18	Charles	Victoria	NJ	43675	02/14/02	Stock	$ 333.05	$ 17,318.60
19								

One person's record

Figure 11.1 Example of a data list

- The data for one person or unit, called a *record,* goes across a row.
- Place a label, or *field name,* for the data in each column above the first row of data. The field name format (i.e., font, cell border, alignment, capitalization style, etc.) should be different from that of the data entries. Excel uses these labels to find and perform operations on the data.
- The data for each record must correspond to the labels or field names in the first row, or the column labels for the list.
- Put only one list on a given worksheet.
- Do not put blank rows or columns within the list.

- If there is other data on the worksheet, such as headings or summary data, leave at least one blank row or column between that data and the list.
- Avoid storing data to the left or right of the list, since filtering can hide that data.
- All column labels (or field names) must fit in one cell above the data. Thus, you must format long field names with the Wrap Text feature. Click Format, Cells, click the Alignment tab, and select the Wrap text option.

▶ To add a new record to a list, click Insert, Rows at the appropriate place in the list and add the data. You can also click Data, Form so that the Data Form dialog box opens, as shown in Figure 11.2.

▶ The data form, which is like the Form object in Access, displays the names for every data field you have created in the list. It also lets you view all of the information for each record, one record at a time. By using the data form, you can add new records, delete records, edit records, move to the next or previous record, and find records based on criteria that you apply.

▶ To add a new column or field, click Insert, Columns, and add the appropriate field name and data.

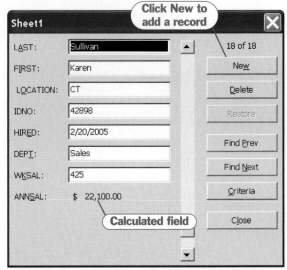

Figure 11.2 Data Form dialog box

TRY it OUT e11-1

1. Open the file **E11-1,** a personnel list, from the Data CD.

2. Click somewhere in the table, and click **Data, Form,** and **New.**

3. In the dialog box, enter the following information for each field:
LAST: Sarbanes	**FIRST:** Karen
LOCATION: CT	**IDNO:** 42999
HIRED: 02/20/05	**DEPT:** Sales
WKSAL: $425.00	

4. Click **New** and **Close.**

5. Add a column to the right of **Column H.**

6. In the new column, click **Format, Cells, Alignment,** and check the **Wrap text** option. Click **OK.**

7. Label the column **DATE OF LAST PERFORMANCE REVIEW.** Adjust column width.

8. Click **Data, Form** and use the scroll bar to view the previous records.

9. Close the Data Form dialog box.

10. Leave the file open.

Sort a List

▶ Excel allows you to sort the data in a list according to the criteria you specify. For example, you can sort the data alphabetically, numerically, or according to groups (e.g., all those who work in the states of New York or Connecticut).

▶ To sort data, select a cell in the field by which you want to sort. Click Data, Sort. The Sort dialog box opens, as shown in Figure 11.3. In the box labeled Sort by, select the field name by which you want Excel to sort the data. You can also sort records by several fields in successive order.

▶ Check the box to indicate whether you want to sort in ascending or descending order. If you want to arrange the data alphabetically, from smallest to largest or from oldest to most recent, select Ascending. If you select Descending, the reverse order results.

▶ Once you sort a list, the original order of the data is lost. You can preserve the original order of the data list by creating a field name called Record Number (or any name that indicates the numbers below it are in sequence). Then number each record sequentially. Later, when you want to sort the data back to the original order, you can sort by Record Number.

▶ To undo a sort, click Edit, Undo Sort.

Figure 11.3 Sort dialog box

TRY it OUT e11-2

1. Continue to work in the open file or open **E11-2** from the Data CD.

2. Click any cell in the list.

3. Click **Data, Sort.** In the box labeled Sort by, select **LAST.** If necessary, click the **Ascending** button. Click **OK.**

4. Click **Edit, Undo Sort.**

5. Click **Data, Sort.** In the box labeled Sort by, select **HIRED.** If necessary, click the **Ascending** button. Click **OK.**

6. Insert a column to the left of **Column A** and enter the column heading: **RECORD**

NUMBER and format the heading for Wrap Text. Enter consecutive numbers in the column, beginning with **1** by entering the first two values and using the fill handle.

7. Click in the **LOCATION** column and click **Data, Sort.** In the box labeled Sort by, select **LOCATION.** Make sure to click the **Ascending** button. In the box labeled Then by, select **LAST.** Make sure to click the **Ascending** button. Click **OK.**

8. Re-sort the list by **RECORD NUMBER.**

9. Keep the file open.

Use Subtotals with Lists and Ranges

▶ Excel provides a quick way to obtain a *subtotal,* a summary of a subset of data that is arranged in a list. You should sort the data for which you want to create a subtotal according to the relevant criterion, so that data in each subgroup appears together. For example, you can create subtotals of salaries by department or by location.

▶ To create a subtotal, click Data, Subtotals to open the Subtotal dialog box, as shown in Figure 11.4.

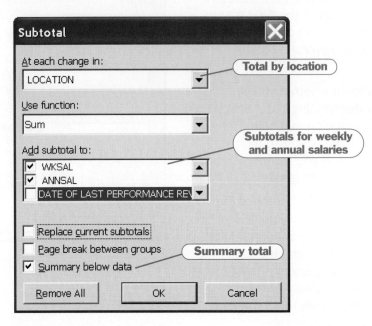

Figure 11.4 Subtotal dialog box

▶ In the box labeled At each change in, select the field name of the data that determines the groups for which you will obtain subtotals.

▶ In the box labeled Use function, select the mathematical operation you want to perform. You can select from Sum, Count, Average, Max, Min, Product, or several statistical functions.

▶ In the box labeled Add subtotal to, select the data on which you want to perform the mathematical function.

▶ Check the box Replace current subtotals, if prior subtotals have been computed and you want to replace them.

▶ Check the box Page break between groups if you want each of the subtotals to appear on a separate page.

▶ Check the box Summary below data if you want to compute a grand total.

▶ Click OK.

▶ You can use the outline controls on the far left column of a subtotaled list to hide or show the elements in the subtotaled list, as shown in Figure 11.5. Click the Hide Detail button to collapse the data so that just the subtotal shows. Click the Show Detail button to display the data that makes up a subtotal.

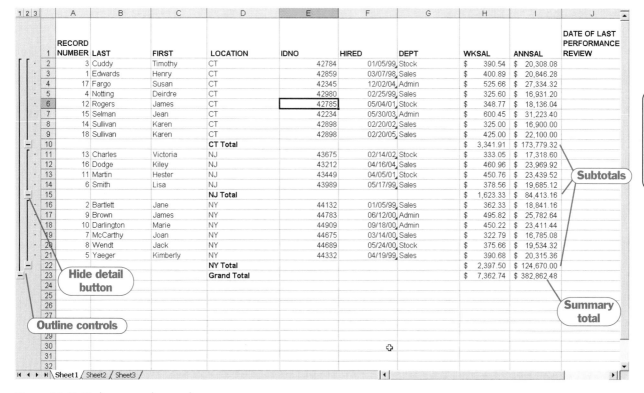

Figure 11.5 Outline controls on a list

▶ If you want to remove subtotals, click Data, Subtotals, and click the Remove All button in the Subtotals dialog box.

T R Y *it* O U T *e11-3*

1. Continue to work in the open file or open **E11-3** from the Data CD.

2. Click **Data, Sort.** Sort the list by **LOCATION** and then by **LAST.** Click **OK.**

3. Click **Data, Subtotals.**

4. In the Subtotal dialog box, in At each change in, select **LOCATION.**

5. In the Use function box, select **Sum,** if not already selected.

6. In the Add subtotal to box, check **WKSAL** and **ANNSAL** and remove any other settings.

7. Check **Summary below data,** if not already selected, remove any other

selections, and click **OK**. *Note: Your dialog box should look like Figure 11.4.*

8. As shown in Figure 11.5, click each **Hide Detail** button in the far left column, starting with those on the right in Column Level 2 and then in Column Level 1. Then click the **Show Detail** buttons in succession, starting with Column Level 1 and then Column Level 2.

9. Click **Data, Subtotals,** and then click the **Remove All** button, to remove subtotals.

10. Close and save the file.

R E H E A R S A L

 GOAL
To use the list, sort, and subtotal functions in Excel on a personnel list

SETTING THE STAGE/WRAPUP
File name: **11.1personnel**

TASK 1

WHAT YOU NEED TO KNOW

▶ Businesses need to keep database information on their employees to store essential facts, such as when individual employees were hired, their rates of compensation, and the departments in which they work. The record of all employees and their associated information is called a *personnel list*. The database functions in Excel allow you to manipulate the list to arrange the data in different ways and to summarize different components of the list.

▶ In this Rehearsal activity, you will work with the Occasions Event Planning personnel list. You will add new records to the list, sort the list, and add subtotals to create a report of salaries according to office location.

▼ DIRECTIONS

1. Open the file **11.1personnel,** which displays as shown on the facing page, from the Data CD.

2. Sort the list in ascending order by date hired.

3. Add a column to the left of **Column A**. Label it **RECORD NUMBER,** format as per other column headings, and use the fill handle to number each record from 1 to 14.

4. Change the labels for **Column D** to OFFICE LOCATION and **Column H** to WEEKLY SALARY.

5. Set alignment for all columns to Wrap text.

6. Format the column for **WEEKLY SALARY** in **Accounting style.**

7. Add a column to the right of **Column H** labeled **ANNUAL SALARY.** Format the column in the **Accounting style.**

8. Enter a formula to calculate the annual salary for each record.

9. Add the following employee records to the end of the list and fill the record numbers down for each new employee:

LAST	FIRST	OFFICE LOCATION	IDNO	DATE HIRED	DEPT	WEEKLY SALARY
Smith	Rebecca	CA	20749	6/24/05	Sales	455
Trent	Robert	OR	21980	6/30/05	Sales	435

10. Click **Data**, **Form** to add the following new employees' records, number 17 and 18, to the list using a data form:

LAST	FIRST	OFFICE LOCATION	IDNO	DATE HIRED	DEPT	WEEKLY SALARY
Leary	Gina	CA	20998	7/15/05	Sales	455
Orroz	James	WA	23999	8/30/05	Sales	430

Continued on next page

11. Fill the Annual Salary down for the new employees, if necessary.

12. Sort the list according to two fields: first by **OFFICE LOCATION** and then by **LAST** (name) in ascending order.

13. Obtain a subtotal for the weekly and annual salaries according to office locations. In addition, obtain grand totals.

14. Print the worksheet.

15. Collapse the data so that only the subtotals for each region show in the report. Print the report.

16. Expand the data so that all of the elements in the original database are visible.

17. Remove the subtotals.

18. Re-sort the list so that it is in order by **RECORD NUMBER**.

19. Sort the list according to annual salaries with the highest salary on top.

20. Save and close the file.

	A	B	C	D	E	F	G	H	I	J	K	L	M
1	LAST	FIRST	LOCATION	IDNO	HIRED	DEPT	WKSAL						
2	Birney	Mary	CA	20456	2/15/2004	Sales	650						
3	Darby	Marge	OR	21567	6/1/1999	Admin	625						
4	Ajello	Anthony	WA	23143	3/2/2000	Sales	460						
5	Kearney	Sharon	CA	21980	8/24/2001	Sales	455						
6	Weeks	David	OR	21486	9/25/1999	Admin	480						
7	Cacher	William	CA	20998	4/13/2000	Sales	490						
8	Gilchrest	Cindy	OR	21222	5/15/2000	Sales	445						
9	Lakoff	Brian	WA	23886	5/15/1999	Admin	500						
10	Williams	Todd	CA	20648	2/15/2004	Admin	650						
11	Carey	Barbara	WA	23846	9/24/2001	Sales	445						
12	Sanderson	David	OR	21778	8/28/2000	Sales	465						
13	Penney	Jason	CA	20846	2/2/2003	Sales	565						
14	Murphy	Janelle	WA	23112	6/15/1999	Sales	480						
15	Gibbons	Dorothy	OR	21668	6/15/1999	Sales	495						
16													
17													

Enter column heading and formula for ANNSAL

Cues for Reference

Add a Record to a List
1. Click **Insert, Row.**
2. Enter appropriate data to correspond to field names in first row.
   or
1. Click **Data, Form,** and **New.**
2. Enter data for each field name in dialog box.
3. Click **Close.**

Sort a List
1. Click **Data, Sort.**
2. Select field name by which you want Excel to sort data.
3. Click **Ascending** or **Descending.**
4. Click **OK.**

Obtain Subtotals
1. Click cell in database.
2. Click **Data, Subtotals.**
3. Select **field name** to sort by in At each change in box.

4. Select **function** in Use function box.
5. Select **field for subtotals** in Add subtotal to box.
6. Check boxes that apply: **Replace current subtotals, Page break between groups,** and **Summary below data.**
7. Click **OK.**

Remove Subtotals
1. Click **Data, Subtotals.**
2. Click **Remove All.**

GOALS

To generate various real estate lists using the filtering functions in Excel

To practice using the following skill sets:

★ Define and apply filters
  ★ AutoFilter
  ★ Advanced Filter

TASK 2

WHAT YOU NEED TO KNOW

Define and Apply Filters

▶ A *filter* allows you to display only the data you want from a data list. For example, certain data may be confidential or you might want to present only a portion of the data on a printout or report. You have already learned how to use AutoFilter to perform some of these actions. In this lesson, you learn how to create and apply custom filters.

AutoFilter

▶ One way to customize the information you select for display is to use AutoFilter to create a specified range of values as the criteria for filtering.

▶ Click Data, select Filter, and click AutoFilter. List arrows appear next to each field name, as shown in Figure 11.6.

▶ Click the list arrow next to the field name you want to filter.

	A	B	C	D	E	F	G	H
1								
2								
3								
4								
5								
6								
7								
8	LOCATION ▼	TOWN ▼	LISTED ▼	TYPE ▼	BR ▼	BATHS ▼	PRICE ▼	
9	122 Maple Drive	Claremont	1-Sep	Sort Ascending	3	2	$ 145,000.00	
10	11 Singletary Road	Claremont	1-Oct	Sort Descending	2	1	$ 200,000.00	
11	25 Arbor Way	Kingston	15-Aug	(All)	4	2.5	$ 250,000.00	
12	16 Leeward Street	Londonderry	12-Sep	(Top 10...)	4	3	$ 280,000.00	
13	114 First Avenue	Kingston	15-Oct	(Custom...) A-frame	3	2	$ 260,000.00	
14	33 Vista Road	Tiverton	11-Sep	Cape	3	2	$ 255,000.00	
15	110 Grand Avenue	Kingston	1-Oct	Colonial Ranch	1	1	$ 189,000.00	
16	98 Lake Street	Tiverton	25-Aug	Colonial	3	2	$ 270,000.00	
17	733 Ocean Drive	Kingston	30-Oct	Cape	4	3	$ 290,000.00	
18	71 King Street	Claremont	20-Sep	Cape	2	1	$ 195,000.00	
19	18 Stone Path	Londonderry	14-Sep	Ranch	3	2	$ 240,000.00	
20	46 Camden Street	Tiverton	30-Sep	Cape	3	2	$ 245,000.00	
21	7 Sloan Street	Londonderry	1-Nov	Colonial	3	1	$ 265,000.00	
22	68 Edgarton Drive	Tiverton	15-Nov	Ranch	2	2	$ 243,000.00	
23	62 Center Street	Kingston	12-Nov	Cape	3	2	$ 260,000.00	
24								

Drop-down list with filter options

Click All to redisplay all records

AutoFilter list arrows

Figure 11.6 AutoFiltered list with list displayed for Type

▶ To create special filters, click Custom. The Custom AutoFilter dialog box opens, as shown in Figure 11.7. Enter or select the filtering criteria you want to use in each of the boxes. For example, you may want to display records for which the data equals, is greater than, or is less than a specified value.

▶ You can also click And to add another condition. This will result in items that meet both conditions. If you click Or and add another condition, it will result in items that meet either condition.

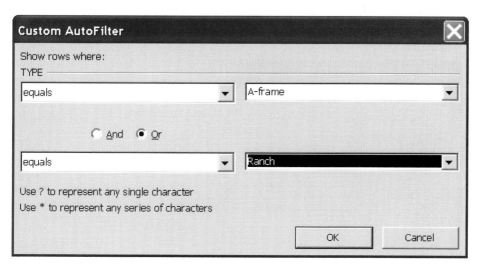

Figure 11.7 Custom AutoFilter dialog box

▶ Click OK. Only the records that meet the filtering criteria you selected will appear. The other records remain in the data list, but are hidden by Excel. To show all of the records again, click the list arrow next to the field name you are using to filter the data and click All, as shown in Figure 11.6. Another way to show all of the records again is to click Data, select Filter, and click AutoFilter to deselect it.

T R Y _it_ O U T _e11-4_

1. Open **E11-4,** a real estate list, from the Data CD.

2. Select any cell in this list. Click **Data,** select **Filter,** and click **AutoFilter.**

3. Click the **list arrow** next to **TYPE.** Select **A-frame.**

4. Click the **list arrow** next to **TYPE** and select **(All).**

5. Click the **list arrow** next to **TYPE** and select **Custom.**

6. In the Custom AutoFilter dialog box, select TYPE **equals,** if not already selected. Click the **list arrow** in the box on its right and select **A-frame.**

7. Click the **Or** button. In the next box, click **equals.** Click the **list arrow** in the box on its right and select **Ranch.**

8. Click **OK.** The records with Ranch and A-Frame types appear.

9. Click the **list arrow** next to **TYPE.** Select **(All).**

10. Leave the file open.

Advanced Filter

▶ Another way to specify filtering criteria is to use the Advanced Filter feature in Excel. The Advanced Filter allows you to name more complex criteria for filtering and to copy the filtered records to another location on the worksheet. You can then view the filtered records, as well as the original data list, at the same time. You can also manipulate the data in the filtered list (for example, sort or delete records) without changing the original data list. In contrast to AutoFilter, list arrows do not appear next to each field name when you use the Advanced Filter.

▶ To use the Advanced Filter, click a cell in the data list. Then click Data, select Filter, and click Advanced Filter. The Advanced Filter dialog box opens, as shown in Figure 11.8.

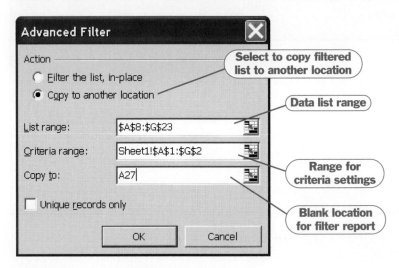

Figure 11.8 Advanced Filter dialog box

▶ You must first specify whether you want Excel simply to filter the records in the current location of the worksheet or to filter and copy them to a new location. Click the appropriate Action button in the dialog box.

▶ Next, select the range that contains the data you want to filter. The field names should be included in this range. You can enter the cell references, or click the Collapse Dialog Box button and select the appropriate cells. Then click the Expand Dialog Box button to redisplay the Advanced Filter dialog box.

▶ Specify the range of cells on the worksheet that contains the filtering criteria. This means that beforehand, you must create a duplicate of the field names of the original data list. The values of the specific filtering criteria for an Advanced Filter are entered under the relevant field names in the location called the *criteria range,* as shown in Figure 11.9. In the figure, the criteria range is in the solution file for E11-5 and is located at the top of the data list so new entries to the data list do not overlap it.

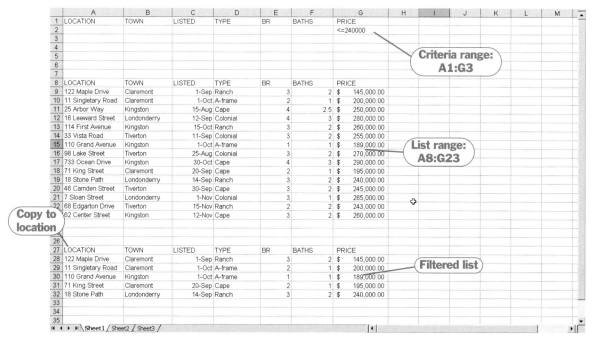

Figure 11.9 Example of a list range, criteria range, and filtered list

▶ You can enter one or more criteria, and Excel displays only the records meeting all of those criteria. If you enter a specific value under a field name, Excel filters only records matching that criterion. Other operators used to set criteria are given in the table below:

SYMBOL	EXAMPLE	RESULT
= (equal to)	=A-frame	Lists all A-frame houses
<> (not equal to)	<>Ranch	Lists all houses except ranches
> (greater than)	>$210,000	Lists all houses with selling prices greater than $210,000
< (less than)	<$200,000	Lists all houses with selling prices less than $200,000
>= (greater than or equal to)	>=$200,000	Lists all houses with selling prices of $200,000 or higher
<= (less than or equal to)	<=$190,000	Lists all houses with selling prices of $190,000 or less

▶ To place the filtered list in another location, specify the first cell or the range of cells for the Copy to location that will contain the filtered data. You cannot select another worksheet as a destination for the filtered data, but you can copy it to another worksheet later.

▶ To deactivate filtering, click Data, select Filter, and click Show All.

1. Continue to work in the open file or open **E11-5** from the Data CD.

2. Copy the field names in **Row 8** to **Row 1.** In Cell G2, under the field name PRICE, enter <=240000.

3. Click **Data,** select **Filter,** and click **Advanced Filter.**

4. Click the **Copy to a another location** button.

5. If the list range is not automatically entered, click the **Collapse Dialog Box** button and select the data list, **Cells A8:G23.** Click the **Expand Dialog Box** button.

6. For the Criteria range, click the **Collapse Dialog Box** button and select the criteria range, **Cells A1: G2.** Click the **Expand Dialog Box** button.

7. In Copy to, enter A27.

8. Click **OK.**

9. Print only the filtered list in Cells **A27:G32.**

10. Close and save the file.

R E H E A R S A L

TASK 2

GOAL
To generate various real estate lists using the filtering functions in Excel

SETTING THE STAGE/WRAPUP
File name: **11.2FourCorners**

WHAT YOU NEED TO KNOW

▶ A *real estate list* is a data list that contains a real estate company's current inventory of homes and

apartments for sale or rent. By using the filtering functions in Excel, you can select properties according to the criteria specified by buyers or real estate brokers.

▶ It is essential for brokers to be able to answer the questions of prospective buyers about their inventory of homes. In this Rehearsal activity, you apply custom filters to create various reports from the data in the real estate list for Four Corners Realty.

▼ DIRECTIONS

1. Open **11.2FourCorners** from the Data CD, as shown in Illustration A on the facing page.

2. Add the following listings to the data list by clicking **Data, Form:**

LOCATION	TOWN	LISTED	TYPE	BR	BATHS	PRICE
12 Loring Drive	Bakersfield	July 30	Cape	3	2	$262,000
33 Wayside Road	Tilton	July 31	Ranch	3	2	$272,000

3. Use the Custom feature of AutoFilter to create a list of three-bedroom properties priced at $270,000 or less. Copy and paste this list to another worksheet, adjust column width, and print the report. Label the worksheet tab: **3br<=270.**

4. On the original worksheet, remove all of the filters.

5. Copy the field names to **Row 1.**

6. Use the Advanced Filter to generate a list of all properties in Farmington that are priced at $240,000 or less. Place the criteria range above the data list, as shown in Illustration B. Cut and paste the filtered list to another worksheet and label the worksheet tab appropriately.

7. Clear the criteria entries. Use the Advanced Filter to generate a list of all Contemporary homes with four bedrooms priced under $350,000. Add a new worksheet and copy the filtered list there. Label the worksheet tab appropriately.

8. On the original worksheet, clear the criteria entries. Use the Advanced Filter to generate a list of three-bedroom homes priced under $280,000. Filter the list on the original worksheet. Sort the resulting filtered list by date from most recent to less recent and print the report.

9. Remove the filter and clear the criteria using Show all.

Continued on next page

Illustration A

	A	B	C	D	E	F	G
4	LOCATION	TOWN	LISTED	TYPE	BR	BATHS	PRICE
5	11 Neeland Way	Farmington	6-May	Tudor	2	2	$ 189,000.00
6	212 Conran Street	Santa Ana	15-May	Ranch	3	2	$ 265,000.00
7	89 Second Street	Bakersfield	1-Jun	Ranch	4	3	$ 300,000.00
8	55 Brighton Road	Farmington	30-May	Cape	3	2	$ 245,000.00
9	67 Lithgow Drive	Farmington	10-Jun	Contemporary	4	3	$ 330,000.00
10	8 Rolling Hills Road	Santa Ana	20-May	Tudor	3	2	$ 280,000.00
11	88 Mountain Drive	Santa Ana	14-Jun	Contemporary	3	2	$ 289,000.00
12	43 Brook Road	Bakersfield	2-Jun	Cape	2	1	$ 235,000.00
13	65 Summer Street	Farmington	1-Jul	Ranch	3	2	$ 265,000.00
14	10 Forsyth Street	Tilton	3-Jun	Cape	4	2	$ 370,000.00
15	14 King Street	Tilton	20-Jun	Contemporary	3	2	$ 280,000.00
16	5 Holly Road	Farmington	19-May	Ranch	2	1	$ 239,000.00
17	200 Winston Drive	Bakersfield	28-Jun	Tudor	3	2	$ 260,000.00
18	314 Third Avenue	Bakersfield	19-May	Ranch	4	3	$ 305,000.00
19	6 Ridley Drive	Santa Ana	30-Jun	Contemporary	4	2	$ 297,000.00
20	95 Simon Street	Tilton	27-May	Ranch	4	2	$ 338,000.00
21	14 Pine Street	Bakersfield	28-Jun	Cape	2	1	$ 239,000.00
22	73 George Street	Tilton	3-Jul	Ranch	3	2	$ 259,000.00
23	68 Corcoran Drive	Bakersfield	20-Jul	Contemporary	3	2	$ 259,000.00

Sheet1 / Sheet2 / Sheet3

Illustration A

Illustration B

	A	B	C	D	E	F	G
1	LOCATION	TOWN	LISTED	TYPE	BR	BATHS	PRICE
2		Farmington					<=240000
3							
4	LOCATION	TOWN	LISTED	TYPE	BR	BATHS	PRICE
5	11 Neeland Way	Farmington	6-May	Tudor	2	2	$ 189,000.00
6	212 Conran Street	Santa Ana	15-May	Ranch	3	2	$ 265,000.00
7	89 Second Street	Bakersfield	1-Jun	Ranch	4	3	$ 300,000.00
8	55 Brighton Road	Farmington	30-May	Cape	3	2	$ 245,000.00
9	67 Lithgow Drive	Farmington	10-Jun	Contemporary	4	3	$ 330,000.00
10	8 Rolling Hills Road	Santa Ana	20-May	Tudor	3	2	$ 280,000.00
11	88 Mountain Drive	Santa Ana	14-Jun	Contemporary	3	2	$ 289,000.00
12	43 Brook Road	Bakersfield	2-Jun	Cape	2	1	$ 235,000.00
13	65 Summer Street	Farmington	1-Jul	Ranch	3	2	$ 265,000.00
14	10 Forsyth Street	Tilton	3-Jun	Cape	4	2	$ 370,000.00
15	14 King Street	Tilton	20-Jun	Contemporary	3	2	$ 280,000.00
16	5 Holly Road	Farmington	19-May	Ranch	2	1	$ 239,000.00
17	200 Winston Drive	Bakersfield	28-Jun	Tudor	3	2	$ 260,000.00
18	314 Third Avenue	Bakersfield	19-May	Ranch	4	3	$ 305,000.00
19	6 Ridley Drive	Santa Ana	30-Jun	Contemporary	4	2	$ 297,000.00
20	95 Simon Street	Tilton	27-May	Ranch	4	2	$ 338,000.00
21	14 Pine Street	Bakersfield	28-Jun	Cape	2	1	$ 239,000.00
22	73 George Street	Tilton	3-Jul	Ranch	3	2	$ 259,000.00
23	68 Corcoran Drive	Bakersfield	20-Jul	Contemporary	3	2	$ 259,000.00
24	12 Loring Drive	Bakersfield	30-Jul	Cape	3	2	$ 262,000.00
25	33 Wayside Road	Tilton	31-Jul	Ranch	3	2	$ 272,000.00

Sheet1 / 3BR<=270 / Sheet3

Illustration B

10. Use the Advanced Filter to generate a list of all Cape Cod-style homes with three or more bedrooms and two baths priced less than $280,000. Add a new worksheet, and cut and paste the filtered list to the worksheet and label the worksheet tab appropriately. Sort the resulting filtered list by price from the lowest to the highest.

11. Return to the real estate list sheet and sort the list by town and then by date listed. Use subtotals (sums) to find the total value of listings for each town and the total value of all real estate listings. Print a copy of this report.

12. Save and close the file.

TASK 3

GOALS

To manage an inventory list using group and outline, data validation, and database functions

To practice using the following skill sets:

* Add group and outline criteria to ranges
  * Group data
  * View and remove groups
  * Outline data
* Use data validation
  * Error messages
* Use database functions

WHAT YOU NEED TO KNOW

Add Group and Outline Criteria to Ranges

▶ Under certain circumstances, you might want to display only a subset or a summary of information in a data list. For example, when the data list is very large, you might want to display only certain similar items from that subset. Or, you might want to show only the subtotals or results of other calculations that Excel has performed on a set of records. To do so, you can use the Group and Outline feature in Excel.

Group Data

▶ One way that you can manage a list is to display a subset of a list by grouping records.

▶ To create a group, first select the records in the data list that will comprise the group. Click Data, select Group and Outline, and click Group.

▶ The Group dialog box opens, as shown in Figure 11.10. Click Rows or Columns, depending on which defines the nature of your group, and click OK. You can create groups within groups by applying the above procedures to the smallest group first, and then successively larger groups.

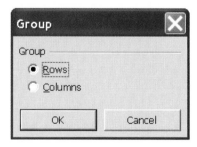

Figure 11.10 Group dialog box

1. Open the file **E11-6,** an inventory list, from the Data CD.

2. Select **Cells A5:G7.**

3. Click **Data,** select **Group and Outline,** and click **Group.**

4. In the Group dialog box, select **Rows,** if not already selected, and click **OK.**

5. Select **Cells A5:G14.**

6. Click **Data,** select **Group and Outline,** and click **Group.**

7. In the Group dialog box, select **Rows,** if not already selected, and click **OK.**

8. Select **Cells A5:G20.**

9. Click **Data,** select **Group and Outline,** and click **Group.**

10. In the Group dialog box, select **Rows,** if not already selected, and click **OK.**

11. Leave the file open.

View and Remove Groups

▶ You can use the group criteria to display or hide parts of a larger list, as shown in Figure 11.11. Notice the Hide Detail buttons that appear in the columns to the left of the list. When you click the Hide Detail button, Excel removes the group from view. When you click the Show Detail button, the group reappears.

1 2 3 4		A	B	C	D	E	F	G
	1	**TIME-OUT SPORTING GOODS**						
	2	**INVENTORY--Soccer**						
(Hide Accessories detail)								
	4	Item No.	Description	Color	Department	Quantity in Stock	Cost	Valuation
	5	21-202	Sports bags	Black	Accessories	20	$ 17.50	$ 350.00
	6	21-203	Sports bags	Navy	Accessories	15	$ 17.50	$ 262.50
	7	21-204	Sports bags	Green	Accessories	18	$ 17.50	$ 315.00
	8	24-160	Soccer T's	White	Clothing	25	$ 5.00	$ 125.00
	9	24-161	Soccer T's	Gray	Clothing	18	$ 5.00	$ 90.00
	10	24-162	Soccer T's	Black	Clothing	15	$ 5.00	$ 75.00
	11	28-430	Sweat Pants	Black	Clothing	24	$ 13.50	$ 324.00
	12	28-431	Sweat Pants	Blue	Clothing	23	$ 13.50	$ 310.50
	13	28-450	Crew Top	Black	Clothing	25	$ 11.50	$ 287.50
	14	28-451	Crew Top	Blue	Clothing	22	$ 11.50	$ 253.00
	15	23-301	Soccer balls	White	Sporting	25	$ 7.50	$ 187.50
(Hide Accessories and Clothing detail)	16		balls	Black trim	Sporting	30	$ 7.50	$ 225.00
	17		balls	Red trim	Sporting	23	$ 7.50	$ 172.50
	18	25-132	Shin guards	Standard	Sporting	22	$ 8.25	$ 181.50
	19	25-149	Elbow guards	Standard	Sporting	35	$ 8.55	$ 299.25
	20	25-155	Knee pads	Standard	Sporting	39	$ 9.35	$ 364.65
(Hide all)	21							

Figure 11.11 Example of grouped data

▶ To remove a group, select the data in the group. Then click Data, select Group and Outline, and click Ungroup.

1. Continue to work in the open file or open **E11-7** from the Data CD.

2. Click the **Hide Detail** button in **Column 3**, **Column 2**, and **Column 1**.

3. Click the **Show Detail** button in **Column 1**, **Column 2**, and **Column 3**.

4. Select **Cells A5:G20**.

5. Click **Data**, select **Group and Outline**, and click **Ungroup**. Select **Rows**, if not already selected, and click **OK**.

6. Select **Cells A5:G14**.

7. Click **Data**, select **Group and Outline**, and click **Ungroup**. Select **Rows**, if not already selected, and click **OK**.

8. Select **Cells A5:G7**.

9. Click **Data**, select **Group and Outline**, and click **Ungroup**. Select **Rows**, if not already selected, and click **OK**.

10. Leave the file open.

Outline Data

▶ The outlining functions in Excel work just like the grouping functions, but apply only to data lists that contain formulas. You saw this feature earlier when outline features were automatically included after subtotals were applied.

▶ To outline data, click Data, select Group and Outline, and click Auto Outline. Excel automatically groups any data that is summarized in the worksheet, as shown in Figure 11.12. You can click the Hide and Show Detail buttons, as you did above, to collapse and expand the data.

▶ To remove an outline, click Data, select Group and Outline, and click Clear Outline. The outline symbols no longer appear on the worksheet.

	A	B	C	D	E	F	G	
1	TIME-OUT SPORTING GOODS							
2	INVENTORY--Soccer							
3								
4	Item No.	Description	Color	Department	Quantity in Stock	Cost	Valuation	
5	21-202	Sports bags	Black	Accessories	20	$ 17.50	$ 350.00	
6	21-203	Sports bags	Navy	Accessories	15	$ 17.50	$ 262.50	
7	21-204	Sports bags	Green	Accessories	18	$ 17.50	$ 315.00	
8	24-160	Soccer T's	White	Clothing	25	$ 5.00	$ 125.00	
9	24-161	Soccer T's	Gray	Clothing	18	$ 5.00	$ 90.00	
10	24-162	Soccer T's	Black	Clothing	15	$ 5.00	$ 75.00	
11	28-430	Sweat Pants	Black	Clothing	24	$ 13.50	$ 324.00	
12	28-431	Sweat Pants	Blue	Clothing	23	$ 13.50	$ 310.50	
13	28-450	Crew Top	Black	Clothing	25	$ 11.50	$ 287.50	
14	28-451	Crew Top	Blue	Clothing	22	$ 11.50	$ 253.00	
15	23-301	Soccer balls	White	Sporting	25	$ 7.50	$ 187.50	
16	23-302	Soccer balls	Black trim	Sporting	30	$ 7.50	$ 225.00	
17	23-303	Soccer balls	Red trim	Sporting	23	$ 7.50	$ 172.50	
18	25-132	Shin guards	Standard	Sporting	22	$ 8.25	$ 181.50	
19	25-149	Elbow guards	Standard	Sporting	35	$ 8.55	$ 299.25	
20	25-155	Knee pads	Standard	Sporting	39	$ 9.35	$ 364.65	
21								
22	TOTAL						$ 3,822.90	
23								

Hide column details

Hide row details

Figure 11.12 Outlined data list

EXCEL

1. Continue to work in the open file or open **E11-8** from the Data CD.

2. In **Cell A22,** enter TOTAL.

3. In **Cell G22,** apply the AutoSum feature to obtain the sum of the Valuation column.

4. Click **Data,** select **Group and Outline,** and click **Auto Outline.**

5. Click the **Hide Detail** button that appears over **Column G.**

6. Print the report.

7. Click the **Hide Detail** button in **Column 1.**

8. Click **Data,** select **Group and Outline,** and click **Clear Outline.**

9. Keep the file open.

Use Data Validation

▶ *Data validation* is a feature that helps you ensure that the correct data is entered on a worksheet or in a data list by specifying what data is valid for particular cells or cell ranges. You can also create messages to alert the person entering the data that there is an error.

▶ Some of the ways that you can specify valid entries include the following:

- Restrict entries to whole numbers, percentages, or text.
- Define a list of valid entries.
- Limit the number of characters that you can enter.
- Compare the entry to a formula in another cell to determine if it is valid.

▶ To use data validation, select the range of data that is subject to validation. Click Data, Validation. The Data Validation dialog box opens, as shown in Figure 11.13.

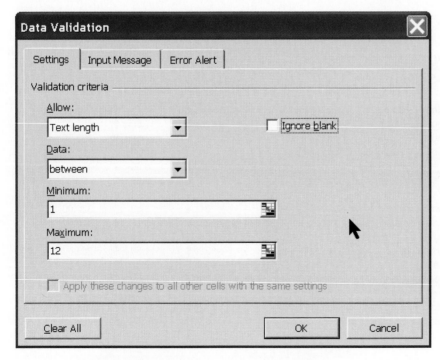

Figure 11.13 Data Validation dialog box

► Click the Settings tab. In the Allow box, select the type of entries that are permitted.

► For whole numbers, decimals, dates, and times, you can specify the values that are valid, such as the Minimum and Maximum values. For text, you can specify the length that is permissible.

► If you select List, you can designate a worksheet location that contains the specific values that you can enter. If the list is not long, you can enter the values in the dialog box, separated by commas.

► If you select Custom, you can write a formula to test the validity of a data entry.

TRY it OUT e11-9

1. Continue to work in the open file or open **E11-9** from the Data CD.

2. Select the range **B5:B30.** *Note: We are providing for additional data in this column.*

3. Click **Data, Validation,** and the **Settings** tab.

4. In the Allow box, select **Text length.**

5. In the Data box, select **between,** if it is not already selected.

6. In the Minimum box, enter **1.**

7. In the Maximum box, enter **12.**

8. Deselect the Ignore blank box.

9. Click **OK.**

10. In **Cell B21,** insert a row and enter **Soccer Sweatshirts** and press the **Enter** key. Notice the error message that appears. Click **Cancel** on the message.

11. Keep the file open.

Error Messages

► The standard error message that appears when validation requirements are not met is shown in Figure 11.14.

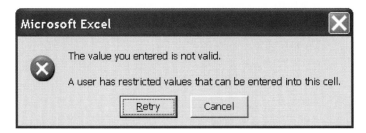

Figure 11.14 Standard Error message

► If you want to create a message that provides information about the data entry error, click Data, Validation and click the Error Alert tab, as shown in Figure 11.15. In Style, select the action you want Excel to take when a mistake in entry is made. In Title, enter the title of the error message you want to display. In Error message, enter the text describing the nature of the error. Click OK.

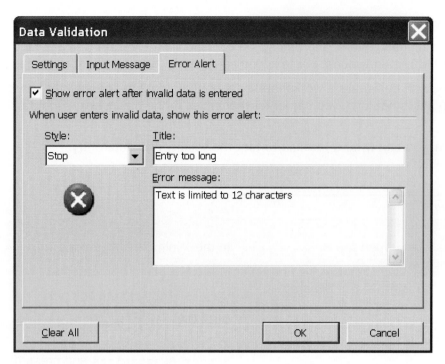

Figure 11.15 Error Alert tab

TRY *it* **OUT** *e11-10*

1. Continue to work in the open file or open **E11-10** from the Data CD.

2. Click **Cell B5.** Click **Data, Validation** and click the **Error Alert** tab.

3. In the box labeled Style, select **Stop**.

4. In the box labeled Title, enter **Entry too long.**

5. In the box labeled Error message, enter: **Text is limited to 12 characters.** Click **OK.**

6. In **Cell B21,** enter: **Referee Uniforms** and press the **Enter** key. Notice the error message that appears.

7. Close and save the file.

Locate Invalid Data

▶ As shown in Figure 11.15, by default, the Show error alert after invalid data is entered box is checked in the Data Validation dialog box, on the Error Alert tab. Therefore, the error message will appear and not allow an invalid entry. However, if you have deselected this option, or if you set validation tests after data is entered, you may wish to locate invalid data or the areas on a worksheet that have validation settings.

▶ To locate the areas on a spreadsheet that have validation settings, click Edit, Go To, or F5, and click the Special button. Select Data Validation on the Go To Special dialog box that appears, as shown in Figure 11.16. The columns that have validation settings will be shaded in blue.

▶ If you had data entered before you made validation settings, you can circle the invalid data. Click Tools, Formula Auditing, Show Formula Auditing Toolbar. On the toolbar, click the Circle Invalid Data button, and the entries that do not meet validation specifications will be circled in red.

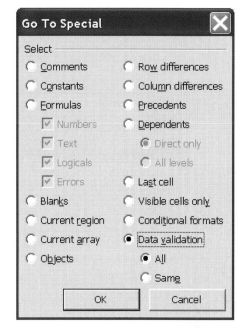

Figure 11.16 Go To Special dialog box

TRY*it*OUT *E11-11*

1. Open **E11-11** from the Data CD.

2. Click **F5**. Click **Special** and select **Data Validation** on the Go To Special dialog box.

3. Click **OK**. The data validation areas will be highlighted in blue.

4. To detect invalid data, click **Tools, Formula Auditing,** and **Show Formula Auditing Toolbar.**

5. Click the **Circle Invalid Data button.** The invalid data will be circled in red.

6. In Cell B14, click **Data, Validation** to view the settings, then click **OK** to close the dialog box. Change "Shoulder Pads" to **Shldr Pads**.

7. The inventory quantities will have to be depleted and should not be changed at this time.

8. Click the **Clear Validation Circles** button.

9. Close and save the file.

Use Database Functions

▶ Data lists can be summarized and analyzed using Excel's *database functions* as shown in the Insert Functions dialog box in Figure 11.17. There are twelve database functions ranging from simple totals to statistical measures. Examples of summary data that might be requested for an inventory database are shown in Figure 11.18.

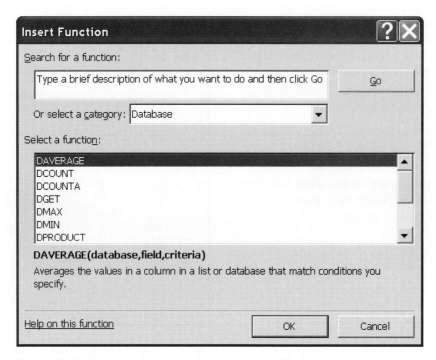

Figure 11.17 Insert Function dialog box—database functions

Number of items in Sporting goods	
Average value of Sporting inventory	
Average value of Clothing inventory	
Value of Sporting and Clothing inventory	

Figure 11.18 Examples of database summary items

▶ Most database functions require a database or list range and a criteria range, similar to the Advanced Filter dialog box that we used earlier. Therefore, when using either database functions or Advanced Filter, it is necessary to create a criteria range above the data list.

▶ For example, to find the count of a specific type of record or of all the records with number values in the fields, use the DCOUNT function. As shown in Figure 11.19, to find the number of items in the Sporting goods department you must specify the database range, provide a column with numbers to count, and provide the criteria range that contains the department criteria.

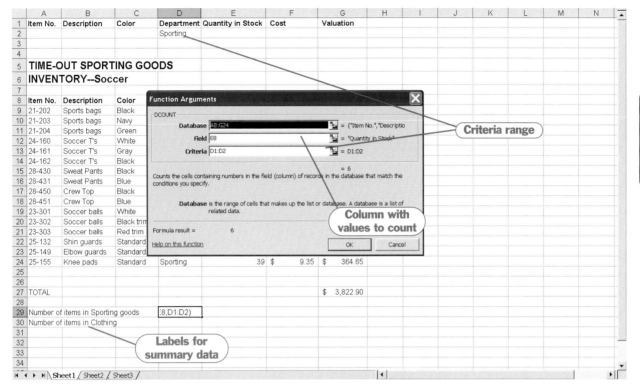

Figure 11.19 DCOUNT function dialog box entries

▶ If you will be entering several database functions, it is more efficient to name the database range and use the name of the range in the formulas. As shown in Figure 11.20, the DAVERAGE function averages the valuations for the department specified in the criteria range.

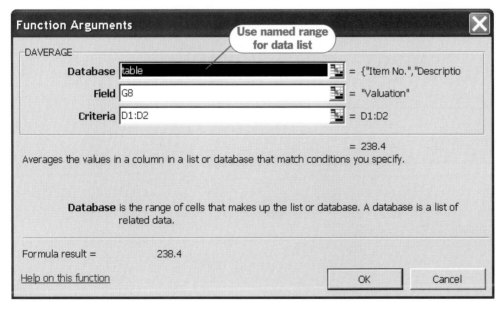

Figure 11.20 DAVERAGE function dialog box using named table range

▶ It is important to note that to display the results of several database functions using the same field with different values, you must create a new criteria area, so that your existing formulas will not change. For example, if you wish to count by different departments, you will have to provide a Department criteria range for each summary formula, as shown in Figure 11.21.

			Department	Department		Department	
			Sporting	Clothing		Clothing	
						Sporting	
TIME-OUT SPORTING GOODS							
INVENTORY--Soccer							

Figure 11.21 Three Department criteria ranges for different summary formulas

▶ In some cases, you may wish to set criteria for several items across the criteria range or for several items in a column. In that case, you just select the field names and criteria that apply for the criteria range. As shown in Figures 11.21 and 11.22, to find the sum of valuations in the Sporting and Clothing departments, use the DSUM function and select the column and the criteria for both departments shown in the criteria range

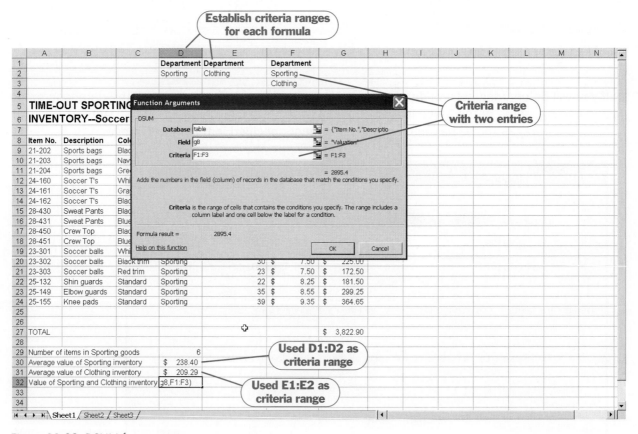

Figure 11.22 DSUM function

1. Open **E11-12** from the Data CD.

2. Notice the summary labels at the bottom and the criteria range at the top of the data list.

3. Find the number of items in the Sporting inventory:
   a. In the criteria range, in **Cell D2,** enter `Sporting`.
   b. In **Cell D29,** click the **Insert function** button.
   c. Select the **Database** category and the **DCOUNT** function, then click **OK.**
   d. In the Database box, click the **Collapse dialog box** button and select the database range **A8:G24.** Click the Expand dialog box button.
   e. In the Field box, enter the column heading location for **Quantity in Stock,** `E8`.
   f. In the Criteria box, click the **Collapse dialog box** button to select the criteria range **D1:D2.** Click the **Expand dialog box** button.
   g. Click **OK.**

4. Insert a name for the database range **A8:G24;** name it `Table`.

5. In Cell **D30,** use the DAVERAGE function to find the average valuation of Sporting goods items. Use the range name for the database argument (Table), use the same criteria range as you did in Step 3, but change the field value to **G8.**

6. In Cell **D31,** use the DAVERAGE function to find the average valuation of Clothing goods items. Use the same database and column, but enter `Clothing` in **E2** and use **E1:E2** as the criteria range.

7. In Cell **D32,** use the DSUM function to find the total valuation of the Clothing and Sporting goods items. Enter `Clothing` and `Sporting` in **F2** and **F3,** respectively, and change the criteria range to **F1:F3.**

8. Format money values in **D30:D32** for **Currency.**

9. Save and close the file.

REHEARSAL

TASK 3

 GOAL
To manage an inventory list using group and outline, data validation, and database functions.

SETTING THE STAGE/WRAPUP
File name: **11.3Inventory**

WHAT YOU NEED TO KNOW

▶ Companies that sell products and goods must maintain an *inventory list* to keep track of their stock items. They need to know how many units are on hand, the cost of each item, its descriptive information, and other information, such as suggested retail price.

▶ In this Rehearsal activity, you create data validation tests for the inventory list for the Baseball Department in the suburban Time Out Sporting Goods store. You also apply Group and Outline criteria and use filters to generate four summary reports that will answer questions about stock on hand. Summary data will also be calculated using database functions.

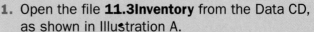

▼ DIRECTIONS

1. Open the file **11.3Inventory** from the Data CD, as shown in Illustration A.

2. Enter the formula for the **Valuation** column. *Hint: valuation=quantity in stock * cost.* Use the fill handle to fill in the rest of the values.

3. Select the range in **A1:A30** and set data validation for **Item No.** so that only numerical entries between 5000 and 9999 are permitted. Create an appropriate error message.

4. Test the data validation by entering a value of **4000** in **Cell A25.** Click **Cancel** on the error message.

5. Set data validation for the **Description** column so that only text 12 or fewer characters in length is permitted. Create an appropriate error message.

6. Test the data validation by entering **Baseball t-shirts** in **Cell B19.** Click **Cancel** on the error message.

7. Set data validation for **Cost** so that no values greater than $100.00 are permitted. Create an appropriate error message.

8. Test the data validation by changing the value in **Cell F19** to $200. Click **Cancel** on the error message.

9. Create a group that includes all equipment (baseballs, bats, gloves, and helmets).

10. Create a group that contains all of the items in the inventory.

11. Hide the portion of the inventory that includes equipment. Print a report that lists the inventory for accessories (pants and sports bags).

12. Show all of the details in the inventory list. Remove all of the groups.

13. Apply outline criteria to the inventory list.

Continued on next page

14. Hide the details in the list so that **Quantity in Stock** and **Cost** are not visible. Print the report.

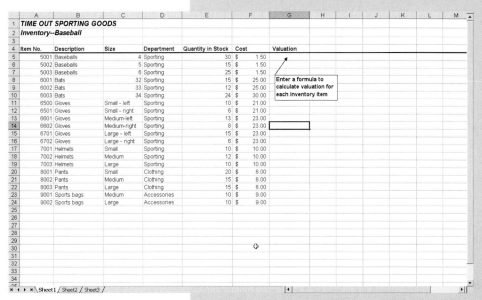

Illustration A

15. Use Advanced Filter to create a report of all the items in inventory that need to be reordered and place the report at the bottom of the sheet. Insert three rows above the inventory for the criteria range, as shown in Illustration B, and copy the column headings to **row 1.** Reordering occurs when the quantity on hand drops below one dozen, or 12 units. Move the report to Sheet2, create a heading, and print the report.

16. Find subtotals (sums) for the valuation of each department in the inventory and for the total inventory. Copy and paste the report to **Sheet 3.** Print a copy of the report. Redo the subtotals on **Sheet3,** and find the Average valuation for each department. Remove the subtotals from **Sheet1.**

17. On **Sheet 1,** add the following labels under the data list in **Cells C29** and **C30,** as shown in Illustration B:

```
Number of items in Sporting Inventory
Total Valuation of inventory costing $10 or more
```

18. You may wish to name the database range.

19. Use the **DCOUNT** function in **Cell G29** to find the summary data. Use the Department field for the criteria range and the Cost field for the column data. Format the results in **General** number format.

20. Use the **DSUM** function in Cell **G30** to find the summary data. Use the Cost field in the criteria range and the Valuation column for column data. Format for **Currency.**

21. Save and close the file.

	A	B	C	D	E	F	G	H	I
1	Item No.	Description	Size	Department	Quantity in Stock	Cost	Valuation		
2				Sporting	<12	>=10			
3									
4	*TIME OUT SPORTING GOODS*								
5	*Inventory--Baseball*								
6									
7	Item No.	Description	Size	Department	Quantity in Stock	Cost	Valuation		
8	5001	Baseballs	4	Sporting	30	$ 1.50	$ 45.00		
9	5002	Baseballs	5	Sporting	15	$ 1.50	$ 22.50		
10	5003	Baseballs	6	Sporting	25	$ 1.50	$ 37.50		
11	6001	Bats	32	Sporting	15	$ 25.00	$ 375.00		
12	6002	Bats	33	Sporting	12	$ 25.00	$ 300.00		
13	6003	Bats	34	Sporting	24	$ 30.00	$ 720.00		
14	6500	Gloves	Small - left	Sporting	10	$ 21.00	$ 210.00		
15	6501	Gloves	Small - right	Sporting	6	$ 21.00	$ 126.00		
16	6601	Gloves	Medium-left	Sporting	13	$ 23.00	$ 299.00		
17	6602	Gloves	Medium-right	Sporting	8	$ 23.00	$ 184.00		
18	6701	Gloves	Large - left	Sporting	15	$ 23.00	$ 345.00		
19	6702	Gloves	Large - right	Sporting	6	$ 23.00	$ 138.00		
20	7001	Helmets	Small	Sporting	10	$ 10.00	$ 100.00		
21	7002	Helmets	Medium	Sporting	12	$ 10.00	$ 120.00		
22	7003	Helmets	Large	Sporting	10	$ 10.00	$ 100.00		
23	8001	Pants	Small	Clothing	20	$ 8.00	$ 160.00		
24	8002	Pants	Medium	Clothing	15	$ 8.00	$ 120.00		
25	8003	Pants	Large	Clothing	15	$ 8.00	$ 120.00		
26	9001	Sports bags	Medium	Accessories	10	$ 9.00	$ 90.00		
27	9002	Sports bags	Large	Accessories	10	$ 9.00	$ 90.00		
28									
29				Number of items in Sporting Inventory			15		
30				Total Valuation of inventory items costing $10 or more			$ 3,017.00		
31									
32									
33									
34									
35									
36									

Insert blank rows and use for criteria range for Advanced filter and Database functions

 Enter summary labels

 Enter database function formulas

Illustration B

 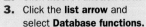

PERFORMANCE

WHAT YOU NEED TO KNOW

Act I

Trilogy Productions is assessing its personnel costs for three offices, Los Angeles, New York, and London. Open the file **11p1.Pers** from the Data CD and organize the data to enable an analysis of the employee expenses associated with each office.

Follow these guidelines:

✻ Label **Column H** ANNSAL and format the column for the Accounting style. Write the formula for annual salary in **Cell H5** and fill in the values for the rest of the employees.

✻ Create data validation for the following columns:

- **IDNO** should be a whole number between 1000 and 9999. Create an error alert message for this column.

- **HIRED** should be a date greater than May 30, 1996. Create an error alert message for this column.

- **WKSAL** should be a decimal number between $400 and $1500. Create an error alert message for this column.

✻ Insert the following new records by clicking **Data, Form:**

LAST	FIRST	LOCATION	IDNO	HIRED	DEPT	WKSAL
Bergen	Cory	New York	1022	3/20/05	Production	$515
Molina	Tracy	Los Angeles	2044	10/30/05	Marketing	$585

✻ Copy the data list to **Sheet2** and **Sheet3** and adjust column widths.

✻ On **Sheet2**, generate a report summarizing weekly and annual salaries by location.

- Sort the list first according to location and then by date hired. Each should be in ascending order.

- Obtain subtotals (sums) for **WKSAL** and **ANNSAL** for each location, as well as a grand total. Collapse the data so that only the subtotals and grand total show. Remove all irrelevant field names. Label the report with an appropriate title as shown in the illustration.

TRILOGY PRODUCTIONS PAYROLL BY LOCATION		
LOCATION	**WKSAL**	**ANNSAL**
London Total	$ 3,990.00	$ 207,480.00
Los Angeles Total	$ 4,680.00	$ 243,360.00
New York Total	$ 5,095.00	$ 264,940.00
Grand Total	$ 13,765.00	$ 715,780.00

✴ On **Sheet3**, generate a report summarizing weekly and annual salaries by departments.

- Sort the list according to the departments in which people work and then by location.

- Obtain subtotals (sums) for **WKSAL** and **ANNSAL** for each department. Collapse the data so that only the subtotals and grand total show. Label the report with an appropriate title.

✴ On **Sheet1,** copy column headings to **Row 1** to create a criteria range. Use Advanced Filter to create a report showing employees who earn more than $650 per week. Place the report in **A30** and add a report heading in **C29.**

✴ Rename worksheet tabs appropriately.

✴ Print a copy of the workbook. Close and save the file.

Act II

An inventory list for the Luggage Department in Odyssey Travel Gear's Boston store is found in the file **11p2.Inven** on the Data CD. You will conduct several analyses, using database functions and other database tools, to determine the cost of the inventory for several categories of items. You will also assess categories of items for which merchandise needs to be replenished.

Follow these guidelines:

✴ Format **Column F** in Accounting style. Write the formula for the valuation of goods in **Cell F5.** Fill in the values for the rest of the column.

✴ Generate a report of all items for which stock quantities are five or fewer, as shown in the illustration on the next page. Create a criteria range and use Advanced Filter to conduct this analysis. Copy the report to **Sheet2.** Delete all irrelevant columns. Label the sheet appropriately and create a report heading.

ODYSSEY TRAVEL GEAR
Stock Report: Items for which quantities are 5 or less

Item No.	Description	Size	Quantity in Stock
2003	Carry-on bag	20"	2
3002	Expandable bag	27"	3
4002	Garment bag	23"	2
5002	Duffle bag	30"	5
6004	Wheels bag	32"	4

EXCEL

✴ Generate a report of all items that meet airline specifications for carry-on bags, 27" or less. Use any filtering technique you prefer to conduct this analysis. Copy the report to **Sheet3.** Label the sheet appropriately and create a report heading. Delete any irrelevant columns.

✴ Copy this last report to a new sheet that you insert. Sort the list in this report according to description and then cost. Use subtotals (Sum) to summarize the Valuation column by description. The data should be outlined. Collapse the data so that only the total Valuation figures are given for each type of item. Label the sheet appropriately and create a report heading.

✴ Print a copy of the three reports.

✴ On **Sheet1,** add the following labels in **B32** and **B33:**

Total valuation of luggage greater than 27" in size

Total valuation of luggage equal to or less than 27" in size

✴ In Cells **F32** and **F33,** use database function formulas to provide the summary data.

Data Analysis

In this lesson, you will learn to use several Excel features to analyze data and create financial reports. Among these are PivotTables and PivotCharts, automated tools, and scenarios. You will learn to format and resize graphics and charts, and to use the Solver add-in to perform analysis.

Upon completion of this lesson, you should have mastered the following skill sets:

✴ Create PivotTables and PivotTable reports
  ✴ Modify and format PivotTables
✴ Create PivotCharts and PivotChart reports from a PivotTable
✴ Data analysis with automated tools and charts
  ✴ Forecast or project linear values
  ✴ Chart forecast data
  ✴ Format and modify charts

✴ Create and display scenarios
✴ Use the Solver add-in Create, format, and resize graphics
  ✴ Use cropping, sizing, and rotating tools
  ✴ Control image contrast and brightness

Terms
Software-related
PivotTable
PivotTable report
PivotChart
PivotChart report
What-if analysis
FORECAST
Analysis Toolpak
Trendline
Scenario
Solver
Cropping
Rotate tool
Document-related
Personnel list
Sales forecast
Aging report
Budget

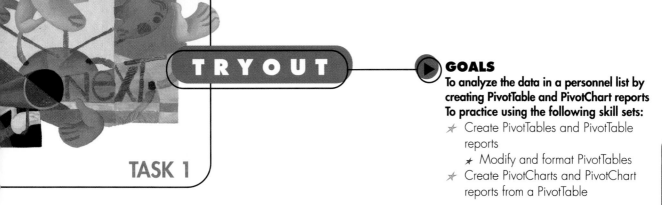

TRYOUT

GOALS

To analyze the data in a personnel list by creating PivotTable and PivotChart reports
To practice using the following skill sets:

* ✳ Create PivotTables and PivotTable reports
  * ✶ Modify and format PivotTables
* ✳ Create PivotCharts and PivotChart reports from a PivotTable

TASK 1

WHAT YOU NEED TO KNOW

Create PivotTables and PivotTable Reports

▶ Excel contains a powerful tool for data analysis called a PivotTable. A *PivotTable* is an interactive function that allows you to manipulate data in a list in order to summarize, analyze, or arrange it in a specific way. With the PivotTable feature, you can work with data using different functions (for example, Sum, Average, Maximum), select which portions of the data to view, and rearrange (or "pivot") the layout of your summary. An example of a PivotTable is shown in Figure 12.1 and the options for one of the fields are shown in Figure 12.2.

	A	B	C	D	E
1	LOCATION	(All) ▼			
2					
3	Sum of WKSAL	DEPT ▼			
4		Admin	Production	Sales	Grand Total
5	Total	3348.9	2740.35	4632.09	10721.34
6					

List boxes to pivot or change data display

Figure 12.1 Sample PivotTable

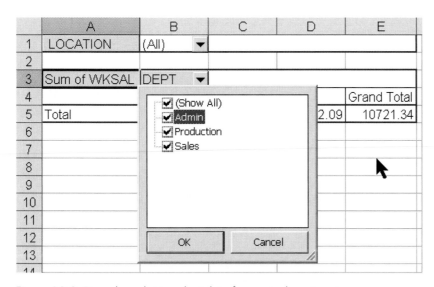

Figure 12.2 Drop-down list to select data from one department

▶ These features are especially useful when you have a large database or list and want to analyze trends or select a portion of the information for a closer look. When you have completed your PivotTable analysis, you can generate a report that contains its contents. It is important to remember that no matter how you pivot or rearrange the data, the original data in your worksheet remains intact.

▶ To create a PivotTable, first click a cell in the data list. Click Data, PivotTable and PivotChart Report. The PivotTable and PivotChart Wizard opens and guides you through the following sequence of steps:

- Step 1 of the PivotTable and PivotChart Wizard, as shown in Figure 12.3, asks you to select the data source you want to analyze. Select a data list or database contained in an Excel workbook or an external data source. Then select whether you want to create a table or chart. For this section of the lesson, select PivotTable and click Next.

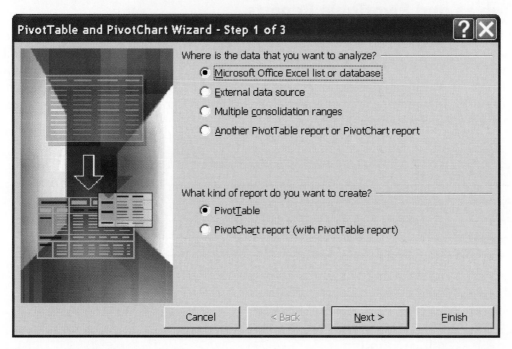

Figure 12.3 PivotTable and PivotChart Wizard—Step 1

- Step 2 of the Wizard, as shown in Figure 12.4, asks you to identify the range of the data you want to use. If the data is in an active list, the range of cells it occupies is indicated by default. You can change the default range or click Browse if you want to locate data that is contained in another file. Then click Next.

Figure 12.4 PivotTable and PivotChart Wizard—Step 2

- Step 3 of the Wizard, as shown in Figure 12.5, asks you to select the destination for the PivotTable report. Indicate whether you want it to go to a new or existing worksheet. If you select a new worksheet, Excel puts the result on a new sheet in your workbook. Click Finish.

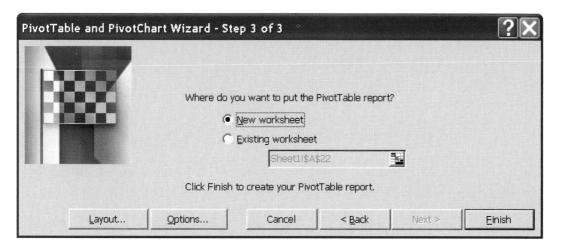

Figure 12.5 PivotTable and PivotChart Wizard—Step 3

▶ The layout view of the PivotTable appears, as shown in Figure 12.6.

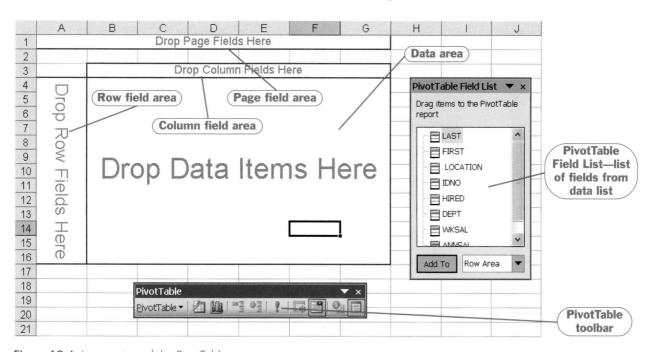

Figure 12.6 Layout view of the PivotTable

▶ This screen contains the following components:

- The PivotTable toolbar, as shown in the lower portion of Figure 12.6, contains buttons that activate a number of commands, including formatting the PivotTable report, making a chart, selecting the function to apply to the data, and refreshing the data. (See also Figure 12.9.)

- The PivotTable Field List, at the right in Figure 12.6, includes the field names from the original data list. You can drag-and-drop the field names you need to the appropriate locations on the PivotTable layout.

- The upper-left portion of the screen contains the different sections, or drop zones, into which you can drag-and-drop data and field names. You can place field names from the original data list in rows or columns or you can use them to label a page. When you drag-and-drop a field name in any part of this screen, a small replica of the layout appears next to the mouse pointer with the shaded region indicating exactly where Excel will place the field name. The sections are:

  a. Page area—The data field you place in the page area is the data that will be displayed in the PivotTable. It acts as a filter. For example, if you have a list of employees and each employee is in one of three locations, you could use Location as the page field. This would give you a report showing the employees in one of the locations. If you change the location, you could view each of the other employee lists.

  b. Row area—Creates row labels for each unique item within the page field. For example, to count employees in each department at each location, you could use Department as the row field. The PivotTable would then automatically count the number in each department for the location selected. This same analysis could be done using the column area.

  c. Column area—Creates column labels for each unique item within the page field. This is similar to the row field; it is a category used to summarize the data. For example, if you want to find out the salaries for each department, at each location, you could use DEPT as the column field. This same analysis could be done using the row area.

  d. Data area—The field name for the data to analyze or summarize goes in the section labeled Drop Data Items Here. Weekly Salary would be the data field used to get a summary of salaries, by department, in each location. In Figure 12.7, LOCATION is in the Page field, DEPT is in the Column field, and WKSAL is being dragged to the Data field. You must always put at least one data field in the data area.

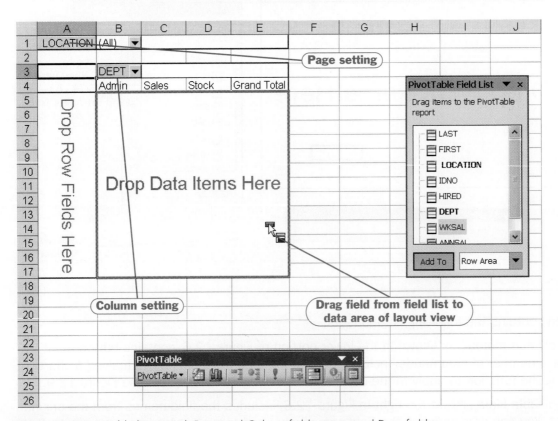

Figure 12.7 PivotTable layout with Page and Column field settings and Data field in process

▶ An alternate way to set up the layout of a PivotTable is to click Layout in Step 3 of the Wizard. The Layout dialog box opens, as shown in Figure 12.8. Click and drag the field names you want to their appropriate locations in the layout section.

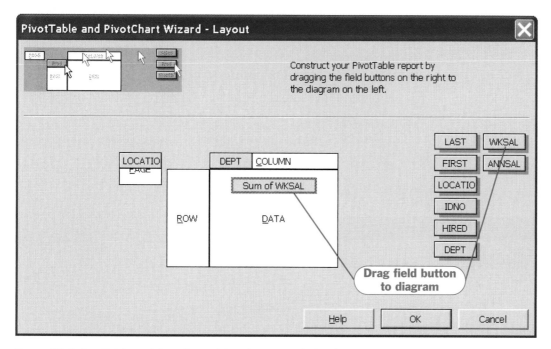

Figure 12.8 PivotTable and PivotChart Wizard—Layout dialog box

T R Y *it* O U T *e12-1*

1. Open **E12-1**, a personnel list, from the Data CD. Click any cell in the data list.

2. Click **Data, PivotTable and PivotChart Report.**

3. In Step 1 of the PivotTable and PivotChart Wizard, click **Microsoft Office Excel list or database,** if necessary, and click **PivotTable** as the kind of report you want to create. Click **Next.**

4. In Step 2 of the Wizard, the range of cells should already be designated as **A1:H19.** Enter that range if it does not appear in the Range box. Click **Next.**

5. In Step 3 of the Wizard, click **New worksheet**, if necessary. Click **Finish.**

6. Drag the following field buttons from the PivotTable field list to the designated locations:
   a. Drag **LOCATION** to the Page Fields area.
   b. Drag **DEPT** to the Column Fields area.
   c. Drag **WKSAL** to the Data Items area. (This action automatically creates the Sum function.)
   d. Leave the Row Fields area blank.

7. Click the list arrow for **LOCATION,** click **DE,** and click **OK.**

8. Click the list arrow for **DEPT,** select only **Sales,** and click **OK.**

9. Keep the file open.

Modify and Format PivotTables

▶ A useful feature of PivotTables lets you easily modify them by using the drag-and-drop technique. For example, to add another field name or additional data to the PivotTable, drag it from the PivotTable field list and drop it in the appropriate place on the PivotTable layout. When you first begin, try to keep your PivotTable simple. Adding too many field names or data fields can make the report difficult to interpret.

Note: The PivotTable field list appears only when a cell in the PivotTable is active.

▶ You can remove field names or data from the PivotTable by dragging them to a blank portion of the worksheet. To undo your most recent change to a PivotTable, click Edit, Undo Pivot.

▶ You can activate many editing features for a PivotTable from the PivotTable toolbar, as shown in Figure 12.9.

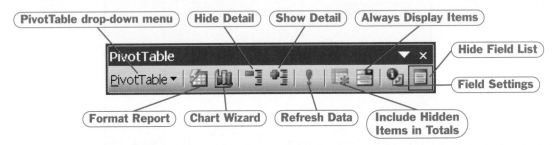

Figure 12.9 PivotTable toolbar

▶ To change which summary function is operating on the data, click the Field Settings button on the PivotTable toolbar or double-click the name of the data. The PivotTable Field dialog box opens, as shown in Figure 12.10. Insert the name of the data you want to summarize in the Name box and select the function (such as Average, Minimum, Maximum, and so forth) you want to apply in the Summarize by box. Click OK.

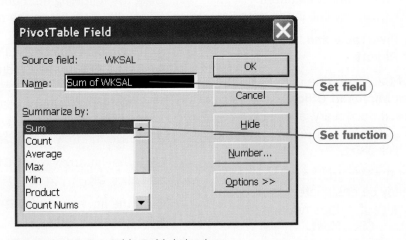

Figure 12.10 PivotTable Field dialog box

▶ To apply an automatic format to the PivotTable, click the Format Report button on the PivotTable toolbar. You can select from eleven formats or choose None from the AutoFormat dialog box, as shown in Figure 12.11. Click OK.

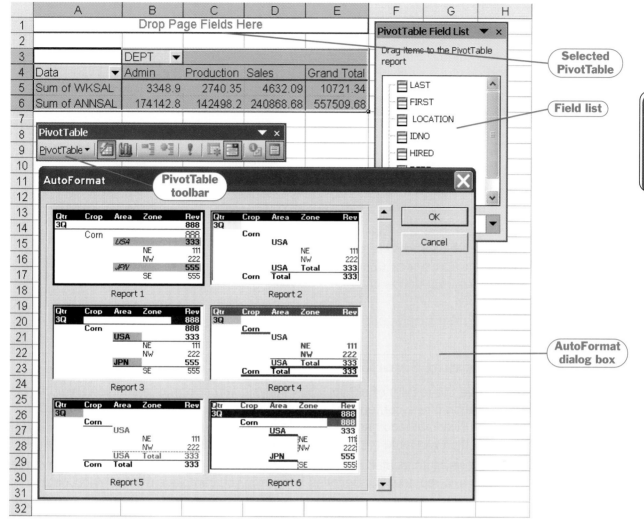

Figure 12.11 AutoFormat dialog box

▶ If the data in the original list changes, you can update the PivotTable by clicking the Refresh Data button on the PivotTable toolbar. The different buttons on the PivotTable toolbar function only when a cell in the PivotTable is active.

▶ You can reactivate the PivotTable and PivotChart Wizard by clicking the PivotTable drop-down menu on the PivotTable toolbar and clicking Wizard.

▶ You can print the results of a PivotTable analysis in the form of a *PivotTable report*. Click a cell in the worksheet that contains the PivotTable and click File, Print, or click the Print button on the toolbar.

TRY it OUT e12-2

1. Continue to work in the open file.

2. Click **Edit, Undo Pivot.** The PivotTable appears with all departments.

3. From the PivotTable field list, click and drag **ANNSAL** to the data area where **Sum of WKSAL** is located.

Continued on next page

4. Click **LOCATION** on the PivotTable and drag it to a blank portion of the worksheet.

5. Click **Sum of WKSAL,** and then the Field Settings button on the PivotTable toolbar. Sum of WKSAL should appear in the Name box. In the Summarize by box, click **Average** and click **OK.**

6. Repeat Step 5 to change **Sum of ANNSAL** to an average function. Click **OK.**

7. On Sheet 1, change the value in **Cell G2** to: $500. Go back and click somewhere in the PivotTable, watch the Sales department, and click the **Refresh Data** button on the PivotTable toolbar.

8. Click the **Format Report** button on the PivotTable toolbar (see Figure 12.11). Click **Report 3** as the format and click **OK.**

9. Select **Columns B** and **C** and click the **Currency Style** format button. Adjust column width, if necessary.

10. Keep the file open.

Create PivotCharts and PivotChart Reports from a PivotTable

▶ It is often helpful to see the results of a PivotTable analysis in the form of a chart. A *PivotChart* is a graphical representation of the contents of a PivotTable. To create a PivotChart, click a cell in the PivotTable. On the PivotTable toolbar, click the Chart Wizard button (see Figure 12.9). A graph of the data in the PivotTable appears on a new worksheet.

- As Figure 12.12 shows, data located in the rows of the PivotTable are placed on the x-axis of the chart. Usually, the x-axis represents categories into which you can place the numerical data.

- Information in the Data Items area of the PivotTable is represented on the y-axis. The y-axis usually displays numerical values such as dollars or frequency counts.

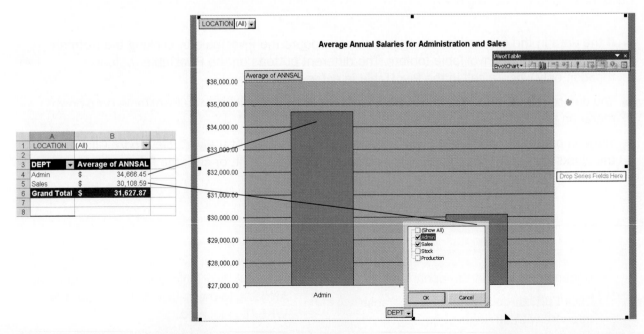

Figure 12.12 Creating a PivotChart from a PivotTable

▶ You can change the type of chart that appears by clicking the Chart Wizard button on the Standard toolbar or by selecting the chart and clicking Chart, Chart Type. Common graph types are column, bar, line, and pie charts.

▶ You can make changes in labels for axes, legends, and other aspects of the chart format by clicking the Chart Wizard button and following the steps in the Wizard, or by selecting the chart and clicking Chart, Chart Options. Some of the reasons you may edit your chart are:

- A chart should have a title that explains the information that is represented.

- The x- and y-axes should be properly labeled.

- If you are presenting more than one data type, then columns, bars, lines, or pie slices will be distinguished by appearing with different colors. Make sure there is a legend that accurately describes what data each color represents. You can also change the formatting of a chart by double-clicking the relevant portion and selecting a color or other style options from the dialog boxes that open.

▶ PivotCharts contain many of the interactive features that are found in PivotTables. For example, you can add and remove field names from the layout of the chart. Field names also appear with drop-down menus that allow you to select different values for a given field.

▶ You can print the results of a PivotChart analysis in the form of a *PivotChart report.* To create the report, select the worksheet that contains the PivotChart. Then click File, Print or click the Print button on the toolbar.

EXCEL

T R Y *i t* O U T *e12-3*

1. Continue to work in the open file or open **E12-3** from the Data CD.

2. Click **Average of WKSAL** on the PivotTable and drag it to a blank spot on the worksheet.

3. Click in the PivotTable and click the **Chart Wizard** button on the PivotTable toolbar. The chart should appear on a new sheet.

4. Right-click the **chart legend** to activate it. Select **Clear** to delete the legend, since there is only one type of data represented in this graph.

5. Click the list arrow for DEPT. Select only **Admin** and **Sales.** Click **OK.**

6. Click **Chart, Chart Options.** In the **Titles** tab of the Chart Options dialog box, enter the following in the Chart title box: `Average Annual Salaries for Administration and Sales.` Click **OK.**

7. Click and drag **LOCATION** from the PivotTable field list to the Page Fields section of the PivotChart. (If the field list is not displayed, click the Show field list button on the Pivot Table toolbar.) View the averages for DE and NJ. Return the Location setting to All.

8. Save the worksheet **E12Pivot.** Close the file.

REHEARSAL

TASK 1

GOAL
To analyze the data in a personnel list by creating a PivotTable and PivotChart report

SETTING THE STAGE/WRAPUP
File name: 12.1Personnel

WHAT YOU NEED TO KNOW

▶ You have already learned that businesses usually keep a *personnel list,* a record of all employees and their associated information. Businesses often need to analyze the data in a personnel list. For example, how many employees work in each department or office location, or the payroll totals for specific departments or office locations. A PivotTable and/or PivotChart analysis is an excellent way to conduct these data analyses.

▶ In this Rehearsal activity, you will conduct several analyses of the data contained in the personnel list for Occasions Event Planning. You will produce a PivotTable report of average weekly salaries, by department, for each office location. You will also produce a PivotChart report showing annual salaries for each department with all locations combined. Finally, you will produce a PivotChart report that shows the number of employees who work in each department.

▼ DIRECTIONS

1. Open **12.1Personnel** from the Data CD. Use the illustration on the next page to guide you through the sequence of steps below.

2. Sort the list by **LAST** (name).

3. Format **Column G** using the Accounting style.

4. Label **Column H** ANNSAL. Write a formula to compute annual salary in **Column H** and format in Accounting style. Fill in the values for all of the employees.

5. Create a PivotTable report on a new sheet to summarize the average weekly salaries of employees for each department and office location. Use the following settings for the PivotTable layout screen:
   a. Drag **LOCATION** to the Page Fields area.
   b. Drag **DEPT** to the Column Fields area.
   c. Drag **WKSAL** to the Data Items field.
   d. Change the function for weekly salaries from Sum to **Average.**

6. Format the report using one of the AutoFormats provided by Excel and format the numbers for **Currency.** Create a PivotTable report for each of the three locations. Print each report.

7. Modify the PivotTable by dragging the ANNSAL field to the WKSAL location. Change the function for annual salaries from Sum to **Average.** Print a copy of this report.

8. Drag the Average of WKSAL off the PivotTable. Create a PivotChart from this table that shows average annual salaries for each department for all locations combined. Use a **column graph** to display the data. Title the chart Average Annual Salary by Department.

9. Print the PivotChart report.

Continued on next page

10. Use the PivotChart to find the number of employees in each department across all locations. (*Hint:* Return to the PivotTable and change Average of ANNSAL to **Count of ANNSAL** with the Field Settings button. Format the numbers in **General** format.)

11. Change the graph to a **pie chart** using the Chart Wizard button on the PivotTable toolbar. Title the chart **Number of Employees by Department**, and add the values as Data Labels.

12. Print the PivotChart report.

13. Save the **12.1Personnel** file.

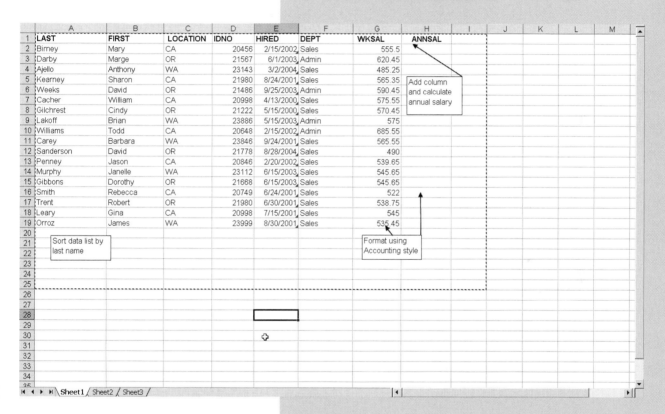

	A	B	C	D	E	F	G	H	I	J	K	L	M
1	LAST	FIRST	LOCATION	IDNO	HIRED	DEPT	WKSAL	ANNSAL					
2	Birney	Mary	CA	20456	2/15/2002	Sales	555.5						
3	Darby	Marge	OR	21567	6/1/2003	Admin	620.45						
4	Ajello	Anthony	WA	23143	3/2/2004	Sales	485.25						
5	Kearney	Sharon	CA	21980	8/24/2001	Sales	565.35	Add column					
6	Weeks	David	OR	21486	9/25/2003	Admin	590.45	and calculate					
7	Cacher	William	CA	20998	4/13/2000	Sales	575.55	annual salary					
8	Gilchrest	Cindy	OR	21222	5/15/2000	Sales	570.45						
9	Lakoff	Brian	WA	23886	5/15/2003	Admin	575						
10	Williams	Todd	CA	20648	2/15/2002	Admin	685.55						
11	Carey	Barbara	WA	23846	9/24/2001	Sales	565.55						
12	Sanderson	David	OR	21778	8/28/2004	Sales	490						
13	Penney	Jason	CA	20846	2/20/2002	Sales	539.65						
14	Murphy	Janelle	WA	23112	6/15/2003	Sales	545.65						
15	Gibbons	Dorothy	OR	21668	6/15/2003	Sales	545.65						
16	Smith	Rebecca	CA	20749	6/24/2001	Sales	522						
17	Trent	Robert	OR	21980	6/30/2001	Sales	538.75						
18	Leary	Gina	CA	20998	7/15/2001	Sales	545						
19	Orroz	James	WA	23999	8/30/2001	Sales	535.45						
20													
21	Sort data list by						Format using						
22	last name						Accounting style						
23													
24													
25													
26													
27													
28													
29													
30													
31													
32													
33													
34													
35													

Sheet1 / Sheet2 / Sheet3 /

Create a PivotTable

1. Click cell on worksheet containing data list.
2. Click **Data, PivotTable and PivotChart Report.**
3. In Step 1 of Wizard, select data source and select PivotTable as type of report. Click **Next.**
4. In Step 2, enter range of cells to include in analysis or accept default range. Click **Next.**
5. In Step 3, select location for PivotTable. Click **Finish.**
6. Drag field names from PivotTable Field list to Page Fields, Row Fields, or Column Fields areas on layout screen.
7. Drag field name for data you are analyzing to Data Items area on layout screen.
8. To change function used to operate on data, click data field name and click **Field Settings** button on PivotTable toolbar.

Create a PivotChart

1. If you already have created a PivotTable:
   a. Click cell in PivotTable and click **Chart Wizard** button on PivotTable toolbar.
   b. Click **Chart Wizard** button on toolbar to make changes to layout and contents of chart.
2. If you have not yet made a PivotTable:
   a. Click **Data, PivotTable and PivotChart Report.**
   b. In Step 1, select data source and select **PivotChart** as type of report you want to create. Click **Next.**
   c. In Step 2, enter range of cells to include in analysis or accept default range. Click **Next.**
   d. In Step 3, select location for PivotChart. Click **Finish.**
   e. Drag field names from PivotTable field list to Page Field or Category Field areas on layout screen.
   f. Drag field name for data you are analyzing to Data Items area on layout screen.

Change the Function in a PivotTable and/or PivotChart Report

1. Click data field name on which you are operating.
2. Click **Field Settings** button on PivotTable toolbar.
3. Make sure field name for data appears in Name box.
4. Select operation you want from Summarize by box.
5. Click **OK.**

Print a PivotTable/PivotChart Report

1. Click cell in worksheet that contains PivotTable or PivotChart.
2. Click **File, Print,** or click **Print** button.

Format a PivotTable

1. Click cell in PivotTable.
2. Click **Format Report** button 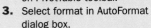 on PivotTable toolbar.
3. Select format in AutoFormat dialog box.
4. Click **OK.**

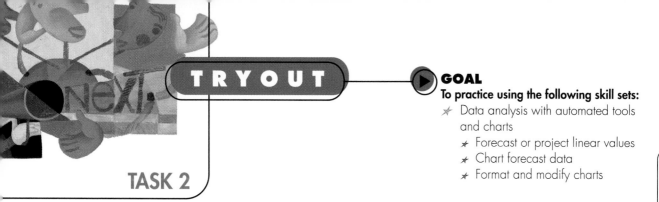

TRYOUT

GOAL
To practice using the following skill sets:
* Data analysis with automated tools and charts
  * Forecast or project linear values
  * Chart forecast data
  * Format and modify charts

TASK 2

EXCEL

WHAT YOU NEED TO KNOW

Data Analysis with Automated Tools and Charts

▶ Before business managers make important financial decisions, they often want to evaluate the impact of several possible courses of action. Past data is generally used in conjunction with a set of formulas or models to make predictions about future outcomes. For example, a business might want to assess the impact changing interest rates for past due accounts may have on company revenues. Or, a business might want to create a *sales forecast,* a projection of future sales based on past performance. Actual sales are then compared to the sales forecast.

▶ Excel contains a powerful set of commands called *what-if analysis* tools that allow you to assess how changes in data affect outcomes. Many of these tools, such as Scenarios, a feature, or *FORECAST,* a statistical function, are always available in Excel. Others, such as Analysis Toolpak and Solver, are add-in programs that are part of your software installation, but must be installed if needed.

Forecast or Project Linear Values

▶ FORECAST is a what-if analysis function that allows you to project future data values based on data that you have already obtained. For example, suppose you have a list of sales figures for each of six months. Excel can compute the projected values for a subsequent month or months. Excel uses a statistical process called regression analysis to forecast data.

▶ To forecast data values, click the cell where you want the forecast value to appear. Then click the Insert Function button.

▶ In the Insert Function dialog box that opens, as shown in Figure 12.13, select All or Statistical in the Or select a category box. In the Select a function box, choose FORECAST. The Function Arguments dialog box opens, as shown in Figure 12.14.

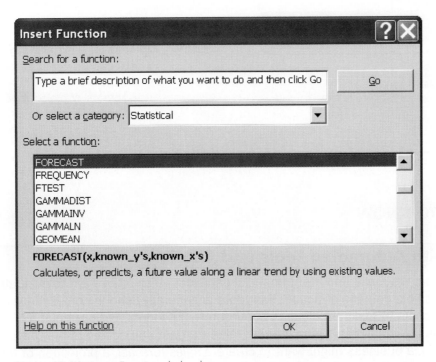

Figure 12.13 Insert Function dialog box

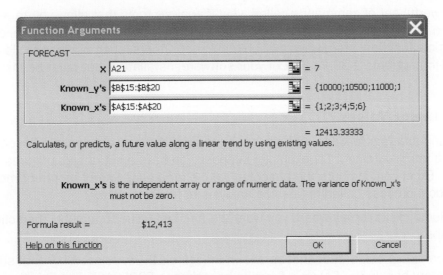

Figure 12.14 Function Arguments dialog box

▶ Refer to the worksheet illustrated in Figure 12.15 and fill in the values as follows:

- In the box labeled X, enter the cell reference for the data point that is associated with the prediction you are making (for example, the month for which you are seeking a forecast sales value). As an alternative, click the Collapse Dialog Box button and click the cell for the data point. Then click the Expand Dialog Box button.

- In the box labeled Known_y's, enter or select the cells that contain the known data of the type you are predicting (for example, past sales figures).

- In the box labeled Known_x's, enter or select the cells that contain known data corresponding with the y-values (for example, months). The x-values must be in numerical form in order for this analysis to work.

- If you will be copying the formula down a range, make the range of Known_x and Known_y data absolute by selecting the range and pressing F4 in the Function Arguments dialog box.

- Arrange the data so that each x-value is in the same row (or column) as its corresponding y-value. In other words, pair the data, as shown in Figure 12.15. Click OK.

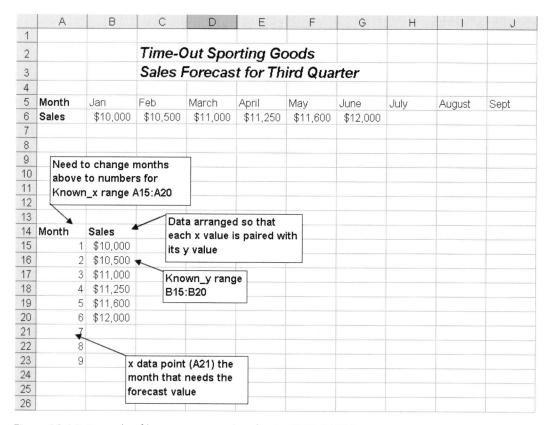

Figure 12.15 Example of how to arrange data for the FORECAST function

▶ When creating a paired data list, as in Figure 12.15, you can use the Transpose feature in Excel. The Transpose feature changes a horizontal range of data to a vertical range or vice versa. Copy the horizontal data, click the new location, use Paste Special, Transpose to copy, and transpose the horizontal data to vertical data.

▶ To create more sophisticated analyses, Excel provides the *Analysis Toolpak,* which is an add-in feature. Add-in features are optional and can be installed as needed. FORECAST uses a linear regression formula but you can customize the formula and find additional information using the Regression feature in the Analysis Toolpak.

1. Open the file **E12-4,** a sales forecast worksheet, from the Data CD.

2. Select the range **B6:G6.** Click the **Copy** button on the toolbar.

3. Click **Cell B15.** Click **Edit, Paste Special, Transpose,** and click **OK.**

4. Click **Cell B21.**

5. Click the **Insert Function** button.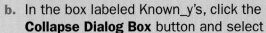

6. Select **Statistical** from the Or select a category list box.

7. Select **Forecast** from the Select a function box and click **OK.**

8. In the Function Arguments dialog box, do the following:
   a. In the box labeled X, click the **Collapse Dialog Box** button and click **Cell A21.** Click the **Expand Dialog Box** button.
   b. In the box labeled Known_y's, click the **Collapse Dialog Box** button and select the range **B15:B20.** Click the **Expand Dialog Box** button. Select the range and press **F4** to make it an absolute reference.
   c. In the box labeled Known_x's, click the **Collapse Dialog Box** button and select the range **A15:A20.** Click the **Expand Dialog Box** button. Select the range and press **F4** to make it an absolute reference.
   d. Click **OK.**

9. Use the fill handle to fill in the values for **Cells B22:B23.**

10. Format **Cells B21:B23** for Currency style with no decimals.

11. Copy **Cells B21:B23.** Select **Cell H6.** Click **Edit, Paste Special,** and click the **Values** and **Transpose** options. Click **OK.** Format **H6:J6** for currency with no decimals.

12. Keep the file open.

Chart Forecast Data

▶ Once you have the forecast values, you might want to display the information in the form of a chart. Simply select the data in the table you have completed, click the Chart Wizard button, and follow the steps in the Wizard.

▶ You can also add a *trendline,* a graphic representation of any tendencies or patterns shown in the data, as shown in Figure 12.16. Excel offers the option of displaying several types of trends, including a linear, logarithmic, or exponential trend. Since the FORECAST function returns its projected data based on an equation using linear regression, choose the linear trendline.

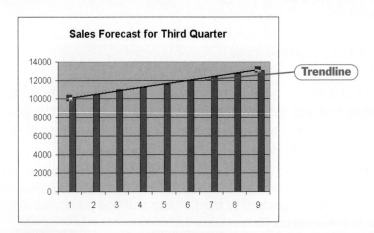

Figure 12.16 Example of a linear trendline for forecasted data

▶ To insert a trendline into a chart, first click the chart to activate it. Then click Chart, Add Trendline to open the Add Trendline dialog box, as shown in Figure 12.17.

- In the Type tab, select the kind of trendline you want to add to the chart.

- In the box labeled Based on series, select the name of the data for which you want to add the trendline.

- Click OK.

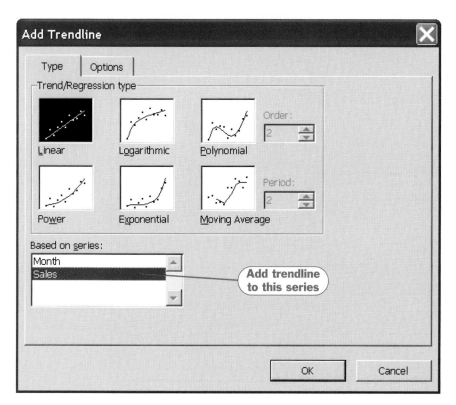

Figure 12.17 Add Trendline dialog box

T R Y i t O U T *e12-5*

1. Continue to work in the open file or open **E12-5** from the Data CD.

2. Select the range **A14:B23.** Click the **Chart Wizard** button.

3. Select the **Column** chart type in Step 1 and click **Next.**

4. In Step 2, the data range should already be selected. Select **Series in: Columns,** if not already selected, and click **Next.**

5. In Step 3, click the Titles tab, if necessary, title the chart `Sales Forecast for Third Quarter` and click **Finish.**

6. Click the chart to activate it, if necessary. Click the **legend** and delete it.

7. Click **Chart, Add Trendline.** In the Type tab, click **Linear,** if not already selected. In the Based on series box, click **Sales** and then click **OK.**

8. Keep the file open.

Format and Modify Charts

▶ As discussed in Lesson 6, every object on a chart can be formatted using the Format Chart Area dialog box, as shown in Figure 12.18. You can open the dialog box by double-clicking a chart or any object in a chart. Or, you can also right-click any object on a chart and select the Format command from the shortcut menu. The dialog box will vary depending on which chart object you want to format.

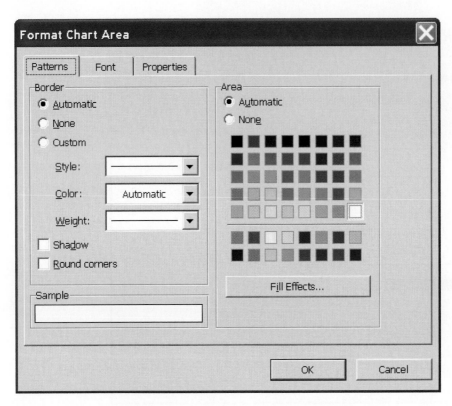

Figure 12.18 Format Chart Area dialog box

▶ You can modify axis labels using a range of labels from elsewhere in the worksheet, by setting the range for Category (X) axis labels on the Source Data dialog box on the Series tab, as shown in Figure 12.19.

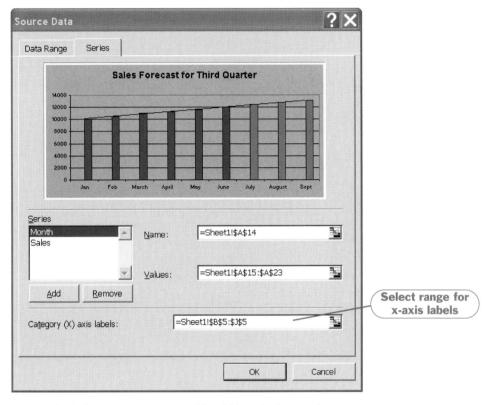

Figure 12.19 Source Data page in Chart Wizard—Series tab

TRY *it* OUT *e12-6*

1. Continue to work in the open file or open **E12-6** from the Data CD.

2. Click the chart to activate it.

3. Click **Chart, Source Data,** and then click the **Series** tab.

4. In the Category (X) axis labels box, click the **Collapse Dialog Box** button and select **B5:J5.** Click the **Expand Dialog Box** button. Click OK.

5. Double-click the Category Axis, select the **Font** tab if necessary, and change the font size to **8** points. Click **OK.**

6. Double-click the Value Axis, select the **Font** tab if necessary, and change the font size to **8** points. Click **OK.**

7. Double-click each of the last three columns of the chart and format them in dark **pink.**

8. Double-click the title, select the **Font** tab if necessary, and change the font to **Arial, Bold, 14 point.** Click **OK.** Place your cursor at the end of the title and press **Enter.** Add a second line to the title that reads Actual – Projected.

9. Select the word **Actual,** right-click it, select **Format Chart Title,** and change the color to **Plum.** Change the color of the word **Projected** to **Pink.**

10. Double-click the chart area and format the chart area color to light **gray.**

11. Close and save the file.

REHEARSAL

TASK 2

GOAL
To create a sales forecast and add a trendline to a chart

SETTING THE STAGE/WRAPUP
File name: **12.2Sales**

WHAT YOU NEED TO KNOW

▶ Randall's Gift Mart would like to create a sales, cost, and gross profit forecast for the fourth quarter. In this Rehearsal activity, you will use data for the first three quarters to forecast data for the fourth quarter. You will create and modify charts to display the results and trends for the year.

▼ DIRECTIONS

1. Open the file **12.2Sales** from the Data CD. Use Illustration A on the next page as a guide to the following steps.

2. Create a table for forecasting data:
   a. In **Cell A15,** enter numbers in the Months column from 1 to 12.
   b. Transpose all the data in the range **B6:J7** to the data list.

3. Forecast the sales figure for months 10, 11, and 12.
   a. In **Cell B24,** enter the FORECAST formula.
   b. Use **A24** as the X target value. Use **B15:B23** as the Known_y range and make it an absolute reference.
   c. Use **A15:A23** as the Known_x range and make it an absolute reference.
   d. Copy the formula for months 11 and 12 and format the result so that it is consistent with the rest of the data table.

4. Use a similar procedure to forecast the Cost figure for months 10, 11, and 12. (*Hint:* The X value and Known_x range stays the same but the Known_y values are obtained from the Cost column.)

5. Use the Paste Special feature with the Values and Transpose options to copy and paste the forecasted values to **Cell K6:M7.**

6. Calculate the Gross Profit line for all months and calculate the totals for the year in column N.

7. Create a column chart to represent sales and gross profit for the year:
   a. Use a non-adjacent selection of data including months and sales in **B5:M6** and gross profit in **B8:M8.**
   b. Label the chart `Sales and Gross Profit 2005.`
   c. Label the x-axis `Months.`

Continued on next page

   d. Label the y-axis `Thousands.`

   e. Place the chart on a new sheet named `Column Chart.`

8. Use the Source Data feature on the Chart menu to change the Series 1 name in the legend to `Sales` and the Series 2 name to `Gross Profit.`

9. Enhance the chart as follows, and as shown in Illustration B on the next page:

   a. Format the projected sales columns in **Gold.**

   b. Format the projected gross profit columns in light **Green.**

   c. Select the title and add a second line to read `Actual - Projected.`

   d. Format Actual in **Blue** and Projected in **Green.**

   e. Select the sales columns and add a linear trendline.

   f. Select the gross profit columns and add a linear trendline.

10. Print a copy of each chart.

11. Save and close the file.

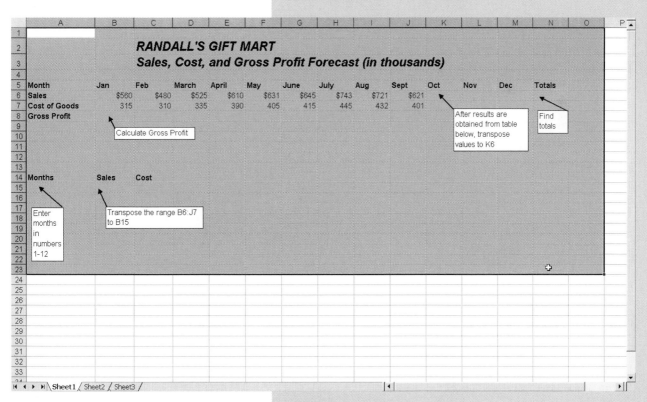

Illustration A

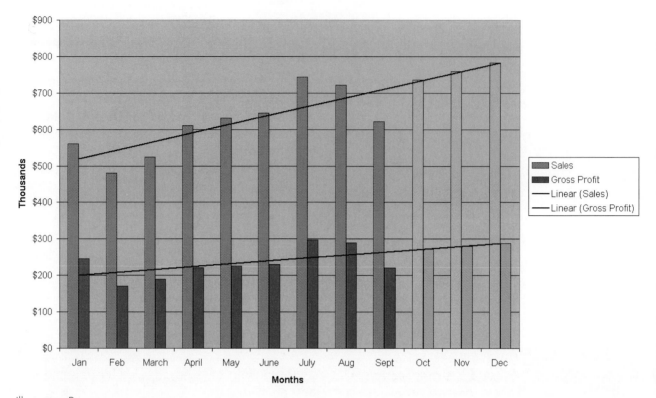

Sales and Gross Profit 2005
Actual - Projected

Illustration B

Cues for Reference

Use the FORECAST Function
1. Click cell where you want result of FORECAST to appear.
2. Click **Insert Function** button.
3. Select **Statistical** from Or select category list box.
4. Click **FORECAST** in Select a function box. Click **OK**.
5. In X box, enter cell reference for data associated with FORECAST value (usually a label).
6. In Known_y's box, enter cell references for known data of type you are predicting.

7. In Known_x's box, enter cell references for known data associated with y's. (Data must be numeric.)
8. Click **OK**.
Note: If the FORECAST function formula is to be copied to additional unknown values, you must make the Known_y and Known_x ranges absolute by pressing F4 after you select the range in the Arguments dialog box.

Transpose Data
1. Select data to transpose.
2. Click **Copy**.
3. Click a location for data.

4. Click **Paste Special, Transpose.**
5. Click **OK**.

Add a Trendline
1. Data should be in a chart.
2. Click chart to make it active.
3. Click **Chart, Add Trendline.**
4. Select type of trendline.
5. Click **OK**.

Format Charts
1. Double-click chart object.
2. Change settings on Format dialog box.
3. Click **OK**.

TRYOUT

GOALS

To create and analyze worksheets using Scenario and Solver features and to chart the results

To practice using the following skill sets:

* Create and display scenarios
* Use the Solver add-in
* Create, format, and resize graphics
    * Use cropping, sizing, and rotating tools
    * Control image contrast and brightness

EXCEL

TASK 3

WHAT YOU NEED TO KNOW

Create and Display Scenarios

▶ A very useful tool in the what-if analysis group is a scenario. A *scenario* is a way to explore the impact of changing data values on numerical outcomes. For example, a company might want to explore the impact of changing specific income or expense values on an overall budget. Or, a business can examine how mailing statements on different dates affects late fees for delinquent accounts. In some instances, a business might want to develop a best- and worst-case scenario before making a financial decision.

▶ To create a scenario, click Tools, Scenarios to open the Scenario Manager dialog box, as shown in Figure 12.20. Click Add to start a new scenario.

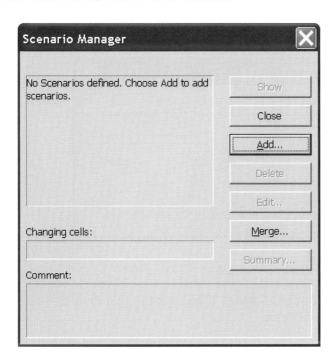

Figure 12.20 Scenario Manager dialog box

▶ In the Add Scenario dialog box, as shown in Figure 12.21, enter a name for the scenario in the top box. In the Changing cells box, enter the cell reference for the data you want to change. You can add a description of your scenario to the Comment box. Click OK.

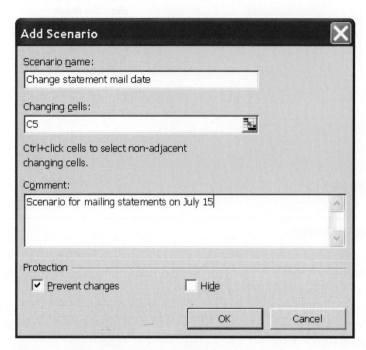

Figure 12.21 Add Scenario dialog box

▶ The Scenario Values dialog box opens, as shown in Figure 12.22. Enter the value for the data you want to change and click OK.

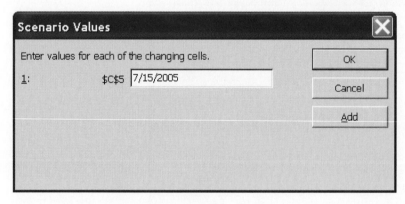

Figure 12.22 Scenario Values dialog box

▶ The Scenario Manager dialog box opens again. If you want to add another scenario, click Add and repeat the actions in the last two steps.

▶ To create a report with the outcomes of different scenarios, click Summary in the Scenario Manager dialog box. The Scenario Summary dialog box opens, as shown in Figure 12.23. Select Scenario summary. You will notice that you can also summarize the results of the scenario using a PivotTable. In the Result cells box, enter the cell references for the data of which you want to see results. In this case, you want to see how the change in statement date will change the late fees values in column H. Click OK.

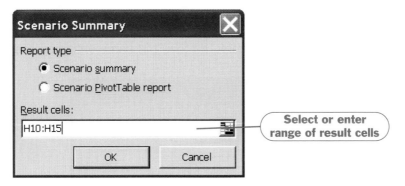

Figure 12.23 Scenario Summary dialog box

▶ Excel summarizes the results of all of the scenarios in a formatted table on a new worksheet, called Scenario Summary, as shown in Figure 12.24.

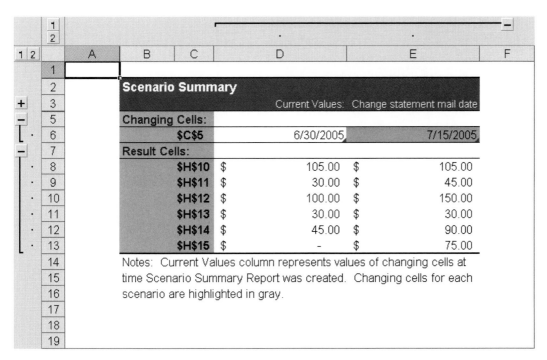

Figure 12.24 Scenario Summary report

▶ Once you have created scenarios, you can show, close, edit, delete, or merge your scenarios from the Scenario Manager dialog box, as shown in Figure 12.25. The merge feature allows you to merge scenarios from another workbook that has the same changing and target cells.

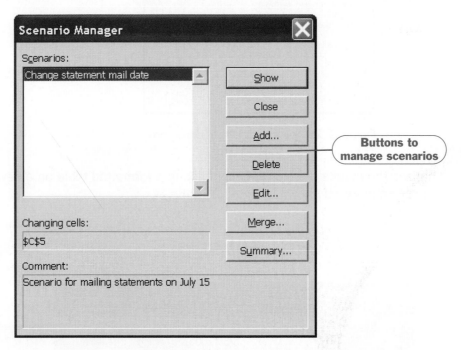

Figure 12.25 Scenario Manager dialog box—Management tools

T R Y _it_ O U T _e12-7_

1. Open the file **E12-7** from the Data CD. _Note:_ Click **Enable Macros** to be able to use this file properly. If the security for your system is set to a high level, Enable Macros will not work. See your administrator or see the information on changing security levels under Digital Signatures for Macro Projects on page 90.

2. Click the sheet labeled **June,** if not already displayed.

3. Click **Tools, Scenarios.**

4. In the Scenario Manager dialog box, click **Add.**

5. In the Add Scenario dialog box, enter the following:
   a. In the Scenario name box, enter **Change statement mail date.**

   b. In the Changing cells box, enter **c5.**
   c. In the Comment box, enter **Scenario for mailing statements on July 15** and click **OK.**

6. In the Scenario Values dialog box, enter **7/15/2005** and click **OK.**

7. In the Scenario Manager dialog box, click **Summary.**

8. In the Scenario Summary dialog box, select **Scenario summary**, if necessary, as the report type. In Result cells, select or enter the range **H10:H15.** Click **OK.**

9. Note the impact on late fees by mailing the statements two weeks later.

10. Close and save the file.

Solver Add-in

▶ The *Solver* feature is another what-if analysis tool that will modify values in changing cells to match a target value or optimal value. However, Solver is one of the optional add-in features that Excel provides on CD-ROM that must be added to your installation as needed. Analysis Toolpak, mentioned earlier, is also an add-in feature. To add in Solver, click Tools, Add-Ins and select Solver Add-in and click OK, as shown in Figure 12.26.

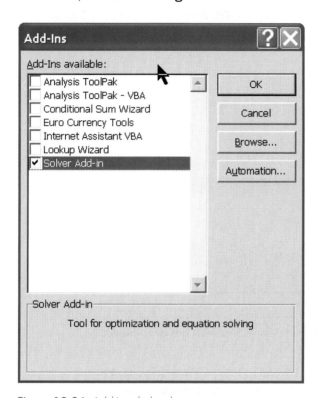

Figure 12.26 Add-Ins dialog box

▶ Solver works with a group of cells that are directly or indirectly related to the formula in the target cell. It will adjust the values in the changing cells you specify—called the adjustable cells—to produce the result you specify from the target cell formula. For example, if a company has budgeted expenses and finds that the company wants the total to be a specific value, Solver can be used to adjust the expenses to meet the target value.

▶ Place your cursor in the target cell and click Tools, Solver. The Solver Parameters dialog box appears, as shown in Figure 12.27. The target cell should be a cell with a formula; in this case, there is a Sum formula in the cell. The budget for 2005 came to $185,030 and the target given is $180,000. Enter the target cell value, enter the changing cells, which are the expense items, and then click Solve.

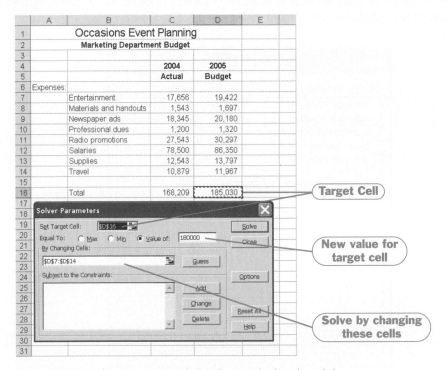

Figure 12.27 Solver Parameters dialog box and related worksheet

▶ The Solver Results dialog box appears, as shown in Figure 12.28, and the changing cells are changed on your worksheet to meet the target. You now have the option to Keep Solver Solution, Restore Original Values, or Save the Solver solution as a Scenario.

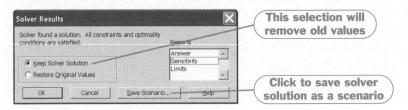

Figure 12.28 Solver Results dialog box

▶ If you select Save Scenario, the Save Scenario dialog box appears, as shown in Figure 12.29. Name the scenario and click OK.

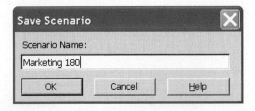

Figure 12.29 Save Scenario dialog box

1. Open **E12-8** from the Data CD.

2. If necessary, click **Tools, Add-Ins,** select **Solver Add-in,** then click **OK**.

3. Click **Tools, Solver.**

4. Click **Cell D16,** the target cell.

5. Click the **Value of** option and enter 180000.

6. In the By Changing Cells box, click the **Collapse Dialog** button and select the changing range **D7:D14,** if necessary.

7. Click **Solve.** Note the changes in the cells.

8. Click **Save Scenario** in the **Solver Results** dialog box.

9. Name the Scenario **Marketing 180.** Click **OK.**

10. Click **Restore Original Values.** Click **OK.**

11. Repeat Steps 2–9 and set up a scenario for a target of $175000. Name the scenario **Marketing 175.**

12. Click **Tools, Scenarios,** and click the **Summary** button. Click **OK** and view the summary.

13. Management has informed you that the budget for $175,000 is the one that will be accepted. Click on Sheet1. Click **Tools, Scenarios** and in the Scenario Manager dialog box, click **Marketing 175** and click the **Show** button.

14. Select the **Marketing 180** scenario and click the **Delete** button. Close the dialog box.

15. Save and close the file.

Create, Format, and Resize Graphics

▶ As discussed in Lesson 6, you can add and modify graphics using the Drawing toolbar, as shown in Figure 12.30. You can use the shapes or lines from the toolbar or click the AutoShapes button to view a menu and submenus of shapes. Select a button or shape to draw or format an object. You can drag the shape to size and move and size it by clicking on the shape to view and using its handles. Right-click a graphic to display the shortcut menu, which includes a Format command for that specific graphic.

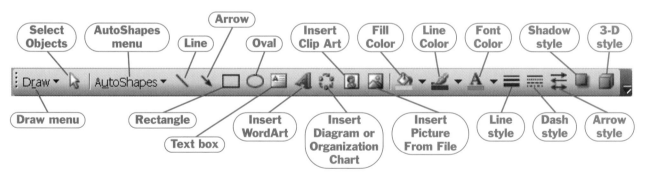

Figure 12.30 Drawing toolbar

▶ An important consideration is that although you can place graphics or drawing objects anywhere on a worksheet or chart, the graphics disappear when you select a chart. To display, create, and modify graphics, click outside the chart to deselect it. An example of the text box and arrow graphics is shown in Figure 12.31.

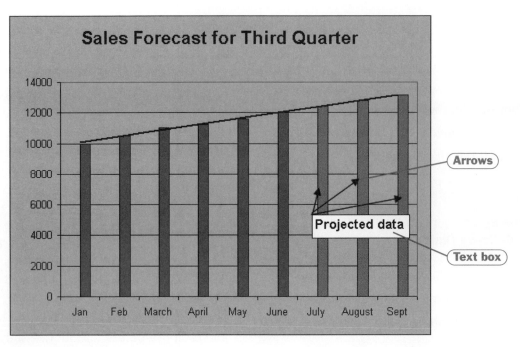

Figure 12.31 Example of graphics

Use Cropping, Rotating, and Resizing Tools with Graphics

▶ To add interest to your worksheets, you can add pictures or graphics using the Insert, Pictures command, as discussed in Lesson 6. You can search for clip art or pictures using the Clip Art task pane, as shown in Figure 12.32.

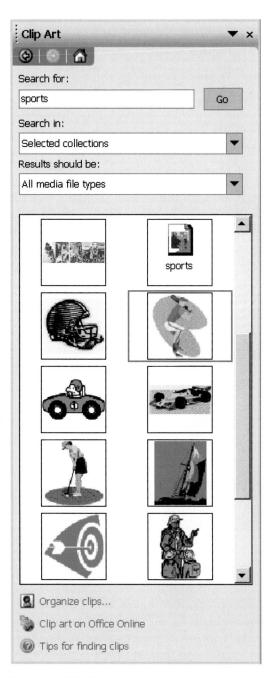

Figure 12.32 Clip Art task pane

▶ When you insert a picture from a file or clip art, the Picture toolbar will display, as shown in Figure 12.33. If a company has digital pictures of its retail store, merchandise items, and so forth, they can be used in reports.

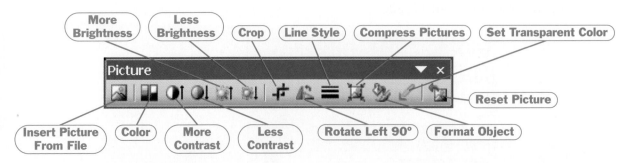

Figure 12.33 Picture toolbar

▶ There are two ways that you can use to change the size of a picture—resizing and *cropping.* Resizing changes the dimensions of the picture by stretching or shrinking it using the handles on the object. When an object is selected, white handles display around the edges and a *rotate tool* displays at the top of the graphic, as shown in Figure 12.34. You can change the orientation or angle of the graphic by using the rotate tool or you can flip the graphic using the Rotate 90 degrees button on the Picture toolbar.

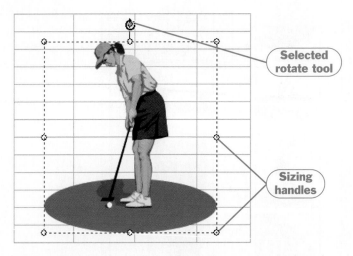

Figure 12.34 Clip art with handles and rotating tool selected

▶ If you change the size of a picture by cropping, it reduces the size of the picture by removing the vertical or horizontal edges. This may be used for emphasis or to remove unwanted portions. You can crop a picture using the Crop button on the Picture toolbar. When you select the picture you want to crop and click the Crop button, crop handles appear. Position the tool over a cropping handle and do one of the following:

- To crop one side, drag the center handle on that side inward.
- To crop equally on two sides at once, hold down the Ctrl key as you drag the center handle on either side inward, as shown in Figure 12.35.
- To crop equally on all four sides at once, hold down the Ctrl key as you drag a corner handle inward.

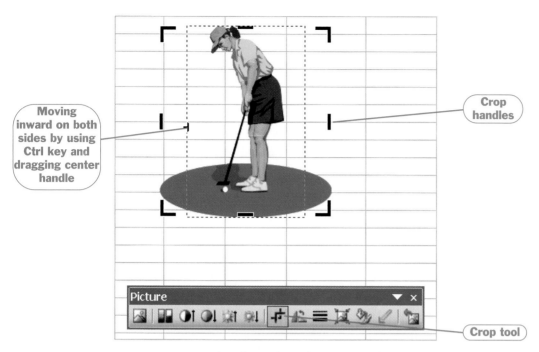

Moving inward on both sides by using Ctrl key and dragging center handle

Crop handles

Crop tool

Figure 12.35 Crop handles and equal cropping on both sides in process

▶ Click the Crop button again to stop the crop procedure. You can undo this operation if you are not satisfied with the results. If you are satisfied, click the Compress Pictures button on the Picture toolbar to delete the cropped parts of the picture from the file completely. When you click the Compress Pictures button, the Compress Pictures dialog box displays, as shown in Figure 12.36, where you can make additional settings. When you click OK, a warning message displays, as shown in Figure 12.37, to give you another opportunity to Apply or Cancel the compression.

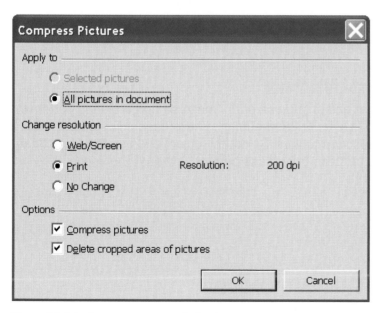

Figure 12.36 Compress Pictures dialog box

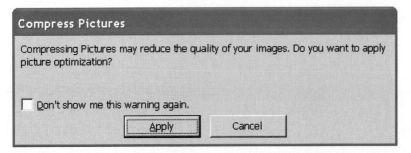

Figure 12.37 Compress message

TRY it OUT *e12-10*

1. Continue to work in the open file or open E12-10 from the Data CD.

2. Click **Insert, Picture** and click **Clip Art.** Enter **Sports** as the search text and click **Go.**

3. Click the golf image to insert it. Note the handles and rotate tool.

4. Practice rotating the image. Click **Undo** to return to original position.

5. Press the **Rotate Left 90°** button until it is in its original position.

6. Clip the **Crop** button on the Picture toolbar, click one vertical edge of the picture, press the **Ctrl** key, and move inward to narrow the image on both sides. Click the **Crop** button.

7. If the image is satisfactory, click the **Compress Pictures** button and click **OK.** Click **Apply** to compress the picture.

8. Move and size the object into the chart on the Jan-Feb-March columns as shown in Figure 12.38 on the next page.

9. Repeat Steps 3–8 to insert the baseball image as shown in Figure 12.38.

10. Keep the file open.

Control Image Contrast and Brightness

▶ You can control the contrast and brightness of an image so that it blends better with its surroundings. As shown in Figure 12.38, the images have been adjusted using the contrast and brightness buttons on the Picture toolbar. Select the object and use the More Contrast, Less Contrast, More Brightness, or Less Brightness buttons to adjust the image.

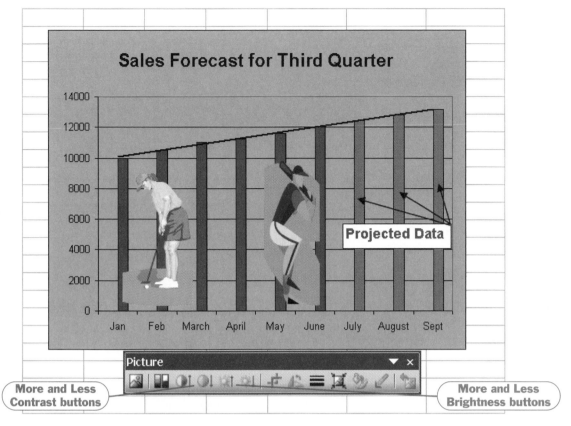

Figure 12.38 Sample of images adjusted using contrast and brightness controls

---

TRY *it* **OUT** *e12-11*

1. Continue to work in the open file or open **E12-11** from the Data CD.

2. If necessary, click **View, Toolbars, Picture** to display the Picture toolbar.

3. Select the golf image and press the **Less Contrast** button several times.

4. Click the **More Contrast** button several times.

5. Click the **More Brightness** button and the **Less Brightness** button several times.

6. After you see the effect of each button, adjust the image so that it blends into the background better.

7. Adjust the contrast and brightness of the baseball image so that it blends into the background better.

8. Close and save the file.

REHEARSAL

TASK 3

 GOAL
To create and analyze several worksheets using the Scenario and Solver features, and to chart the results

SETTING THE STAGE/WRAPUP
File names: 12.3Aging
            12.3Budget

WHAT YOU NEED TO KNOW

▶ You have already learned that an *aging report* is a financial document that shows an analysis of how many days payments from customers are overdue. Scenarios can be very helpful to a business that is trying to determine the effect of changing its credit terms and the interest rates that apply to overdue accounts.

▶ A *budget* is a proposal for future income and expenses used by a business as a guide for the next business period. The scenario and Solver tools are valuable for use in preparing a reasonable budget.

▶ In this Rehearsal activity, Time Out Sporting Goods has asked you to analyze two worksheets it has prepared. You create a scenario for the accounts receivable aging reports for Time Out Sporting Goods. You examine the effect of changing both the credit terms given to all customers from 20 days to 30 days and of raising the interest rate for some delinquent accounts. On the budget worksheet, you create worst-, average-, and best-case scenarios for the budget using the Solver feature. In addition, you will chart the results using graphics.

DIRECTIONS

1. Open the file **12.3Aging** from the Data CD, as shown in Illustration A.

2. On the September sheet, create a scenario for changing three items: the terms for payment in **Cell D6** and the interest rates for 60 and 90 days in **Cells C27** and **C28**. Use the **Ctrl** key to select each of the nonadjacent cells. Label the scenario `Terms and Interest Rates—Sept`.

3. Change **D6** to 30 days, **C27** to .020 and **C28** to .030. Create a scenario summary that shows the impact of the changes on the late fees in the range **H10:H16**.

4. Bold the **H16** line on the Scenario summary sheet; note the increase in fees with this scenario.

5. Rename the new sheet `Scenario–Sept Interest + Terms`.

6. Repeat Steps 2, 3, and 4 above for the Oct sheet. Label it `Scenario–Oct Interest + Terms`.

7. Open the file **12.3Budget** from the Data CD as shown in Illustration B.

8. On the Budget Scenarios sheet, create three Solver solutions and save them as scenarios. You will be changing the Net Income after Taxes to a worst-, average-, and best-case scenario. The changing cells for all Solver scenarios are **D8**, **D9**, **D11**, and **D13**. Use the **Ctrl** key to select nonadjacent changing cells. Save each Solver solution as a scenario with the names and the target cell (D14) values listed below: *Note: Restore the original values after you create and save each Solver solution as a scenario.*
   Worst   111000
   Average   115000
   Best   120000

9. Create a scenario summary that shows the impact of the three changes on the data in the range **D7:D14**.

Continued on page 172

Illustration A

	INVOICE NUMBER	INVOICE DATE	CUSTOMER	DATE DUE	DAYS UNPAID	INVOICE AMOUNT	INTEREST RATE	LATE FEE	AMOUNT DUE
			Time Out Sporting Goods						
			Accounts Receivable Aging Report						
Current Date:			10/31/2005						
Terms for payment:			20	days					
100	07/15/05	KM Dept Store		08/04/05	88.00	$ 4,000.00	0.015	$ 60.00	$4,060.00
110	07/22/05	Channel		08/11/05	81.00	$ 3,000.00	0.015	$ 45.00	$3,045.00
115	07/29/05	Champ's		08/18/05	74.00	$ 11,000.00	0.015	$ 165.00	$11,165.00
120	08/17/05	Morton's		09/06/05	55.00	$ 2,000.00	0.010	$ 20.00	$2,020.00
133	08/22/05	ABC Sports		09/11/05	50.00	$ 8,000.00	0.010	$ 80.00	$8,080.00
145	09/10/05	Quality Dept. Stores		09/30/05	31.00	$ 12,000.00	0.010	$ 120.00	$12,120.00
		Total				$ 40,000.00		$ 490.00	$ 40,490.00

Scenario: Compare results to 30 days

UNPAID DAYS	INTEREST RATE
1	0.000
15	0.050
30	0.010
60	0.015
90	0.020

Scenario: Compare to changing to .02 at 60 days and .03 for 90 days

Illustration A

Illustration B

Time Out Sporting Goods
Budget Analysis - 2005

	Actual 2003	Actual 2004	Budget Proposals 2005
Income:			
Net Sales	1,548,911	1,647,778	1,664,256
Less: Cost of Goods Sold	1,002,543	1,045,212	1,055,664
Gross Profit	546,368	602,566	608,592
Expenses:	413,341	446,049	450,509
Net Income before Taxes	133,027	156,517	158,082
Less: Taxes	39,908	46,955	47,425
Net Income after Taxes	93,119	109,562	110,658

Create scenarios using the Solver feature that change the Net Income after Taxes to Best Case: $120,000, Average Case: $115,000 or Worst Case: $111,000

Budget Scenarios / Sheet2 / Sheet3 /

Illustration B

10. As shown in Illustration C, copy the labels from **A7:A14** from the Budget sheet to **C11** on the Scenario Summary sheet.

11. Adjust the size of the column and reformat the labels so that they match the Scenario Summary sheet, as illustrated.

12. Create a column chart using the column headings and Net Sales figures.
    - Title the chart `Time Out Sporting Goods Budget Proposals-2005.`
    - Title the x-axis `Net Sales.`
    - Save the chart on a new sheet titled `Net Sales Chart.`
    - Enhance the chart as follows:
        - Delete the legend.
        - Format each column in a different color.

13. Add a graphic in a blank area of the chart. Adjust the rotation, cropping, brightness, or contrast to create the best appearance.

14. Repeat Steps 12 and 13 to create a chart showing Net Income after Taxes. Title the new sheet `Net Income Chart.` Use a different graphic. Add a text box and an arrow to the chart pointing to the Best Case value. Enter text: `Company Goal.`

15. Format the text box by changing the font and fill color.

16. Print copies of the Scenario Summary and each chart.

17. Save and close both files.

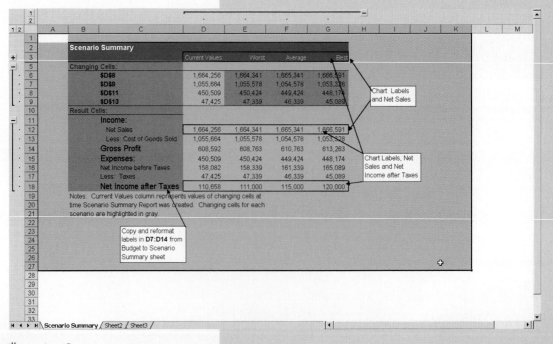

Illustration C

Cues for Reference

Create a Scenario
1. Click **Tools, Scenario.**
2. Click **Add** in Scenario Manager dialog box.
3. In Add Scenario dialog box, enter name for scenario. In Changing cells box, enter cell reference for data you want to change.
4. In Scenario Values dialog box, enter new value for data you want to change. Click **OK.**
5. In Scenario Manager dialog box, click **Summary.**
6. In Result cells box, enter cell references for data for which you want to see results.

Add-in Solver
1. Click **Tools, Add-Ins.**
2. Select **Solver Add-in.**
3. Click **OK.**

Create Solver Results
1. Select the target cell.
2. Click **Tools, Solver.**
3. Set the target using the **Value of, Min,** or **Max** option.

4. Click the **Collapse Dialog** button and select the changing range.
5. Click **Solve.**

Show the Results:
6. Click the **Show** button.

Remove the Results:
7. Click **Edit, Undo.**

Save as a Scenario
1. Click **Save Scenario** in the Solver Results dialog box.
2. Name the scenario. Click **OK.**
3. Click **Restore Original Values.** Click **OK.**

Add Graphics to Charts
1. The chart should not be selected.
2. Click **View, Toolbars, Drawing** to display the Drawing toolbar.
3. Click the desired graphic object button.
4. Click and drag to size and place object.

Format Graphics
1. Right-click the graphic object.
2. Select **Format.**

3. Modify formats.
4. Click **OK.**

Crop and Compress Graphics
1. Select the object.
2. Click the **Crop** button on the Picture toolbar.
3. Drag the crop handles as necessary to crop vertically or horizontally.
4. Click the **Crop** button again.
5. Click the **Compress** button on the Picture toolbar.
6. Make any additional settings. Click **OK** twice.

Change Brightness and Contrast for Graphics
1. Select the object.
2. Click the **More Brightness** button or **Less Brightness** button on the Picture toolbar.
or
Click the **More Contrast** button or **Less Contrast** button on the Picture toolbar.

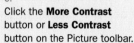

PERFORMANCE

SETTING THE STAGE/WRAPUP

Act I File name:

    12p1.TrilPersonnel

Act II File name:

    12p2.OdySales

Act III File name:

    12p3.ALSAging

WHAT YOU NEED TO KNOW

Act I

Trilogy Productions is assessing its personnel costs for three offices; New York, Los Angeles, and London. Open the file **12p1.TrilPersonnel** from the Data CD. Create the appropriate PivotTable and PivotChart reports so that management can make an analysis of employee expenses by department and location.

Follow these guidelines:

✴ Prepare the worksheet:

    ✴ Label **Column H** ANNSAL.

    ✴ Format the column in Accounting style.

    ✴ Enter the formula for annual salary in **Cell H2** and fill in the values for the rest of the employees.

    ✴ Sort the list first by LOCATION and then by date HIRED. Each should be in ascending order.

✴ Create a PivotTable that shows average ANNSAL by location and department. *(Hint: Put LOCATION in the Columns field and DEPT in the Rows field.)* Format all appropriate cells in Currency format with no decimals.

✴ Use one of the AutoFormats to format the report and print it.

✴ Remove LOCATION from the PivotTable and print a new report that shows average annual salaries by department.

✴ Go to the sheet with the data list and change the WKSAL entry for Judy Harris to $850.00

✴ Go to the sheet with the PivotTable and use the PivotTable toolbar to refresh the data.

✴ Click in the PivotTable and create a PivotChart showing average ANNSAL by department, as shown in the illustration on the next page.

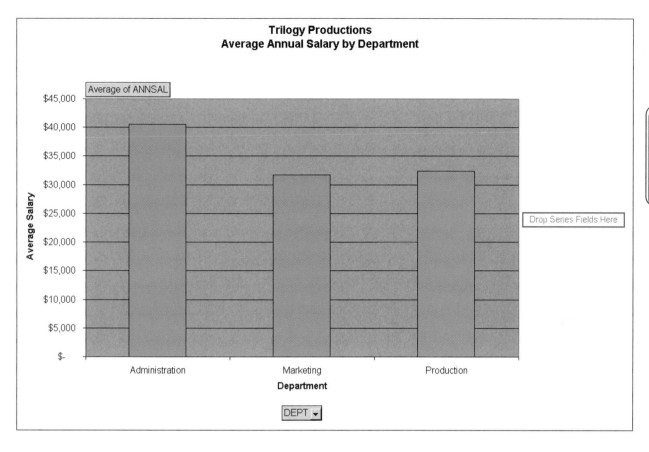

* Title the chart `Trilogy Productions Average Annual Salary by Department`
* Label the x-axis `Department.`
* Label the y-axis `Average Salary.`
* Place the chart on a new sheet entitled `Average Salary Chart.`
* Delete the legend and format the columns so they are green.
* Print the PivotChart report.
* Save your work.

Act II

Odyssey Travel Gear is preparing a sales, cost, and gross profit forecast for the third quarter. Open the file **12p2.OdySales** from the Data CD. Create and print the forecast for the third quarter, including a chart with a trendline.

Follow these guidelines:

* Arrange the data in a table that represents the months by numbers and transposes the three data columns. Use FORECAST to project the values for the last three months. Use absolute references for the ranges so that the formula can be copied to each month below. Copy and transpose the data for the last quarter back to the worksheet as values.

* Use the tabular version of the forecast to create a column chart that shows the data. Label the chart `Sales Forecast for the Third Quarter`, as illustrated below.

* Label the x-axis `Month.`

* Label the y-axis `Sales ($).`

* Change the values on the x-axis from numbers to the names of the months.

* Format the columns that represent the forecast data with a different color. Add a text box that labels the columns for July, August, and September as `Forecast Sales.`

* Add a text box that labels the columns for preceding months as `Actual Sales.`

* Format the text boxes with an appropriate fill color.

* Add a linear trendline on the chart for the Sales series.

* Increase the font size of the chart title.

* Print the chart.

* Save your work.

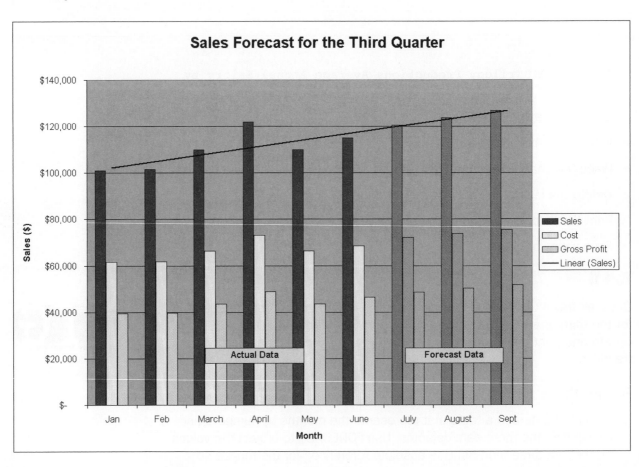

Act III

The Air Land Sea Travel Group is conducting an analysis to assess the impact of changing interest rates on past due accounts. Open the file **12p3.ALSAging** from the Data CD. Create two scenarios using the Solver feature according to the guidelines below and create charts to present the data.

Follow these guidelines:

* On the Aging sheet, create the first scenario so that the interest rates for accounts past due appear as follows:

DAYS UNPAID	INTEREST RATE
1	0.000
30	0.010
60	0.020
90	0.030

* Label the scenario `Interest Rate Change 1`.

* For the second scenario, the interest rate for accounts past due should appear as follows:

DAYS UNPAID	INTEREST RATE
1	0.000
30	0.020
60	0.030
90	0.040

   Label the scenario `Interest Rate Change 2`.

* Create a scenario summary showing the impact of these changes on the late fees, including the total of the fees. Name the sheet `Scenario Summary - Late Fees`.

* Create a scenario summary showing the impact of these changes on the total amount due. Name the sheet `Scenario Summary - Total Due`.

* On the Expense Budget sheet, use the Solver feature to create three scenarios for total expenses. The scenarios will be saved with the names and target values below:

Below Average	$625,000
Average	$655,000
Above Average	$700,000

- Create a scenario summary comparing the three scenarios for the data in **D7:D17.** Replace the cell labels in the scenario summary with the expense labels. Format the expense labels to match the summary sheet. Name the sheet `Scenario Summary - Expenses 2005.`

- Create a column chart of the labels and totals of the actual and projected data columns on a sheet named Column Chart, as illustrated below. Add a title `AirLandSea Travel Group - Projected Expense Scenarios 2005.`

- Format the three scenario columns in a different color than the actual data. Add an appropriate graphic, crop or rotate it, if necessary, and modify its brightness and contrast. Add a text box to the current values column and indicate that it represents 2004 values. See the illustration.

- Print a copy of the workbook.

- Save and close the file.

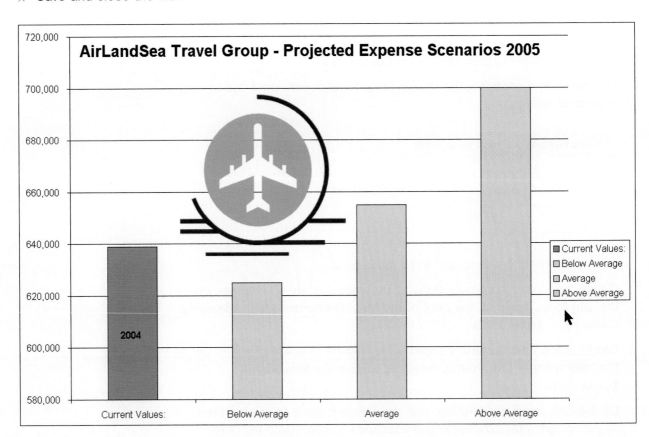

Marketing and Sales Reports

In this lesson, you will learn to import data from other sources such as external databases and the Web, into Excel. You will also learn to export data from Excel to other applications and to publish your worksheets to the Web. This ability to move data across different applications is helpful in producing and sharing various types of marketing and sales reports.

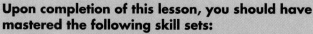

Upon completion of this lesson, you should have mastered the following skill sets:

- Import data into Excel from external sources
  - Obtain data from an external file
  - Obtain data using other methods
  - Obtain data from a Web page
- Export data from Excel
- Publish and edit Web workbooks and worksheets
  - Add interactivity to a Web page
- Retrieve external data and create queries

- Delete and edit database queries
- Structure worksheets using XML
  - Add an XML map to a workbook and modify XML view options
  - Map XML elements to a worksheet
  - Import XML Data into XML Spreadsheets
- Create Extensible Markup Language (XML) Web queries

Terms
Software-related
- Importing data
- Exporting data
- Interactivity
- Round-tripping
- Query
- Microsoft Query
- Extensible Markup Language (XML)
- Schema
- Map

 GOALS

To create a Web page for marketing purposes by importing and exporting data.

To practice using the following skill sets:

✴ Import data into Excel
  ✴ Obtain data from an external file
  ✴ Obtain data using other methods
  ✴ Obtain data from a Web page
✴ Export data from Excel
✴ Publish and edit Web workbooks and worksheets
  ✴ Add interactivity to a Web page

EXCEL

WHAT YOU NEED TO KNOW

Import Data into Excel

▶ The data you need to conduct analyses and create marketing and sales reports may be found in a variety of locations, such as a corporate database, a file created in an application other than Excel, or on the Web. Instead of reentering the data, you can import the data into your Excel worksheet and then conduct analyses or create reports. *Importing data* is the process of bringing information into Excel from a source other than an Excel file.

Obtain data from an External File

▶ Excel can read data written in several other file formats. Among them are the following:

- Access
- dBASE
- Lotus 1-2-3
- SQL Server
- FoxPro
- Paradox
- Quattro Pro
- Web pages (HTML)
- Oracle
- Text

▶ In most cases, you can bring external data into Excel by opening a blank worksheet and clicking Data, selecting Import External Data, and clicking Import Data. The Select Data Source dialog box opens, as shown in Figure 13.1.

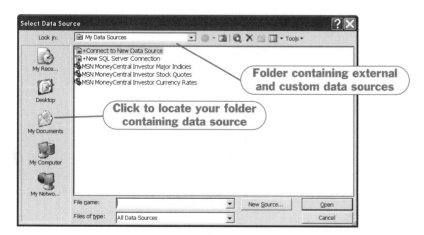

Figure 13.1 Select Data Source dialog box

▶ If the data you want to import is in a file on your computer or network drive, click the My Data Sources list arrow and select the location that holds your file. The data source may be in the My Documents folder. Select one of the file types in the Files of type drop-down menu. Select the file you want to import and click Open. The Import Data dialog box opens, as shown in Figure 13.2.

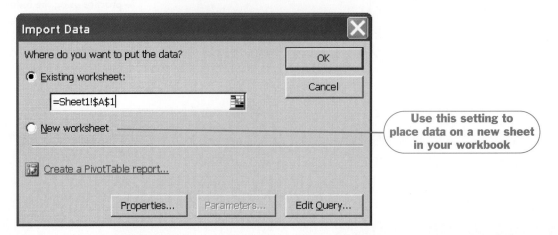

Figure 13.2 Import Data dialog box

▶ If you want to place the data on your current worksheet, click Existing worksheet. Enter or click the cell on your worksheet where you want the data range to start and click OK. If you want the data to appear on a new worksheet, click New worksheet and click OK. Excel adds a new worksheet to your workbook and places the data, beginning in the upper-left cell.

TRY*it* OUT *e13-1*

1. Open a blank Excel worksheet and click **Cell A1.**

2. Click **Data,** select **Import External Data,** and click **Import Data.**

3. In the Select Data Source dialog box, click the **My Data Sources** list arrow and locate the drive that contains the Data CD.

4. In the Files of type drop-down menu, click **Access Databases.** Click the file E13-1Homes. This is an Access database file with the extension .mdb. Click **Open.**

5. In the Import Data dialog box, click **Existing worksheet** and enter or click **Cell A1** as the destination for the imported data, if not already selected. Click **OK.** The Access file appears in the worksheet.

6. Close the file. Do not save.

Obtain Data using Other Methods

▶ You can also bring data into Excel by other means. Many applications, such as Access, offer the option of saving a file in an Excel format. For example, if you have a file open in Access, you can click Export and choose Excel as your file format. Select a location in which to save your file. After you close the file, you can reopen and work on it in Excel.

▶ Or, use the Copy and Paste features to import text files in table format into Excel. For example, if the data is in a Word file, open the file, select the data, and click the Copy button. Make sure Excel is open in another window. Click the Paste button to place the data in its appropriate location on the Excel worksheet.

▶ Alternatively, you can drag and drop the data from Word into Excel. Open the Word and Excel windows so that they are both visible on the screen. (Right-click the taskbar to tile the windows.) Select the data you want to import from the Word document. Hold down the Ctrl key and drag the data to the Excel worksheet, as shown in Figure 13.3.

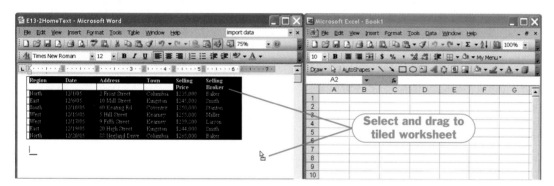

Figure 13.3 Tiled Excel and Word documents—Drag table from Word to Excel

TRY *it* OUT e13-2

1. Open a blank Excel worksheet.

2. Open the Word file **E13-2HomesText** from the Data CD. The text data is in a table format.

3. Right-click the **taskbar** and click **Tile Windows Vertically.**

4. Select the entire table in the Word document.

5. Hold down the **Ctrl** key and drag the data to the Excel worksheet.

6. Adjust column widths, if necessary.

7. Close both files. Do not save.

Obtain Data from a Web Page

▶ You can also import data from a Web page written in HTML (Hypertext Markup Language) into Excel with the drag-and-drop method. Follow these steps:
- Open both the HTML page and Excel.
- Arrange the windows so that they are both visible on the screen.
- Select the data you want to import from the HTML page.
- Hold down the Ctrl key and drag the data to the Excel worksheet.

T R Y *i t* O U T *e13-3*

1. Open a blank Excel worksheet.

2. Use Word or your browser to open the file **E13-3Web** from the Data CD. This file is in HTML format.

3. Right-click the **taskbar** and click **Tile Windows Vertically.**

4. Select the entire table on the Web page.

5. Hold down the **Ctrl** key and drag the table from the HTML document to Excel.

6. Adjust cell width, if necessary.

7. Click the cells with the numeric data and notice that you can edit the values.

8. Close both files. Do not save.

Export Data from Excel

▶ You can send data from Excel to many other applications, such as databases or text files, with a process that is called *exporting data.*

▶ To export data from Excel, click File, Save As. Click the list arrow in the Save as type box. A number of file type options appear, including other spreadsheet, text, and database formats, as shown in Figure 13.4. Select the file format of the application you want and save the file. You should then be able to use the data originally created in Excel in the other application. If you are saving the worksheet as a Text (tab delimited) file for use in Word, you can only save one sheet at a time. This file type does not support multiple-page workbooks.

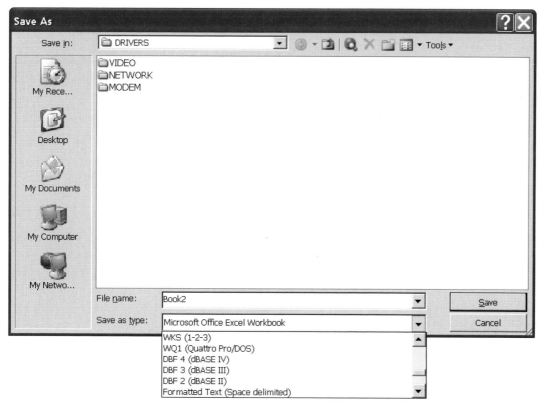

Figure 13.4 Save As file options

▶ For the other Office applications, it is generally better to import the Excel file from within the other application. Refer to Lesson 6, in the Access unit, to learn how to import an Excel file into an Access database. The Excel data should be in the form of a list, as discussed in Excel Lesson 11, with consistent data and column headings. Arrange the data in rows, with a label in each column above the first row of data, and no blank rows or columns. Save and close the Excel file, then switch to Access to import the file.

▶ If you want to use Excel data in your contact list in Outlook, you must first name the data range in Excel. Then, switch to Outlook, and use the File, Import and Export command to start the Import File Wizard. You can select Excel as the type of file and, if necessary, you can map the fields in the Excel file to the Outlook fields.

▶ If worksheets are to be used in PowerPoint presentations, they can be copied and pasted from Excel to PowerPoint, or they can be imported directly from within PowerPoint.

1. Open the Excel file **E13-4** from the Data CD.

2. Click **File, Save As.**

3. In the Save as type drop-down menu, click **Text (Tab delimited).** Name the file `13-4Text` and click **Save.**

4. Click **OK** at the warnings that you can only save the current sheet and you may lose Excel formats and features. If prompted to preserve worksheet format, click **Yes.** Close the file.

5. Switch to Word and open the file **13-4Text.** Notice that the graphic, formats, and layout do not appear.

6. Realign the columns of data using the **Tab** key, if necessary.

7. Click **File, Save** and notice the message that prompts you to save the file in Word format. Click **Yes.**

8. Close the file.

Publish and Edit Web Worksheets and Workbooks

▶ Businesses often publish financial reports to the Web to disseminate information to customers, shareholders, employees, and the general public. You do not need to know HTML to create a Web page from your Excel workbook.

▶ To save an Excel file as a Web page, open the Excel workbook you want to publish. Click File, Save as Web Page. The Save As dialog box opens, as shown in Figure 13.5.

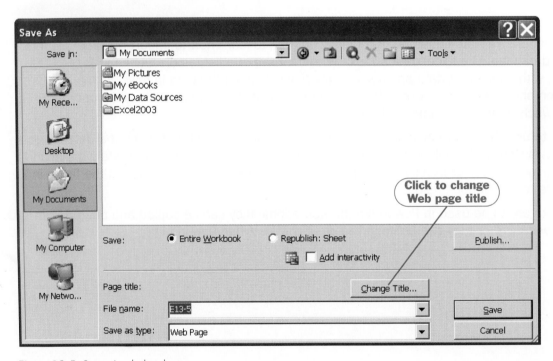

Figure 13.5 Save As dialog box

▶ Click Change Title to add a title to the Web page you are publishing. The Set Page Title dialog box opens, as shown in Figure 13.6. Enter the title you want and click OK.

Figure 13.6 Set Title dialog box

▶ Interactivity means that viewers of the Web page can manipulate the data in a browser. Adding interactivity will be discussed in the next section. If you want to publish the entire workbook and do not want to add interactivity to the Web page, select Entire Workbook, leave the Add interactivity box blank, name the file, and click Save. If you want to publish portions of a workbook, or if you want to remove interactivity from portions of a workbook, click Publish. The Publish as Web Page dialog box opens, as shown in Figure 13.7.

Figure 13.7 Publish as Web Page dialog box

▶ In the Choose box, select whether you want to publish the entire workbook, a specific worksheet, specific items on a worksheet (such as a chart or filtered list), or a range of cells on a worksheet. Since you can publish only one item at a time, you must repeat the publishing steps described here to publish multiple items from a workbook.

▶ In the File name box, enter the path to the location for your Web page. Or, you can click Browse to find and select the location. If you want to republish the page automatically after making changes in the Excel file, check the AutoRepublish every time this workbook is saved checkbox.

▶ To view the page after it is published, check the Open published web page in browser box. Click Publish.

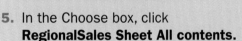

T R Y *it* **O U T** *e13-5*

1. Open the Excel file **E13-5** from the Data CD.

2. Click **File, Save as Web Page.**

3. Click the **Change Title** button to change the title. Enter **Four Corners Realty** and click **OK.**

4. Click the **Publish** button.

5. In the Choose box, click **RegionalSales Sheet All contents.**

6. In the Viewing options section, make sure Add interactivity with is not checked.

7. In the File name box, enter **C:\My Documents\E13-5.htm** or enter the correct path to your data files.

8. Check **Open published web page in browser.**

9. Click the **Publish** button. You can view your Web page in the browser.

10. Close the page and the file. Do not save.

Add Interactivity to a Web Page

▶ If you want to add *interactivity* to your Web page so that users can work in the worksheet, you must choose different options in the Publish as Web Page dialog box.

- In the Viewing options section, select Add interactivity with.
- Select the type of interactivity you want—Spreadsheet, PivotTable, or Charts.

Note: Persons working with your page must have Internet Explorer 4.1 or later and must also have a license to use Office.

▶ To edit your Web page, you can use a process called *round-tripping,* which routes you to Office from your browser and back again, after edits are complete.

- If you have saved your Excel worksheet as a Web page, open the published page in a browser and click Edit on the browser toolbar.
- You can choose from several applications to edit, including Word, Excel, and Notepad. Select one.
- Make the changes to your Web page. Click File, Save on the browser toolbar.
- Close the browser.

1. Open **E13-6** from the Data CD.

2. Click **File, Save as Web Page.**

3. Click the **Publish** button.

4. In the Choose box, click **RegionalSales Sheet All contents.**

5. In the Viewing options section, check **Add interactivity with** and select **Spreadsheet functionality,** if not already selected.

6. Click **Change** and enter `Four Corners Realty` for the title. Click **OK.**

7. In the File name box, enter `c:\My Documents\ E13-6.htm` or enter the correct path to the data files.

8. Check **Open published web page in browser**, if not already selected.

9. Click **Publish.** You can view your Web page in the browser.

10. Within the browser, sort the regions alphabetically using the **Sort Ascending** button.

11. Change the data in **Cell B16** to `10`.

12. Click **File, Save As** on the browser toolbar. Click **Yes** if prompted to overwrite the existing file.

13. Close the page. Close the file.

REHEARSAL

TASK 1

 GOAL
To create a Web page for marketing purposes by importing and exporting data

SETTING THE STAGE/WRAPUP
File names: 13.1Seniors.mdb
13.1Seniors.xls
13.1Competition.htm

WHAT YOU NEED TO KNOW

▶ In-Shape Fitness Centers maintain an Access database of all of their members. The membership coordinator would like to give a special, one-time promotional discount of 15% off the monthly membership fees of all members who are age 55 and over. She also found information about a competitor's discounts on a Web page. She would like to include all of this information on a Web page published by In-Shape Fitness Centers.

▶ In this Rehearsal activity, import the In-Shape Fitness Centers' Access database into Excel, then perform the appropriate analyses in Excel to calculate the one-time promotional discount. Import their competitor's information from an HTML page. After creating the Excel report with some of the information from the competitor's page, publish it to a Web page for In-Shape Fitness Centers.

▼ DIRECTIONS

1. The file **13.1Seniors** on the Data CD is an Access database file. Import this file into a blank worksheet in Excel, starting in **Cell B5.** Use Illustration A on the next page as a guide for this activity.

2. In **Cell A2,** enter and format the title **IN-SHAPE FITNESS CENTERS.**

3. Insert the current date in **Cell C1.**

4. In **Cell I5,** create a new column labeled **Age.** Enter a formula to calculate each member's approximate age in **Cell I6.** *(Hint: Use the YEAR function to compute the difference in years between two dates, e.g., =YEAR (C1) -YEAR (G6). Make sure the date in **Cell C1** is an absolute cell reference and that the result is in the Number format with no decimal places.)*

5. Use the fill handle to fill in the rest of the values for each member.

6. Sort the data by age, so that the oldest members are at the top of the list.

7. Delete the records of members who are less than 55 in age.

8. Label **Cell J5** **15% Discount** and set Wrap Text Alignment.

9. Write a formula in **Cell J6** that computes 15% of the individual's membership fee and fill in the values for each member.

10. Label **Cell K5** **Promo Fee** and set Wrap Text Alignment. Compute the promotional membership fee by subtracting the discount from each membership fee.

11. Format the column in Accounting style and fill in the values for each member.

Continued on next page

12. Create another Age column. Insert a column to the right of the Age column and label the column **Age**. Copy the data from Column I and used paste special values to place the age values in the new column.

13. Delete today's date and all the columns except the second Age column, Member Fee, 15% Discount, and Promo Fee.

14. Save the file as **13.1Seniors.xls.**

15. Use Word or your browser to open the HTML file **13.1Competition** on the Data CD. Copy only the table data to your Excel worksheet, below the worksheet data.

16. In the Excel worksheet, add labels and format the column labels and data as shown in Illustration B.

17. Format all labels for bold and set an appropriate font size.

18. Publish the worksheet as a Web page and add a title: **In-Shape Fitness Centers Promotion.** View the Web page in a browser. Use the browser editor to make any changes in formatting you think are necessary.

19. Save and close the file.

	A	B	C	D	E	F	G	H	I	J	K	L
1												
2		**IN-SHAPE FITNESS CENTERS**			Enter and format title					Add new column headings		
3												
4				Enter today's date here								
5		MemID	Name	Address	City/Town	Gender	Date of Birth	Member Fee	Age	15% Discount	Promo Fee	
6		1	Smith, Harry	32 Pine Ridge	Centerville	M	04/12/1940	$65				
7		2	Neely, Caren	114 First Avenue	Townsend	F	06/16/1960	$75				
8		3	Hanson, Neal	15 Rawley Street	Centerville	M	12/02/1982	$75				
9		4	Gretel, Conor	33 King Street	Springfield	M	11/04/1973	$75		Enter formulas		
10		5	Henry, Grace	782 Main Avenue	Springfield	F	03/15/1945	$65				
11		6	Stanton, Joan	89 Forest Avenue	Townsend	F	05/07/1976	$75				
12		7	Rogers, Thomas	201 Fox Run	Centerville	M	09/23/1977	$75				
13		8	Topher, Eric	52 Queen Street	Springfield	M	10/01/1943	$65				
14		9	Loring, Stephen	11 Brigham Street	Centerville	M	01/25/1980	$75		Insert another Age column and copy and paste values to new column		
15		10	Prouty, Shannon	2 Lyme Street	Townsend	F	08/04/1949	$75				
16		11	Houston, Debra	57 North Street	Springfield	F	12/16/1939	$65				
17		12	Gingrich, John	45 Elm Street	Centerville	M	04/27/1944	$65				
18		13	Deutsch, Lyle	6 Hancock Road	Townsend	M	06/14/1963	$75				
19		14	Manion, Kris	86 Noon Street	Centerville	F	11/17/1968	$75				
20		15	O'Connor, Timothy	19 Newtown Road	Townsend	M	05/19/1979	$75				
21		16	Mary Ann Popper	54 Carling Road	Centerville	F	07/10/1950	$75				
22		17	Brian Drury	234 Edinboro Drive	Springfield	M	01/31/1985	$75				
23		18	Vincent Ryan	76 North Street	Springfield	M	10/12/1982	$75				
24		19	Diana Wilson	876 Potter Drive	Townsend	F	09/25/1948	$75				
25												
26												
27				Copy competitor's rates below data								
28												

Illustration A

Illustration B

	A	B	C	D	E	F	G
1							
2	**IN-SHAPE FITNESS CENTERS**						
3	**15% off Fees for All Members 55 or over**						
4							
5	Member Fee	Age	15% Discount	Promo Fee			
6	$65	65	9.75	$ 55.25			
7	$65	64	9.75	$ 55.25			
8	$65	61	9.75	$ 55.25			
9	$65	60	9.75	$ 55.25			
10	$65	59	9.75	$ 55.25			
11	$75	56	11.25	$ 63.75			
12	$75	55	11.25	$ 63.75			
13							
14	**We give better discounts than our competition!**						
15							
16		**Competition's Discounts**					
17		65 and over	15%				
18		60-64	10%				
19		55-59	5%				
20							

Callouts in illustration:
- Insert labels in Rows 3, 14, and 16
- Center headings and data
- Format Table data to match worksheet above

Import Data to Excel
1. Open blank Excel worksheet and click **Data**, select **Import External Data**, and click **Import Data.**
2. Click **My Data Sources** list arrow, browse to your file location and select the file.
3. Click **Open.**
4. Indicate whether you want the data to go to an existing or a new worksheet.
5. Click **OK.**

Getting Data from a Web Page
1. Open HTML page and open Excel.
2. Arrange windows so that both are visible on screen.

3. Select data you want to import from HTML page.
4. Hold down **Ctrl** and drag data to Excel worksheet.

Export Data from Excel
1. Click **File, Save As.**
2. Specify new file type for Excel file.
3. Click **OK.**
4. Open file in alternate application.

Publish Worksheets and Workbooks to the Web
1. Click **File, Save as Web Page.**
2. Click **Publish.**

3. In Choose box, select whether to publish workbook, worksheet, or specific range of cells.
4. In Viewing options section, decide if you want to add interactivity and what type.
5. Click **Change** to add a title to Web page.
6. In the File name box, enter or select location in which you want to save your file.
7. Check any other options you want to enable, such as AutoRepublish or Open web page in browser.
8. Click **Publish.**

TRYOUT

TASK 2

GOALS

To create a sales report that retrieves data from an external source, an XML data file, and from the Web.

To practice using the following skill sets:

✳ Retrieve external data and create queries

✳ Delete and edit database queries

✳ Structure worksheets using XML

✳ Add an XML map to a workbook and modify XML view options

✳ Map XML elements to a worksheet

✳ Import XML Data into XML Spreadsheets

✳ Create Extensible Markup Language (XML) Web queries

WHAT YOU NEED TO KNOW

Retrieve External Data and Create Queries

▶ A useful way to obtain external data in Excel is to create a query. A *query* is a text file that includes information about a data source and information you would like to extract from it. Instead of importing the whole database as you did earlier in this lesson, you can specify which portions of a database you want. In other words, you can ask questions of, or "query," the database. You can also filter and sort the data, according to the criteria you specify, before the data is imported into Excel.

▶ You can save queries if you want to extract the same information from a database in the future. If you apply a saved query at a later time, any changes to the database are reflected in the query results. You can also share saved queries with other users. *Note: Queries have .odc or .dgy file extensions*.

▶ The easiest way to create a query is to use the Microsoft Query feature, which contains the Query Wizard. *Microsoft Query* is an application that allows you to retrieve specified information from external sources and is automatically activated when you initiate a query. If it does not activate, you will be asked if you wish to install it.

▶ To create a query, first open an Excel worksheet. Click Data, select Import External Data, and click New Database Query. The Choose Data Source dialog box opens, as shown in Figure 13.8. Make sure the box Use the Query Wizard to create/edit queries is checked. Select the type of file you want to access and click OK.

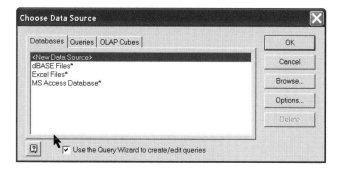

Figure 13.8 Choose Data Source dialog box

► The Select Database dialog box opens, as shown in Figure 13.9. Find the location that contains the file you want to access, select the file name, and click OK.

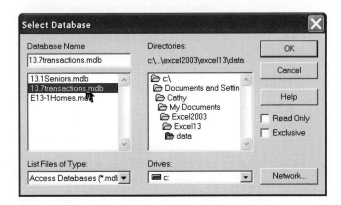

Figure 13.9 Select Database dialog box

► The Query Wizard - Choose Columns dialog box opens, as shown in Figure 13.10. Click the plus sign to the left of the database name and all of the field names in the database appear. To bring a field into Excel, select it and click the > button to bring it into the Columns in your query box. Use the up and down buttons on the far right to change the order of the fields. Click Next.

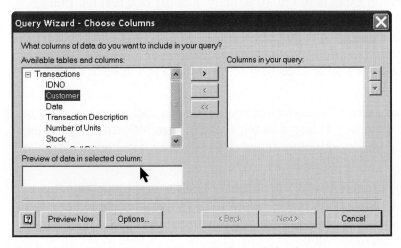

Figure 13.10 Query Wizard - Choose Columns dialog box

► The Query Wizard - Filter Data dialog box, shown in Figure 13.11, gives you the opportunity to filter the data. You can select more than one criteria by selecting the And or Or radio buttons. Select your filtering criteria and click Next. Simply click Next if you do not want to filter the data.

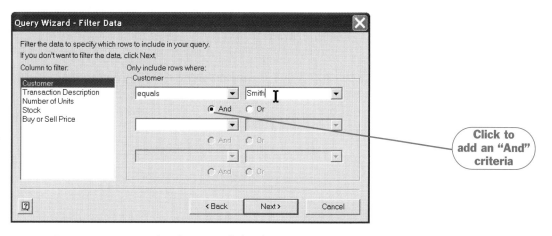

Figure 13.11 Query Wizard - Filter Data dialog box

▶ The next dialog box gives you the opportunity to sort the data. Select your sorting criteria and click Next, or just click Next if you do not want to sort the data.

▶ The Query Wizard - Finish dialog box opens, as shown in Figure 13.12. Click Save Query if you want to save the query for future use. Select the location in which you want to save it in the Save As dialog box that opens. *Note: Queries are usually saved in the Queries folder.* Indicate whether you want to place the results of the query in an Excel worksheet or if you want to edit or view the data in the query. Click Finish. At that point, the Import Data dialog box requests a placement for the results of the query, as shown in Figure 13.12B.

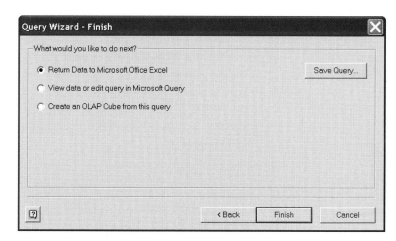

Figure 13.12 Query Wizard - Finish dialog box

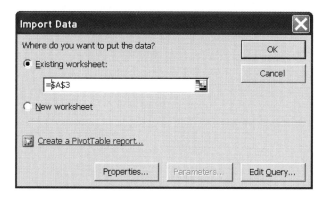

Figure 13.12B Import Data dialog box

Note: When you initiate Microsoft Query, it runs in the background while you work on your Excel worksheet. You can view it or minimize it like any other window that appears in the taskbar at the bottom of your screen.

▶ When you create a query and click a cell that contains data from an external source, the External Data toolbar appears, as shown in Figure 13.13. If it does not display, click View, Toolbars, External Data. If you click the Refresh Data button, data linked to an external source will be updated if there have been any changes to the original database.

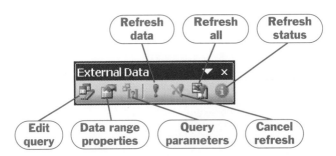

Figure 13.13 External Data toolbar

T R Y i t O U T e13-7

1. Open a new Excel worksheet. Click **Data,** select **Import External Data,** and click **New Database Query.**

2. In the Choose Data Source dialog box, click **MS Access Database*.** Click **OK.**

3. In the Select Database dialog box, locate the Access file **13.7transactions** on the Data CD and click **OK.**

4. Click the plus sign to the left of **Transactions.** Move the following field names to the **Columns in your query** section: "Customer," "Transaction Description," "Number of Units," "Stock," and "Buy or Sell Price." Click **Next.**

5. Filter the data so that only the records for customer Smith are selected.
   a. In Columns to filter, select **Customer.**
   b. In Only include rows where, select **equals.**
   c. Enter **Smith** in the next box on the right. Select **And.**

6. Filter the data so that only the records where the Transaction Description is Buy are selected.
   a. In Columns to filter, select **Transaction Description.** A new screen should appear.
   b. In Only include rows where, select **equals.**
   c. Enter **Buy** in the next box on the right.
   d. Click **Next.**

7. Click **Next** to skip the sorting.

8. Select **Return Data to Microsoft Office Excel,** if not already selected. Click **Finish.**

9. In the Import Data dialog box, enter **=$A$3** as the cell reference in the existing worksheet. Click **OK.** The results of the query appear in Excel.

10. Save the file as **E13-7.** Keep the file open.

Delete and Edit Database Queries

▶ If you need to delete a database query, click the name box and select the named range for the query, as shown in Figure 13.14. When you press the Delete key, you are prompted to confirm the deletion of the query.

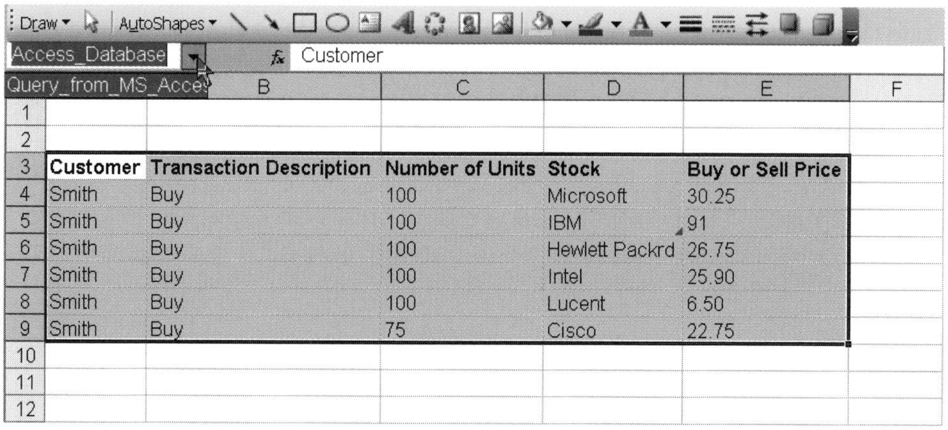

Access_Database | Customer

Query_from_MS_Acce	B	C	D	E	F
1					
2					
3 Customer	Transaction Description	Number of Units	Stock	Buy or Sell Price	
4 Smith	Buy	100	Microsoft	30.25	
5 Smith	Buy	100	IBM	91	
6 Smith	Buy	100	Hewlett Packrd	26.75	
7 Smith	Buy	100	Intel	25.90	
8 Smith	Buy	100	Lucent	6.50	
9 Smith	Buy	75	Cisco	22.75	
10					
11					
12					

Figure 13.14 Selected query range

▶ Microsoft Query and the Query Editor let you edit the query to display other information. To edit an existing query, click Data, select Import External Data, and click Edit Query, or use the Edit Query button on the External Data toolbar. You are returned to the Query Wizard in the Choose Columns screen (see Figure 13.10), where you can begin to change your query selections.

TRY *it* OUT *e13-8*

1. Continue to work in the open file or open **E13-8** from the Data CD.
2. In B1 enter `Wilson-Jones Brokerage Company` and format the title in bold and in a larger font.
3. Copy the data on Sheet1 to **Sheet2** and **Sheet3.**
4. On Sheet2, click **Insert, Name, Define,** and select the **Query_from_MS_Access_Database Sheet2.**
5. Click **Delete,** and **Close.** Notice that the data remains, however, query parameters have been deleted.
6. Switch to **Sheet3** and click within the query results. Click **Data,** select **Import External Data,** and click **Edit Query.**
7. Click **Next** in the Query Wizard - Choose Columns dialog box.
8. Filter the data so that only the **Sell** records for customer Hudson are selected.
   a. In Columns to filter, select **Customer.**
   b. In Only include rows where, select **equals.**
   c. Enter `Hudson` in the next box on the right. Select **And.**
   d. In Columns to filter, select **Transaction Description.**
   e. In Only rows where, select **equals.**
   f. Enter `Sell` in the next box on the right.
   g. Click **Next** two times to complete the query.
9. Select **Return Data to Microsoft Office Excel** and click **New Worksheet.** Click **Finish.** The results of the query appear in Excel on Sheet4.
10. Switch to **Sheet1.**
11. Close and save the file.

Structure Worksheets Using XML

▶ Many Web pages now use *Extensible Mark-Up Language (XML)* as a format for presenting data. XML, like HTML, is a commonly used language that employs tags to define, transmit, validate, and intepret structured data. Because XML can be read by a variety of applications, and because it is widely used, you can now share data more easily through the Web by identifying and extracting specific data from business documents. For example, an invoice that contains the name and address of a customer, a Web page with stock market quotes, or a report that contains last quarter's financial results can be passed to a database or reused elsewhere, outside of the workbook.

▶ You can save any Excel file in XML format (in the Save As Type option) for eventual publication to the Web, or you can take advantage of XML format to locate data on a Web page. There are two XML formats in Excel: XML Spreadsheet or XML Data, as shown in Figure 13.15. Worksheet data for transfer to other applications should be saved as XML Data.

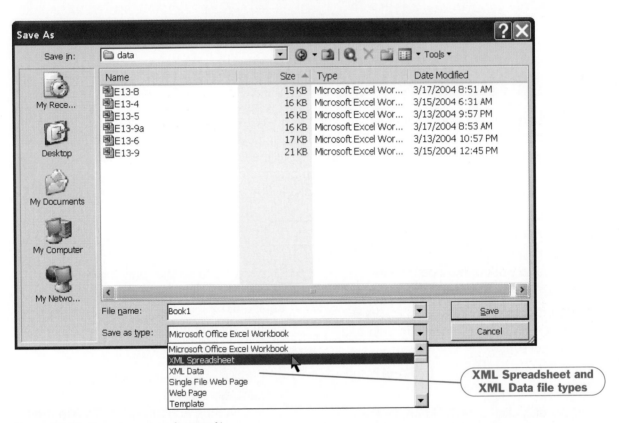

Figure 13.15 Save As options for XML files

▶ The procedure to import XML Data files into an Excel workbook involves the use of schemas. A *schema* can be thought of as tags that store information, such as file properties, data formats, layout, column titles, and so forth, which define the structure of the workbook. A schema, which is an .xsd file, is generally created by a firm's IT or Information Technology department and provided as part of the structure for XML Data and spreadsheet files. A sample of an .xsd file, or schema, is shown in Figure 13.16, as it appears in Notepad.

```
<?xml version="1.0" encoding="UTF-8" standalone="no"?>
    <xsd:schema xmlns:xsd="http://www.w3.org/2001/XMLSchema" xmlns="urn:NetSales"
        targetNamespace="urn:NetSales" elementFormDefault="qualified">
        <xsd:element name="Root">
            <xsd:complexType mixed="false">
                <xsd:sequence minOccurs="0" maxOccurs="1">
                    <xsd:element minOccurs="0" maxOccurs="unbounded" name="NetSales">
                        <xsd:complexType mixed="false">
                            <xsd:sequence minOccurs="0" maxOccurs="1">
                                <xsd:element type="xsd:date" name="Date"/>
                                <xsd:element type="xsd:string" name="Store"/>
                                <xsd:element type="xsd:decimal" name="SportingGoods"/>
                                <xsd:element type="xsd:decimal" name="Accesssories"/>
                                <xsd:element type="xsd:decimal" name="Clothing"/>
                                <xsd:element type="xsd:decimal" name="Total"/>
                            </xsd:sequence>
                        </xsd:complexType>
                    </xsd:element>
                </xsd:sequence>
            </xsd:complexType>
        </xsd:element>
    </xsd:schema>
```

Figure 13.16 Sample of a schema, or .xsd file

▶ Once you have obtained a custom XML schema for your spreadsheet, you can add it to your Excel worksheet and save the file as an XML Spreadsheet. You drag the elements from the schema onto your spreadsheet to define or map the structure of the workbook. When you save a workbook in the XML Spreadsheet format, and add an XML schema, Excel will create an XML *map* (or structure). Generally, this is only done once. Thereafter, XML Data can be imported into the mapped spreadsheet using the same schema.

Add an XML Map to a Workbook and Modify XML View Options

▶ To add a schema to an Excel spreadsheet, select the cell to receive the schema, and click Data, select XML, and click XML Source. The XML Source task pane will display, as shown in Figure 13.17. *Note: There are no XML maps in a workbook until they are added.*

Figure 13.17 XML Source task pane and options button

▶ To add a schema, click the XML Maps button, and the XML Maps dialog box displays, as shown in Figure 13.18. When you click the Add button, the Select XML Source dialog box displays, as shown in Figure 13.19. You then locate and select the schema, or .xsd file, and click Open. You can then choose to rename, delete or cancel the schema using the buttons in the XML Maps dialog box, or accept the schema by clicking OK.

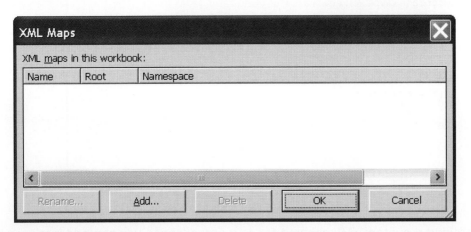

Figure 13.18 XML Maps dialog box

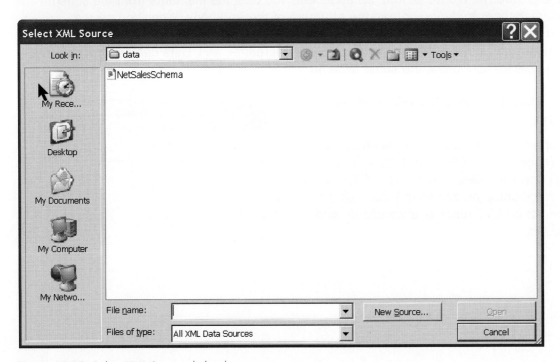

Figure 13.19 Select XML Source dialog box

▶ Once you add the XML schema, it becomes the XML Map for the workbook and is displayed in the XML Source task pane, as shown in Figure 13.20.

Figure 13.20 XML Source task pane with XML map

▶ The Options button menu displays settings you can choose for the XML Source task pane, as shown in Figure 13.17. The Automatically Merge Elements When Mapping feature should be checked so that when an XML element or folder is dragged to an XML list, or a table of data in an XML file, it automatically expands to all the columns included in the folder. If the active cell is not in the XML list, when you select the Hide Borders of Inactive List command, the borders of the XML list will not be displayed.

1. Open **E13-9** from the Data CD.

2. Click **Data, XML, XML Source.**

3. On the XML Source task pane, click the **XML Maps** button.

4. Click the **Add** button and locate the **NetSalesSchema** file on the Data CD.

5. Select the file and click **Open.**

6. Select the schema and click the **Rename** button on the XML Maps dialog box; change "Root_Map" to **NetSalesByStore**. Click **OK.**

7. Click the **Options** button on the XML Source task pane.

8. Check that the **Automatically Merge Elements When Mapping** and the **My Data Has Headings** options are activated.

9. Save the file as an XML Spreadsheet and name it **E13-Sales**.

10. Keep the file open.

Map XML Elements to a Worksheet

▶ Once the XML map is added to a worksheet, you can drag the elements to the location on the spreadsheet to receive XML Data with the same configuration. In the file with the XML Map, select the folder representing the parent data element from the XML Source task pane. All the child elements in that folder will automatically be selected. Drag the folder to the first location on the spreadsheet to receive the data list, as shown in Figure 13.21. Individual child elements may be dragged to the worksheet or elements may be deleted on the worksheet, by selecting and deleting the column.

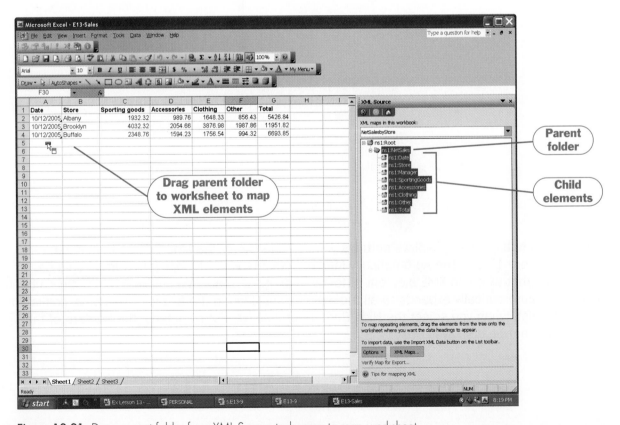

Figure 13.21 Drag parent folder from XML Source task pane to map worksheet

1. Continue to work in **E13-Sales** or open it from the Data CD.

2. Click on the **NetSales** parent element, which will select all the child elements in the folder.

3. Drag the folder to **A5** on the worksheet. Notice the border of the XML list area.

4. Click in **Cell C6,** and note that the Manager data is not required for this worksheet.

5. Right-click and select **Delete, Column.**

6. Note that the XML list is now matched to the worksheet.

7. Save the file and keep it open.

Import XML Data into XML Spreadsheets

▶ To import data into the XML list, the data should be saved as an XML Data file and should be created with the same XML map. In practice, the template for the XML Data would be provided for users in remote locations. To import XML Data into an XML Spreadsheet, click Data, XML, Import and select the XML Data file from the Import XML dialog box as shown in Figure 13.22. Click Import and the data list will appear in the XML Spreadsheet file.

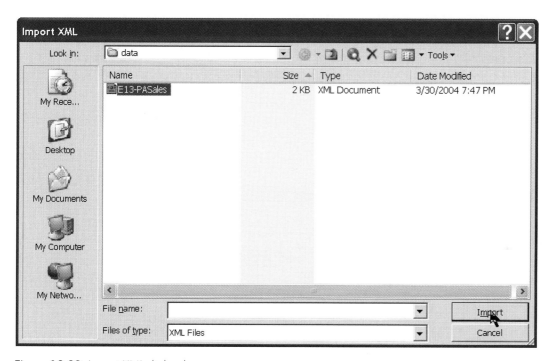

Figure 13.22 Import XML dialog box

▶ If there is XML list data in the same worksheet as regular Excel ranges, you should convert the XML list data to an Excel range so that all data may be analyzed as one list. To convert XML list data, right-click anywhere in the list, select List, and click Convert to Range. Click Yes to confirm the conversion. After the list is converted to an Excel range, you can delete the column headings from the XML list.

1. Continue to work in **E13-Sales** or open **E13-11** from the Data CD.

2. Click **Cell A6** and click **Data,** select **XML,** and click **Import.**

3. On the Data CD, locate and select **E13-PASales,** an XML Data file with the same XML map as in E13-Sales.

4. Click **Import.** The data list will flow into the XML Spreadsheet.

5. Right-click anywhere in the XML list, and select **List, Convert to Range.** Click **Yes** to confirm.

6. Delete row 5 containing the XML list headings.

7. Format all numeric data for currency.

8. Save and close the file.

Create Extensible Markup Language (XML) Web Queries

▶ You can obtain data from Web pages using a Web query. Query data can be imported to a worksheet where you can analyze it and use it in reports as with any other data in Excel. When you create a query you can later refresh or update data that you import to your worksheet. For example, as stock quotes or sales figures on the Web change, you can update them in your worksheet and include them in any formulas you create.

▶ To create a Web query you need to have an Internet connection. Click Data, select Import External Data, and click New Web Query to connect to the Internet and display the New Web Query dialog box, as shown in Figure 13.23. In the Address box, enter the Web address that contains the data you want to import and click Go.

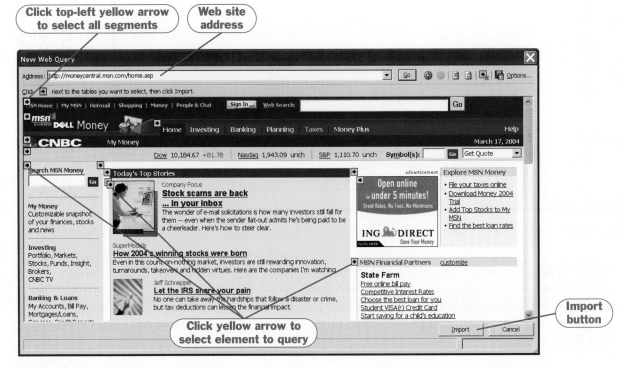

Figure 13.23 New Web Query dialog box

▶ Select the tables you want to import by clicking the yellow arrows that appear next to the tables on the Web page. As you click each arrow, it turns into a green checkmark. Once you select your data, click Import.

Note: If you want to import the whole page, click the yellow arrow in the upper left corner.

▶ The Import Data dialog box opens, as shown in Figure 13.24. Indicate whether you want the data to go into an Existing worksheet or a New worksheet. Click OK. To update the data in the table, click the Refresh Data button on the External Data toolbar.

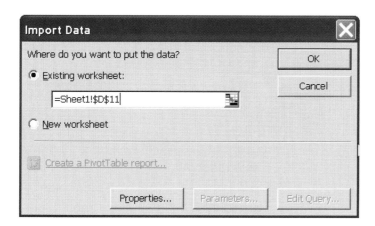

Figure 13.24 Import Data dialog box

▶ You can also bring data into Excel from a Web page using a shortcut. Right-click the data on the Web page and choose the Export to Excel option. This activates a Web query.

T R Y *it* O U T *e13-12*

Note: You need an Internet connection to complete this Try it Out.

1. Open **E13-12** from the Data CD.

2. Click **Data**, select **Import External Data,** and click **New Web Query.**

3. In the New Web Query dialog box, enter `http://moneycentral.msn.com` and click **Go.**

4. On the Money Central Web site, locate the box entitled "Get Quote" and enter **MSFT** (the Microsoft stock symbol) in the Symbol(s) box at the left. Click **Go.**

5. Click the yellow arrow next to the table of Microsoft data that includes the last price.

6. Click **Import.**

7. In the Import Data dialog box, indicate that you want to place the data starting in **Cell D11** of the existing worksheet. Click **OK.**

8. In **Cell F3** enter `Last Price` and in **Cell G3** enter `Current Value.`

9. In **Cell F4** enter a reference to the last price in the imported chart (*Hint: =F11*).

10. In **Cell G4** enter the formula that gives the total current valuation of the customer's Microsoft stock (*Hint: number of shares*current price*).

11. Format **F4** and **G4** for currency.

12. Save and close the file.

13. Reopen the file at another time, select a cell in the imported data area, and click the **Refresh Data** button on the External Data toolbar.

REHEARSAL

TASK 2

GOAL

To create a sales report that retrieves data from an external source, an XML Data file, and from the Web

SETTING THE STAGE/WRAPUP

File name: **13.2ForeignOrders.mdb**
13.2Conversion.xls
13.2Orderschema.xsd
13.2Argentina.xml

WHAT YOU NEED TO KNOW

▶ Time Out Sporting Goods maintains a database of its transactions in several foreign countries. A manager wants to create a summary report of all sales that took place in Brazil, Spain, and Mexico during one month. In addition, the sales representative in Argentina has sent an XML Data file with the sales from that country. As part of the report, the current currency conversion rates should be placed on the Excel worksheet.

▶ On the currency conversion Web site used in this Rehearsal, the current currency rates are quoted "In U.S. dollars" and "Per U.S. dollar." Use the appropriate "Per U.S. dollar" rate multiplied by the U.S. dollar amount to calculate the foreign currency equivalent. If you want to obtain the U.S. equivalent of foreign funds, use the "In U.S. dollars" rate and multiply by the foreign currency amount.

▼ DIRECTIONS

Part A

1. Open a blank Excel workbook. Refer to Illustration A.

2. The file **13.2ForeignOrders** on the Data CD is an Access database file. Create a query to import data from this file to your Excel workbook.

3. In your query, include all of the columns in the database except for ID.

4. Filter the data in your query so that only the orders from Brazil are imported.

5. Place the data starting in **Cell A5** of the Excel worksheet. Use Illustration A as a guide.

6. In **A2** label the top of the sheet `Sales in Brazil: March`. Format the title in **14 pt. bold.**

7. In **Cells F4** and **F5,** enter `Total Due U.S.$.` Format in **bold.** In **Cell F6,** enter the formula that computes the total amount due for each order. Format the column for U.S. currency and fill in the values for **F7:F12.**

8. In **Cells G4** and **G5,** enter `Conversion Factor`. Format in **bold** and adjust the column width if necessary.

9. In **Cells H4** and **H5,** enter `Total Due Reals`. Format in **bold.** Format cells **H6:H11** for commas.

10. Rename the sheet `Sales-Brazil`.

11. Make three copies of the sheet in the workbook and rename them `Sales-Spain`, `Sales-Mexico`, and `Sales-Argentina`.

Continued on next page

► In this Rehearsal activity, create a query for Time Out Sporting Goods to obtain data from the database and import it into Excel (Part A). Add an XML schema to the worksheet for Portugal, map the worksheet, import the XML Data file, and convert the XML list to a range (Part B). Also, create a Web query to obtain currency conversion rates that you can update periodically (Part C).

12. Edit the worksheet title, in **Cell A2**, for each country and the Total Due, in Column H, for the foreign currency using the heading indicated:
Spain = `Total Due Euros`
Mexico = `Total Due Mexican Pesos`
Argentina = `Total Due Argentine Pesos`

13. Edit the query on the Spain and Mexico sheets to locate orders from those countries. Argentina data will be obtained from another source.

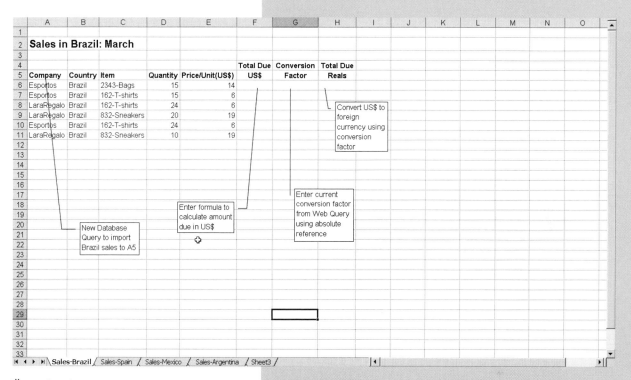

Illustration A

Part B (Refer to Illustration B)

14. On a blank worksheet in the same workbook, create a Web query to find the conversion factors to change the U.S. dollars to other currencies. One place to find the current currency conversion rates is
http://moneycentral.msn.com/investor/market/rates.asp

*Note: If you use the suggested Web site, the entire table of conversion rates is labeled with the yellow arrow, rather than individual rates. Have the query place the currency conversion table in **Cell A16.** The solution file will vary from current data obtained from the Internet. If you do not have Internet access, copy the data from **13.2conversion** on the Data CD to **Cell A16.***

Continued on next page

15. Copy the query results to the **Brazil, Spain, Mexico, and Argentina** sheets in **A16.** Switch back to the **Brazil** sheet and group the four sheets.

16. In **Cell G6** enter a reference to the Per U.S. Dollar conversion factor for the Brazilian Real (=$C$19 as per Illustration B) and make it an absolute reference. Fill in the value for the rest of the column.

17. In **Cell H6,** enter a formula to multiply the Total Due U.S.$ data by the Conversion Factor to convert to Brazilian Reals. Fill in the values for the rest of the column.

18. Ungroup the sheets and on the Spain and Mexico sheets, change the reference in **Cell G6** to the appropriate Per US$ conversion rate, using an absolute reference, and copy it for all data. Delete any unnecessary formulas.

19. Save the file; name it 13.2ForeignOrders.

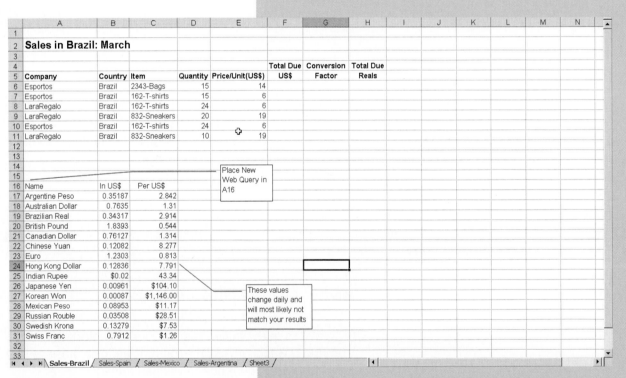

Illustration B

Continued on next page

Part C (Refer to Illustration C.)

20. Switch to the **Sales-Argentina** worksheet. The data for Argentina must be imported from an XML Data file that is structured by an orders schema.

21. Add the XML Source file **13.2Orderschema** to the worksheet, as shown in Illustration C. Rename the Root_Map to `Argentina`.

22. Map the **Orders** parent element to **Cell A6.** *Note:* The NS2 reference is an automatically numbered name space indicator, which may be different on your system.

23. Import the XML Data file **13.2Argentina** into the XML list in **Cell A7.**

24. Convert the XML list to a range. Delete the XML list headings in **Row 6.**

25. Change the reference in **Cell G6** to the appropriate Per US$ conversion rate for the Argentine Peso, using an absolute reference, and copy it for all data. Check that formulas are correct for all items.

26. Group all sheets, set the print range for **A1:I15**, and print the workbook.

27. Save and close the file.

28. Reopen the file at another time. On the **Brazil** sheet, click **Cell A16** and click the **Refresh Data** button on the External Data toolbar. Check the changes in the conversion rates.

29. Save and close the file.

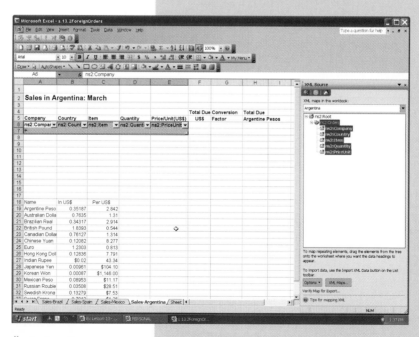

Illustration C

Retrieve External Data with Queries

1. Open an Excel worksheet.
2. Click **Data,** select **Import External Data,** and click **New Database Query.**
3. In Choose Data Source dialog box, select file type and click **OK.**
4. In Select Database dialog box, select name and click **OK.**
5. In Query Wizard - Choose Columns dialog box, click plus sign to left of database name. Move each of fields you want into Columns in your query section. Click **Next.**
6. Filter data, if needed. Click **Next.**
7. Sort data, if needed. Click **Next.**
8. In Query Wizard - Finish dialog box, indicate whether you want to save query and if you want to place it in an Excel worksheet. Click **Finish.**

Edit Database Query

1. Position mouse cursor within external data range.
2. Click **Data,** select **Import External Data,** and click **Edit Query.**

3. Edit Query Wizard settings as necessary.
4. Complete Query Wizard - Finish dialog box, as indicated in Step 8 above. Click **Finish.**

Create Web Queries

1. Click **Data,** select **Import External Data,** and click **New Web Query.**
2. In New Web Query dialog box, enter Web address that contains data you want to import in Address box. Click **Go.**
3. Select tables you want to import by clicking yellow arrows next to tables on Web page. Click **Import.**
4. Indicate whether you want data to go to existing or new worksheet. Click **OK.**
5. Click **Refresh Data** button on External Data toolbar if you want to update data in table.

Delete External Data Ranges

1. Click **Insert, Name,** and **Define.**
2. Select data range to delete.
3. Press **Delete.**

Add XML Map to Spreadsheet

1. Click **Data, XML,** and **XML Source.**
2. In the XML Source task pane, click the **XML Maps** button.
3. On the XML Maps dialog box, click the **Add** button.
4. Locate and select the .xsd file. Click **Open.** Click **OK.**

Rename XML Map

1. In the XML Maps dialog box, click the **Rename** button.
2. Enter the new name and click **OK.**

Map XML Elements

1. Select the parent element in the XML Source task pane.
2. Drag it to the worksheet.
3. Modify by deleting columns, if necessary.

Import XML Data to Spreadsheet

1. Click **Data, XML** and **Import.**
2. In the Import XML dialog box, locate and select the XML Data file.
3. Click **Import** button. 🖼

Convert XML List to a Range

1. Right-click in the XML list range.
2. Click **List, Convert to range.**

PERFORMANCE

SETTING THE STAGE/WRAPUP

Act I File names:

> 13p1.travel.doc
> 13p1.national.xls

Act II File name:

> 13p2.orders.mdb
> 13p2.orderschema.xls
> 13p2.Mexico.xml

EXCEL

WHAT YOU NEED TO KNOW

Act I

A marketing analyst for the Air Land Sea Travel Group would like to publish a Web page that provides information about the regions of the world to which the company's customers travel. The page will also include similar information from a national data bank. The company data is currently in a text file. The national data is on the Web. You will import the relevant information from these sources to an Excel file and then publish the worksheet as a Web page.

Follow these guidelines:

✳ The file that contains the company information is a Word file, **13p1.travel.doc,** on the Data CD. Copy and paste the table data into Excel and make any necessary adjustments to the format of the table.

✳ Insert a line below Mexico, as shown in the illustration on the next page, and compute the total number of travelers who went to North America. Add an indented label for the subtotal. Calculate the number of travelers who went overseas and add an indented label. Compute the total number of travelers for all destinations at the bottom of the table and label it. Add a column to the table for % of total, as shown in the illustration. Enter a formula, using an absolute reference, to calculate the percentage of total travelers who went to each destination. Format for percents with one decimal place.

	A	B	C	D
1	Air, Land, Sea Travel			
2				
3	**Where did our customers travel in 2003?**			
4				
5	**Destination**	**Number of Customers**	**% of Total**	
6	Canada	230		
7	Mexico	220		
8	**Subtotal to North America**			
9	Europe	500		
10	Central America	200		
11	Caribbean	635		
12	South America	270		
13	Africa	80		
14	Middle East	75		
15	Asia	226		
16	Oceania	59		
17	**Subtotal to Overseas**	2045		
18	Grand Total			
19				
20				

✻ Obtain information about national travel statistics from http://tinet.ita.doc.gov.

✻ Use the Outbound Travel from the U.S. link and open the Select Destinations Visited by U.S. Resident Travelers report. (Choose the View for Free option and use the most current data. If you do not have Internet access, use the data in the **13p1.national** file, found on the Data CD.)

✻ Import the table into your Excel worksheet. Delete all columns from the national data except Country and the Total travelers for the current year, expressed in thousands. Analyze the data with subtotals and a total. Add labels as you did with the company data. Add a column for % of Total and enter and copy the formula. Add a note to the bottom of the report providing the name of the Web site as the source for the national data.

✻ Add text to label all information on the page for viewers. Add any clip art or formatting that you think will make the page attractive and readable.

✻ Save the file as a Web page and name it **13p1.travel.** Open and view your page in a browser. Make any modifications you think are necessary to improve the page. (You can use round-tripping to edit in Excel from your browser.)

✻ Print the page.

✻ Close and save the file.

Act II

Odyssey Travel Group has an Access database that keeps track of all orders. A portion of that database is available in **13p2.orders** on the Data CD. A manager would like to obtain a summary of the sales orders originating in Brazil, Canada, and Argentina for the month of June.

For this exercise, you will import the database information into Excel and filter the data three times to show the orders from each country on a separate worksheet. You will also add information about Brazil's currency to compute the total amount due for each order. You will create a Web query to obtain the current currency conversion factor and use it for future updates of the information.

In addition, you have just received XML Data from the Mexican representative with orders from that country. The sales from Mexico will be added to the worksheet after an XML map is added to the spreadsheet.

Follow these guidelines:

⚹ Open a worksheet in Excel and create a database query linked to the Access file **13p2.orders.** Include the Company, Country, Item, Quantity, and Price/Unit data.

⚹ First, you will create a report showing the Sales Order Summary for Brazil, as shown in the illustration on the next page. Enter a title for the worksheet that includes the company name and the report title. Add columns to the table that are labeled `Total Due (US $)`, `Conversion Factor, and Total Due (Reals)`. *Note: Brazil's currency is the real.* Format the labels and adjust the column widths to make your table attractive and readable. Name the worksheet tab.

⚹ Create a Web query to locate the conversion factor for U.S. dollars to Brazilian reals. A good source for this information is http://moneycentral.msn.com/investor/market/rates.asp.

⚹ Fill in the data and formulas for the columns **Conversion Factor** and **Total Due (Reals)**. Be sure to make the conversion factor an absolute reference so that it will fill in correctly, as shown in the illustration.

	A	B	C	D	E	F	G	H
1			**Odyssey Travel Gear**					
2			Sales Orders from Brazil					
3						Total Due	Conversion	Total Due
4	Company	Country	Item	Quantity	Price/Unit (US$)	US$	Factor	(Reals)
5	Brazilia	Brazil	27" Suitcas	20	24.00	$480.00	2.878	1,381.44
6	Nuevo	Brazil	27" Wheels	15	25.00	$375.00	2.878	1,079.25
7	Brazilia	Brazil	27" Suitcas	25	24.00	$600.00	2.878	1,726.80
8	Nuevo	Brazil	Tote	25	14.00	$350.00	2.878	1,007.30
9	Nuevo	Brazil	Tote	15	14.00	$210.00	2.878	604.38
10	Brazilia	Brazil	32" Suitcas	10	27.00	$270.00	2.878	777.06
11								
12								
13								
14								
15	Name	In US$	Per US$					
16	Argentine Peso	0.35112	2.848					
17	Australian Dollar	0.7551	1.324					
18	Brazilian Real	0.34746	2.878					
19	British Pound	1.8242	0.548					
20	Canadian Dollar	0.76138	1.313					
21	Chinese Yuan	0.12082	8.277					
22	Euro	1.2012	0.833					
23	Hong Kong Dollar	0.12836	7.791					
24	Indian Rupee	0.0229	43.67					
25	Japanese Yen	0.00948	105.5					
26	Korean Won	0.00087	1,148					
27	Mexican Peso	0.08972	11.146					
28	Russian Rouble	0.03504	28.54					
29	Swedish Krona	0.13074	7.649					
30	Swiss Franc	0.76711	1.304					
31								

* Edit the query and use grouping and copying to create additional worksheets for Argentina and Canada.

* Copy the worksheet once again and change the headings to create a report for Mexico. Add the **13p.2orderschema** to the worksheet and map the elements to the report. Import the **13p.2Mexico** XML Data file. Convert the XML list to a range and complete formulas and formatting for this report, including naming the worksheet tab.

* Open the file at another time and refresh the currency data.

PERFORMANCE

SETTING THE STAGE/WRAPUP
File names:

Job 1: **Salesinv.xls**
        Salesinv.tmp
        musicmaxlogo.tif
Job 2: **12345wil.xls**
        12346ott.xls
Job 3: **emplist.xls**
        emplist3.xls
Job 4: **emplist4.xls**
        musicmaxlogo.tif
Job 5: **emplist5.xls**
        musicmaxlogo.tif
Job 6: **funding6.xls**
Job 7: **flyer7.xls**
        musicmaxlogo.tif
Job 8: **wilmington.xls**
        mktgsales.xls
        fayetteville.doc
        charlotte.xml
        RevenueSchema.xsd
        Annualreport8.xls
        musicmaxlogo.tif
Job 9: **annualreport9.xls**
        musicmaxlogo.tif

MusicMax is a company that has three retail stores in North Carolina: Fayetteville, Charlotte, and their main store and offices in Wilmington. Their stores sell sheet music, small musical instruments, records, albums, CDs, and miscellaneous supply items for musicians and music collectors. In addition, they produce a weekly flyer and have a Web site that generates mail order, telephone, and online sales orders.

You have been asked to do spreadsheet tasks to revise some procedures and forms, consolidate data for annual reports, manage employee data, analyze loan possibilities for a large purchase, and prepare charts and reports for management.

The data for each task is located on the Data CD in the Final Project folder. Include your name and task number as part of the footer on each worksheet.

JOB 1: Create a Sales Invoice Template

MusicMax would like to enhance the Sales Invoice they have developed for mail order customers. They already provide sales incentives by offering free shipping for orders over $100. However, they would also like to include an incentive table that shows an increasing discount depending on the amount of the sale. You will add the new table, add a company logo, add formulas, and save the invoice as a template.

FOLLOW THESE GUIDELINES:

1. Use the **Salesinv.xls** file from the Data CD.

2. Add the **Musicmaxlogo.tif** file to the left of the company header on the invoice, as illustrated.

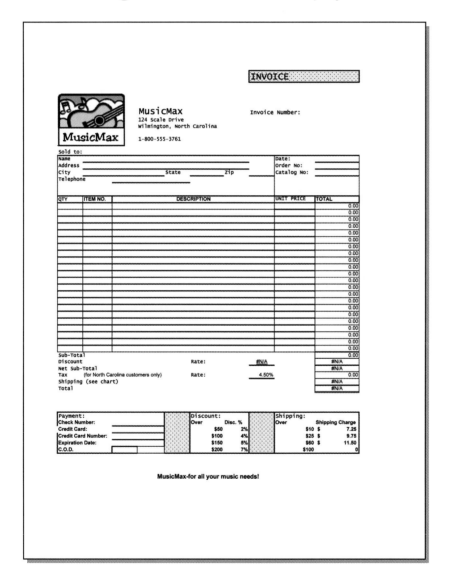

3. Insert new rows for `Discount` and `Net Sub-Total`.

4. Add a Discount table in **F49** as shown and format the table and invoice.

5. Enter test data in **row 18** as follows:
   `QTY: 2`
   `ITEM NO: 343T`
   `DESCRIPTION: Music Stands`
   `UNIT PRICE: 40.00`

6. Enter formulas as follows:
   a. **J18:J39**—Formula to calculate total per item.
   b. **J40**—Sub-Total.
   c. **H41**—Discount Rate: Use a lookup function to find discount rate according to value in Sub-Total. Format for Percent.
   d. **J41**—Discount.
   e. **J42**—Net Sub-Total.
   f. **J43**—Tax: Use an If statement to find sales tax if value in State box, F13, is NC. (*Hint: Use quotation marks for "NC."*)
   g. **J44**—Shipping: Use a lookup function to find shipping cost based on Net Sub-Total value.

7. Format QTY, Unit Price, and Total columns appropriately.

8. Use Print Preview to check formats and appearance of invoice.

9. Delete test data.

10. Print a copy of the template.

11. Save the invoice as a template file, **Salesinv.xlt.**

JOB 2:   Create Invoices Using a Template

Use the sales invoice template to create invoices for the sales orders that were telephoned in this morning; use today's date. Save each invoice using the invoice number, followed by the first three letters of the customer's last name.

FOLLOW THESE GUIDELINES:

1. Use the template file created in Job 1 to create invoice #12345 for the following:
   ```
   Denise Williams
   435 Pinewood Drive
   Southport, NC 28461
   910-555-9821
   Order No:  1432     Catalog No: 53C
   1  B4323  Guitar for the Absolute Beginner  @  44.95
   1  B4976  FastTrack Guitar Method-Book 1    @   7.95
   1  SM437  The Eagles-Acoustic Classics      @  19.95
   C.O.D.
   ```

2. Use the template file created in Job 1 to create invoice #12346 for the following:
   ```
   Marcus Otterbeck
   465 Spring Terrace
   Reston, VA  20194
   703-555-5476
   Order No:  none    Catalog No: 55G
   2  E2342  Behind-the-Neck Headphones           @  19.99
   4  E7643  Folding Headphones with Controls     @   9.99
   1  A7543  DVD Audio-West Side Story            @  12.99
   2  SM643  Billy Joel: Fantasies and Delusions  @  16.95
   VISA 6575 5555 5544 3332    Expiration 8/31/07
   ```

3. Print a copy of each invoice. Save and close the files.

JOB 3: Customize an Employee List

MusicMax has three stores and an administrative office located at the main store. The administrative staff has a marketing group that manages the online, telephone, and mail order sales. Employee records are handled by the human resources administrator.

The employee list needs to be updated and customized for ease of use. This requires making data validation settings, creating a custom menu, and adding macros for frequently used operations.

FOLLOW THESE GUIDELINES:

1. Use the **emplist.xls** file from the Data CD.

2. Enter a formula to calculate ANNUAL SAL for each employee. Format columns **J** and **K** for commas.

3. Add data validation settings for **Rows 2** to **25** for the STATE (two-letter Post Office designation), DEPT (create list of the departments in **N1:N4**), and WKLY SAL (minimum 300.00, maximum 999.99) fields. Add appropriate error messages. Check settings.

4. Add a custom menu, named **Employees**, with the following commands from the Data and Tools menus:
   a. **Data, Form**
   b. **Data, Subtotals**
   c. **Data, Sort Ascending**
   d. **Tools, Protect Worksheet**

5. Use the Data Form, shown in the illustration, to enter records for two new employees as follows:
   ```
   Ruiz, Carlos   (Male)
   65 Rally Drive
   Fayetteville, NC  28301
   2/24/85, Sales Department, $385 per week

   Thompson, Keisha (Female)
   400 Carson Road
   Wilmington, NC  28401
   6/18/82, Human Resources, $410 per week
   ```

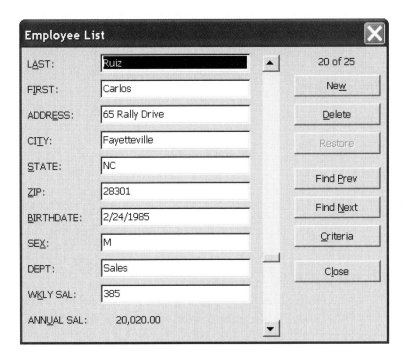

6. Sort the worksheet in **ascending** order by **last name**.

7. Give the range `A1:K30` the name `EMPLOYEES`.

8. Set the Print range for the worksheet data and select print settings for landscape mode and to fit the worksheet to one sheet wide.

9. Print the worksheet.

10. Protect the worksheet.

11. Save the file as **emplist3.xls** and close the file.

JOB 4:   Summarize Employee List Data

MusicMax management has requested various summary information to better analyze its payroll expenses. You will use Excel data list features including subtotals, filters, database functions, pivot tables, and charts to produce these reports.

FOLLOW THESE GUIDELINES:

1. Use your saved file from the previous project or open **emplist4.xls** from the Data CD.

2. Unprotect the worksheet.

3. Use AutoFilter to display only Sales staff from all locations. Print the list. Restore all data.

4. Use AutoFilter to display all personnel in the Wilmington location. Print the list.

5. Remove AutoFilter.

6. Sort the list by **DEPT** in **Ascending order.**

7. Create subtotals of weekly and annual salaries by department. Adjust column widths to display subtotal labels and print a copy of the report. Use the outline feature to hide the details and print a copy of the department totals and grand total, as shown in the illustration. Remove all subtotals.

1 2 3		I	J	K
	4	DEPT	WKLY SAL	ANNUAL SAL
+	8	Administration Total	2,025.00	105,300.00
+	11	Human Resources Total	935.00	48,620.00
+	14	Marketing Total	950.00	49,400.00
+	32	Sales Total	7,585.00	394,420.00
·	33			-
·	34	Grand Total	11,495.00	597,740.00
−	35			
	36			

8. Insert rows above the list for criteria and add database summary labels below the list in **A32** for the following:
   a. Average Annual Salary – Charlotte
   b. Average Annual Salary – Fayetteville
   c. Average Annual Salary – Wilmington

9. Enter database function formulas to find the summary results in **D32:D34.**

10. Create a PivotTable with the CITY, DEPT, WKLY SAL, and ANNUAL SAL data to find the sum of the weekly and annual salaries by department for all cities. Format the data for currency and add a report heading and the company logo, as shown in the illustration. Name the sheet appropriately.

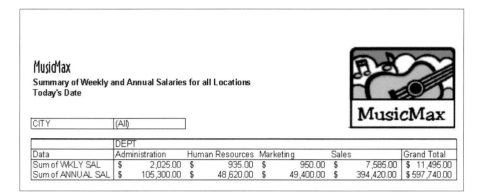

MusicMax
Summary of Weekly and Annual Salaries for all Locations
Today's Date

CITY	(All)					
	DEPT					
Data	Administration	Human Resources	Marketing	Sales		Grand Total
Sum of WKLY SAL	$ 2,025.00	$ 935.00	$ 950.00	$	7,585.00	$ 11,495.00
Sum of ANNUAL SAL	$ 105,300.00	$ 48,620.00	$ 49,400.00	$	394,420.00	$ 597,740.00

11. Copy the PivotTable to a new sheet and change the City setting to Wilmington and hide or remove the ANNUAL SAL data. Create a PivotChart based on the weekly salary report from the Wilmington store. Add an appropriate title and the company logo to the chart. Name the sheet appropriately. Print a copy of the chart.

12. Protect the sheet.

13. Save and close the file.

JOB 5:   Analyze Employee Salaries for Annual Salary Increase

MusicMax management wants you to prepare an analysis of the salaries of its employees by department in anticipation of annual salary raises. They would like to see the impact on each salary if they increased their weekly payroll to $13,000.

FOLLOW THESE GUIDELINES:

1. Use your saved file from the previous project or open **emplist5.xls** from the Data CD.

2. Copy the Employee List excluding the criteria range and summary formulas to a new sheet.

3. Delete columns so that only the LAST, DEPT, and WKLY SAL columns remain.

4. Add appropriate titles, formats, sheet title, and the company logo. Add column headings as shown in the illustration.

MusicMax				
Annual Salary Increase Proposal				**MusicMax**
Today's date				
LAST	**DEPT**	**WKLY SAL**	**PERCENTAGE OF TOTAL**	**PROPOSED SALARY**
Fallin	Administration	650.00		
Kung	Administration	675.00		
Minotti	Administration	700.00		
Ingrams	Human Resources	525.00		
Thompson	Human Resources	410.00		
Quincy	Marketing	475.00		
Resta	Marketing	475.00		
Able	Sales	450.00		
Bender	Sales	460.00		
Cruz	Sales	425.00		
Darcy	Sales	385.00		
Ericson	Sales	450.00		
Grogan	Sales	400.00		
Hickory	Sales	550.00		
Jacobsen	Sales	525.00		
Linwood	Sales	460.00		
Nestor	Sales	450.00		
Obrien	Sales	450.00		
Perez	Sales	550.00		
Ruiz	Sales	385.00		
Satturna	Sales	450.00		
Tremain	Sales	410.00		
Unitas	Sales	400.00		
Warren	Sales	385.00		

5. Presently, the total salaries are $11,495. Enter a formula to divide each weekly salary by the total to find the PERCENTAGE OF TOTAL. Format the values for two-place percents.

6. In the **PROPOSED SALARY** column, clear the validation settings and enter a formula to multiply each percentage by 13000.

7. Create subtotals by DEPT and a grand total.

8. Align column headings for number values to the right.

9. Preview and print the worksheet.

10. Name the worksheet tab "Salary Analysis."

11. Protect the worksheet.

12. Close and save the file.

JOB 6:   Analyze Purchase Options for New Equipment

MusicMax is interested in buying a new server, enhancing their current network, and adding new software to manage inventory for its stores. The computer consultants have submitted an estimate of $70,000 for the main portion of this upgrade. Management is interested in comparing various scenarios for funding this project. They are considering a one-, two-, or three-year loan and wish to estimate the monthly payment using 5% and 6% rates.

FOLLOW THESE GUIDELINES:

1. Open **funding6.xls** from the Data CD.
2. Enter a formula in **B7** to calculate the monthly payment using the PMT function.
3. Set up a series of scenarios as follows:

SCENARIO NAME	CHANGE B5 TO:	CHANGE B6 TO:
12mos5%	12	.05
12mos6%	12	.06
24mos5%	24	.05
24mos6%	24	.06
36mos5%	36	.05
36mos6%	36	.06

4. Create a scenario summary showing the changing cell in **B7.**
5. Add labels in the scenario summary in **column B** to indicate the Months, Rate, and Payment values.
6. Copy the titles from Sheet1 to the Scenario Summary sheet.
7. Print a copy of the Scenario Summary.
8. Close and save the file.

JOB 7:   Create a Web Query for a Company Newsletter

MusicMax produces a flyer that is available in its stores that contains the new releases for the month on one side and the top 20 from the Billboard Top 50 list on the other side. They would like to create a Web Query to obtain these results monthly from the Billboard.com Web site and set up their flyer pages with the data.

FOLLOW THESE GUIDELINES:

1. In a new workbook, create four worksheets titled:
   SideOne-Top20
   SideTwo-New Rock Releases
   Top 50 Query
   New Rock Releases Query

2. Set up headings and formats for each sheet, using appropriate titles, using the headings for the first sheet shown in the illustration as an example.

| This Week | Last week | Weeks on chart | "Title," Artist Imprint \| Catalog No. \| Promotion Label | | Peak Position |

3. On the Top 50 Query sheet, create a Web query to import the Top 50 list from the Billboard.com site. (On www.Billboard.com, click the Singles & Tracks link under the Charts heading, and the Top 50 radio button under the The Billboard Hot 100 heading. Import the table.)

4. Copy the Top 20 Tracks from the list and paste link it to the SideOne-Top20 sheet in the appropriate location.

5. On the New Rock Releases Query sheet, create a Web query to import the new releases for the week following the current week in the Rock/Pop/R&B category. (On www.Billboard.com, click the New Releases link under the Artists & Music heading to locate the week and category desired. Import the data.)

6. Copy the new release list and paste link it to the SideTwo-New Rock Releases worksheet in the appropriate location.

7. Format data as needed.

8. Print a copy of the SideOne-Top 20 and SideTwo-New Rock Releases worksheets.

9. Save the file as **flyer7.xls** and close the file.

10. Refresh the data in a week to create an updated flyer.

JOB 8: Assemble Annual Report Data

The data reporting system and network between MusicMax stores is not yet operational; therefore financial data must be assembled from each location into one report. The Wilmington store and the Marketing department that conducts online, telephone, and mail order sales have submitted annual Revenue, Cost of Goods Sold, and Expense data in Excel format. The Charlotte store has sent its report in an XML data file and the Fayetteville data is in a Word file.

The data must be placed into one Excel file on separate sheets where it will be modified, summarized, and consolidated. Use the names of the files as the sheet names for each set of store or sales data.

FOLLOW THESE GUIDELINES:

1. Use the **wilmington.xls, mktgsales.xls, fayetteville.doc, charlotte.xml,** and **RevenueSchema.xsd** files from the Data CD.

2. Open the **wilmington.xls** file and save it as `annualreport8.xls`. Name the sheet.

3. Open **mktgsales.xls** and copy the data to Sheet2 in the annualreport8 file. Name the sheet.

4. Open **fayetteville.doc** in Word and copy the data to Sheet3 in the annualreport8 file. Name the sheet. Format the data as in the other sheets using Format Painter.

5. Add two additional worksheets; name them `Charlotte` and `Consolidated Data`.

6. On the Charlotte sheet, add the **RevenueSchema** to the file and map the data to Row 5 of the spreadsheet. Import the **charlotte.xml** file into the worksheet. Convert the list to a range. Correct column headings and add appropriate worksheet titles. All worksheets should have the data in the same locations.

7. Group the Wilmington, MktgSales, Fayetteville, and Charlotte sheets.

8. On the Consolidated Data sheet, insert a column in Column D. Label it `Gross Profit` and set format for text wrap. Label Column F `Net Profit`.

9. Enter formulas to calculate Gross Profit and Net Profit for all months on all sheets.

10. Copy Column A data and the column headings from any sheet to the Consolidated Data sheet. Change the second title to `Consolidated Revenue Report`.

11. Consolidate the data from each of the sheets onto the Consolidated Data sheet.

12. Group all sheets and find the totals of the columns. Include single and double-line borders.

13. On the Consolidated Data sheet, add the company logo and format the report data and headings to make a good appearance for an annual report. For example, use color and eliminate abbreviations. Values should be formatted for commas with no decimals, using dollar signs for totals. A portion of a sample solution is shown in the illustration.

	A	B	C	D	E	F
1						
2	**MusicMax**					
3	**Consolidated Revenue Report**					
4	**For the fiscal year ended June 30, 2005**					
5						
6					**MusicMax**	
7	**Month**	**Revenue**	**Cost of Goods Sold**	**Gross Profit**	**Expenses**	**Net Profit**
8	July	548,539	220,876	327,663	243,171	84,492
9	August	392,544	158,964	233,580	175,190	58,390
10	September	417,351	169,209	248,142	184,119	64,023
11	October	450,825	181,882	268,943	200,833	68,110
12	November	495,651	199,892	295,759	219,552	76,207
13	December	551,026	223,607	327,419	243,935	83,484
14	January	426,628	172,662	253,966	188,555	65,411
15	February	474,207	191,432	282,775	210,225	72,550
16	March	374,736	149,709	225,027	166,437	58,590
17	April	413,907	168,032	245,875	183,636	62,239
18	May	452,210	181,566	270,644	199,765	70,879
19	June	499,500	202,944	296,556	222,185	74,371
20	**Totals**	**$ 5,497,124**	**$ 2,220,775**	**$ 3,276,349**	**$ 2,437,603**	**$ 838,746**
21						

Wilmington / MktgSales / Charlotte / Fayetteville \ Consolidated Data /

14. Print the workbook.

15. Save and close the file.

JOB 9:   Analyze Annual Data Using Charts and Percentage Analysis

MusicMax management would like to use the data on the Consolidated Data sheet to create additional reports that will analyze and compare the various sales centers and display the results using charts. All charts should be on separate chart sheets that are named for the type of chart and the data presented. All the summary reports will be part of an annual report, for fiscal year 2005, that will be presented to the stockholders of this private company.

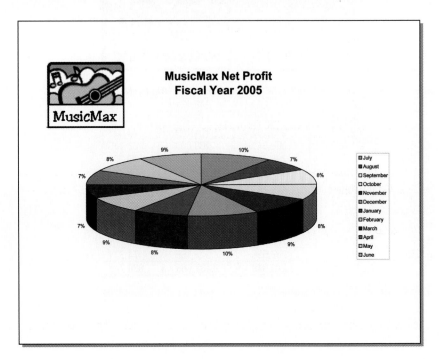

FOLLOW THESE GUIDELINES:

1. Use the file from JOB 8 or open **annualreport9.xls** from the Data CD.

2. Using the Consolidated Data sheet, create the following on new sheets:
   a. Pie Chart of Monthly Net Profit showing percentages for each month, as shown in the illustration on the previous page.
   b. Pie Chart of Monthly Revenue showing percentages for each month.

3. On a new sheet, show the totals from each sales center and the grand totals for the company. Label the sheet **Revenue by Sales Center.** *(The grand totals should match those on the Consolidated Data sheet.)* A sample of the sheet is shown in the illustration.

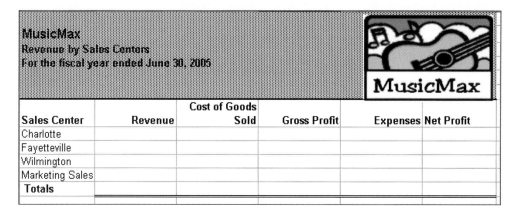

Sales Center	Revenue	Cost of Goods Sold	Gross Profit	Expenses	Net Profit
Charlotte					
Fayetteville					
Wilmington					
Marketing Sales					
Totals					

4. Using the Revenue by Sales Centers sheet, create a column chart showing the data from all sales centers with the data series arranged by column. Add appropriate titles and the company logo.

5. Print copies of the charts and the Revenue by Sales Center sheet.

6. Save and close the file.

JOB 10:   Prepare Final Project for Review

Label a folder for the Final Project and include your name and other identification required by your instructor.

Arrange printed reports in the order they were assigned.

Provide a copy of your solution files on disk or a reference to their location on the network, if applicable.

GLOSSARY

3-D references A cell reference in a formula that refers to calculating values in a cell or cells in the same location on a group of worksheets in a workbook.

Absolute (cell) reference In Excel, a reference to a particular cell or group of cells that must remain constant even if you copy the contents or formula in one cell to another cell.

Accept changes To decide that a modification of information should remain on a worksheet.

Account An accounting form used to summarize increases and decreases in an item.

Account Statement A monthly summary of the increases and decreases in an account.

Accounts payable Creditors that a business owes money to.

Accounts receivable Customers that owe money to a business.

Accounts receivable aging report A financial document that shows an analysis of how many days payments from customers are overdue.

Active cell The cell in use or the cell that is ready to receive text or a formula.

Active (cell) reference The row and column location of the active cell, which appears in the name box.

Aging report A report prepared to analyze the number of days a company's Accounts Receivable accounts are overdue.

Align center Text alignment in which text is centered between the margins.

Align left Text alignment in which text is even at the left margin and uneven at the right margin.

Align right Text alignment in which text is uneven at the left margin and even at the right margin.

Analysis Toolpak Add-in feature that includes regression and other data analysis features.

Annual interest Interest rate for the use of money expressed on an annual basis.

AutoComplete The automatic completion of an entry in an Excel column using previously entered column data.

AutoFill The Excel feature that allows you to drag, copy and fill data.

AutoFilter A feature that requires a data table and that allows you to filter lists using arrows that appear at every column heading.

AutoFit Feature to widen columns to fit the longest data in that column.

AutoFormat A feature that provides a predefined format applied to a report, a form, a worksheet, or a table.

AutoShapes Built-in graphic objects, found on the Drawing toolbar that you can place and size.

AutoSum A feature that automatically adds the selected numbers in a column.

Balance sheet A financial report that shows the value of the business, its Assets, Liabilities and Capital, on a specific date.

Benefits statement Report by an employer stating benefits offered or provided to employees.

Bonus table A data table that defines the extra money paid to employees based on some measure of performance.

Border A variety of line styles that border the edge of a cell or range of cells.

Budget An analysis of the projected income and expenses for a future period.

Business form A document format that is developed for an activity that occurs often.

Category labels Identifies values in a chart data series as shown on the horizontal or x-axis.

Cell A location on a worksheet that contains text, values, or formulas.

Cell address The location of a cell as identified by the column letter and row number.

Cell comment A notation or documentation added to a cell in a worksheet.

Cell coordinate The column letter and row number given to a cell. For example, A1 is the coordinate for the cell in the first row, first column.

Cell cursor In spreadsheets, the heavy line that outlines a cell and indicates the active cell.

Chart A visual representation of data. The terms graph and chart are interchangeable.

Chart sheet A separate sheet created to display a chart on a full page.

Chart Wizard A software assistant that steps you through the creation of a chart.

Column Vertical area for data that is identified by letter across a spreadsheet grid.

Column chart Compares individual or sets of values using the proportional height of the columns.

Combination chart A custom chart that plots the data series using two different chart types.

Conditional format The application of specific formats if the content of a cell or range of cells meets certain criteria.

Consolidated budget A business document that shows the planned or actual income and expenses from several departments or companies.

Consolidated income statement An Income Statement that is made up of data from various subsidiaries or divisions.

Criteria range A separate area of the worksheet created using the column headings of a data table that contains criteria for an advanced filter.

Cropping A tool on the Picture Toolbar used to reduce the size of a picture by removing vertical or horizontal edges.

Currency conversion table A data table that contains foreign exchange rates for the money of different countries, as well as any computations based on those rates.

Custom menu A set of buttons and commands grouped into a user-created drop-down menu.

Custom number format A user-created format that specifies how Excel displays numbers within a cell.

Database functions Formulas used to analyze and/or summarize a data list.

Data consolidation A way to combine the information from different workbooks or worksheets and store it in another workbook or worksheet.

Data list A columnar table of data with column headings—used for database functions.

Data series Is a group of values in a chart identified by a label.

Data validation A feature that helps to ensure that the correct data is entered on a worksheet or in a data list.

Dependents Cells containing formulas that reference the cell you are auditing.

Depreciation schedule An accounting record that shows the cost of an asset over its estimated useful life.

Destination file Receives data from another file.

Divisional sales report A summary of sales figures for each department of a company.

Drag-and-drop A method of moving text using the mouse. Text is "dragged" from its original location and dropped into its new location.

Edit mode Double-click a cell or press F2 to go into worksheet edit mode.

Embedded chart Is a chart object that is placed on a worksheet.

Embedded file An object placed into a destination file that becomes part of that file, but can be edited in its source application.

Evaluate Formula A function that allows you to see the step-by-step calculations that a formula performs.

Expense report A report of money spent by an employee on business travel or expenses.

Exporting data Sending data from Excel to other applications.

Extensible Mark-Up Language (XML) A format for putting structured data in a text file; allows for the exchange of data between different applications.

Field name Label for a particular column of data in a list.

Fill handle The rectangular indicator at the bottom right corner of a cell that is used with AutoFill.

Filter An Excel function that allows you to display only the data specified by certain criteria.

Financial functions Are used to analyze loans, calculate payments, and compute depreciation on assets.

Find and Replace A feature that scans a document and searches for occurrences of specified text, symbols, or formatting and replaces it with other specified text, symbols, or formatting.

Folder A subdivision of a drive that you create to hold files that are related to each other.

Footer The same text or graphic appearing at the bottom of every page or every other page in a document.

FORECAST A what-if analysis that allows you to project future data values based on data that you have already obtained.

Format Painter An Office feature that allows you to copy formats from one set of data to another.

Formula An instruction to the computer to calculate data in a certain way.

Formula bar The formula bar is under the toolbar and shows the entry of data and provides formula assistance.

Freeze Panes Used to keep headings or row data in view when scrolling through a large worksheet.

Function In spreadsheets, a built-in formula that performs special calculations automatically.

Function arguments The cell addresses that make up the data for the function formula.

FV (future value) function Used to calculate the future value of a series of equal payments, at a fixed interest rate, for a specific number of payments.

General ledger Contains the major accounts of a business.

Graphic A line, circle, or box that has been created, or an image or illustration that is imported into the publication.

Group sheets Selecting multiple worksheets as a group so that you can make entries on all sheets simultaneously.

Header The same text appearing at the top of every page or every other page in a document.

HLOOKUP An Excel lookup function used when the data are arranged horizontally in a table.

Hyperlink A shortcut that allows you to jump to another location in another workbook, a file on your hard drive or network, or an Internet address.

IF statement A logical function that tests a condition and performs one action if it is true and another if it is false.

Importing data Bringing information into Excel from a source other than an Excel file.

Income statement A financial report that shows Income, Expenses and Profits for the period..

Insert Function button Used to select and enter a function name and arguments in a formula.

Integration The sharing or combining of data between Office XP applications.

Interactivity A feature added to an Excel file published to a Web page that allows viewers to manipulate data in their browsers.

Inventory list A data list kept by a company to keep track of products and goods, including stock on hand, cost of goods, and other information, such as suggested retail price.

Journal A record of business transactions in chronological order.

Label In spreadsheets, a text entry.

Label prefix Numeric labels are entered with an apostrophe ('), which serves as the label prefix.

Left-alignment To position text along the left margin. See *Align Left*.

Legend The identification of a chart data series showing the colors of the series markers.

Line chart Compares individual sets of values with lines connecting the points of data.

Linked file A shortcut to source file data placed in a destination file. All data changes will update in both locations.

Listing agent In a real estate office, the agent who contracts with the homeowner to sell the property.

Locked cells Specific cells in a worksheet to which protection has been added.

Macro A series of actions you record to allow you to complete a task quickly and efficiently.

Map define the structure of a workbook by dragging the elements of a schema onto the worksheet.

Menu bar Appears at the top of the Excel screen and contains lists of commands for each category of features or items on the menu.

Merge and Center button Centers text over a range of selected cells.

Merge cells Removing the dividing lines between cells to create a single, larger cell. This is also referred to as joining cells.

Merging workbooks incorporating changes made by users into a single workbook.

MHTML An encapsulated aggregate document that includes all the elements of a Web site in a single file.

Microsoft Query An application that allows you to retrieve specified information from external sources.

Name box On the Formula bar, the name box shows the cell address of the active cell.

Named range A label applied to a specified range of cells.

Negative numbers Result of a calculation that is a value less than zero.

Nonadjacent selection A selection of worksheet data that is not contiguous accomplished using the Ctrl key.

Nper Number of payments.

Numeric label In spreadsheets, text that begins with a number. Numeric labels cannot be calculated.

Office Clipboard A memory area of the computer where data is stored temporarily.

Order of mathematical operations Formulas are executed in the following order: parentheses, exponents, multiplication and division, and addition and subtraction.

Orientation On charts, the plotting of data in a chart by row or column layout.

Page break Is the location on a page where one page ends and another begins.

Password A sequence of letters and/or numbers that must be entered before access to a worksheet or workbook is allowed.

Paste Link option Connecting the data from one location to another so that if the original data is changed it updates on the linked location.

Paste values A paste option that allows you to paste only the values, not the formulas of copied data.

Payroll register A worksheet that calculates employee's salary, taxes, and net pay.

Personnel list A record of all employees in a business and their associated information.

Pie chart Circular graphs used to show the relationship of each value in a data range to the total of the range.

PivotChart A graphical representation of the contents of a PivotTable.

PivotChart report A print-out of a PivotChart analysis.

PivotTable An interactive tool that allows you to manipulate data in a list in order to summarize, analyze, or arrange it in tabular form.

PivotTable report A print-out of a PivotTable analysis.

PMT (payment) function Used to calculate a loan payment based on the principal (present value of loan), interest rate, and number of payments.

Portfolio A group of investments owned by a person or business.

Precedents Cells that are referenced in a formula.

Principal Present value of a loan.

Print Titles Use to print row or column titles for a large worksheet that prints on more than one page.

Professional invoice An invoice or bill sent for services such as legal, accounting or consulting services.

Properties Facts about a file that provide identification or information for using, sorting, or organizing the file.

Protection A feature of Excel that allows another user to read data but not make any changes to it until protection is removed.

Purchase order A form sent by a firm to a vendor to request shipment of items listed on the order.

PV (present value) function Use to calculate the present value of a series of equal payments, at a fixed interest rate, for a specific number of payments.

Quarterly Every three months, or four times a year.

Quarterly budget A statement of income and expenses prepared every three months.

Query A text file that contains information about a data source and the information to extract from it.

Range In spreadsheet applications, one or more contiguous cells.

Rate Interest rate per period.

Real estate list A data list that contains a company's current inventory of properties for sale and/or rent.

Reciprocal Used to calculate the result of subtracting a percentage discount. Subtract the discount percent from 100% to get the reciprocal.

Record The data for one person or unit in a list; it goes across a row in Excel.

Regional sales analysis A financial analysis of sales figures for different sales territories.

Reimbursement A request to be paid for money spent on business expenses.

Reject changes To decide that a modification of information should not be made to a worksheet.

Relative (cell) reference In spreadsheets, cell references that change relative to their new locations when a formula is copied.

Report Manager An Excel add-in program that allows you to create printed reports containing information from different sections of a workbook; it includes scenarios.

Research tools A task pane that provides resources for research.

Revenue Income or monies received by a business.

Right-alignment To position text along the right margin. See *Align right*.

Rotate tool The tool that appears above a graphic to change its orientation or angle.

Round-tripping A feature that allows you to edit an HTML document in a browser using Notepad, Word, or FrontPage.

Row Horizontal area for data that is identified by a number along the side of a spreadsheet grid.

S&P 500 Standard and Poor's 500 stock index is a weighted index made up of the stock prices of 500 blue chip stocks, which reflects market trends.

Sales commission analysis A study of sales performance over a specified period of time in order to identify notable patterns or to select individuals who are above or below certain goals important to a business.

Sales forecast A projection of future sales based on past performance.

Sales invoice A bill prepared by a seller and sent to the customer when goods are supplied, which details items sold and terms of the sale.

Sales journal A record of sales transactions.

Scenario A what-if analysis that allows you to explore the impact of changing data values on numerical outcomes.

Schedule of accounts payable A list prepared monthly of the balances of creditor accounts.

Schedule of accounts receivable A list prepared monthly of the balances of customer accounts.

Schema Tags that store information such as file properties, data formats, layout, column titles, etc., which define the structure of a workbook.

Scroll bars Located at the right and bottom of the screen and used to move to different areas of the worksheet that are not displayed.

Selling agent In a real estate office, the agent who sells a listed property. The listing and selling agent can be the same person.

Serial value The numeric value of a date which allows you to use dates in formulas and represents the number of days from January, 1900 to the date entered.

Series A list of numbers or text that is in a sequential arrangement that can be produced using AutoFill.

Series labels Identifies charted values and appears in the legend.

Shared workbook A workbook that a number of users can edit.

Source file Provides the data for integrating into another file.

Split cells Reversing the merge cells process and returning cells to their normal size.

Status bar The status bar at the bottom of the Excel screen displays the condition of worksheet calculations and settings.

Straight-line depreciation A method of calculating the loss in value in an asset by dividing the cost of an asset less the scrap value by the estimated useful life.

Structured data Formatted data, such as worksheets, that can be imported into Access.

Style A set of formatting characteristics that can be applied to a paragraph or selected text.

Subtotal A summary of a subset of data that is arranged in a list.

SUM In spreadsheet and database applications, a function used to add numbers in a range or values in a field.

Tab scrolling buttons Allow you to scroll hidden worksheets into view.

Task pane A new feature that displays on start up, on the right side of the screen, and shows options pertinent to the task at hand.

Tax status The number of dependents and marital status of employees, which is used for payroll tax calculations.

Template A workbook that serves as an outline or guide, into which you can place data.

Terms Credit terms given to a buyer that may involve discounts for early payment.

Title bar The shaded bar at the top of a dialog box or application window that displays the title of the box, or the name of the file, and the application.

Toolbar A bar with buttons, located under the menu bar, provides quick access to common features.

Tracer arrows The lines Excel creates in a worksheet to identify dependents and precedents of audited cells.

Track changes The ability to view modifications made to a file by other users.

Transaction A business event or activity that changes the financial status of a business.

Trendline A graphic representation of any tendencies or patterns in data, presented in a chart.

Trial balance A list of all the accounts in a business consisting of debit and credit balances, which must equal to show that the books are in balance.

Value A numeric entry on a worksheet that is able to be calculated.

Vendor A supplier or merchant that provides your company with goods or services.

Visual Basic Editor A module in Excel within which macros are recorded using the programming language Visual Basic.

VLOOKUP An Excel lookup function used when the data are arranged vertically in a table.

Watch Window A feature that displays a window on the screen to watch the values and formulas in selected cells.

Web page Is a location on an Internet server, part of the World Wide Web, which can be reached and identified by a Web address.

What-if analysis A group of commands that allows the user to assess how changes in data or formulas affect outcomes; includes forecasting and scenarios.

Workbook An Excel file made up of several worksheets.

Working folder The default location for saving and opening files.

Worksheet An accounting term for a columnar analysis that uses the Trial Balance and end-of-year adjustments to develop the data for the Income Statement and Balance Sheet reports.

Worksheet One page in an Excel workbook.

Workspace A shared location in which you can store several workbooks.

X-axis In spreadsheet charting, the horizontal scale that typically displays the data series.

Y-axis In spreadsheet charting, the vertical scale that typically displays the scale values.

INDEX